SCHOOL AND SOCIETY THROUGH SCIENCE FICTION

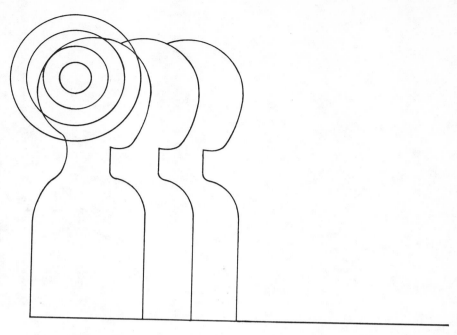

SCHOOL AND SOCIETY THROUGH SCIENCE FICTION

Joseph D. Olander
Florida International University

Martin Harry Greenberg
Florida International University

Patricia Warrick
University of Wisconsin

Rand McNally College Publishing Company/Chicago

Current printing (last digit)
15 14 13 12 11 10 9 8 7 6 5 4 3 2 1

Copyright © 1974 by Rand McNally College Publishing Company
All Rights Reserved
Printed in U.S.A.
Library of Congress Card Number 74-12644

To Cookie, Sally, and Jim

TABLE OF CONTENTS

Manhood at its best is the heart and mind natural to man; propriety is the road man travels. How sad it is when the man quits his road and does not follow it; when he loses the heart and mind natural to him and does not know how to seek it out. If one of his chickens or dogs is lost, he knows how to seek it out; but when the heart and mind natural to him is lost, he does not know how to seek it out. The procedures of education are nothing more than a seeking out of that lost heart and mind.

—MENCIUS
Kao Pu-hai (6A:11)

INTRODUCTION

The story of Prometheus is a long-forgotten one, but it is a myth worth reviving in the twentieth century. The old Greek tale is meaningful for studying the dilemma of modern humanity and for elaborating the role of science fiction in the study of school and society.

Prometheus was an extremely original, creative, and bold Titan. He dared to steal fire from Mount Olympus in order to give it to mortal man. For this, Zeus condemned him to almost eternal torment consisting of the daily consumption of his liver by hungry vultures. After a long cosmic period, Hercules killed the vultures and Zeus accepted the death of Chiron in Prometheus's stead. Some felt that Prometheus was unjustly condemned. Others, like Diogenes, felt that the punishment was fitting, for Prometheus had brought to man the techniques that resulted in the complication of life.

The dilemma of Prometheus bears striking similarities to the dilemma facing us in the latter half of the twentieth century. Prometheus was possessed of originality, daring, and creativity; indeed, his prowess knew no bounds. He took it upon himself to behave limitlessly within the formidable variety of his qualities, and for this unrestrained behavior he was severely punished.

Societies are complex organizations of yet more complex beings. As a result of the developments in science and technology, societies and their members have developed the Promethean qualities of creativity, originality, and daring. These qualities have given rise to a staggering potential for change. The magnitude and rate of change continue to increase and set the tone for modern life.

Yet, in order to avoid the fate of Prometheus, this potential for change cannot go uncontrolled. It needs to be controlled. Merely to control, however, is insufficient; the control must also guide and direct change. One of the major purposes of social structure and tradition is to control and guide this Promethean change which is mankind's peculiar quality.

The decade of the 1960s witnessed social change on an unprecedented scale. Sexual mores loosened, the meaning and significance of the college degree was transformed, the role of authority underwent a profound shift in the direction of a loss of legitimacy which startled the members of the previous generation—in short, future shock was upon us. The current decade promises social change of even greater magnitude. Social structure and tradition appear unable to restrain Prometheus. In addition, individuals respond to increases in social change in different ways. Some rely more heavily on tradition in the face of uncertainty and complexity; others reject tradition and seek entirely new ways of behaving and thinking. The different responses to social change simply compound existing problems and generate new ones.

In order to deal with the Promethean qualities of change, a Promethean literature is needed—a literature which is original, daring, and creative; a literature which, above all, *accepts change as normal.* Such a literature is science fiction. Donald Wollheim, in *The Universe Makers,* defines science fiction as ". . . that branch of fantasy, which, while not true of present-day knowledge, is rendered plausible by the reader's recognition of the scientific possibilities of it being possible at some future date or at some uncertain period in the past."[1] In other words science fiction is a literature concerned with change.

Judith Merril, another science fiction critic, classifies science fiction as speculative fiction, composed of "stories whose objective is to explore, to discover, to learn, by means of projection, extrapolation, the nature of the universe, of man, of reality." She defines speculative fiction as "the mode which makes use of the traditional 'scientific method' (observation, hypothesis, experimentation) to examine some postulated approximation of reality, by introducing a given set of changes—imaginary or inventive—into the common background of 'known facts,' creating an environment in which the

---

1. Donald Wollheim, *The Universe Makers* (New York: Harper and Row, 1971), p. 10.

responses and perceptions of the characters will reveal something about the inventions, the characters, or both."[2]

The science fiction short story is particularly well suited to the overall pedagogical purpose of this book. Unlike a novel, which may involve complicated subplots and subthemes, a good short story aims to produce *one single effect* by revealing a theme or a basic idea. This theme, however, must be developed in the context of an action. Hence the theme arises from a meaningful situation, a conflict, or complication, that sets the story in motion. The theme is revealed when further incidents are raveled and unraveled in the course of the *plot.* The plot necessarily involves the development of *character* and a narrative technique or style, which also contribute to the theme. Finally, the basic idea is revealed by, and through, a background that harmonizes with the action and characters. Accordingly, the science fiction short stories contained in this book have been selected not only with a view towards their conceptual merit for the study of the relationship between school and society but also with serious consideration of these preceding qualities of good fiction.

Social science aims to produce right answers to the problems regarding school and society; science fiction is a literature which may help to provide *right questions* about these problems. Since right answers to wrong questions may not be especially meaningful, it is important to ask about the application of science fiction to the study of the social foundations of education and its problems.

Science fiction can contribute to this study in several distinct ways. First, it is an effective tool for analyzing the elements of, and solutions to, problems. Its effectiveness can be demonstrated by comparing science fiction with modern, rational methods for analyzing solutions to problems. Such methods involve at least four categories of calculations which constitute the major criteria for judging the feasibility of proposed solutions to problems. Each of these calculations falls along a continuum and includes:

---

2. Judith Merril, "What Do You Mean: Science? Fiction?," in *SF: The Other Side of Realism,* ed. Thomas Clareson (Bowling Green: University Popular Press, 1971), p. 60.

1. The Technological Calculus (Impossibility ↔ Possibility)
2. The Economic Calculus (Benefits ↔ Costs)
3. The Legal Calculus (Lawful ↔ Unlawful)
4. The Political Calculus (Agreement ↔ Disagreement)

Each of these calculations needs to be made in order to approach problem-solving as a logical structure of thought. The technological calculus, which ranges from impossibility to possibility, raises the question of whether one has the technological capability to solve a problem. Technological capability not only relates to the availability of "hardware," such as tools, equipment, and machinery, but also involves the availability of conceptual tools, such as theories, principles, and concepts. Problems in education most frequently involve questions of both hardware and knowledge.

The economic calculus, which ranges from benefits to costs, asks one major question: Is it worthwhile to solve a problem in a particular way? The answer is usually measured in terms of social costs and benefits, which include money, resources, time, opportunity, and degrees of social organization and disorganization. The haunting refrain of the economic calculus runs through every major problem in education.

The legal calculus, which ranges from lawful to unlawful, highlights to what extent solutions to problems are congruent with the social concept of what is lawful and of what is thereby clothed with the garment of the legitimate power of the community. Many problems in education turn on these concepts.

Finally, the political calculus emphasizes the significance of the human trait of disagreement in the problem-solving process. It ranges from agreement to disagreement and focuses on the importance of sustaining agreement between human beings about solutions to problems. The political calculus is particularly important in the study of school and society. People disagree not only on how problems in education are to be solved, but also on what social values and norms are to be used in defining and evaluating them.

Technological, economic, legal, and political calculations are therefore involved in the analysis of problems affecting school and society. Once these considerations are made, they become assumptions in the approach to solving these problems and, from a methodological perspective, limitations on the nature of problematic inquiry. At this stage, inquiry usually stops; implementation of the solution begins. If the assumptions upon which the solution is based are incorrect, the problem may not only go unsolved; additional problems may also be generated. This condition is especially likely to occur with complex social problems regarding the school.

As a tool for analyzing problems, science fiction does not suffer from these limitations. Inquiry is subject only to the boundaries of the human imagination, and science fiction writers are therefore much freer than social scientists to conceptualize and write about sociological possibilities which may be solutions to the problems in education.

But the advantage of science fiction involves much more than the expansion of the ranges within which technological, economic, legal, and political calculations can be made about the social dimensions of problems in education and their solutions. More importantly, the science fiction writer is able *to assess the consequences of these calculations* by creating a fictional world through which he can evaluate not only solutions to problems but also the very definitions of the problems themselves.

While the term *science fiction* is usually associated with the twentieth century, the use of a fictional world as a tool for inquiry about existing worlds and for evaluating alternative worlds is a very traditional technique. For example, during the fourth century B.C., Plato developed his model for a perfect society in *The Republic*. Similarly, in sixteenth-century England, Sir Thomas More assessed alternative political and social conditions in his *Utopia*.

These two examples of classical speculative fiction are the forerunners of contemporary science fiction which attempts to evaluate and criticize society. By depicting the potential development of trends in society today and by conceptualizing alternatives to those trends, science fiction offers the student of school and society a methodological tool by which man and his relationships —actual and possible—can be studied. The unique contribution of science fiction is that it, by definition, need not limit itself to what has been in the past or is now possible. Any alternative which can be conceived by man's mind may be utilized. The *possibility* of ideas simply reinforces their *probability,* and the link between the present and the future becomes the human imagination. Science fiction is indeed Promethean.

The second contribution which science fiction can make to the study of school and society is the effective capturing of the discreteness of life. Modern life is diverse and complex. It is also characterized by large structures, such as the corporation, the city, government, and mass media, and by all-encompassing processes, such as industrialization, urbanization, and bureaucratization. In an analysis of the problems which these conditions generate, social scientists often become preoccupied with the study of "macrosystems," "macrostructures," and "macroprocesses." Diversity, structure, and process are difficult to capture theoretically. Science fiction provides a convenient lens through which diversity can be appreciated and understood, and structure and process simplified and clarified. The conditions of modern life not only can be intellectualized more meaningfully; they can also be emotionally experienced. Empathizing with the characters of a story allows a reader to experience the world depicted by science fiction. Thus "heart-learning" as well as "head-learning" is developed. Both forms of learning are necessary in the study of school and society.

Science fiction's third contribution to the study of school and society is optimism. Often the thorough study of problems in education leads to intellectual despair about the ability of the individual to cope with the conditions of modern life and its problems. Certainly, mainstream literature reflects man-alone, man-unaided, and man-alienated themes. The model of the twentieth-century individual depicted in this literature is the anti-hero, pessimistic about his ability to cope with modern society and fatalistic about his destiny. He views the future with horror and despair.

Science fiction writers, on the other hand, have a deep, abiding faith in humanity and in its invincibility. For them, the individual really is important; he is neither unaided, nor alone, nor alienated. To be sure, some science fiction writers postulate a rather problematic future; but there is still a future ahead that is worth seeking. The future is not something which merely happens; it must be created. Harlan Ellison put the matter epigrammatically:

> The world you were born into is going nuts. Just check around if you think I'm wrong. . . .
>   Not Christ nor man nor governments of men will save you . . . writers about tomorrow must stop living in yesterday and

work from their hearts and their guts and their courage to tell us about tomorrow, before all the tomorrows are stolen away from us . . . no one will come down from the mountain to save your lily-white hide or your black ass. God is within you. Save yourselves.[3]

Science fiction then presents to man not only a future in which he can have faith but also a feeling of faith in himself. This perspective, woven throughout science fiction, is refreshing in the context of other bodies of literature which prophesy doom. Here again science fiction emerges as a Promethean literature, for the English adjectival cognate for life-giving is "promethean."

To assert that a thread of optimism is woven throughout science fiction does not imply that science fiction writers are naive. On the contrary, they are well aware of the potential dangers, as well as promise, of science and technology. The fourth contribution which science fiction can make to the study of school and society is its ability to function as a warning device for the development of future problems.

Educational problems are not mysterious; they can be analyzed and forecast. But in order to achieve these objectives, two important elements must be assessed: *predisposing* factors and *precipitating* factors. Predisposing factors are those which create a problematic situation; precipitating factors are those which actually make the problem obvious to a large number of people. Most social science perspectives on educational problems deal with how society responds to social situations *after* they become problems; hence precipitating factors are the focus of concern.

Science fiction, however, has the distinction of being able to discern the predisposing factors in the present world which lead to problems in the future. Instead of merely describing a situation—as good narrative fiction does—science fiction writers engage in diagnosis, which is primarily concerned with determining the symptoms of a problem. From a diagnosis of trends, a writer then proceeds to another step, which is a concern for the *etiology* of the situation, or the search for causes and the development of the problematic condition. Frequently, science fiction writers proceed to still another

---

3. Quoted in Wollheim, op. cit., p. 107.

7

step and engage in *prognosis,* or an attempt to offer an evaluative prediction and treatment of the problem.

Through this mode of analysis, science fiction does not apply the methods of past sociology to future educational problems; rather, it is developing future sociology for present and future educational problems. Diagnosis, etiology, and prognosis—these are the trademarks of good science fiction. Happily, they are also the ingredients of good social science analysis of educational problems.

It is possible to name a fifth contribution of science fiction to the study of school and society: its capacity, as a body of literature, to make us aware of and comfortable with change. Educational problems are inextricably bound up with change, and science fiction is unparalleled as a system of ideas concerned with understanding and evaluating change. In fact, Brian Aldiss, a leading science fiction writer, has classified science fiction as the "subliterature of change"—the "literary mode of today."[4] The importance of science fiction to school and society in this connection cannot be overstated. Since science fiction has reflected, if not shaped, the world of today—a world of science and technology—it is hardly surprising to note that science fiction can also make us aware of the consequences of science and technology for the human condition. In this sense, science fiction has produced a major proposition whose testing continues as humanity rushes toward the future: *changes in the modes of life result in changes in the goals and purposes of living.* This proposition is of special significance in its application to the study of school and society. Changes in the organizational techniques which are applied to social relationships result in changes in social goals and values. Future shock is not an inexorable condition; it is merely the price which people must pay for ignorance of science fiction's major proposition.

Science fiction not only can contribute to the study of school and society in a collective sense but also can help to develop attitudes towards educational problems on the part of the individual

---

4. Brian Aldiss, *The Shape of Further Things: Speculations on Change* (Garden City, N. Y.: Doubleday, 1971), pp. xi, 41.

as he asks the question: What can I do to help solve educational problems?

One attitude which can be developed from the application of science fiction to social problems is "anti-scapegoatism." The term *scapegoat* has come to mean any person who has to bear the blame for the misfortunes of, or calamities absorbed by, others. The term has been traced back to the ancient Hebrews, who loaded their "sins" onto the back of a goat and then sent it into the desert. The principle is still with us today. Many educational problems are apt to be "explained" by reference to "scapegoat theories." The literature of science fiction is anti-scapegoat. It reminds us that problems simply do not go away by themselves. It also develops a particularly severe posture toward the conditions which give rise to problems and admits of no projection technique like the scapegoat in the search for explanations. Indeed, one of the standard plot techniques in science fiction is to employ the *android* (an artificial man or woman programmed to have human emotions) as a surrogate for the blacks, Jews, Indians, or other oppressed groups, in order to expose bigotry, racism, and the scapegoat syndrome.

Another attitude is a healthy skepticism toward experts who propound solutions to educational problems. These experts tend to be technicians, administrative specialists, economists, bureaucrats, and a variety of academicians, including scientists. Their discussions of educational problems frequently put a premium upon the values of efficiency, cost-effectiveness, rationality, and long-range planning. In a word, they are concerned primarily about the "stomach" of educational problems. Unlike experts, science fiction writers are concerned about the "soul" of educational problems by addressing themselves primarily to fundamental human and social values and basic human dilemmas. Expertise generates a particular kind of authority towards educational problems. Science fiction is a refreshing change from it.

In addition, it is important that an individual not be content with understanding a particular educational problem but look rather at the general sociological condition from which the problem is generated. Whereas social scientists will very likely be content with an objective description and explanation of particular educational problems, science fiction writers explicitly take positions of diagnosis, etiology, and prognosis in relation to underlying trends which give rise to educational problems.

This difference in methodological approach to school and society on the part of the science fiction writer stems from his explicit avowal of a set of values from which his inquiry proceeds. The aim of the social scientist is to develop, on the basis of value neutrality, a set of lawlike propositions about the nature of educational problems. Ideally, such propositions take the form $2 + 2 = 4$. But the science fiction writer deals with hypothetical imperatives and explicitly argues on behalf of propositions which take the forms: "since you want 4, then do . . ."; "if you want 4, then do . . ."; or "if you don't want 4, then don't do . . ."

The richness of the kinds of propositions which science fiction writers depict in their stories coincides with the richness and conflicting diversity in the principles that are an integral part of American culture which affects the school. Among these principles may be included upper mobility, the popular vote, freedom of expression, freedom of belief, love of leisure, a desire to have one's way of life emulated, a distrust of big government, frugality and industriousness, sovereignty of the people, individualism, freedom from the past, agreeability in the association of ideas, equal opportunity, humanitarianism, dominance of women, party government, glorification of the common people, ingenuity and invention, high standards of living, belief in the evolutionary process, emphasis on efficiency, freedom of relationships, openness, humor, and so *ad infinitum*. These contradictory values and principles are permeated with a generous materialistic philosophy. An American espouses materialism and capitalism, yet he accedes to the highest moral and cultural practices of the world. Science fiction writers work with these sets of values and attempt to point out the if-then, since-then dimensions of them in relation to school and society.

The organization of this book respects the classifications normally found in texts in the field of the social foundations of education. Not all teachers in this field may agree with the boundary criteria for such classifications. Therefore, the materials in the book allow the teacher to bring his own theoretical insights to bear upon the major subjects involved in his course. He can use the materials in relation to lectures, discussion, and the major textbooks in the field in a creative way and avoid following traditional paradigms in teaching about the social foundations of education. Since this is a book about alternative school and social worlds, it is most appropriate that the teacher develop alternative conceptual worlds to deal with them.

1.
THE PURPOSES OF EDUCATION

Just as a "child is father to the man," so, too, a nation's educational system is made up not only of current ideas and technology but also of vestiges of the past. One cannot hope to understand the changes which the American educational system is undergoing without a serious consideration of the traditions and educational patterns that went before it. American educational practices are as much a legacy of the past as they are a response to new challenges.

What is taught in the schools, how it is taught, and how education is organized are extensions of the purposes of education as reflected in American ideas and philosophy regarding education. The nature of that philosophy, we have come to observe, is not based upon abstract educational speculation; rather, it has emerged from, and is rooted in, the social, economic, and political conditions of American life. The conditions of this life encouraged, at the beginning of our nation, easy and somewhat utopian optimism due to the liberation of Americans from the "Old World." What speculation existed was couched in terms of rather natural influences, such as economic and geographical factors, upon the American school system. The greater part of thinking about the purposes of American education arose in relation to specific issues and controversies.

Over time, several distinct themes became woven throughout the purposes of American education, but these were supplanted by other themes as social, economic, and political dynamics dictated. For example, the purposes of early American education were inextricably bound up with theology. The early leaders of the American colonies were largely clergymen. It was quite natural for religious values to dominate the purposes of education at that time. Education has become secularized today. Moreover, the individualism of the eighteenth century was eventually de-emphasized by the enormous extension of government regulation and by a willingness to permit government a wide field of influence in education. Furthermore, the belief that individualism was based on natural rights was replaced by the utilitarian idea that the aims of education should serve the "greatest good for the greatest number."

Thus the purposes of American education have varied according to the social, economic, and political development of the nation. But this is not to say that these purposes have not had a common motif. Consistent threads have been apparent. They can be summarized by the following premises: (1) that education should *serve the political values* of the country; (2) that education should help to *develop effective members* of society; (3) that education should help to *develop intellectual abilities* of thinking and analysis in the student, thus enabling him to become employable; (4) that education should be *founded on the traditions of society;* (5) that education should *stress the integration of theory with practice;* and (6) that education should be *available to all people.*

These premises, which seem to inhere in the major purposes of American education, are ambiguous and thus tend to generate conflict and disagreement not only as to what they *really* mean but also as to how they can best be achieved. Figure A depicts levels of conflict over factors related to an educational system.

The educational system generates a great deal of conflict in American society. This conflict can exist over personalities, educational issues, how the school is organized, how students are taught, what students are taught, and the purposes of education. As Figure A shows, the highest level of conflict is likely to be over the funda-

Figure A

High Conflict

Purposes of Education
What Is Taught
Educational Methods
Educational Organization
Educational Issues
Personalities

Low Conflict

mental purposes of education; at least this has been historically true.

But perhaps conflict is inevitable in the educational system. After all, the school system is embedded in society. Whatever happens in society and whatever conflict exists there is bound to be reflected in the school system.

Moreover, the history of American education reveals a path of development between two essentially competing purposes. Figure B represents this development.

Figure B

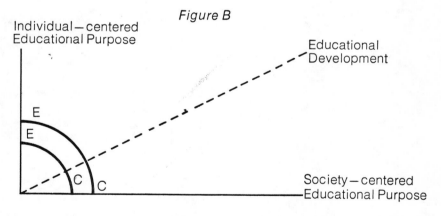

Individual—centered
Educational Purpose

Educational
Development

E

E

C   C

Society—centered
Educational Purpose

There is competition between education that is individual-centered and education which is society-centered. The basic premise of the former is equality; of the latter, system capability. Thus there exists a dialectic between "E" (equality) and "C" (system capability). This dialectic generates social conflict over the nature and purpose of education, over the allocation of scarce resources to varying purposes of education, and over the content of curriculum as it relates to these purposes.

All this is not to suggest that this competition between equality and system capability is negative; indeed, a democratic society thrives on competing interests, ideas, and values. What this analysis does suggest for the student of the social foundations of education is that the *public* (social) and *private* (individual) purposes of education may be in conflict and that the resolution of this conflict determines the future development of education.

PROFESSION

Isaac Asimov

American education has been subjected to a variety of criticisms throughout its history. These criticisms include:

1. Charges of *subversion and communist influence.* The schools proved to be an inviting target for right-wing extremists, especially during the McCarthy era in the early 1950s. The most prominent organization dedicated to erasing the "evils of communism" from the schools was the National Council for American Education, who attacked both teachers and their textbooks as tools of the communist conspiracy. While a few teachers were members of the Communist party, so were a few doctors, plumbers, and carpenters. This type of criticism remains with us today, although the "subversion" charges are not normally directed at a particular group.

2. Opposition to the increasing *costs* of education. This criticism often arises when school bond issues or similar devices are placed before the public. Cities like Youngstown, Ohio, have had their public education systems paralyzed by the failure at the polls of bond issues. Persons whose children have grown up and couples without children have protested what they feel to be the "unfairness" of tax laws which "force" them to contribute to the expenses of school operations. Special educational programs for the disadvantaged have also drawn the fire of critics, who see them as discriminatory because they will not be of direct benefit to their own children.

3. The schools are *destroying traditional values.* This charge most often refers to religious values. The struggle over the teaching of evolutionary theory was one example of this feeling. The banning of religious observances in some schools has also brought criticisms of the educational system, rather than of the judicial system whose dictates the schools were observing.

4. The schools are charged with *incompetency*. The furor over "why Johnny can't read" along with the still too high drop-out rate in the schools are two manifestations of this criticism. On a more general level, the Russian launching of Sputnik in the late 1950s forced a reexamination of our educational system. The question of why the United States was not first in space was often answered by pointing out deficiencies in education, especially in the areas of science and engineering. The charge of incompetency continues to be raised, in spite of the fact that research has shown that each generation of Americans is better educated and more knowledgeable than the one before.

5. The schools are *"tools of the establishment"* and are *dehumanizing* the student. This charge, usually associated with spokesmen of the New Left, holds that the schools support monopolistic capitalism and the exploitation of the average American, in that they inculcate the young with traditional values which need to be changed. Furthermore, say these critics, the schools, through their emphasis on competition and achievement, place students in the position of "winners" and "losers." They argue that this is dehumanizing and degrading, forcing the students to lose a sense of compassion, and making them feel, in the words of a famous football coach, that "winning isn't everything, it's the *only* thing."

These critics argue for a new, more humanistic type of educational system. Open classrooms, the elimination of grading, and a greater role for students in determining curriculum are some of the steps advocated. In "Profession" author Isaac Asimov creates a society which does away with traditional education by means of advanced technology. Everyone can read in this society, because the government has devised a method for mass "education." It is a highly specialized society, like our own, but with some important differences. It dispenses with schools, teachers, guidance counselors, even organized education. But like all educational systems, it too is subject to criticism!

FOR FURTHER THOUGHT OR DISCUSSION

1. Which criticisms of American education do you consider valid?

2. What does the ending of the story tell you about the nature of the learning process?

3. What alternative systems of education work better than our own?

4. Examine the radical critique of American education. Are our schools dehumanizing?

5. Are schools *reflective* of our society, or do they *create* the society we live in?

6. Is the system of education in the story totalitarian or egalitarian?

PROFESSION   *Isaac Asimov*

George Platen could not conceal the longing in his voice. It was too much to suppress. He said, "Tomorrow's the first of May. Olympics!"

He rolled over on his stomach and peered over the foot of his bed at his roommate. Didn't *he* feel it, too? Didn't *this* make some impression on him?

George's face was thin and had grown a trifle thinner in the nearly year and a half that he had been at the House. His figure was slight but the look in his blue eyes was as intense as it had ever been, and right now there was a trapped look in the way his fingers curled against the bedspread.

George's roommate looked up briefly from his book and took the opportunity to adjust the light-level of the stretch of wall near his

"Profession" by Isaac Asimov, published in *Astounding Science Fiction*. Copyright © 1957 by Street and Smith Publications, Inc. Reprinted by permission of the author.

chair. His name was Hali Omani and he was a Nigerian by birth. His dark brown skin and massive features seemed made for calmness, and mention of the Olympics did not move him.

He said, "I know, George."

George owed much to Hali's patience and kindness when it was needed, but even patience and kindness could be overdone. Was this a time to sit there like a statue built of some dark, warm wood?

George wondered if he himself would grow like that after ten years here and rejected the thought violently. No!

He said defiantly, "I think you've forgotten what May means."

The other said, "I remember very well what it means. It means nothing! You're the one who's forgotten that. May means nothing to you, George Platen, and," he added softly, "it means nothing to me, Hali Omani."

George said, "The ships are coming in for recruits. By June, thousands and thousands will leave with millions of men and women heading for any world you can name, and all that means nothing?"

"Less than nothing. What do you want me to do about it, anyway?" Omani ran his finger along a difficult passage in the book he was reading and his lips moved soundlessly.

George watched him. Damn it, he thought, yell, scream; you can do that much. Kick at me, do anything.

It was only that he wanted not to be so alone in his anger. He wanted not to be the only one so filled with resentment, not to be the only one dying a slow death.

It was better those first weeks when the Universe was a small shell of vague light and sound pressing down upon him. It was better before Omani had wavered into view and dragged him back to a life that wasn't worth living.

Omani! He was old! He was at least thirty. George thought: Will I be like that at thirty? Will I be like that in twelve years?

And because he was afraid he might be, he yelled at Omani, "Will you stop reading that fool book?"

Omani turned a page and read on a few words, then lifted his head with its skullcap of crisply curled hair and said, "What?"

"What good does it do you to read the book?" He stepped forward, snorted "More electronics," and slapped it out of Omani's hands.

Omani got up slowly and picked up the book. He smoothed a crumpled page without visible rancor. "Call it the satisfaction of curiosity," he said. "I understand a little of it today, perhaps a little more tomorrow. That's a victory in a way."

"A victory. What kind of a victory? Is that what satisfies you in life? To get to know enough to be a quarter of a Registered Electronician by the time you're sixty-five?"

"Perhaps by the time I'm thirty-five."

"And then who'll want you? Who'll use you? Where will you go?"

"No one. No one. Nowhere. I'll stay here and read other books."

"And that satisfies you? Tell me! You've dragged me to class. You've got me to reading and memorizing, too. For what? There's nothing in it that satisfies me."

"What good will it do you to deny yourself satisfaction?"

"It means I'll quit the whole farce. I'll do as I planned to do in the beginning before you dovey-lovied me out of it. I'm going to force them to—to——"

Omani put down his book. He let the other run down and then said, "To what, George?"

"To correct a miscarriage of justice. A frame-up. I'll get that Antonelli and force him to admit he—he——"

Omani shook his head. "Everyone who comes here insists it's a mistake. I thought you'd passed that stage."

"Don't call it a stage," said George violently. "In my case, it's a fact. I've told you——"

"You've told me, but in your heart you know no one made any mistake as far as you were concerned."

"Because no one will admit it? You think any of them would admit a mistake unless they were forced to? ——Well, I'll force them."

It was May that was doing this to George; it was Olympics month. He felt it bring the old wildness back and he couldn't stop it. He didn't want to stop it. He had been in danger of forgetting.

He said, "I was going to be a Computer Programmer and I *can* be one. I could be one today, regardless of what they say analysis shows." He pounded his mattress. "They're wrong. They *must* be."

"The analysts are never wrong."

"They *must* be. Do you doubt my intelligence?"

"Intelligence hasn't one thing to do with it. Haven't you been told that often enough? Can't you understand that?"

George rolled away, lay on his back and stared somberly at the ceiling.

"What did you want to be, Hali?"

"I had no fixed plans. Hydroponicist would have suited me, I suppose."

"Did you think you could make it?"

"I wasn't sure."

George had never asked personal questions of Omani before. It struck him as queer, almost unnatural, that other people had had ambitions and ended here. Hydroponicist!

He said, "Did you think you'd make *this?*"

"No, but here I am just the same."

"And you're satisfied. Really, really satisfied. You're happy. You love it. You wouldn't be anywhere else."

Slowly, Omani got to his feet. Carefully, he began to unmake his bed. He said, "George, you're a hard case. You're knocking yourself out because you won't accept the facts about yourself. George, you're here in what you call the House, but I've never heard you give it its full title. Say it, George, say it. Then go to bed and sleep this off."

George gritted his teeth and showed them. He choked out, "No!"

"Then I will," said Omani, and he did. He shaped each syllable carefully.

George was bitterly ashamed at the sound of it. He turned his head away.

For most of the first eighteen years of his life, George Platen had headed firmly in one direction, that of Registered Computer Programmer. There were those in his crowd who spoke wisely of Spationautics, Refrigeration Technology, Transportation Control, and even Administration. But George held firm.

He argued relative merits as vigorously as any of them, and why not? Education Day loomed ahead of them and was the great fact of their existence. It approached steadily, as fixed and certain as the calendar—the first day of November of the year following one's eighteenth birthday.

After that day, there were other topics of conversation. One could discuss with others some detail of the profession, or the virtues of one's wife and children, or the fate of one's space-polo team, or one's experience in the Olympics. Before Education Day, however, there was only one topic that unfailingly and unwearyingly held everyone's interest, and that was Education Day.

"What are you going for? Think you'll make it? Heck, that's no good. Look at the records; quota's been cut. Logistics now——"

Or Hypermechanics now—— Or Communications now—— Or Gravitics now——

Especially Gravitics at the moment. Everyone had been talking about Gravitics in the few years just before George's Education Day because of the development of the Gravitic power engine.

Any world within ten light-years of a dwarf star, everyone said, would give its eyeteeth for any kind of Registered Gravitics Engineer.

The thought of that never bothered George. Sure it would; all the eyeteeth it could scare up. But George had also heard what had happened before in a newly developed technique. Rationalization and simplification followed in a flood. New models each year; new types of gravitic engines; new principles. Then all those eyeteeth gentlemen would find themselves out of date and superseded by later models with later educations. The first group would then have to settle down to unskilled labor or ship out to some backwoods world that wasn't quite caught up yet.

Now Computer Programmers were in steady demand year after year, century after century. The demand never reached wild peaks; there was never a howling bull market for Programmers; but the demand climbed steadily as new worlds opened up and as older worlds grew more complex.

He had argued with Stubby Trevelyan about that constantly. As best friends, their arguments had to be constant and vitriolic and, of course, neither ever persuaded or was persuaded.

But then Trevelyan had had a father who was a Registered Metallurgist and had actually served on one of the Outworlds, and a grandfather who had also been a Registered Metallurgist. He himself was intent on becoming a Registered Metallurgist almost as a matter of family right and was firmly convinced that any other profession was a shade less than respectable.

"There'll always be metal," he said, "and there's an accomplishment in molding alloys to specification and watching structures grow. Now what's a Programmer going to be doing. Sitting at a coder all day long, feeding some fool mile-long machine.

Even at sixteen, George had learned to be practical. He said simply, "There'll be a million Metallurgists put out along with you."

"Because it's good. A good profession. The best."

"But you get crowded out, Stubby. You can be way back in line. Any world can tape out its own Metallurgists, and the market for advanced Earth models isn't so big. And it's mostly the small worlds that want them. You know what percent of the turnout of Registered Metallurgists get tabbed for worlds with a Grade A rating. I looked it up. It's just 13.3 percent. That means you'll have seven chances in eight of being stuck in some world that just about has running water. You may even be stuck on Earth; 2.3 percent are."

Trevelyan said belligerently, "There's no disgrace in staying on

Earth. Earth needs technicians, too. Good ones." His grandfather had been an Earth-bound Metallurgist, and Trevelyan lifted his finger to his upper lip and dabbed at an as yet nonexistent mustache.

George knew about Trevelyan's grandfather and, considering the Earth-bound position of his own ancestry, was in no mood to sneer. He said diplomatically, "No intellectual disgrace. Of course not. But it's nice to get into a Grade A world, isn't it?

"Now you take Programmers. Only the Grade A worlds have the kind of computers that really need first-class Programmers so they're the only ones in the market. And Programmer tapes are complicated and hardly any one fits. They need more Programmers than their own population can supply. Its just a matter of statistics. There's one first-class Programmer per million, say. A world needs twenty and has a population of ten million, they have to come to Earth for five to fifteen Programmers. Right?

"And you know how many Registered Computer Programmers went to Grade A planets last year? I'll tell you. Every last one. If you're a Programmer, you're a picked man. Yes, sir."

Trevelyan frowned. "If only one in a million makes it, what makes you think *you'll* make it?"

George said guardedly, "I'll make it."

He never dared tell anyone; not Trevelyan; not his parents; of exactly what he was doing that made him so confident. But he wasn't worried. He was simply confident (that was the worst of the memories he had in the hopeless days afterward). He was as blandly confident as the average eight-year-old kid approaching Reading Day—that childhood preview of Education Day.

Of course, Reading Day had been different. Partly, there was the simple fact of childhood. A boy of eight takes many extraordinary things in stride. One day you can't read and the next day you can. That's just the way things are. Like the sun shining.

And then not so much depended upon it. There were no recruiters just ahead, waiting and jostling for the lists and scores on the coming Olympics. A boy or girl who goes through the Reading Day is just someone who has ten more years of undifferentiated living upon Earth's crawling surface; just someone who returns to his family with one new ability.

By the time Education Day came, ten years later, George wasn't even sure of most of the details of his own Reading Day.

Most clearly of all, he remembered it to be a dismal September day with a mild rain falling. (September for Reading Day; November for Education Day; May for Olympics. They made nursery rhymes out of it.) George had dressed by the wall lights, with his parents far more excited than he himself was. His father was a Registered Pipe Fitter and had found his occupation on earth. This fact had always been a humiliation to him, although, of course, as anyone could see plainly, most of each generation must stay on Earth in the nature of things.

There had to be farmers and miners and even technicians on Earth. It was only the late-model, high-specialty professions that were in demand on the Outworlds, and only a few millions a year out of Earth's eight billion population could be exported. Every man and woman on Earth couldn't be among that group.

But every man and woman could hope that at least one of his children could be one, and Platen, Senior, was certainly no exception. It was obvious to him (and, to be sure, to others as well) that George was notably intelligent and quick-minded. He would be bound to do well and he would have to, as he was an only child. If George didn't end on an Outworld, they would have to wait for grandchildren before a next chance would come along, and that was too far in the future to be much consolation.

Reading Day would not prove much, of course, but it would be the only indication they would have before the big day itself. Every parent on Earth would be listening to the quality of reading when his child came home with it; listening for any particularly easy flow of words and building that into certain omens of the future. There were few families that didn't have at least one hopeful who, from Reading Day on, was the great hope because of the way he handled his trisyllabics.

Dimly, George was aware of the cause of his parents' tension, and if there was any anxiety in his young heart that drizzly morning, it was only the fear that his father's hopeful expression might fade out when he returned home with his reading.

The children met in the large assembly room of the town's Education hall. All over Earth, in millions of local halls, throughout that month, similar groups of children would be meeting. George felt depressed by the grayness of the room and by the other children, strained and stiff in unaccustomed finery.

Automatically, George did as all the rest of the children did. He found the small clique that represented the children on his floor of the apartment house and joined them.

Trevelyan, who lived immediately next door, still wore his hair childishly long and was years removed from the sideburns and thin, reddish mustache that he was to grow as soon as he was physiologically capable of it.

Trevelyan (to whom George was then known as Jaw-jee) said, "Bet you're scared."

"I am not," said George. Then, confidentially, "My folks got a hunk of printing up on the dresser in my room, and when I come home, I'm going to read it for them." (George's main suffering at the moment lay in the fact that he didn't quite know where to put his hands. He had been warned not to scratch his head or rub his ears or pick his nose or put his hands into his pockets. This eliminated almost every possibility.)

Trevelyan put *his* hands in his pockets and said, "My father isn't worried."

Trevelyan, Senior, had been a Metallurgist on Diporia for nearly seven years, which gave him a superior social status in his neighborhood even though he had retired and returned to Earth.

Earth discouraged these re-immigrants because of population problems, but a small trickle did return. For one thing the cost of living was lower on Earth, and what was a trifling annuity on Diporia, say, was a comfortable income on Earth. Besides, there were always men who found more satisfaction in displaying their success before the friends and scenes of their childhood than before all the rest of the Universe besides.

Trevelyan, Senior, further explained that if he stayed on Diporia, so would his children, and Diporia was a one-spaceship world. Back on Earth, his kids could end anywhere, even Novia.

Stubby Trevelyan had picked up that item early. Even before Reading Day, his conversation was based on the carelessly assumed fact that his ultimate home would be in Novia.

George, oppressed by thoughts of the other's future greatness and his own small-time contrast, was driven to belligerent defense at once.

"My father isn't worried either. He just wants to hear me read because he knows I'll be good. I suppose your father would just as soon not hear you because he knows you'll be all wrong."

"I will not be all wrong. Reading is *nothing*. On Novia, I'll *hire* people to read to me."

"Because *you* won't be able to read yourself, on account of you're *dumb!*"

"Then how come I'll be on Novia?"

And George, driven, made the great denial. "Who says you'll be on Novia? Bet you don't go anywhere."

Stubby Trevelyan reddened. "I won't be a Pipe Fitter like your old man."

"Take that back, you dumbhead."

"You take *that* back."

They stood nose to nose, not wanting to fight but relieved at having something familiar to do in this strange place. Furthermore, now that George had curled his hands into fists and lifted them before his face, the problem of what to do with his hands was, at least temporarily, solved. Other children gathered round excitedly.

But then it all ended when a woman's voice sounded loudly over the public address system. There was instant silence everywhere. George dropped his fists and forgot Trevelyan.

"Children," said the voice, "we are going to call out your names. As each child is called, he or she is to go to one of the men waiting along the side walls. Do you see them? They are wearing red uniforms so they will be easy to find. The girls will go to the right. The boys will go to the left. Now look about and see which man in red is nearest to you—"

George found his man at a glance and waited for his name to be called off. He had not been introduced before this to the sophistications of the alphabet, and the length of time it took to reach his own name grew disturbing.

The crowd of children thinned; little rivulets made their way to each of the red-clad guides.

When the name "George Platen" was finally called, his sense of relief was exceeded only by the feeling of pure gladness at the fact that Stubby Trevelyan still stood in his place, uncalled.

George shouted back over his shoulder as he left, "Yay, Stubby, maybe they don't want you."

That moment of gaiety quickly left. He was herded into a line and directed down corridors in the company of strange children. They all looked at one another, large-eyed and concerned, but beyond a snuffling, "Quitcher pushing" and "Hey, watch out" there was no conversation.

They were handed little slips of paper which they were told must remain with them. George stared at his curiously. Little black marks of different shapes. He knew it to be printing but how could anyone make words out of it? He couldn't imagine.

He was told to strip; he and four other boys who were all that now remained together. All the new clothes came shucking off and four eight-year-olds stood naked and small, shivering more out of embarrassment than cold. Medical technicians came past, probing them, test-

27

ing them with odd instruments, pricking them for blood. Each took the little cards and made additional marks on them with little black rods that produced the marks, all neatly lined up, with great speed. George stared at the new marks, but they were no more comprehensible than the old. The children were ordered back into their clothes.

They sat on separate little chairs then and waited again. Names were called again and "George Platen" came third.

. He moved into a large room, filled with frightening instruments with knobs and glassy panels in front. There was a desk in the very center, and behind it a man sat, his eyes on the papers piled before him.

He said, "George Platen?"

"Yes, sir," said George in a shaky whisper. All this waiting and all this going here and there was making him nervous. He wished it were over.

The man behind the desk said, "I am Dr. Lloyed, George. How are you?"

The doctor didn't look up as he spoke. It was as though he had said those words over and over again and didn't have to look up any more.

"I'm all right."

"Are you afraid, George?"

"N—no, sir," said George, sounding afraid even in his own ears.

"That's good," said the doctor, "because there's nothing to be afraid of, you know. Let's see, George. It says here on your card that your father is named Peter and that he's a Registered Pipe Fitter and your mother is named Amy and is a Registered Home Technician. Is that right?"

"Y—yes, sir."

"And your birthday is February 13, and you had an ear infection about a year ago. Right?"

"Yes, sir."

"Do you know how I know all these things?"

"It's on the card, I think, sir."

"That's right." The doctor looked up at George for the first time and smiled. He showed even teeth and looked much younger than George's father. Some of George's nervousness vanished.

The doctor passed the card to George. "Do you know what all those things there mean, George?"

Although George knew he did not he was startled by the sudden request into looking at the card as though he might understand now through some sudden stroke of fate. But they were just marks as before and he passed the card back. "No, sir."

"Why not?"

George felt a sudden pang of suspicion concerning the sanity of this doctor. Didn't he know why not?

George said, "I can't read, sir."

"Would you like to read?"

"Yes, sir."

"Why, George?"

George stared, appalled. No one had ever asked him that. He had no answer. He said falteringly, "I don't know, sir."

"Printed information will direct you all through your life. There is so much you'll have to know even after Education Day. Cards like this one will tell you. Books will tell you. Television screens will tell you. Printing will tell you such useful things and such interesting things that not being able to read would be as bad as not being able to see. Do you understand?"

"Yes, sir."

"Are you afraid, George?"

"No, sir."

"Good. Now I'll tell you exactly what we'll do first. I'm going to put these wires on your forehead just over the corners of your eyes. They'll stick there but they won't hurt at all. Then, I'll turn on something that will make a buzz. It will sound funny and it may tickle you, but it won't hurt. Now if it does hurt, you tell me, and I'll turn it off right away, but it won't hurt. All right?"

George nodded and swallowed.

"Are you ready?"

George nodded. He closed his eyes while the doctor busied himself. His parents had explained this to him. They, too, had said it wouldn't hurt, but then there were always the older children. There were the ten- and twelve-year-olds who howled after the eight-year-olds waiting for Reading Day, "Watch out for the needle." There were the others who took you off in confidence and said, "They got to cut your head open. They use a sharp knife that big with a hook on it," and so on into horrifying details.

George had never believed them but he had had nightmares, and now he closed his eyes and felt pure terror.

He didn't feel the wires at his temple. The buzz was a distant thing, and there was the sound of his own blood in his ears, ringing hollowly as though it and he were in a large cave. Slowly he chanced opening his eyes.

The doctor had his back to him. From one of the instruments a strip of paper unwound and was covered with a thin, wavy purple line. The doctor tore off pieces and put them into a slot in another machine.

He did it over and over again. Each time a little piece of film came out, which the doctor looked at. Finally, he turned toward George with a queer frown between his eyes.

The buzzing stopped.

George said breathlessly, "Is it over?"

The doctor said, "Yes," but he was still frowning.

"Can I read now?" asked George. He felt no different.

The doctor said, "What?" then smiled very suddenly and briefly. He said, "It works fine, George. You'll be reading in fifteen minutes. Now we're going to use another machine this time and it will take longer. I'm going to cover your whole head, and when I turn it on you won't be able to see or hear anything for a while, but it won't hurt. Just to make sure I'm going to give you a little switch to hold in your hand. If anything hurts, you press the little button and everything shuts off. All right?"

In later years, George was told that the little switch was strictly a dummy; that it was introduced solely for confidence. He never did know for sure, however, since he never pushed the button.

A large smoothly curved helmet with a rubbery inner lining was placed over his head and left there. Three or four little knobs seemed to grab at him and bite into his skull, but there was only a little pressure that faded. No pain.

The doctor's voice sounded dimly. "Everything all right, George?"

And then, with no real warning, a layer of thick felt closed down all about him. He was disembodied, there was no sensation, no universe, only himself and a distant murmur at the very ends of nothingness telling him something—telling him—telling him—

He strained to hear and understand but there was all that thick felt between.

Then the helmet was taken off his head, and the light was so bright that it hurt his eyes while the doctor's voice drummed at his ears.

The doctor said, "Here's your card, George. What does it say?"

George looked at his card again and gave out a strangled shout. The marks weren't just marks at all. They made up words. They were words just as clearly as though something were whispering them in his ears. He could *hear* them being whispered as he looked at them.

"What does it say, George?"

"It says—it says—'Platen, George. Born 13 February 6492 of Peter and Amy Platen in . . .'" He broke off.

"You can read, George," said the doctor. "It's all over."

"For good? I won't forget how?"

"Of course not." The doctor leaned over to shake hands gravely. "You will be taken home now."

It was days before George got over this new and great talent of his. He read for his father with such facility that Platen, Senior, wept and called relatives to tell the good news.

George walked about town, reading every scrap of printing he could find and wondering how it was that none of it had ever made sense to him before.

He tried to remember how it was not to be able to read and he couldn't. As far as his feeling about it was concerned, he had always been able to read. Always.

At eighteen, George was rather dark, of medium height, but thin enough to look taller. Trevelyan, who was scarcely an inch shorter, had a stockiness of build that made "Stubby" more than ever appropriate, but in this last year he had grown self-conscious. The nickname could no longer be used without reprisal. And since Trevelyan disapproved of his proper first name even more strongly, he was called Trevelyan or any decent variant of that. As though to prove his manhood further, he had most persistently grown a pair of sideburns and a bristly mustache.

He was sweating and nervous now, and George, who had himself grown out of "Jaw-jee" and into the curt monosyllabic gutterality of "George," was rather amused by that.

They were in the same large hall they had been in ten years before (and not since). It was as if a vague dream of the past had come to sudden reality. In the first few minutes George had been distinctly surprised at finding everything seem smaller and more cramped than his memory told him; then he made allowance for his own growth.

The crowd was smaller than it had been in childhood. It was exclusively male this time. The girls had another day assigned them.

Trevelyan leaned over to say, "Beats me the way they make you wait."

"Red tape," said George. "You can't avoid it."

Trevelyan said, "What makes *you* so damned tolerant about it?"

"I've got nothing to worry about."

"Oh, brother, you make me sick. I hope you end up Registered Manure Spreader just so I can see your face when you do." His somber eyes swept the crowd anxiously.

George looked about, too. It wasn't quite the system they used on the children. Matters went slower, and instructions had been given out at the start in print (an advantage over the pre-Readers). The names Platen and Trevelyan were well down the alphabet still, but this time the two knew it.

Young men came out of the education rooms, frowning and uncomfortable, picked up their clothes and belongings, then went off to analysis to learn the results.

Each, as he came out, would be surrounded by a clot of the thinning crowd. "How was it?" "How'd it feel?" "Whacha think ya made?" "Ya feel any different?"

Answers were vague and noncommittal.

George forced himself to remain out of those clots. You only raised your own blood pressure. Everyone said you stood the best chance if you remained calm. Even so, you could feel the palms of your hands grow cold. Funny that new tensions came with the years.

For instance, high-specialty professionals heading out for an Outworld were accompanied by a wife (or husband). It was important to keep the sex ratio in good balance on all worlds. And if you were going out to a Grade A world, what girl would refuse you? George had no specific girl in mind yet; he wanted none. Not now! Once he made Programmer; once he could add to his name, Registered Computer Programmer, he could take his pick, like a sultan in a harem. The thought excited him and he tried to put it away. Must stay calm.

Trevelyan muttered, "What's it all about anyway? First they say it works best if you're relaxed and at ease. Then they put you through this and make it impossible for you to be relaxed and at ease."

"Maybe that's the idea. They're separating the boys from the men to begin with. Take it easy, Trev."

"Shut up."

George's turn came. His name was not called. It appeared in glowing letters on the notice board.

He waved at Trevelyan. "Take it easy. Don't let it get you."

He was happy as he entered the testing chamber. Actually happy.

The man behind the desk said, "George Platen?"

For a fleeting instant there was a razor-sharp picture in George's mind of another man, ten years earlier, who had asked the same question, and it was almost as though this were the same man and he, George, had turned eight again as he stepped across the threshold.

But the man looked up and, of course, the face matched that of the sudden memory not at all. The nose was bulbous, the hair thin and stringy, and the chin wattled as though its owner had once been grossly overweight and had reduced.

The man behind the desk looked annoyed. "Well?"

George came to Earth. "I'm George Platen, sir."

"Say so, then. I'm Dr. Zachary Antonelli, and we're going to be intimately acquainted in a moment."

He stared at small strips of film, holding them up to the light owlishly.

George winced inwardly. Very hazily, he remembered that other doctor (he had forgotten the name) staring at such film. Could these be the same? The other doctor had frowned and this one was looking at him now as though he were angry.

His happiness was already just about gone.

Dr. Antonelli spread the pages of a thickish file out before him now and put the films carefully to one side. "It says here you want to be a Computer Programmer."

"Yes, doctor."

"Still do?"

"Yes, sir."

"It's a responsible and exacting position. Do you feel up to it?"

"Yes, sir."

"Most pre-Educates don't put down any specific profession. I believe they are afraid of queering it."

"I think that's right, sir."

"Aren't you afraid of that?"

"I might as well be honest, sir."

Dr. Antonelli nodded, but without any noticeable lightening of his expression. "Why do you want to be a Programmer?"

"It's a responsible and exacting position as you said, sir. It's an important job and an exciting one. I like it and I think I can do it."

Dr. Antonelli put the papers away, and looked at George sourly. He said, "How do you know you like it? Because you think you'll be snapped up by some Grade A planet?"

George thought uneasily: He's trying to rattle you. Stay calm and stay frank.

He said, "I think a Programmer has a good chance, sir, but even if I were left on Earth, I know I'd like it." (That was true enough. I'm not lying, thought George.)

"All right, how do you know?"

He asked it as though he knew there was no decent answer and George almost smiled. He had one.

He said, "I've been reading about Programming, sir."

"You've been *what?*" Now the doctor looked genuinely astonished and George took pleasure in that.

"Reading about it, sir. I bought a book on the subject and I've been studying it."

"A book for Registered Programmers?"

"Yes, sir."

"But you couldn't understand it."

"Not at first. I got other books on mathematics and electronics. I made out all I could. I still don't know much, but I know enough to know I like it and to know I can make it." (Even his parents never found that secret cache of books or knew why he spent so much time in his own room or exactly what happened to the sleep he missed.)

The doctor pulled at the loose skin under his chin. "What was your idea in doing that, son?"

"I wanted to make sure I would be interested, sir."

"Surely you know that being interested means nothing. You could be devoured by a subject and if the physical makeup of your brain makes it more efficient for you to be something else, something else you will be. You know that, don't you?"

"I've been told that," said George cautiously.

"Well, believe it. It's true."

George said nothing.

Dr. Antonelli said, "Or do you believe that studying some subject will bend the brain cells in that direction, like that other theory that a pregnant woman need only listen to great music persistently to make a composer of her child. Do you believe that?"

George flushed. That had certainly been in his mind. By forcing his intellect constantly in the desired direction, he had felt sure that he would be getting a head start. Most of his confidence had rested on exactly that point.

"I never——" he began, and found no way of finishing.

"Well, it isn't true. Good Lord, youngster, your brain pattern is fixed at birth. It can be altered by a blow hard enough to damage the cells or by a burst blood vessel or by a tumor or by a major infection—— each time, of course, for the worse. But it certainly can't be affected by your thinking special thoughts." He stared at George thoughtfully, then said, "Who told you to do this?"

George, now thoroughly disturbed, swallowed and said, "No one, doctor. My own idea."

"Who knew you were doing it after you started?"

"No one. Doctor, I meant to do no wrong."

"Who said anything about wrong? Useless is what I would say. Why did you keep it to yourself?"

"I—I thought they'd laugh at me." (He thought abruptly of a recent exchange with Trevelyan. George had very cautiously broached the thought, as of something merely circulating distantly in the very

Two men entered on catfeet and got on either side of George. They pinned his arms to his sides. One of them used an air-spray hypodermic in the hollow of his right elbow and the hypnotic entered his vein and had an almost immediate effect.

His screams cut off and his head fell forward. His knees buckled and only the men on either side kept him erect as he slept.

They took care of George as they said they would; they were good to him and unfailingly kind—about the way, George thought, he himself would be to a sick kitten he had taken pity on.

They told him that he should sit up and take some interest in life; and then told him that most people who came there had the same attitude of despair at the beginning and that he would snap out of it.

He didn't even hear them.

Dr. Ellenford himself visited him to tell him that his parents had been informed that he was away on special assignment.

George muttered, "Do they know——"

Ellenford assured him at once, "We gave no details."

At first George had refused to eat. They fed him intravenously. They hid sharp objects and kept him under guard. Hali Omani came to be his roommate and his stolidity had a calming effect.

One day, out of sheer desperate boredom, George asked for a book. Omani, who himself read books constantly, looked up, smiling broadly. George almost withdrew the request then, rather than give any of them satisfaction, then thought: What do I care?

He didn't specify the book and Omani brought one on chemistry. It was in big print, with small words and many illustrations. It was for teen-agers. He threw the book violently against the wall.

That's what he would be always. A teen-ager all his life. A pre-Educate forever and special books would have to be written for him. He lay smoldering in bed, staring at the ceiling, and after an hour had passed, he got up sulkily, picked up the book, and began reading.

It took him a week to finish it and then he asked for another.

"Do you want to take the first one back?" asked Omani.

George frowned. There were things in the book he had not understood, yet he was not so lost to shame as to say so.

But Omani said, "Come to think of it, you'd better keep it. Books are meant to be read and reread."

It was that same day that he finally yielded to Omani's invitation that he tour the place. He dogged at the Nigerian's feet and took in his surroundings with quick hostile glances.

The place was no prison certainly. There were no walls, no locked doors, no guards. But it was a prison in that the inmates had no place to go outside.

It was somehow good to see others like himself by the dozen. It was so easy to believe himself to be the only one in the world so— maimed.

He mumbled, "How many people here anyway?"

"Two hundred and five, George, and this isn't the only place of the sort in the world. There are thousands."

Men looked up as he passed, wherever he went; in the gymnasium, along the tennis courts; through the library (he had never in his life imagined books could exist in such numbers; they were stacked, actually stacked, along long shelves). They stared at him curiously and he returned the looks savagely. At least *they* were no better than he; no call for *them* to look at him as though he were some sort of curiosity.

Most of them were in their twenties. George said suddenly, "What happens to the older ones?"

Omani said, "This place specializes in the younger ones." Then, as though he suddenly recognized an implication in George's question that he had missed earlier, he shook his head gravely and said, "They're not put out of the way, if that's what you mean. There are other Houses for older ones."

"Who cares?" mumbled George, who felt he was sounding too interested and in danger of slipping into surrender.

"You might. As you grow older, you will find yourself in a House with occupants of both sexes."

That surprised George somehow, "Women, too?"

"Of course. Do you suppose women are immune to this sort of thing?"

George thought of that with more interest and excitement than he had felt for anything since before that day when— He forced his thought away from that.

Omani stopped at the doorway of a room that contained a small closed-circuit television set and a desk computer. Five or six men sat about the television. Omani said, "This is a classroom."

George said, "What's that?"

"The young men in there are being education. Not," he added, quickly, "in the usual way."

"You mean they're cramming it in bit by bit."

"That's right. This is the way everyone did it in ancient times."

This was what they kept telling him since he had come to the House but what of it? Suppose there had been a day when mankind had not known the diatherm-oven. Did that mean he should be satisfied to eat meat raw in a world where others ate it cooked?

He said, "Why do they want to go through that bit-by-bit stuff?"

"To pass the time, George, and because they're curious."

"What good does it do them?"

"It makes them happier."

George carried that thought to bed with him.

The next day he said to Omani ungraciously, "Can you get me into a classroom where I can find out something about programming?"

Omani replied heartily, "Sure."

It was slow and he resented it. Why should someone have to explain something and explain it again? Why should he have to read and reread a passage, then stare at a mathematical relationship and not understand it at once? That wasn't how other people had to be.

Over and over again, he gave up. Once he refused to attend classes for a week.

But always he returned. The official in charge, who assigned reading, conducted the television demonstrations, and even explained difficult passages and concepts, never commented on the matter.

George was finally give a regular task in the gardens and took his turn in the various kitchen and cleaning details. This was represented to him as being an advance, but he wasn't fooled. The place might have been far more mechanized than it was, but they deliberately made work for the young men in order to give them the illusion of worthwhile occupation, of usefulness. George wasn't fooled.

They were even paid small sums of money out of which they could buy certain specified luxuries or which they could put aside for a problematical use in a problematical old age. George kept his money in an open jar, which he kept on a closet shelf. He had no idea how much he had accumulated. Nor did he care.

He made no real friends though he reached the stage where a civil good day was in order. He even stopped brooding (or almost stopped) on the miscarriage of justice that had placed him there. He would go weeks without dreaming of Antonelli, of his gross nose and wattled neck, of the leer with which he would push George into a boiling quicksand and hold him under, till he woke screaming with Omani bending over him in concern.

Omani said to him on a snowy day in February, "It's amazing how you're adjusting."

But that was February, the thirteenth to be exact, his nineteenth birthday. March came, then April, and with the approach of May he realized he hadn't adjusted at all.

The previous May had passed unregarded while George was still in his bed, drooping and ambitionless. This May was different.

All over Earth, George knew, Olympics would be taking place and young men would be competing, matching their skills against one another in the fight for a place on a new world. There would be the holiday atmosphere, the excitement, the news reports, the self-contained recruiting agents from the worlds beyond space, the glory of victory or the consolations of defeat.

How much of fiction dealt with these motifs; how much of his own boyhood excitement lay in following the events of Olympics from year to year; how many of his own plans——

George Platen could not conceal the longing in his voice. It was too much to suppress. He said, "Tomorrow's the first of May. Olympics!"

And that led to his first quarrel with Omani and to Omani's bitter enunciation of the exact name of the institution in which George found himself.

Omani gazed fixedly at George and said distinctly, "A House for the Feeble-minded."

George Platen flushed. Feeble-minded!

He rejected it desperately. He said in a monotone, "I'm leaving." He said it on impulse. His conscious mind learned it first from the statement as he uttered it.

Omani, who had returned to his book, looked up. "What?"

George knew what he was saying now. He said it fiercely, "I'm leaving."

"That's ridiculous. Sit down, George, calm yourself."

"Oh, no. I'm here on a frame-up, I tell you. This doctor, Antonelli, took a dislike to me. It's the sense of power these petty bureaucrats have. Cross them and they wipe out your life with a stylus mark on some card file."

"Are you back to that?"

"And staying there till it's all straightened out. I'm going to get to Antonelli somehow, break him, force the truth out of him." George was breathing heavily and he felt feverish. Olympics month was here and he couldn't let it pass. If he did, it would be the final surrender and he would be lost for all time.

Omani threw his legs over the side of his bed and stood up. He was nearly six feet tall and the expression on his face gave him the look of a concerned Saint Bernard. He put his arm about George's shoulder, "If I hurt your feeling——"

George shrugged him off. "You just said what you thought was the truth, and I'm going to prove it isn't the truth, that's all. Why not? The door's open. There aren't any locks. No one ever said I couldn't leave. I'll just walk out."

"All right, but where will you go?"

"To the nearest air terminal, then to the nearest Olympics center. I've got money." He seized the open jar that held the wages he had put away. Some of the coins jangled to the floor.

"That will last you a week maybe. Then what?"

"By then I'll have things settled."

"By then you'll come crawling back here," said Omani earnestly, "with all the progress you've made to do over again. You're mad, George."

"Feeble-minded is the word you used before."

"Well, I'm sorry I did. Stay here, will you?"

"Are you going to try to stop me?"

Omani compressed his full lips. "No, I guess I won't. This is your business. If the only way you can learn is to buck the world and come back with blood on your face, go ahead. —Well, go ahead."

George was in the doorway now, looking back over his shoulder. "I'm going,"—he came back to pick up his pocket grooming set slowly— "I hope you don't object to my taking a few personal belongings."

Omani shrugged. He was in bed again reading, indifferent.

George lingered at the door again, but Omani didn't look up. George gritted his teeth, turned and walked rapidly down the empty corridor and out into the night-shrouded grounds.

He had expected to be stopped before leaving the grounds. He wasn't. He had stopped at an all-night diner to ask directions to an air terminal and expected the proprietor to call the police. That didn't happen. He summoned a skimmer to take him to the airport and the driver asked no questions.

Yet he felt no lift at that. He arrived at the airport sick at heart. He had not realized how the outer world would be. He was surrounded by professionals. The diner's proprietor had had his name inscribed on the plastic shell over the cash register. So and so, Registered Cook. The man in the skimmer had his license up, Registered Chauffeur. George felt the bareness of his name and experienced a kind of nakedness because of it; worse, he felt skinned. But no one challenged him. No one studied him suspiciously and demanded proof of professional rating.

George thought bitterly: Who would imagine any human being without one?

He bought a ticket to San Francisco on the 3 A.M. plane. No other plane for a sizable Olympics center was leaving before morning and he wanted to wait as little as possible. As it was, he sat huddled in the waiting room, watching for the police. They did not come.

He was in San Francisco before noon and the noise of the city struck him like a blow. This was the largest city he had ever seen and he had been used to silence and calm for a year and a half now.

Worse, it was Olympics month. He almost forgot his own predicament in his sudden awareness that some of the noise, excitement, confusion was due to that.

The Olympics boards were up at the airport for the benefit of the incoming travelers, and crowds jostled around each one. Each major profession had its own board. Each listed directions to the Olympics Hall where the contest for that day for that profession would be given; the individuals competing and their city of birth; the Outworld (if any) sponsoring it.

It was a completely stylized thing. George had read descriptions often enough in the newsprints and films, watched matches on television, and even witnessed a small Olympics in the Registered Butcher classification at the county seat. Even that, which had no conceivable Galactic implication (there was no Outworlder in attendance, of course) aroused excitement enough.

Partly, the excitement was caused simply by the fact of competition, partly by the spur of local pride (oh, when there was a home-town boy to cheer for, though he might be a complete stranger), and, of course, partly by betting. There was no way of stopping the last.

George found it difficult to approach the board. He found himself looking at the scurrying, avid onlookers in a new way.

There must have been a time when they themselves were Olympic material. What had *they* done? Nothing!

If they had been winners, they would be far out in the Galaxy somewhere, not stuck here on Earth. Whatever they were, their professions must have made them Earth-bait from the beginning; or else they had made themselves Earth-bait by inefficiency at whatever high-specialized professions they had had.

Now these failures stood about and speculated on the chances of newer and younger men. Vultures!

How he wished they were speculating on him.

He moved down the line of boards blankly, clinging to the outskirts of the groups about them. He had eaten breakfast on the strato and he wasn't hungry. He was afraid, though. He was in a big city during the confusion of the beginning of Olympics competition. That was protection, sure. The city was full of strangers. No one would question George. No one would care about George.

No one would care. Not even the House, thought George bitterly. They cared for him like a sick kitten, but if a sick kitten up and wanders off, well, too bad, what can you do?

And now that he was in San Francisco, what did he do? His thoughts struck blankly against a wall. See someone? Whom? How? Where would he even stay? The money he had left seemed pitiful.

The first shamefaced thought of going back came to him. He could go to the police— He shook his head violently as though arguing with a material adversary.

A word caught his eye on one of the boards, gleaming there: *Metallurgist.* In smaller letters, *nonferrous.* At the bottom of a long list of names, in flowing script, *sponsored by Novia.*

It induced painful memories: himself arguing with Trevelyan, so certain that he himself would be a Programmer, so certain that a Programmer was superior to a Metallurgist, so certain that he was following the right course, so certain that he was clever—

So clever that he had to boast to that small-minded, vindictive Antonelli. He had been so sure of himself that moment when he had been called and had left the nervous Trevelyan standing there, so cocksure.

George cried out in a short, incoherent high-pitched gasp. Someone turned to look at him, then hurried on. People brushed past impatiently pushing him this way and that. He remained staring at the board, openmouthed.

It was as though the board had answered his thought. He was thinking "Trevelyan" so hard that it had seemed for a moment that of course the board would say "Trevelyan" back at him.

But that *was* Trevelyan, up there. And *Armand* Trevelyan (Stubby's hated first name; up in lights for everyone to see) and the right hometown. What's more, Trev had wanted Novia, aimed for Novia, insisted on Novia; and this competition was sponsored by Novia.

This had to be Trev; good old Trev. Almost without thinking, he noted the directions for getting to the place of competition and took his place in line for a skimmer.

Then he thought somberly: Trev made it! He wanted to be a Metallurgist, and he made it!

George felt colder, more alone than ever.

There was a line waiting to enter the hall. Apparently, Metallurgy Olympics was to be an exciting and closely fought one. At least, the illuminated sky sign above the hall said so, and the jostling crowd seemed to think so.

It would have been a rainy day, George thought, from the color of the sky, but San Francisco had drawn the shield across its breadth from bay to ocean. It was an expense to do so, of course, but all expenses were warranted where the comfort of Outworlders was concerned. They would be in town for the Olympics. They were heavy spenders. And for each recruit taken, there would be a fee both to Earth and to the local government from the planet sponsoring the Olympics. It paid to keep Outworlders in mind of a particular city as a pleasant place in which to spend Olympics time. San Francisco knew what it was doing.

George, lost in thought, was suddenly aware of a gentle pressure on his shoulder blade and a voice saying, "Are you in line here, young man?"

The line had moved up without George's having noticed the widening gap. He stepped forward hastily and muttered, "Sorry, sir."

There was the touch of two fingers on the elbow of his jacket and he looked about furtively.

The man behind him nodded cheerfully. He had iron-gray hair, and under his jacket he wore an old-fashioned sweater that buttoned down in front. He said, "I didn't mean to sound sarcastic."

"No offense."

"All right, then." He sounded cozily talkative. "I wasn't sure you might not simply be standing there, entangled with the line, so to speak, only by accident. I thought you might be a——"

"A what?" said George sharply.

"Why, a contestant, of course. You look young."

George turned away. He felt neither cozy nor talkative, and bitterly impatient with busybodies.

A thought struck him. Had an alarm been sent out for him? Was his description known, or his picture? Was Gray-hair behind him trying to get a good look at his face?

He hadn't seen any news reports. He craned his neck to see the moving strip of news headlines parading across one section of the city shield, somewhat lackluster against the gray of the cloudy afternoon sky. It was no use. He gave up at once. The headlines would never concern themselves with him. This was Olympics time and the only news worth headlining was the comparative scores of the winners and the trophies won by continents, nations, and cities.

It would go on like that for weeks, with scores calculated on a per capita basis and every city finding some way of calculating itself into a position of honor. His own town had once placed third in an Olympics covering Wiring Technician; third in the whole state. There was still a plaque saying so in Town Hall.

George hunched his head between his shoulders and shoved his hands in his pocket and decided that made him more noticeable. He relaxed and tried to look unconcerned, and felt no safer. He was in the lobby now, and no authoritative hand had yet been laid on his shoulder. He filed into the hall itself and moved as far forward as he could.

It was with an unpleasant shock that he noticed Gray-hair next to him. He looked away quickly and tried reasoning with himself. The man had been right behind him in line after all.

Gray-hair, beyond a brief and tentative smile, paid no attention to him and, besides, the Olympics was about to start. George rose in his seat to see if he could make out the position assigned to Trevelyan and at the moment that was all his concern.

The hall was moderate in size and shaped in the classical long oval, with the spectators in the two balconies running completely about the rim and the contestants in the linear trough down the center. The machines were set up, the progress boards above each bench were dark, except for the name and contest number of each man. The contestants themselves were on the scene, reading, talking together; one was checking his fingernails minutely. (It was, of course, considered bad form for any contestant to pay any attention to the problem before him until the instant of the starting signal.)

George studied the program sheet he found in the appropriate slot in the arm of his chair and found Trevelyan's name. His number was twelve and, to George's chagrin, that was at the wrong end of the hall. He could make out the figure of Contestant Twelve, standing with his hands in his pockets, back to his machine, and staring at the audience as though he were counting the house. George couldn't make out the face.

Still, that was Trev.

George sank back in his seat. He wondered if Trev would do well. He hoped, as a matter of conscious duty, that he would, and yet there was something within him that felt rebelliously resentful. George, professionless, here, watching. Trevelyan, Registered Metallurgist, Nonferrous, there, competing.

George wondered if Trevelyan had competed in his first year. Sometimes men did, if they felt particularly confident—or hurried. It involved a certain risk. However efficient the Educative process, a preliminary year on Earth ("oiling the stiff knowledge," as the expression went) insured a higher score.

If Trevelyan was repeating, maybe he wasn't doing so well. George felt ashamed that the thought pleased him just a bit.

He looked about. The stands were almost full. This would be a well-attended Olympics, which meant greater strain on the contestants —or greater drive, perhaps, depending on the individual.

Why Olympics, he thought suddenly? He had never known. Why was bread called bread?

Once he had asked his father: "Why do they call it Olympics, Dad?"

And his father had said: "Olympics means competition."

George had said: "Is when Stubby and I fight an Olympics, Dad?"

Platen, Senior, had said: "No. Olympics is a special kind of competition and don't ask silly questions. You'll know all you have to know when you get Educated."

George, back in the present, sighed and crowded down into his seat.

All you have to know!

Funny that the memory should be so clear now. "When you get Educated." No one ever said, "*If* you get Educated."

He always had asked silly questions, it seemed to him now. It was as though his mind had some instinctive foreknowledge of its inability to be Educated and had gone about asking questions in order to pick up scraps here and there as best it could.

And at the House they encouraged him to do so because they agreed with his mind's instinct. It was the only way.

He sat up suddenly. What the devil was he doing? Falling for that lie? Was it because Trev was there before him, an Educee, competing in the Olympics that he himself was surrendering?

He *wasn't* feeble-minded! *No!*

And the shout of denial in his mind was echoed by the sudden clamor in the audience as everyone got to his feet.

The box seat in the very center of one long side of the oval was filling with an entourage wearing the colors of Novia, and the word "Novia" went up above them on the main board.

Novia was a Grade A world with a large population and a thoroughly developed civilization, perhaps the best in the Galaxy. It was the kind of world that every Earthman wanted to live in someday; or, failing that, to see his children live in. (George remembered Trevelyan's insistence on Novia as a goal—and there he was competing for it.)

The lights went out in that section of the ceiling above the audience and so did the wall lights. The central trough, in which the contestants waited, became floodlit.

Again George tried to make out Trevelyan. Too far.

The clear, polished voice of the announcer sounded. "Distinguished Novian sponsors. Ladies. Gentlemen. The Olympics competition for Metallurgist, Nonferrous, is about to begin. The contestants are——"

Carefully and conscientiously, he read off the list in the program. Names. Home towns. Educative years. Each name received its cheers, the San Franciscans among them receiving the loudest. When Trevelyan's name was reached, George surprised himself by shouting and waving madly. The gray-haired man next to him surprised him even more by cheering likewise.

George could not help but stare in astonishment and his neighbor leaned over to say (speaking loudly in order to be heard over the hubbub), "No one here from my home town; I'll root for yours. Someone you know?"

George shrank back. "No."

"I noticed you looking in that direction. Would you like to borrow my glasses?"

"No. Thank you." (Why didn't the old fool mind his own business?)

The announcer went on with other formal details concerning the serial number of the competition, the method of timing and scoring and so on. Finally, he approached the meat of the matter and the audience grew silent as it listened.

"Each contestant will be supplied with a bar of nonferrous alloy of unspecified composition. He will be required to sample and assay the bar, reporting all results correctly to four decimals in percent. All will utilize for this purpose a Beeman Microspectrograph, Model FX-2, each of which is, at the moment, not in working order."

There was an appreciative shout from the audience.

"Each contestant will be required to analyze the fault of his machine and correct it. Tools and spare parts are supplied. The spare part necessary may not be present, in which case it must be asked for, and time of delivery thereof will be deducted from final time. Are all contestants ready?"

The board above Contestant Five flashed a frantic red signal. Contestant Five ran off the floor and returned a moment later. The audience laughed good-naturedly.

"Are all contestants ready?"

The boards remained blank.

"Any questions?"

Still blank.

"You may begin."

There was, of course, no way anyone in the audience could tell how any contestant was progressing except for whatever notations went up on the notice board. But then, that didn't matter. Except for what professional Metallurgists there might be in the audience, none would understand anything about the contest professionally in any case. What was important was who won, who was second, who was third. For those who had bets on the standings (illegal, but unpreventable) that was all-important. Everything else might go hang.

George watched as eagerly as the rest, glancing from one contestant to the next, observing how this one had removed the cover from his microspectrograph with deft strokes of a small instrument; how that one was peering into the face of the thing; how still a third was setting his alloy bar into its holder; and how a fourth adjusted a vernier with such small touches that he seemed momentarily frozen.

Trevelyan was as absorbed as the rest. George had no way of telling how he was doing.

The notice board over Contestant Seventeen flashed: Focus plate out of adjustment.

The audience cheered wildly.

Contestant Seventeen might be right and he might, of course, be wrong. If the latter, he would have to correct his diagnosis later and lose time. Or he might never correct his diagnosis and be unable to complete his analysis or, worse still, end with a completely wrong analysis.

Never mind. For the moment, the audience cheered.

Other boards lit up. George watched for Board Twelve. That came on finally: "Sample holder off-center. New clamp depresser needed."

An attendant went running to him with a new part. If Trevelyan was wrong, it would mean useless delay. Nor would the time elapsed in waiting for the part be deducted. George found himself holding his breath.

Results were beginning to go up on Board Seventeen, in gleaming letters: aluminum, 41.2649; magnesium, 22.1914; copper, 10.1001.

Here and there, other boards began sprouting figures.

The audience was in bedlam.

George wondered how the contestants could work in such pandemonium, then wondered if that were not even a good thing. A first-class technician should work best under pressure.

Seventeen rose from his place as his board went red-rimmed to signify completion. Four was only two seconds behind him. Another, then another.

Trevelyan was still working, the minor constituents of his alloy bar still unreported. With nearly all contestants standing, Trevelyan finally rose, also. Then, tailing off, Five rose, and received an ironic cheer.

It wasn't over. Official announcements were naturally delayed. Time elapsed was something, but accuracy was just as important. And not all diagnoses were of equal difficulty. A dozen factors had to be weighed.

Finally, the announcer's voice sounded, "Winner in the time of four minutes and twelve seconds, diagnosis correct, analysis correct within an average of zero point seven parts per hundred thousand, Contestant Number—*Seventeen*, Henry Anton Schmidt of——"

What followed was drowned in the screaming. Number Eight was next and then Four, whose good time was spoiled by a five part in ten thousand error in the niobium figure. Twelve was never mentioned. He was an also-ran.

George made his way through the crowd to the Contestant's Door and found a large clot of humanity ahead of him. There would be weeping relatives (joy or sorrow, depending) to greet them, newsmen to interview the top-scorers, or the home-town boys, autograph hounds, publicity seekers and the just plain curious. Girls, too, who might hope to catch the eye of a top-scorer, almost certainly headed for Novia (or perhaps a low-scorer who needed consolation and had the cash to afford it).

George hung back. He saw no one he knew. With San Francisco so far from home, it seemed pretty safe to assume that there would be no relatives to condole with Trev on the spot.

Contestants emerged, smiling weakly, nodding at shouts of approval. Policemen kept the crowds far enough away to allow a lane for walking. Each high-scorer drew a portion of the crowd off with him, like a magnet pushing through a mound of iron filings.

When Trevelyan walked out, scarcely anyone was left. (George felt somehow that he had delayed coming out until just that had come to pass.) There was a cigarette in his dour mouth and he turned, eyes downcast, to walk off.

It was the first hint of home George had had in what was almost a year and a half and seemed almost a decade and a half. He was almost amazed that Trevelyan hadn't aged, that he was the same Trev he had last seen.

George sprang forward. *"Trev!"*

Trevelyan spun about, astonished. He stared at George and then his hand shot out. "George Platen, *what* the devil——"

And almost as soon as the look of pleasure had crossed his face, it left. His hand dropped before George had quite the chance of seizing it.

"Were you in there?" A curt jerk of Trev's head indicated the hall.

"I was."

"To see me?"

"Yes."

"Didn't do so well, did I?" He dropped his cigarette and stepped on it, staring off to the street, where the emerging crowd was slowly eddying and finding its way into skimmers, while new lines were forming for the next scheduled Olympics.

Trevelyan said heavily, "So what? It's only the second time I missed. Novia can go shove after the deal I got today. There are planets that would jump at me fast enough—— But, listen, I haven't seen you since Education Day. Where did you go? Your folks said you were on special assignment but gave no details and you never wrote. You might have written."

"I should have," said George uneasily. "Anyway, I came to say I was sorry the way things went just now."

"Don't be," said Trevelyan. "I told you. Novia can go shove—— At that I should have known. They've been saying for weeks that the Beeman machine would be used. All the wise money was on Beeman machines. The damned Education tapes they ran through me were for Henslers and who uses Henslers? The worlds in the Goman Cluster if you want to call them worlds. Wasn't *that* a nice deal they gave me?"

"Can't you conplain to——"

"Don't be a fool. They'll tell me my brain was built for Henslers. Go argue. *Everything* went wrong. I was the only one who had to send out for a piece of equipment. Notice that?"

"They deducted the time for that, though."

"Sure, but I lost time wondering if I could be right in my diagnosis when I noticed there wasn't any clamp depresser in the parts they had supplied. They don't deduct for that. If it had been a Hensler, I would have *known* I was right. How could I match up then? The top winner was a San Franciscan. So were three of the next four. And the fifth guy was from Los Angeles. They get big-city Educational tapes. The best available. Beeman spectrographs and all. How do I compete with them? I came all the way out here just to get a chance at a Novian-sponsored Olympics in my classification and I might just as well have stayed home. I knew it, I tell you, and that settles it. Novia isn't the only chunk of rock in space. Of all the damned——"

He wasn't speaking to George. He wasn't speaking to anyone. He was just uncorked and frothing. George realized that.

George said, "If you knew in advance that the Beemans were going to be used, couldn't you have studied up on them?"

"They weren't in my tapes, I tell you."

"You could have read—books."

The last word had tailed off under Trevelyan's suddenly sharp look.

Trevelyan said, "Are you trying to make a big laugh out of this? You think this is funny? How do you expect me to read some book and try to memorize enough to match someone else who *knows*."

"I thought——"

"You try it. You try——" Then, suddenly, "What's your profession, by the way?" He sounded thoroughly hostile.

"Well——"

"Come on, now. If you're going to be a wise guy with me, let's see what you've done. You're still on Earth, I notice, so you're not a Computer Programmer and your special assignment can't be much."

George said, "Listen, Trev. I'm late for an appointment." He backed away, trying to smile.

"No, you don't." Trevelyan reached out fiercely, catching hold of George's jacket. "You answer my question. Why are you afraid to tell me? What is it with you? Don't come here rubbing a bad showing in my face, George, unless you can take it, too. Do you hear me?"

He was shaking George in frenzy and they were struggling and swaying across the floor, when the Voice of Doom struck George's ear in the form of a policeman's outraged call.

"All right now. *All* right. Break it up."

George's heart turned to lead and lurched sickeningly. The policeman would be taking names, asking to see identity cards, and George lacked one. He would be questioned and his lack of profession would show at once; and before Trevelyan, too, who ached with the pain of the drubbing he had taken and would spread the news back home as a salve for his own hurt feelings.

George couldn't stand that. He broke away from Trevelyan and made to run, but the policeman's heavy hand was on his shoulder. "Hold on, there. Let's see your identity card."

Trevelyan was fumbling for his, saying harshly, "I'm Armand Trevelyan, Metallurgist, Nonferrous. I was just competing in the Olympics. You better find out about him, though, officer."

George faced the two, lips dry and throat thickened past speech.

Another voice sounded, quiet, well-mannered. "Officer. One moment."

The policeman stepped back. "Yes, sir?"

"This young man is my guest. What is the trouble?"

George looked about in wild surprise. It was the gray-haired man who had been sitting next to him. Gray-hair nodded benignly at George.

Guest? Was he mad?

The policeman was saying, "These two were creating a disturbance, sir."

"Any criminal charges? Any damages?"

"No, sir."

"Well, then, I'll be responsible." He presented a small card to the policeman's view and the latter stepped back at once.

Trevelyan began indignantly, "Hold on, now——" but the policeman turned on him.

"All right now. Got any charges?"

"I just——"

"On your way. The rest of you—move on." A sizable crowd had gathered, which now, reluctantly, unknotted itself and raveled away.

George let himself be led to a skimmer but balked at entering.

He said, "Thank you, but I'm not your guest." (Could it be a ridiculous case of mistaken identity?)

But Gray-hair smiled and said, "You weren't but you are now. Let me introduce myself, I'm Ladislas Ingenescu, Registered Historian."

"But——"

"Come, you will come to no harm, I assure you. After all, I only wanted to spare you some trouble with a policeman."

"But why?"

"Do you want a reason? Well, then, say that we're honorary townsmates, you and I. We both shouted for the same man, remember, and we townspeople must stick together, even if the tie is only honorary. Eh?"

And George, completely unsure of this man, Ingenescu, and of himself as well, found himself inside the skimmer. Before he could make up his mind that he ought to get off again, they were off the ground.

He thought confusedly: The man has some status. The policeman deferred to him.

He was almost forgetting that his real purpose here in San Francisco was not to find Trevelyan but to find some person with enough influence to force a reappraisal of his own capacity of Education.

It could be that Ingenescu was such a man. And right in George's lap.

Everything could be working out fine—fine. Yet it sounded hollow in his thought. He was uneasy.

During the short skimmer-hop, Ingenescu kept up an even flow of small-talk, pointing out the landmarks of the city, reminiscing about past Olympics he had seen. George, who paid just enough attention to make vague sounds during the pauses, watched the route of flight anxiously.

Would they head for one of the shield-openings and leave the city altogether?

No, they headed downward, and George sighed his relief softly. He felt safer in the city.

The skimmer landed at the roof-entry of a hotel and, as he alighted, Ingenescu said, "I hope you'll eat dinner with me in my room?"

George said, "Yes," and grinned unaffectedly. He was just beginning to realize the gap left within him by missing lunch.

Ingenescu let George eat in silence. Night closed in and the wall lights went on automatically. (George thought: I've been on my own almost twenty-four hours.)

And then over the coffee, Ingenescu finally spoke again. He said, "You've been acting as though you think I intend you harm."

George reddened, put down his cup and tried to deny it, but the older man laughed and shook his head.

"It's so. I've been watching you closely since I first saw you and I think I know a great deal about you now."

George half rose in horror.

Ingenescu said, "But sit down. I only want to help you."

George sat down but his thoughts were in a whirl. If the old man knew who he was, why had he not left him to the policeman? On the other hand, why should he volunteer help?

Ingenescu said, "You want to know why I should want to help you? Oh, don't look alarmed. I can't read minds. It's just that my training enables me to judge the little reactions that give minds away, you see. Do you understand that?"

George shook his head.

Ingenescu said, "Consider my first sight of you. You were waiting in line to watch an Olympics, and your micro-reactions didn't match what you were doing. The expression of your face was wrong, the action of your hands was wrong. It meant that something, in general, was wrong, and the interesting thing was that, whatever it was, it was nothing common, nothing obvious. Perhaps, I thought, it was something of which your own conscious mind was unaware.

"I couldn't help but follow you, sit next to you. I followed you again when you left and eavesdropped on the conversation between your friend and yourself. After that, well, you were far too interesting an object of study—I'm sorry if that sounds cold-blooded—for me to allow you to be taken off by a policeman. ——Now tell me, what is it that troubles you?"

George was in an agony of indecision. If this was a trap, why should it be such an indirect, roundabout one? And he *had* to turn to someone. He had come to the city to find help and here was help being offered. Perhaps what was wrong was that it was being offered. It came too easy.

Ingenescu said, "Of course, what you tell me as a Social Scientist is a privileged communication. Do you know what that means?"

"No sir."

"It means, it would be dishonorable for me to repeat what you say to anyone for any purpose. Moreover no one has the legal right to compel me to repeat it."

George said, with sudden suspicion, "I thought you were a Historian."

"So I am."

"Just now you said you were a Social Scientist."

Ingenescu broke into loud laughter and apologized for it when he could talk. "I'm sorry, young man, I shouldn't laugh, and I wasn't really laughing at you. I was laughing at Earth and its emphasis on physical science, and the practical segments of it at that. I'll bet you can rattle off every subdivision of construction technology or mechanical engineering and yet you're a blank on social science."

"Well, then what *is* social science?"

"Social science studies groups of human beings and there are many high-specialized branches to it, just as there are to zoology, for instance. For instance, there are Culturists, who study the mechanics of cultures, their growth, development, and decay. Cultures," he added, forestalling a question, "are all the aspects of a way of life. For instance, it includes the way we make our living, the things we enjoy and believe, what we consider good and bad and so on. Do you understand?"

"I think I do."

"An Economist—not an Economic Statistician, now, but an Economist—specializes in the study of the way a culture supplies the bodily needs of its individual members. A Psychologist specializes in the individual member of a society and how he is affected by the society. A Futurist specializes in planning the future course of a society, and a Historian—— That's where I come in, now."

"Yes, sir."

"A Historian specializes in the past development of our own society and of societies with other cultures."

George found himself interested. "Was it different in the past?"

"I should say it was. Until a thousand years ago, there was no Education; not what we call Education, at least."

George said, "I know. People learned in bits and pieces out of books."

"Why, how do you know this?"

"I've heard it said," said George cautiously. Then, "Is there any use in worrying about what's happened long ago? I mean, it's all done with, isn't it?"

"It's never done with, my boy. The past explains the present. For instance, why is our Educational system what it is?"

George stirred restlessly. The man kept bringing the subject back to that. He said snappishly, "Because it's best."

"Ah, but why is it best? Now you listen to me for one moment and I'll explain. Then you can tell me if there is any use in history. Even before interstellar travel was developed——" He broke off at the look of complete astonishment on George's face. "Well, did you think we always had it?"

"I never gave it any thought, sir."

"I'm sure you didn't. But there was a time, four or five thousand years ago, when mankind was confined to the surface of Earth. Even then, his culture had grown quite technological and his numbers had increased to the point where any failure in technology would have meant mass starvation and disease. To maintain the technological level and advance it in the face of an increasing population, more and more technicians and scientists had to be trained, and yet, as science advanced, it took longer and longer to train them.

"As first interplanetary and then interstellar travel was developed, the problem grew more acute. In fact, actual colonization of extra-Solar planets was impossible for about fifteen hundred years because of a lack of properly trained men.

"The turning point came when the mechanics of the storage of knowledge within the brain was worked out. Once that had been done, it became possible to devise Educational tapes that would modify the mechanics in such a way as to place within the mind a body of knowledge ready-made so to speak. But you know about *that*.

"Once that was done, trained men could be turned out by the thousands and millions, and we could begin what someone has since called the "Filling of the Universe." There are now fifteen hundred inhabited planets in the Galaxy and there is no end in sight.

"Do you see all that is involved? Earth exports Education tapes for low-specialized professions and that keeps the Galactic culture unified. For instance, the Reading tapes insure a single language for all of us. ——Don't look so surprised, other languages are possible, and in the past were used. Hundreds of them.

"Earth also exports high-specialized professionals and keeps its own population at an endurable level. Since they are shipped out in a balanced sex ratio, they act as self-reproductive units and help increase the populations on the Outworlds where an increase is needed. Furthermore, tapes and men are paid for in material which we much need and on which our economy depends. *Now* do you understand why our Education is the best way?"

"Yes, sir."

"Does it help you to understand, knowing that without it, interstellar colonization was impossible for fifteen hundred years?"

"Yes, sir."

"Then you see the uses of history." The Historian smiled. "And now I wonder if you see why I'm interested in you?"

George snapped out of time and space back to reality. Ingenescu, apparently, didn't talk aimlessly. All this lecture had been a device to attack him from a new angle.

He said, once again withdrawn, hesitating, "Why?"

"Social Scientists work with societies and societies are made up of people."

"All right."

"But people aren't machines. The professionals in physical science work with machines. There is only a limited amount to know about a machine and the professionals know it all. Furthermore, all machines of a given sort are just about alike so that there is nothing to interest them in any given individual machine. But people, ah— They are so complex and so different one from another that a Social Scientist never knows all there is to know or even a good part of what there is to know. To understand his own specialty, he must always be ready to study people; particularly unusual specimens."

"Like me," said George tonelessly.

"I shouldn't call you a specimen, I suppose, but you are unusual. You're worth studying, and if you will allow me that privilege then, in return, I will help you if you are in trouble and if I can."

There were pin wheels whirring in George's mind. —All this talk about people and colonization made possible by Education. It was as though caked thought within him were being broken up and strewn about mercilessly.

He said, "Let me think," and clamped his hands over his ears.

He took them away and said to the Historian, "Will you do something for me, sir?"

"If I can," said the Historian amiably.

"And everything I say in this room is a privileged communication. You said so."

"And I meant it."

"Then get me an interview with an Outworld official, with—with a Novian."

Ingenescu looked startled. "Well, now——"

"You can do it," said George earnestly. "You're an important official. I saw the policeman's look when you put that card in front of his eyes. If you refuse, I—I won't let you study me."

It sounded a silly threat in George's own ears, one without force. On Ingenescu, however, it seemed to have a strong effect.

He said, "That's an impossible condition. A Novian in Olympics month——"

"All right, then, get me a Novian on the phone and I'll make my own arrangements for an interview."

"Do you think you can?"

"I know I can. Wait and see."

Ingenescu stared at George thoughtfully and then reached for the visiphone.

George waited, half drunk with his new outlook on the whole problem and the sense of power it brought. It couldn't miss. It *couldn't* miss. He would be a Novian yet. He would leave Earth in triumph despite Antonelli and the whole crew of fools at the House for the (he almost laughed aloud) Feeble-minded.

George watched eagerly as the visiplate lit up. It would open up a window into a room of Novians, a window into a small patch of Novia transplanted to Earth. In twenty-four hours, he had accomplished that much.

There was a burst of laughter as the plate unmisted and sharpened, but for the moment no single head could be seen but rather the fast passing of the shadows of men and women, this way and that. A voice was heard, clear-worded over a background of babble. "Ingenescu? He wants me?"

Then there he was, staring out of the plate. A Novian. A genuine Novian. (George had not an atom of doubt. There was something completely Outworldly about him. Nothing that could be completely defined, or even momentarily mistaken.)

He was swarthy in complexion with a dark wave of hair combed rigidly back from his forehead. He wore a thin black mustache and a pointed beard, just as dark, that scarcely reached below the lower limit of his narrow chin, but the rest of his face was so smooth that it looked as though it had been depilated permanently.

He was smiling. "Ladislas, this goes too far. We fully expect to be spied on, within reason, during our stay on Earth, but mind reading is out of bounds."

"Mind reading, Honorable?"

"Confess! You knew I was going to call this evening. You knew I was only waiting to finish this drink." His hand moved up into view and his eye peered through a small glass of a faintly violet liqueur. "I can't offer you one, I'm afraid."

George, out of range of Ingenescu's transmitter could not be seen by the Novian. He was relieved at that. He wanted time to compose himself and he needed it badly. It was as though he were made up exclusively of restless fingers, drumming, drumming——

But he was right. He hadn't miscalculated. Ingenescu *was* important. The Novian called him by his first name.

Good! Things worked well. What George had lost on Antonelli, he would make up, with advantage, on Ingenescu. And someday, when he was on his own at last, and could come back to Earth as powerful a Novian as this one who could negligently joke with Ingenescu's first name and be addressed as "Honorable" in turn—when he came back, he would settle with Antonelli. He had a year and a half to pay back and he——

He all but lost his balance on the brink of the enticing daydream and snapped back in sudden anxious realization that he was losing the thread of what was going on.

The Novian was saying, "——doesn't hold water. Novia has a civilization as complicated and advanced as Earth's. We're not Zeston, after all. It's ridiculous that we have to come here for individual technicians."

Ingenescu said soothingly, "Only for new models. There is never any certainty that new models will be needed. To buy the Educational tapes would cost you the same price as a thousand technicians and how do you know you would need that many?"

The Novian tossed off what remained of his drink and laughed. (It displeased George, somehow, that a Novian should be this frivolous. He wondered uneasily if perhaps the Novian ought not to have skipped that drink and even the one or two before that.)

The Novian said, "That's typical pious fraud, Ladislas. You know we can make use of all the late models we can get. I collected five Metallurgists this afternoon——"

"I know," said Ingenescu. "I was there."

"Watching me! Spying!" cried the Novian. "I'll tell you what it is. The new-model Metallurgists I got differed from the previous model only in knowing the use of Beeman Spectrographs. The tapes couldn't be modified that much, not that much" (he held up two fingers close together) "from last year's model. You introduce the new models only to *make* us buy and spend and come here hat in hand."

"We don't *make* you buy."

"No, but you sell late-model technicians to Landonum and so we have to keep pace. It's a merry-go-round you have us on, you pious Earthmen, but watch out, there may be an exit somewhere." There was a sharp edge to his laugh, and it ended sooner than it should have.

Ingenescu said, "In all honesty, I hope there is. Meanwhile, as to the purpose of my call——"

"That's right, *you* called. Oh, well, I've said my say and I suppose next year there'll be a new model of Metallurgist anyway for us to spend goods on, probably with a new gimmick for niobium assays and nothing else altered and the next year—— But go on, what is it you want?"

"I have a young man here to whom I wish you to speak."

"Oh?" The Novian looked not completely pleased with that. "Concerning what?"

"I can't say. He hasn't told me. For that matter he hasn't even told me his name and profession."

The Novian frowned. "Then why take up my time?"

"He seems quite confident that you will be interested in what he has to say."

"I dare say."

"And," said Ingenescu, "as a favor to me."

The Novian shrugged. "Put him on and tell him to make it short."

Ingenescu stepped aside and whispered to George, "Address him as 'Honorable'."

George swallowed with difficulty. This was it.

George felt himself going moist with perspiration. The thought had come so recently, yet it was in him now so certainly. The beginnings of it had come when he had spoken to Trevelyan, then everything had fermented and billowed into shape while Ingenescu had prattled, and then the Novian's own remarks had seemed to nail it all into place.

George said, "Honorable, I've come to show you the exit from the merry-go-round." Deliberately, he adopted the Novian's own metaphor.

The Novian stared at him gravely. "What merry-go-round?"

"You yourself mentioned it, Honorable. The merry-go-round that Novia is on when you come to Earth to—to get technicians." (He couldn't keep his teeth from chattering; from excitement, not fear.)

The Novian said, "You're trying to say that you know a way by which we can avoid patronizing Earth's mental supermarket. Is that it?"

"Yes, sir. You can control your own Educational system."

"Umm. Without tapes?"

"Y—yes, Honorable."

The Novian, without taking his eyes from George, called out, "Ingenescu, get into view."

The Historian moved to where he could be seen over George's shoulder.

The Novian said, "What is this? I don't seem to penetrate."

"I assure you solemnly," said Ingenescu, "that whatever this is it is being done on the young man's own initiative, Honorable. I have not inspired this. I have nothing to do with it."

"Well, then, what is the young man to you? Why do you call me on his behalf?"

Ingenescu said, "He is an object of study, Honorable. He has value to me and I humor him."

"What kind of value?"

"It's difficult to explain; a matter of my profession."

"The Novian laughed shortly. "Well, to each his profession." He nodded to an invisible person or persons outside plate range. "There's a young man here, a protégé of Ingenescu or some such thing, who will explain to us how to Educate without tapes." He snapped his fingers, and another glass of pale liqueur appeared in his hand. "Well, young man?"

The faces on the plate were multiple now. Men and women, both, crammed in for a view of George, their faces molded into various shades of amusement and curiosity.

George tried to look disdainful. They were all, in their own ways, Novians as well as the Earthman, "studying" him as though he were a bug on a pin. Ingenescu was sitting in a corner, now, watching him owl-eyed.

Fools, he thought tensely, one and all. But they would have to understand. He would *make* them understand.

He said, "I was at the Metallurgist Olympics this afternoon."

"You, too?" said the Novian blandly. "It seems all Earth was there."

"No, Honorable, but I was. I had a friend who competed and who made out very badly because you were using the Beeman machines. His education had included only the Henslers, apparently an older model. You said the modification involved was slight." George held up two fingers close together in conscious mimicry of the other's previous gesture. "And my friend had known some time in advance that knowledge of the Beeman machines would be required."

"And what does that signify?"

"It was my friend's lifelong ambition to qualify for Novia. He already knew the Henslers. He had to know the Beemans to qualify and he knew that. To learn about the Beemans would have taken just a few more facts, a bit more data, a small amount of practice perhaps. With a life's ambition riding the scale, he might have managed this——"

"And where would he have obtained a tape for the additional facts and data? Or has Education become a private matter for home study here on Earth?"

There was dutiful laughter from the faces in the background.

George said, "That's why he didn't learn, Honorable. He thought he needed a tape. He wouldn't even try without one, no matter what the prize. He refused to try without a tape."

"Refused, eh? Probably the type of fellow who would refuse to fly without a skimmer." More laughter and the Novian thawed into a smile and said, "The fellow is amusing. Go on. I'll give you another few moments."

George said tensely, "Don't think this is a joke. Tapes are actually bad. They teach too much; they're too painless. A man who learns that way doesn't know how to learn any other way. He's frozen into whatever position he's been taped. Now if a person *weren't* given tapes but were forced to learn by hand, so to speak, from the start; why, then he'd get the habit of learning, and continue to learn. Isn't that reasonable? Once he has the habit well developed he can be given just a small amount of tape-knowledge, perhaps, to fill in gaps or fix details. Then he can make further progress on his own. You can make Beeman Metallurgists out of your own Hensler Metallurgists in that way and not have to come to Earth for new models."

The Novian nodded and sipped at his drink. "And where does everyone get knowledge without tapes? From interstellar vacuum?"

"From books. By studying the instruments themselves. By *thinking*."

"Books? How does one understand books without Education?"

"Books are in words. Words can be understood for the most part. Specialized words can be explained by the technicians you already have."

"What about reading? Will you allow reading tapes?"

"Reading tapes are all right, I suppose, but there's no reason you can't learn to read the old way, too. At least in part."

The Novian said, "So that you can develop good habits from the start?"

"Yes, yes," George said gleefully. The man was beginning to understand.

"And what about mathematics?"

"That's the easiest of all, sir—Honorable. Mathematics is different from other technical subjects. It starts with certain simple principles and proceeds by steps. You can start with nothing and learn. Its practically designed for that. Then, once you know the proper types of mathematics, other technical books become quite understandable. Especially if you start with easy ones."

"Are there easy books?"

"Definitely. Even if there weren't, the technicians you now have can try to write easy books. Some of them might be able to put some of their knowledge into words and symbols."

"Good Lord," said the Novian to the men clustered about him. "The young devil has an answer for everything."

"I have. I have," shouted George. "Ask me."

"Have you tried learning from books yourself? Or is this just theory with you?"

George turned to look quickly at Ingenescu, but the Historian was passive. There was no sign of anything but gentle interest in his face.

George said, "I have."

"And do you find it works?"

"Yes, Honorable," said George eagerly. "Take me with you to Novia. I can set up a program and direct——"

"Wait, I have a few more questions. How long would it take, do you suppose, for you to become a Metallurgist capable of handling a Beeman machine, supposing you started from nothing and did not use Educational tapes?"

George hesitated. "Well—years, perhaps."

"Two years? Five? Ten?"

"I can't say, Honorable."

"Well, there's a vital question to which you have no answer, have you? Shall we say five years? Does that sound reasonable to you?"

"I suppose so."

"All right. We have a technician studying metallurgy according to this method of yours for five years. He's no good to us during that time, you'll admit, but he must be fed and housed and paid all that time."

"But——"

"Let me finish. Then when he's done and can use the Beeman, five years have passed. Don't you suppose we'll have modified Beemans then which he *won't* be able to use?"

"But by then he'll be expert on learning. He could learn the new details necessary in a matter of days."

"So you say. And suppose this friend of yours, for instance, had studied up on Beemans on his own and managed to learn it; would he be as expert in its use as a competitor who had learned it off the tapes?"

"Maybe not——" began George.

"Ah," said the Novian.

"Wait, let *me* finish. Even if he doesn't know something as well, it's the ability to learn further that's important. He may be able to think up things, new things that no tape-Educated man would. You'll have a reservoir of original thinkers——"

"In your studying," said the Novian, "have you thought up any new things?"

"No, but I'm just one man and I haven't studied long——"

"Yes. ——Well, ladies, gentlemen, have we been sufficiently amused?"

"Wait," cried George, in sudden panic. "I want to arrange a personal interview. There are things I can't explain over the visiphone There are details——"

The Novian looked past George. "Ingenescu! I think I have done you your favor. Now, really, I have a heavy schedule tomorrow. Be well."

The screen went blank.

George's hands shot out toward the screen, as though in a wild impulse to shake life back into it. He cried out, "He didn't believe me. He didn't believe me."

Ingenescu said, "No, George. Did you really think he would?"

George scarcely heard him. "But why not? It's all true. It's all so much to his advantage. No risk. I and a few men to work with—— A dozen men training for years would cost less than one technician. —— He was drunk! Drunk! He didn't understand."

George looked about breathlessly. "How do I get to him? I've got to. This was wrong. Shouldn't have used the visiphone. I need time. Face to face. How do I——"

Ingenescu said, "He won't see you, George. And if he did, he wouldn't believe you."

"He will, I tell you. When he isn't drinking. He——" George turned squarely toward the Historian and his eyes widened. "Why do you call me George?"

"Isn't that your name? George Platen?"

"You know me?"

"All about you."

George was motionless except for the breath pumping his chest wall up and down.

Ingenescu said, "I want to help you, George. I told you that. I've been studying you and I want to help you."

George screamed, "I don't need help. I'm not feeble-minded. The whole world is, but I'm not." He whirled and dashed madly for the door.

He flung it open and two policemen roused themselves suddenly from their guard duty and seized him.

For all George's straining, he could feel the hypo-spray at the fleshy point just under the corner of his jaw, and that was it. The last thing he remembered was the face of Ingenescu, watching with gentle concern.

George opened his eyes to the whiteness of a ceiling. He remembered what had happened. He remembered it distantly as though it had happened to somebody else. He stared at the ceiling till the whiteness filled his eyes and washed his brain clean, leaving room, it seemed, for new thought and new ways of thinking.

He didn't know how long he lay there so, listening to the drift of his own thinking.

There was a voice in his ear. "Are you awake?"

And George heard his own moaning for the first time. Had he been moaning? He tried to turn his head.

The voice said, "Are you in pain, George?"

George whispered, "Funny. I was so anxious to leave Earth. I didn't understand."

"Do you know where you are?"

"Back in the—the House." George managed to turn. The voice belonged to Omani.

George said, "It's funny I didn't understand."

Omani smiled gently, "Sleep again——"

George slept.

And woke again. His mind was clear.

Omani sat at the bedside reading, but he put down the book as George's eyes opened.

George struggled to a sitting position. He said, "Hello."

"Are you hungry?"

"You bet." He stared at Omani curiously. "I was followed when I left, wasn't I?"

Omani nodded. "You were under observation at all times. We were going to maneuver you to Antonelli and let you discharge your aggressions. We felt that to be the only way you could make progress. Your emotions were clogging your advance."

George said, with a trace of embarrassment, "I was all wrong about him."

"It doesn't matter now. When you stopped to stare at the Metallurgy notice board at the airport, one of our agents reported back the list of names. You and I had talked about your past sufficiently so that I caught the significance of Trevelyan's name there. You asked for directions to the Olympics; there was the possibility that this might result in the kind of crisis we were hoping for; we sent Ladislas Ingenescu to the hall to meet you and take over."

"He's an important man in the government, isn't he?"

"Yes, he is."

"And you had him take over. It makes me sound important."

"You *are* important, George."

A thick stew had arrived, steaming, fragrant. George grinned wolfishly and pushed his sheets back to free his arms. Omani helped arrange the bed-table. For a while, George ate silently.

Then George said, "I woke up here once before just for a short time."

Omani said, "I know. I was here."

"Yes, I remember. You know, everything was changed. It was as though I was too tired to feel emotion. I wasn't angry any more. I could just think. It was as though I had been drugged to wipe out emotion."

"You weren't," said Omani. "Just sedation. You had rested."

"Well, anyway, it was all clear to me, as though I had known it all the time but wouldn't listen to myself. I thought: What was it I had wanted Novia to let me do? I had wanted to go to Novia and take a batch of un-Educated youngsters and teach them out of books. I had wanted to establish a House for the Feeble-minded—like here—and Earth already has them—many of them."

Omani's white teeth gleamed as he smiled. "The Institute of Higher Studies is the correct name for places like this."

"Now I see it," said George, "so easily I am amazed at my blindness before. After all, who invents the new instrument models that require new-model technicians? Who invented the Beeman spectrographs, for instance? A man called Beeman, I suppose, but he couldn't have been tape-Educated or how could he have made the advance?"

"Exactly."

"Or who makes Educational tapes? Special tape-making technicians? Then who makes the tapes to train *them?* More advanced technicians? Then who makes the tapes—— You see what I mean. Somewhere there has to be an end. Somewhere there must be men and women with capacity for original thought."

"Yes, George."

George leaned back, stared over Omani's head, and for a moment there was the return of something like restlessness to his eyes.

"Why wasn't I told all this at the beginning?"

"Oh, if we could," said Omani, "the trouble it would save us. We can analyze a mind, George, and say this one will make an adequate architect and that one a good woodworker. We know of no way of detecting the capacity for original, creative thought. It is too subtle a thing. We have some rule-of-thumb methods that mark out individuals who may possibly or potentially have such a talent.

"On Reading Day, such individuals are reported. You were, for instance. Roughly speaking, the number so reported comes to one in ten thousand. By the time Education Day arrives, these individuals are checked again, and nine out of ten of them turn out to have been false alarms. Those who remain are sent to places like this."

George said, "Well, what's wrong with telling people that one out of—of a hundred thousand will end at places like these? Then it won't be such a shock to those who do."

"And those who don't? The ninety-nine thousand nine hundred and ninety-nine that don't? We can't have all those people considering themselves failures. They aim at the professions and one way or another they all make it. Everyone can place after his or her name: Registered something-or-other. In one fashion or another every individual has his or her place in society and this is necessary."

"But we?" said George. "The one in ten thousand exception?"

"You can't be told. That's exactly it. It's the final test. Even after we've thinned out the possibilities on Education Day, nine out of ten of those who come here are not quite the material of creative genius, and there's no way we can distinguish those nine from the tenth that we want by any form of machinery. The tenth one must tell us himself."

"How?"

"We bring you here to a House for the Feeble-minded and the man who won't accept that is the man we want. It's a method that can be cruel, but it works. It won't do to say to a man, 'You can create. Do so.' It is much safer to wait for a man to say, 'I can create, and I will do so whether you wish it or not.' There are ten thousand men like you, George, who support the advancing technology of fifteen hundred worlds. We can't allow ourselves to miss one recruit to that number or waste our efforts on one member who doesn't measure up."

George pushed his empty plate out of the way and lifted a cup of coffee to his lips.

"What about the people here who don't—measure up?"

"They are taped eventually and become our Social Scientists. Ingenescu is one. I am a Registered Psychologist. We are second echelon, so to speak."

George finished his coffee. He said, "I still wonder about one thing."

"What is that?"

George threw aside the sheet and stood up. "Why do they call them Olympics?"

69

THE GREAT INTELLECT BOOM

Christopher Anvil

Education and society are so deeply intertwined today that a *dependency relationship* has developed between them. Society cannot function without education and education, because it must rely on society and government for protection and funds, needs society.

Our schools and colleges are now called upon to perform a whole range of functions which are straining this institution to the breaking point. For one thing, it must socialize youth to take their places in our social, political, and economic systems. It must prepare them to "make a living." Second, schools and colleges help young people to mature, to become "well adjusted" individuals who have "found themselves." The schools work with people at one of the most important and vulnerable times of their lives—adolescence. Third, education prepares the population to accept change, to regard it as normal, and, through applied research at the university level, to benefit society directly. Finally, higher education attempts to discover the fundamental truths of the universe. To perform all of these tasks with excellence, or even adequacy, is asking a great deal. When things go wrong in society, the educational system is one of the first to be singled out for blame.

Among the tasks assigned to the schools by popular mythology is that of turning out "educated" persons. The definition of an educated individual is subject to dispute. Usually, we tend to regard people who act as we want them to act as "educated." In earlier times, to be educated meant to be "civilized"—to enjoy classical music, fine foods, and the more refined things in life. More recently, the definition has referred to a well-rounded person, one with a liberal arts background who has been exposed to a variety of disciplines.

70

"The Great Intellect Boom" examines the consequences of instant intellectuality on a society. It raises important questions concerning the role of education in society—for example, are we becoming so concerned with "book-learning" that we are losing the capability to perform needed manual tasks? In the recent past, there seemed to be developing a strong trend against working with one's hands. Blue-collar occupations grew in disfavor with the expanse of white-collar jobs. It was considered a mark of failure to have to go into manual labor, even if it involved a skill. The country became more and more profession oriented. This attitude, which may have peaked in the late sixties, has given rise to a backlash in the form of the vocational school movement of the seventies.

There seemed to be a recognition that highly educated people were doing less and less *things.* Could it be that education's destiny was to create a class of human beings who just sat around and thought twenty-four hours a day? This story supplies an interesting and humorous answer to this question.

FOR FURTHER THOUGHT OR DISCUSSION

1. Are we producing an overeducated population?

2. What is the status of the vocational school today?

3. If everyone were as smart as the characters in the story, what would be the effect on the educational system?

4. Who determines the worth of a high school diploma or a college degree—is it the schools or society?

5. Can our universities cope with the demands made upon them by society?

6. Is learning, as the story suggests, "an end in itself"? What are the social consequences of this attitude?

THE GREAT INTELLECT BOOM   *Christopher Anvil*

Morton Hommel, Ph.D., director of the Banner Value Drug & Vitamin Laboratories, Inc., proudly put the bottle of yellow capsules on the desk of old Sam Banner, president of the company.

Banner glanced at them dubiously.

"What are they good for, Mort?"

Hommel said, with quiet pride, "They increase intelligence."

Banner looked up.

"What's that again?"

"The drug stimulates intellectual activity. It channels energy from gross physical pursuits into imaginative creativity."

Banner looked at him alertly.

"Have you been taking it?"

"No. But we've carried out exhaustive—"

"It *works?*"

"It's extremely effective."

Banner sat back, and studied the capsules.

"Well, a thing like this would sell to students. Lawyers would want it. Doctors, engineers— Just about everybody could use more brains these days. Quite a market." Then he shook his head. "But it might be that what we've got here is a catastrophe in a bottle. How did we get into this, anyway? I don't remember any work on brain pills."

Hommel winced. "We prefer to think of it as a *drug mediating the enhancement of intellectual activity.*"

"That's what I say. Brain pills. How did we get into this in the first place?"

"Well, you remember that problem of parapl—"

"Put it into words an ordinary human can follow, Mort."

Hommel's face took on the expression of a truck driver faced with a detour off a six-lane highway onto a mountain road. With a visible effort, he said, "I mean, that problem of broken nerve tracts that wouldn't grow together."

"I remember *that*. So what?"

"We thought we had a promising lead. It had seemed satisfactory with experimental animals. What we wanted, of course, was something to stimulate the broken ends of the nerve, to cause them to grow and rejoin. We thought at first this would have to be administered locally; but we found, purely by accident, that it could be given by mouth. When we had every reason to believe that the drug would prove successful, we tried it on a human volunteer. This volunteer . . . ah . . . had evidently lacked proper motivational opportunities for educational develop—"

Banner stared. "He *what*, Mort?"

"He'd lacked the proper motivational opportunities for educa—"

"Was the fellow stupid?"

"Well, I'd hesitate to say he—"

"Mort," said Banner, "a junkyard is a junkyard—whether you decide to call it a junkyard or a 'storage module for preprocessed metals.' Was the fellow stupid, or wasn't he?"

Hommel blew out his breath.

"He wasn't the brightest person I ever met."

"All right. What happened?"

"He'd been badly injured. Yet it certainly seemed, from our previous work, that the drug ought to produce a cure. But it didn't."

"The broken ends of the nerves didn't grow together?"

"No."

Banner nodded sympathetically.

"What then?"

"Well, we were very much disappointed. But we were also surprised, because the patient suddenly seemed to gain insight into his accident. Prior to this time, he'd simply blamed the other drivers."

"How did he get hurt?"

"He was driving in heavy traffic, got on the wrong turnoff, and tried to get back by making a quick U-turn in a cloverleaf intersection."

Banner looked blank.

Hommel said, "Not only that, but he was convinced that the other drivers owed him a lifetime pension. After he'd been treated with our drug, he saw there was another side to the question."

Banner glanced thoughtfully at the capsules. "Maybe we have something here, after all. What happened next?"

"Well, at first we didn't realize what had happened. But we continued treatment, still hoping for a cure. The patient enrolled in a correspondence course and completed his high-school education. Meanwhile, we'd started treatment on another patient, who read comic books at the beginning of the treatment, and was studying medieval history at the end. It began to dawn on us that there might be some connection.

After that, we carried out thorough investigations, and found that there is invariably a marked increase in the patient's intellectual activity. It's no longer possible to think of this as a coincidence. The increase in intellectual activity is caused by our drug."

"Any side effects?"

"In some few patients there's a rash. Occasionally, there's a complaint of a temporary numbness—a sense of being removed from reality. The rash subsides in a day or two after discontinuance of treatment. The numbness fades away in a few hours. Neither reaction seems serious, and neither is especially common."

"How about this increased intelligence? Does it fade away when the patient stops taking the pills?"

"There's a drop, but there's also a residual increase that remains. One of the men on the hospital staff compared intelligence with the amount of traffic a road network will bear. The 'mental traffic' will depend on the mental 'road system'—the number and condition of the brain's nerve cells and connections. The drug speeds up mental 'road building.' When the drug is discontinued, this 'road building' drops back to a much lower level. Those 'roads' only partly finished quickly become unusable. But those already finished remain in use, allowing an increase in 'traffic'—intelligence—over what there was to begin with, although lower than at the peak."

"How much of an increase can there be? What's the limit?"

"We don't know. But it can be substantial, from what we've seen. And happily this all fits right in with the current recognition of the importance of education. Quite a few of our patients have gone back to school or college, where they're all doing well. This drug fits in perfectly with the needs of the day."

Banner shook his head.

"It *sounds* good, Mort. And *maybe* it is. But we want to take a few precautions, just in case. Keep working to see if there are any side effects we don't know about, especially any that build up slowly. And start work on an antidote."

Hommel looked dumbfounded.

"But—an *antidote* to this would be a *stupidity drug*."

"It might be, and it might not. Who knows how it would work? But we'd better find one." Banner smiled suddenly. "By the way, Mort, have you thought what to name this? How about 'Super Mentalline'?"

"Surely we ought to take a more conservative approach."

"With this," said Banner, "that may prove harder than it looks. But we'll see what we can do."

The drug, when it appeared, was modestly advertised. And Hommel thought the label on the bottle *too* restrained:

CEREBROCREATINE
A Mental Stimulant

Take one to two capsules daily as required, for mild stimulation of intellectual activity. Especially recommended for students, teachers, and others engaged in pursuits requiring increased mental activity.

Caution: Some individuals may be allergic to these capsules. Appearance of a rash, or a temporary feeling of numbness, should cause reduction of dosage or discontinuance of use.

Sales got off to a sluggish start, and remained dull until a sensational Sunday supplement article appeared, titled: "Breakthrough in Brains—New Drug Dramatically Boosts I.Q.!"

That got the ball rolling. Soon, brief "special reports" on radio added to the attention. Television news announcers began introducing humorous items on "I.Q. Capsules," for light relief from a steady diet of disasters.

Sales started to pick up.

Students with half a semester's work to do the night before the exam instantly recognized the possibilities. The results were so delightful that the news spread fast.

Sales of Cerebrocreatine began doubling from week to week.

Banner found himself reading with close attention a letter that gave an idea what was going on:

Dear Sir:

I am writing to thank you for your help in passing German I. The night before the midyear exam, I could scarcely tell the difference between "f" and "s" in that weird type they use in our reader. But I ate up about half a bottle of your I.Q. pills, holed up with the text and the reader, and by the time Old Sol crawled up over the treetops next morning, I was a new man, *Ja wohl!*

I'm pretty well covered with red spots right now, and for a while there I kind of felt like I was packed in ice, but I got past the midyear's exam, and it was worth it!

This German, by the way, is interesting, once you get into it.

Yours in *Gemutlichkeit,*

Banner read this letter over and over again, then called Hommel in to find out how work was coming on the antidote.

Hommel was cheerful.

"We've had some brilliant suggestions, and some really stimulating discussions on the subject, and that sort of beginning can lay the groundwork for some genuine high-order achievement later on. I'm sure we'll have real progress to report before long, considering the caliber of the thought that's been shown recently."

Banner frowned.

"That's nice, Mort. But what's been *done* so far?"

"Well, as you realize, this is an extremely difficult problem to deal with. There are a great many ramifications, of really extraordinary subtlety. To put it in layman's language, it pays to clear away the undergrowth before plunging into the thicket."

Banner looked at Hommel attentively, then held out the letter.

"Take a look at this, Mort."

Hommel read the letter quickly, with a faint air of negligent disinterest.

"I'm sorry we didn't have this when I was going to school."

Banner said dryly, "Personally, I'm glad it waited until now." He studied Hommel's expression alertly. "You haven't tried this stuff yourself, Mort?"

"I've made rather extensive use of it. The results have been most gratifying. It's highly stimulating mentally."

"I see. But no actual *work* has been done on the antidote?"

Hommel frowned. "No, I admit, but—"

"Quite a few weeks have gone by."

"I realize that, and we've found some really interesting approaches, that I think should enable us to solve the problem much more rapidly than if we had simply gone at it blindly, more or less by trial and error."

"Maybe. Well, keep at it. And Mort—"

"Yes?"

"If I were you, I'd go a little easy on those pills."

"We've found no harmful side effects, other than those that are strictly temporary."

Banner nodded. "I could be wrong, Mort. But bear in mind that the dosage we suggest on the bottle is 'one to two capsules daily,' and here we have a letter that says, 'I ate up about half a bottle of your I.Q. pills.' We could get something unexpected out of this. If so, we want people here who aren't worried about getting a dose of the same thing themselves. How about your star chemist, Peabody? Is he using the stuff, too?"

"I'm sorry to say Peabody has acquired an irrational distrust of drugs."

"He won't use it himself?"

"No. And I have to admit, he shows up rather poorly by contrast with those who do."

"He does, eh? Well, Mort, do as you think best. But I'd advise you to think this over."

After Hommel had left, Banner called in Peabody.

"I'm told," said Banner, "that you don't think much of our new brain-booster pills."

Peabody looked harassed.

"It isn't that, sir, but I . . . ah . . . I think I'm probably allergic to them."

"Have you tried them?"

"No, sir."

"Don't you feel that, out of loyalty to the company, you ought to eat up at least a bottle a week?"

"I wouldn't want to eat even one capsule a week."

"Why not?"

Peabody shook his head.

"You never know what the side effects may be."

Banner leaned forward.

"What do you think of the work that's been done in finding an antidote?"

"What work? No work *has* been done."

"Even by you?"

"I've groped around some. I've gotten some ideas. But I can't say I've actually accomplished much yet."

"What do you think of the suggestions that have been made?"

"Oh, some of the *suggestions* have been brilliant. They might take a hundred years, all the laboratory facilities and chemists in the country, and a trillion dollars, but some of the suggestions have really sounded good."

"A little impractical, eh?"

Peabody nodded. "Brilliant, though."

"Just between the two of us, Peabody, how many pills do you think the average person who uses this stuff takes?"

"Two with every meal, and two when he goes to bed. That night, he dreams of waking up with an I.Q. of 1,500, and when he gets up he chews up two or three extra for good luck."

"*Does* it make him smarter?"

Peabody scratched his head, and looked exasperated.

"Yes, it does, but—I don't know."

"At least, the pill is useful for learning, isn't it?"

"I suppose so. Everyone says it is. It must be. But is learning supposed to be an end in itself? Once they get started on this stuff, they don't stop."

Banner nodded slowly. "We have to have an antidote."

"There may not *be* an antidote. The effect may be irreversible."

"But we have to look, because that's the only way to find out—and there's another thing that might help, if it's taken care of in time."

"What's that?"

"Where does Hommel keep his personal stock of brain pills?"

Peabody's eyes widened.

"In a drawer of his desk— You mean the Cerebrocreatine?"

"Yes. Now, of course, Peabody, I don't want to suggest that you— or anyone, for that matter—might make up a batch of these pills at considerably reduced strength, and put them in place of the pills Hommel has right now. Naturally, I wouldn't suggest such a thing. Nevertheless, if somebody *did* do that, it might just possibly do some good. Of course, if anyone did do it, he would want to think it over carefully first. Peabody, I admire people who get things *done*. By the way, it seems to me that it's about time you got an increase in salary, isn't it? Yes, I think so. Well, it's been nice weather lately, hasn't it? If we come up with one more drug like this, I think I may just go into the business of manufacturing fishing rods. Of course, there may be something wrong with that, too. If people would chew their food more before they swallow it, they wouldn't *need* so many pills in the first place. And a little exercise wouldn't hurt, either. What the devil are they doing with these things, anyway, Peabody? Are they trying to see who can get to be smartest by eating the most pills?"

Peabody, listening wide-eyed, swallowed hard, opened his mouth, shut it, recovered his breath, and said, "Yes, sir. They seem to use longer words every day."

Banner nodded. "I've always thought there must be a hole in this somewhere. Well, you think over what we've been talking about, and decide what you want to do. The more people we have actually *working* on this antidote, the better."

Peabody squinted in concentration, then nodded determinedly.

As time passed sales climbed to a stunning figure.

Hommel told Banner that he'd evidently reached "some kind of a saturation point with the drug, which no longer seemed to have any effect" on him.

Peabody received a raise.

Hommel reported that a number of his more outstanding men seemed to have "reached the saturation point."

Peabody received a bonus.

Hommel stated exasperatedly that there was "no word of anyone *else* having reached the saturation point"—only he and some of his best men. And wondered why should that be.

Banner wondered aloud if possibly there could be anything about working in a plant where the drug was manufactured that could have anything to do with it.

Hommel seized on the idea as a possible explanation, and determined to look into it once work on the antidote could be got moving. Save for Peabody, this was still on dead center, no one being able to figure out how to put his grandiose research plans into effect.

"The trouble," said Hommel, "is that there are so many very interesting and exciting alternative approaches to the problem—we scarcely know where to start."

"In that case," said Banner, "start anywhere. But for heaven's sake, *start.*"

"Many of the more promising methods might prove prohibitively expensive."

"Then forget about them. That simplifies the problem."

Hommel looked puzzled. "True," he said, as if he could not quite grasp the concept, but recognized somehow that it was valid.

After Hommel had gone out, Banner stared at the closed door, then shook his head.

"Well, if that's brilliance, let's hope it wears off pretty soon."

More time went by.

Work on the antidote got sluggishly under way, by fits and starts, and with baffling setbacks, as if the work were dogged by gremlins.

Banner, meanwhile, tried to rouse, amongst those in high places, some awareness of possible future difficulties. Those in high places were not aroused, except by enthusiasm for Cerebrocreatine.

Meanwhile, in colleges and universities throughout the world, bell-shaped curves were being knocked into weird corrugated forms. Ranks of straight-A students moved triumphantly toward graduation. Newspaper and magazine articles predicting the arrival of the millennium multiplied like rabbits.

Banner, meanwhile, had trouble with his car. Having had it inexpertly repaired while he was away on a trip, now that he was back he called up to get it taken care of, and invited Hommel to come along with him.

"All that needs to be done," said Banner, as they walked onto the company parking lot, "is to adjust the carburetor. That shouldn't take too long. We can have lunch a little early, and if they don't have the work done, we'll come back in their courtesy car. I'd adjust it myself, except that they've made so many improvements in the thing that it scares me every time I look under the hood."

Banner got in, and reached over to open the door for Hommel, who by now was seeming more like his usual self. As Hommel slid in and slammed the door, Banner turned the key in the ignition. The engine choked and gagged into life, to run with a galloping rhythm as clouds of black smoke poured out the tail pipe. Like a malfunctioning oil burner on the move, they pulled out onto the highway.

The drive to town turned into a thrilling trip. The car lacked acceleration, and had a tendency to cough and quit. A police officer soon motioned them to the side, parked in front, red light blinking, walked back to their car.

"You're creating a serious hazard in the area of air pollution."

Banner adopted the humble attitude suitable to the occasion. "I'm very sorry, Officer. I made an appointment to get it fixed, and I'm on my way there right now."

"You realize that it's as essential to maintain a vehicle as to purchase it in the first place?"

"Yes, Officer," said Banner humbly.

Just then, a car streaked past at about seventy.

The officer straightened up, hesitated, then said, "As I look at all this traffic, it's impossible not to imagine what it would be like to strip away wheels, trim, and car bodies, leaving only the engines and tail pipes of all these vehicles, pouring out clouds of gaseous contamination. Such a situation would never be tolerated. Yet, the fact that the contamination is incidental, that one contaminating vehicle moves on, to be replaced by a new one, that the source of contamination is covered by trim, and incidental to the purpose of individualized transportation—all this caused the damage inflicted to be overlooked for decades. One wonders what other sources of trouble are similarly concealed by externals."

Banner opened his mouth, and shut it again.

The officer said, "Not long ago, it was necessary for us to learn some new police procedures, and to assist in acquiring the proper degree of mental readiness, I made considerable use of what are known as 'I.Q. capsules.' Quite a number of surprising thoughts occurred to me, based on things I'd heard or read, and hadn't connected together. Were you aware, for instance, that the civilization of ancient Rome may have collapsed because of contamination of the drinking water with lead, which was extensively used for water pipes? And have you considered that an ingredient used extensively to prevent 'knocking' in modern motor fuels contains lead? Could our air supply be contaminated as was the Romans' water supply?"

The officer shook his head and glanced around. "Rectify that condition as soon as possible. If I should see it again and it hasn't been alleviated, I'll be compelled to give you a summons."

"Yes, Officer," said Banner. "I'm going right down there."

The policeman nodded, got back in his car, and Banner waited for a break in the traffic.

"Those pills of ours, Mort, seem to get around."

"They certainly do. I wonder if there's anything to what he said?"

"I'll be frank to say, I don't know. But I did notice a speeder go past, and he missed it."

They drove into town, and found the car dealer's drive blocked with parked cars. Banner pulled off the road in an adjacent lot where the dealer sold his used cars. Frowning, they got out and walked back.

"It looks to me," said Banner, "as if he has enough work piled up to last for the next three months."

They were walking along a row of used cars, and passed one where a puzzled customer looked into a car's engine compartment, listening to the salesman:

". . . And another thing you might not know, and I wouldn't either, but I've been studying up on it lately, and that's this power brake. Now, you tend to think a power brake *applies power* to the brake, but that's not how it works. What happens here is that the power brakes create a vacuum on *one* side of the piston, while atmospheric pressure—"

The customer looked desperate.

"Look, all I *want*—"

Banner shoved open the door of the showroom, nodded to a group

81

of salemen leaning against the trunk of a new car, and walked past toward a short hall leading to the garage. From behind came the voices of the salesmen:

"... And when he did that, she had him dead to rights."

"Sure. It was the same in Schlumberger vs. Mallroyd."

"Oh, I don't know. The decision there was adverse."

"*Was* it? What do you say, Phil?"

"Well, I'd hesitate to go into that. I'm not far enough in the course to say about that. I *thought* so. But I realize there's a lot involved in that. It depends on whether a higher court—"

Banner shoved open another door, walked down a short hall past the open door of an office where a stack of mail lay unopened on a chair, pushed open another door, and he and Hommel walked past a counter where parts were sold, into the garage itself.

Here they were momentarily struck speechless by a roomful of cars with the hoods up, the mechanics seated at a bench where all the tools had been shoved off onto the floor. The men, comfortably seated at the bench, had books open, writing furiously.

Banner eased through the jam of cars, and peered over their shoulders. They were all working on different pages of separate copies of the same book, a text on calculus. As they filled up the sheets of paper with finished problems, they put them on top of a large stack of such papers, and tore off fresh sheets. Several unopened packs of paper, containing five hundred sheets to the pack, sat on the back of the bench.

From the service manager's cubicle across the room came the ring of a phone, then an obliging voice:

"Sure, bring it right in. We'll get at it first chance we get."

Banner stared across the room, to see the service manager put down the phone, and turn to contemplate a skeleton on a stand. His voice came faintly across the room:

"Clavicle, scapula, sternum, rib; frontal, parietal, occipital, squamous temporal, mastoid temporal, nasal, zygomatic, maxilla, mandible..."

Banner eased through the jammed cars, motioned the stupefied Hommel to follow, shoved open the door to the short hall, walked through, shoved open the door to the salesroom, and was greeted by the words, "Was it ethyl ether, or was it a preparation consisting of ethyl ether? In the one case, what they'd run into..."

Banner stiff-armed the outer door, to find the same salesman and customer standing by the car. The customer, red-faced, was saying heatedly, "...All I'm *in* here for is a car I can use to get to work!"

The salesman nodded.

"But of course you can select a car more intelligently after you learn how they operate. And it's a fascinating study. You'll be surprised, as I was, once you get into it. For instance, were you aware that the present infinitely-variable transmission is a descendant, in a sense, of a development of the 1920s ..."

Banner walked past to his car, got in, opened Hommel's door, then nursed the engine to life.

"Let's hope, Mort, that this place isn't typical."

"It couldn't be."

"You're right. If it was, the country would have collapsed by now."

They finally found a garage that could do the job, but the mechanic was overloaded with work, and it took a long time.

Somehow, the day's experiences didn't seem to augur well for the future.

As time passed, the men working on the antidote began to see the importance of it, and developed a fervor that only Peabody had had before. But it took a long time for this fervor to produce any results.

"I hate to say it," said Hommel, "but it seems to me that this Cerebrocreatine of ours helps study, but somehow prevents *work*."

Banner handed over a newspaper. "Take a look at this, Mort."

Hommel glanced at the paper, to find an article marked in pencil:

SAUGASH AREA BOASTS FOUR COLLEGES!

Saugash, April 22. Work began today on a new neighborhood college, to supplement the Saugash Community College completed here last fall. This brings to four the total of higher educational facilities in the Saugash area, counting Saugash University and Saugash Teachers College.

Dr. Rutherford Dollard Ganst, VI, President of Saugash University, presided at the ground-breaking ceremonies, which were attended by the mayor and many other notables, and a crowd of interested persons estimated at over four thousand.

President Ganst, in a short and memorable address, stated: "Nothing is more important in this day of rapid scientific advance and complex societal change than an informed citizenry. Education alone can create an informed citizenry. Thus the need for education becomes no less vital and urgent than the need for air or water, for food or any other necessity of life. Education has become the basic prerequisite for life today. Nothing is more important. Today, educational qualifications are vital to everyone, from the manual laborer at the bottom, to the head of the great educational system at the top. Employers will not accept the unqualified, because they are seriously lacking in qualifications. Without qualifications there can be no success. Mere ability is no longer enough. Indeed, with sufficient qualifications, one may dispense with ability. It is the *qualifications* that are vital, and only educational institutions may grant qualifications. Thus Education is no longer the necessity of youth alone. Education is now the essential and inescapable concomitant of progress and indeed of existence for every man and every woman of each and every age and condition of life, without exception, from the cradle to the grave. The gigantic dominating growth of our educational system, swelling like a tide to overwhelming proportions never before conceived by the mind of man in all recorded history, cannot be resisted! Nothing can stop it. Nothing can stay it. *Education will be served!* Science requires it. Technology demands it. The towering giants in the field of the hierarchy of education itself mandate it! *Education will conquer all!*"

Hommel looked up dizzily.

Banner said, "When you first told me about this pill, Mort, you said, 'It stimulates intellectual activity. It channels energy from gross physical pursuits into imaginative creativity.' The trouble seems to be that it channels a little too *much* energy."

"But what can we do?"

Banner shook his head.

"Keep working on that antidote."

As the days passed, the situation didn't stand still. On a drive to town one afternoon, Banner and Hommel were nearly run off the road by a truck whose driver was studying at sixty miles an hour. A few minutes later, on the flat farmland below the highway, Hommel saw a farmer driving a tractor, reading a book strapped to the steering wheel in front of him. The tractor ran into an electric pole, the book and the farmer were knocked off. The farmer picked up the book and went on reading.

Banner parked on the shoulder of the road behind a car with a flat tire, and looked where Hommel pointed.

He shook his head, then glanced up, and murmured, "Now, what's *this?*"

The car in front had the left rear tire flat, and three men were standing around the open trunk of the car. They seemed to be arguing in a languid way.

"Oh, no," one of them was saying, "I'm sure the essential thing is to *first* jack up the car."

"You mean, *elevate the car on a jack.*"

"Well, my terminology may have been a little imprecise, but—"

The third man broke in. "It's incorrect, in any case. The essential prerequisite is removal of the tire bolts while application of vehicular weight precludes rotation of the wheel."

"Rotation of the wheel? Yes, yes, we're overlooking something. Due to the fact that the wheels are fastened on opposite sides of the car, they rotate in opposite senses, and to prevent inertial loosening of the fastening nuts or cap screws—cap screws in this case, I presume— the 'handedness' of the screw threads is reversed on opposite sides of the vehicles. Now, to loosen a cap screw successfully, it must be rotated in the proper direction. Yet, the thread is screwed in out of sight in the brake drum. *It is not subject to visual observation.*"

"That *is* important. How can we determine the handedness of the threads?"

A perspiring woman stuck her head out the car window.

"Oh, hurry, *Please* hurry."

One of the men sluggishly got out the jack and stood holding it.

"Does anyone have a text, or repair manual, that might clarify this point?"

The woman put her head out the window again.

"*Please* hurry! The pains are coming closer together!"

One of the men looked around severely.

"Now, don't interrupt. We have a difficult problem here."

The man with the jack leaned it against the bumper, then all three men knelt to scratch diagrams in the dirt on the shoulder of the road.

Banner and Hommel hadn't changed a tire in years, but they could stand it no longer, and got out.

Banner grabbed the jack, and fitted it under the rear bumper. Hommel pulled out a combination tire iron and lug wrench, popped off the wheel cover, and loosened the wheel. Banner jacked the car up. Hommel took the wheel off. Banner got out the spare, and Hommel put it on while Banner put the flat into the trunk, then let down the jack. Hommel banged the wheel cover into place. Banner put the jack in the trunk, Hommel tossed the tire iron inside, and they turned away.

The other three men stood staring. One of them shook a yellow capsule out of a bottle, tossed it into his mouth and swallowed.

"Would you be prepared to do that again? I'm not sure that we've learned all the essential manipulations."

The woman put her head out the window. There was a note of desperate urgency in her voice.

"The pains are getting closer together!"

As the car disappeared down the highway, Banner and Hommel stood staring after it.

"How near, Mort, are we to that antidote?"

Hommel had a haunted look.

"No one could say. Peabody seems to be closest. But he could run into trouble any time. Besides, his solution seems to be the least desirable."

"Don't worry about that," said Banner with feeling. "Just as long as we get it while there's time to use it."

Several more weeks crawled by, so slowly that they seemed like months or years. Meanwhile, the gradual overall disintegration turned into specific failures in production and distribution. Little notice of this appeared in newspapers, general magazines, or on radio or television, which were preoccupied with more intellectual matters, particularly "adjusted voting." Under "adjusted voting" each person would cast a number of votes in accordance with his "intellectual level." The more degrees, the more votes. Television networks were carrying the "Debate of the Century" on this plan, the object of the most acrimonious dispute being how many votes should be allowed for publication in professional journals. No one dared to disagree with the principle of the plan, lest he label himself as "undereducated." To be "undereducated" was a serious business. The social stigma attached to it was about equivalent to having served two terms in prison for robbing gas stations and grocery stores.

In the midst of all this, with consumption of Cerebrocreatine mounting from week to week, with gigantic new campuses looming over the landscape, with the airwaves thick with learned discussions as the means of existence crumbled, Hommel and Peabody walked into Banner's office.

"Well, we've got it. It's practically a stupidity drug, but it *works*."

Banner got the new drug on the market in record time. Advertised as "Super*Aktion*, for active people—instant-acting stimulant to healthful practical activity," it was wholesaled at a very modest profit in "superinhalator bottles," supposed to be used by spraying into the nose and throat.

"For the love of Heaven," said Hommel, "why don't we sell it in *capsules?*"

"It isn't going to sell like wildfire, Mort. Not in the present state of affairs. What one-hundred-percent intellectual is *interested* in healthful practical activity? And what is Cerebrocreatine turning the average person into?"

"I know. We should sell it in some different form. If only—"

Banner shook his head. "Since it will have only a very limited sale, we've got to make the most of it." He picked up a sample inhalator. It was shaped like a small gun, made of violet plastic, with the label on the side of the grip. Banner aimed it across the room, and squeezed the trigger. There was a *squish* sound, and a fine jet of liquid shot out, to leave an oval of tiny droplets on the wall.

Hommel frowned, and looked at the "superinhalator" again.

"When in doubt," said Banner, "rely on human nature. *Real* human nature, with its high points and its low points. Bear in mind, there are likely to be a few unregenerate bullheaded individualists around, regardless of anything formal education can do, even backed up by a thing like Cerebrocreatine."

"I still don't—"

From the window came a rude roar of exhaust, and a screech of brakes.

Banner looked out, to see a truck marked "Central Plumbing" slam to a stop in the drive below. Three men in coveralls jumped out, went around to the rear, yanked out a blow torch, a suction plunger, a coil of wire, and a tool case, and headed for the front door.

Hommel looked out.

"About time. That drain has been plugged for three months." He shook his head dispiritedly. "But I still don't see any way that we can hope—"

From a window down below boomed a rough profane voice:

"Where's the drain? We haven't got the whole — — - — day! Great ——! Look at all these stupid ——!"

There was a faint but distinct *squish squish squish* sound.

Hommel stared at Banner, then at the "superinhalator" on his desk.

Banner said, "Practical men use practical means, Mort."

There was a thunder of feet on the staircase down the hall.

Banner and Hommel went into the hallway, to find a research chemist named Smyth looking around dazedly as he tossed yellow capsules into his mouth and contemplated some complex theoretical problem.

Up the stairs burst a couple of brisk men in gray lab coats, followed by three more in coveralls.

Smyth looked at this crew as at a colony of tame ants that has gotten out of its jar.

One of the men in overalls shifted his blowtorch to the other hand, and aimed a small violet gun at Smyth.

"*Squish!*"

Smyth staggered back against the wall. He sucked in a deep breath, and suddenly his expression changed from dreamy contemplation to astonishment. He banged his fist into his open hand.

"Why am I just standing here *thinking* about it? Why not *do* it?"

He strode off down the corridor in one direction as the plumbers vanished around the corner in the other direction.

From around the corner came a sucking pumping sound, followed by a gurgling noise, more sucking and pumping sounds, a good deal of profanity, then a shout of triumph.

"She's unplugged! O.K., boys, let's go!"

Banner nodded.

"That's more *like* it!"

Hommel looked down the hall where Smyth had disappeared.

"Wait a minute. What's he working on—"

There was a thundering noise on the stairs, then the roar of exhaust.

Smyth came hurrying back up the hall, carrying what looked like a silver-coated round-bottomed flask in one hand, and in the other a small bottle of yellowish oily liquid. From the mouth of the silvered flask came a wisp of whitish vapor.

Hommel stared. "Great, holy, leaping—"

"You see, Mort," said Banner, a little expansively, "we've provided the few remaining practical men with the means to convert *intellectuals* into practical men. They, in turn, will be irritated by the intellectuals around *them*. There's the answer to our problem."

Hommel was watching Smyth.

Smyth vanished into his laboratory.

Banner went on, "The trouble with Cerebrocreatine was that it undermined necessities of life at the same time that it gave us fringe benefits we could get along without. That's not progress. Progress is the product of a new advantage *compounding advantages we already have.*"

He paused as Smyth came out, holding in one gloved hand a shiny rod bearing at its end a clamp. The clamp gripped a small unstoppered bottle of yellowish oily liquid.

Smyth insinuated the rod around the door frame, peered into the room, drew the door almost shut, turned his face away, and tilted the rod.

BAM!

The building jumped. Fire shot out around the edges of the door. Black smoke rolled out behind the flames.

Smyth threw off the smoking glove, sniffed the air, then sucked his fingers.

"Well, *that* didn't work."

He turned away, drew in a deep breath, then went back into his laboratory. There was immediately the whir of a powerful draft sucking up fumes.

"Hm-m-m," said Banner, looking thoughtfully at the partly open door.

Smyth reappeared, unrolling what looked like a small coil of bell wire. He tacked a loop to the door frame, then, still unrolling wire, went back into the laboratory. Wisps of smoke were still trailing out around the top of the door, but this didn't seem to slow him down. He came out, cut the loop, stripped the insulation off the two ends, pounded in another tack, and hammered it flat to hold the two wires. Then he bent the ends of the wires apart, so they wouldn't touch—yet.

Hommel cleared his throat.

"Ah . . . Dr. Smyth . . . I wonder if perhaps . . . a little more theoretical consideration of the thermodynamics of the reaction—?"

"Theoretical considerations be damned," said Smyth. "The only way we're going to find out is to try it and see what products we get."

He raised his left arm over his head, shielding one ear with his shoulder and the other with his fingers, then he touched the bare ends of the two wires together.

BOOM!

The building jumped.

Cracks shot up the wall.

There was a heavy shattering crash from overhead.

As the roar died away, the smash and tinkle of breaking glass could be heard throughout the building.

Smyth shoved the door slightly open, and a grayish cloud poured out. He wafted some of the fumes in his direction, and sniffed cautiously.

His face lit in a triumphant smile.

"*That* saves some time!"

He pulled the door shut, and headed toward the stockroom.

Hommel turned to Banner, "How is *this* an improvement? We were better off with theorists!"

"We've overshot the mark again. This stuff is too strong."

"There's a threshold effect. If you don't use enough, you get no result you can detect."

A small crowd was gathering in the hall to see what was going on. Banner separated Peabody from the pack.

"Peabody, my boy," said Banner, "we've got this last problem pretty well licked, thanks to your antidote. But there's still one little loose end that we've got to take care of."

Peabody looked apprehensive.

"What's that, sir?"

Banner shook his head.

"*Now* we need an antidote for the antidote."

EXAMINATION DAY

Henry Slesar

Historically, the system of public education in the United States has been subjected to a variety of attacks. These include charges that it is incompetent, that it produces people who cannot read, that it attacks religion, and that it is a threat to traditional American values. Moreover, recently the schools have been subjected to a double-barreled attack from both the radical left and the political right. Attacks from the right are not really new, since charges of communist influence and infiltration in the schools have taken place at various times throughout the twentieth century. The focus of this concern has changed in the last few years to the "threat" supposedly emanating from young "radical" teachers who are bringing new lifestyles into the schoolroom. Some feel that the racial unrest in many schools is due to "do-gooder" school boards and teachers. In addition, the stand taken against the Vietnam War by many teachers produced divisions and emotions on the part of parents, just as the war did in most aspects of American life.

On the other hand, the educational system of the country has been attacked in some quarters as being too "establishment," too conservative, and too competition-oriented. This radical critique holds that the schools are tools of the ruling class, indoctrinating students toward a belief in corporate capitalism and forcing them to acquiesce in a system of exploitation.

Therefore, the schools are viewed by some as a dangerous source of governmental and economic power, and by others as a threat to the "American way of life." Sometimes you just cannot win no matter what you do!

In "Examination Day" we see a society in which the educational system is under the thumb of the government and is called upon to serve it in a way that is unprecedented in any country in the world.

The vehicle for the subjugation in the story is the examination, the test—that device so often feared by the pupil, but one that has been deemed necessary to properly evaluate the progress of both the school and the student. There has been comparatively little research done on the effect of testing on the psychological well-being of the student. What is clear is that the examination is of increasing importance to every young man and woman. In many cases it determines the future—entrance to law or medical school, entrance to a good university through the College Entrance Exams, admittance to graduate school through the Graduate Record Exams, even receiving a high school diploma. The examination can be either a way out of poverty and the ghetto or a sentence of marginality for millions. The centrality of examinations is not restricted to America or even to the present. In ancient China, for example, students who failed the civil service exams often committed suicide.

"Examination Day" looks at the most important moment in a young student's life in a society of the future and at the same time raises the issue of the child who learns *too* well.

FOR FURTHER THOUGHT OR DISCUSSION

1. Are examinations necessary to education? What alternatives to exams can you think of?

2. Are schools reflections of society or determinants of society?

3. Is there an "establishment" viewpoint built into the curriculum of most schools?

4. In what ways do schools challenge the *status quo?*

5. In the story, what is so threatening to the government about those who fail the exam?

EXAMINATION DAY *Henry Slesar*

The Jordans never spoke of the exam, not until their son, Dickie, was 12 years old. It was on his birthday that Mrs. Jordan first mentioned the subject in his presence, and the anxious manner of her speech caused her husband to answer sharply.

"Forget about it," he said. "He'll do all right."

They were at the breakfast table, and the boy looked up from his plate curiously. He was an alert-eyed youngster, with flat blond hair and a quick, nervous manner. He didn't understand what the sudden tension was about, but he did know that today was his birthday, and he wanted harmony above all. Somewhere in the little apartment there were wrapped, beribboned packages waiting to be opened, and in the tiny wall-kitchen, something warm and sweet was being prepared in the automatic stove. He wanted the day to be happy, and the moistness of his mother's eyes, the scowl on his father's face, spoiled the mood of fluttering expectation with which he had greeted the morning.

"What exam?" he asked.

His mother looked at the tablecloth. "It's just a sort of Government intelligence test they give children at the age of twelve. You'll be getting it next week. It's nothing to worry about."

"You mean a test like in school?"

"Something like that," his father said, getting up from the table. "Go read your comic books, Dickie."

The boy rose and wandered toward that part of the living room which had been "his" corner since infancy. He fingered the topmost comic of the stack, but seemed uninterested in the colorful squares of fast-paced action. He wandered toward the window, and peered gloomily at the veil of mist that shrouded the glass.

"Why did it have to rain *today?*" he said. "Why couldn't it rain tomorrow?"

His father, now slumped into an armchair with the Government newspaper, rattled the sheets in vexation. "Because it just did, that's all. Rain makes the grass grow."

"Why, Dad?"

"Because it does, that's all."

Dickie puckered his brow. "What makes it green, though? The grass?"

"Nobody knows," his father snapped, then immediately regretted his abruptness.

Later in the day, it was birthday time again. His mother beamed as she handed over the gaily-colored packages, and even his father managed a grin and a rumple-of-the-hair. He kissed his mother and shook hands gravely with his father. Then the birthday cake was brought forth, and the ceremonies concluded.

An hour later, seated by the window, he watched the sun force its way between the clouds.

"Dad," he said, "how far away is the sun?"

"Five thousand miles," his father said.

Dick sat at the breakfast table and again saw moisture in his mother's eyes. He didn't connect her tears with the exam until his father suddenly brought the subject to light again.

"Well, Dickie," he said, with a manly frown, "you've got an appointment today."

"I know, Dad. I hope——"

"Now it's nothing to worry about. Thousands of children take this test every day. The Government wants to know how smart you are, Dickie. That's all there is to it."

"I get good marks in school," he said hesitantly.

"This is different. This is a—special kind of test. They give you this stuff to drink, you see, and then you go into a room where there's a sort of machine——"

"What stuff to drink?" Dickie said.

"It's nothing. It tastes like peppermint. It's just to make sure you answer the questions truthfully. Not that the Government thinks you won't tell the truth, but this stuff makes *sure*."

Dickie's face showed puzzlement, and a touch of fright. He looked at his mother, and she composed her face into a misty smile.

"Everything will be all right," she said.

"Of course it will," his father agreed. "You're a good boy, Dickie; you'll make out fine. Then we'll come home and celebrate. All right?"

"Yes, sir," Dickie said.

They entered the Government Educational Building 15 minutes before the appointed hour. They crossed the marble floors of the great pillared lobby, passed beneath an archway and entered an automatic elevator that brought them to the fourth floor.

There was a young man wearing an insignia-less tunic, seated at a polished desk in front of Room 404. He held a clipboard in his hand, and he checked the list down to the Js and permitted the Jordans to enter.

The room was cold and official as a courtroom, with long benches flanking metal tables. There were several fathers and sons already there, and a thin-lipped woman with cropped black hair was passing out sheets of paper.

Mr. Jordan filled out the form, and returned it to the clerk. Then he told Dickie: "It won't be long now. When they call your name, you just go through the doorway at that end of the room." He indicated the portal with his finger.

A concealed loudspeaker crackled and called off the first name. Dickie saw a boy leave his father's side reluctantly and walk slowly toward the door.

At five minutes of 11, they called the name of Jordan.

"Good luck, son," his father said, without looking at him. "I'll call for you when the test is over."

Dickie walked to the door and turned the knob. The room inside was dim, and he could barely make out the features of the gray-tunicked attendant who greeted him.

"Sit down," the man said softly. He indicated a high stool beside his desk. "Your name's Richard Jordan?"

"Yes, sir."

"Your classification number is 600–115. Drink this, Richard."

He lifted a plastic cup from the desk and handed it to the boy. The liquid inside had the consistency of buttermilk, tasted only vaguely of the promised peppermint. Dickie downed it, and handed the man the empty cup.

He sat in silence, feeling drowsy, while the man wrote busily on a sheet of paper. Then the attendant looked at his watch, and rose to stand only inches from Dickie's face. He unclipped a pen-like object from the pocket of his tunic, and flashed a tiny light into the boy's eyes.

"All right," he said. "Come with me, Richard."

He led Dickie to the end of the room, where a single wooden armchair faced a multi-dialed computing machine. There was a microphone on the left arm of the chair, and when the boy sat down, he found its pinpoint head conveniently at his mouth.

"Now just relax, Richard. You'll be asked some questions, and you think them over carefully. Then give your answers into the microphone. The machine will take care of the rest."

"Yes, sir."

"I'll leave you alone now. Whenever you want to start, just say 'ready' into the microphone."

"Yes, sir."

The man squeezed his shoulder, and left.

Dickie said, "Ready."

Lights appeared on the machine, and a mechanism whirred. A voice said:

"Complete this sequence. One, four, seven, ten . . ."

Mr. and Mrs. Jordan were in the living room, not speaking, not even speculating.

It was almost four o'clock when the telephone rang. The woman tried to reach it first, but her husband was quicker.

"Mr. Jordan?"

The voice was clipped; a brisk, official voice.

"Yes, speaking."

"This is the Government Educational Service. Your son, Richard M. Jordan, Classification 600–115, has completed the Government examination. We regret to inform you that his intelligence quotient has exceeded the Government regulation, according to Rule 84, Section 5, of the New Code."

Across the room, the woman cried out, knowing nothing except the emotion she read on her husband's face.

"You may specify by telephone," the voice droned on, "whether you wish his body interred by the Government or would you prefer a private burial place? The fee for Government burial is ten dollars."

PRIMARY EDUCATION OF THE CAMIROI

R. A. Lafferty

Different societies educate their young in different ways. In primitive societies this function is performed almost solely by the family, with fathers supplying models for their sons and mothers playing this role for their daughters. In other societies, parents play an important role in education both through their interactions with their children and, increasingly, through their interactions with their children's teachers. Teachers and parents both have a vested interest in the same children. The parents want their children to succeed in school, success usually being measured in terms of the report card, while the teacher's professional advancement is partially determined by his or her "success" in helping the child to learn.

Conflicts between parents and teachers are not uncommon. The issue may be over whether or not a student received the correct grade or over a disciplinary problem. In dealing with parents, the teacher is in an awkward position. If the teacher feels that the parents are to blame for a particular problem, care must be taken to ensure that parents do not feel that undue interference in their affairs is taking place. Teachers need to be sensitive to parents' feelings, both for the good of the child and for their own professional security. As the stakes of school achievement rise due to the increasing importance placed on college admission, parents' concern for their children's grades is also rising. Since it is the teacher who determines grades and all that this implies, the seeds of potential conflict between parent and teacher will increase.

Finally, it should be remembered that the child will be in school (in most cases) for at least twelve years. During this time, the teachers come to *replace* parents in terms of the training function.

The potential for conflict thus derives partly from jealousy, since some parents may feel that their children's future is being determined by "others." They may feel that control over their children is passing out of their hands. The teacher must recognize this feeling and work toward a partnership whose beneficiary will be the child.

One vehicle for parent-teacher cooperation is the PTA. The Parent-Teacher Associations have historically been organizations in which the parents played a passive role, receiving information about education from school officials. However, as the problems of education have increased, especially in urban areas, PTAs have become more important as vehicles for protest and controversy. Parents are taking more aggressive postures toward the schools, and this trend is likely to become more pronounced in the future.

In this story, a delegation from a PTA is visiting another culture to observe and learn from its educational system. We have much to learn from the way other societies educate their young. It is necessary for American education to be flexible and open-minded, and not to fear the incorporation of educational methods developed by others.

FOR FURTHER THOUGHT OR DISCUSSION

1. What is the educational significance of "Conclusion A " and Conclusion B " in the story?

2: What are the implications of a curriculum based on the Camiroi system?

3. What is the nature of the parent-teacher relationship? How can it be improved?

4. What social trends are affecting this relationship? In what ways?

5. What is the future of the parent-teacher relationship?

6. What is the present role of the PTA, and what should it be?

PRIMARY EDUCATION OF THE CAMIROI   R. A. Lafferty

ABSTRACT FROM JOINT REPORT TO THE GENERAL DUBUQUE PTA CONCERNING THE PRIMARY EDUCATION OF THE CAMIROI, Subtitled Critical Observations of a Parallel Culture on a Neighboring World, and Evaluations of the other way of education.

Extract from the Day Book:

"Where," we asked the Information Factor at Camiroi City Terminal, "is the office of the local PTA?"

"Isn't any," he said cheerfully.

"You mean that in Camiroi City, the metropolis of the planet, there is no PTA?" our chairman Paul Piper asked with disbelief.

"Isn't any office of it. But you're poor strangers, so you deserve an answer even if you can't frame your questions properly. See that elderly man sitting on the bench and enjoying the sun? Go tell him you need a PTA. He'll make you one."

"Perhaps the initials convey a different meaning on Camiroi," said Miss Munch the first surrogate chairman. "By them we mean —"

"Parent Teachers Apparatus, of course. Colloquial English is one of the six Earthian languages required here, you know. Don't be abashed. He's a fine person, and he enjoys doing things for strangers. He'll be glad to make you a PTA."

We were nonplusssed, but we walked over to the man indicated.

"We are looking for the local PTA, sir," said Miss Smice, our second surrogate chairman. "We were told that you might help us."

"Oh, certainly," said the elderly Camiroi gentleman. "One of you arrest that man walking there, and we'll get started with it."

"Do what?" asked our Mr. Piper.

"Arrest him. I have noticed that your own words sometimes do not convey a meaning to you. I often wonder how you do communicate among yourselves. Arrest, take into custody, seize by any force physical or moral, and bring him here."

"Yes, *sir*," cried Miss Hanks our third surrogate chairman. She enjoyed things like this. She arrested the walking Camiroi man with force partly physical and partly moral and brought him to the group.

"It's a PTA they want, Meander," the elder Camiroi said to the one arrested. "Grab three more, and we'll get started. Let the lady help. She's good at it."

Our Miss Hanks and the Camiroi man named Meander arrested three other Camiroi men and brought them to the group.

"Five. It's enough," said the elderly Camiroi. "We are hereby constituted a PTA and ordered into random action. Now, how can we accommodate you, good Earth people?"

"But are you legal? Are you five persons competent to be a PTA?" demanded our Mr. Piper.

"Any Camiroi citizen is competent to do any job on the planet of Camiroi," said one of the Camiroi men (we learned later that his name was Talarium), "otherwise Camiroi would be in a sad shape."

"It may be," said our Miss Smice sourly. "It all seems very informal. What if one of you had to be World President?"

"The odds are that it won't come to one man in ten," said the elderly Camiroi (his name was Philoxenus). "I'm the only one of this group ever to serve as president of this planet, and it was a pleasant week I spent in the Office. Now to the point. How can we accommodate you?"

"We would like to see one of your schools in session," said our Mr. Piper. "We would like to talk to the teachers and the students. We are here to compare the two systems of education."

"There is no comparison," said old Philoxenus, "— meaning no offense. Or no more than a little. On Camiroi, we practice Education. On Earth, they play a game, but they call it by the same name. That makes the confusion. Come. We'll go to a school in session."

"And to a public school," said Miss Smice suspiciously. "Do not fob off any fancy private school on us as typical."

"That would be difficult," said Philoxenus. "There is no public school in Camiroi City and only two remaining on the Planet. Only a small fraction of one percent of the students of Camiroi are in public schools. We maintain that there is no more reason for the majority of children to be educated in a public school than to be raised in a public orphanage. We realize, of course, that on Earth you have made a sacred buffalo of the public school."

"Sacred cow," said our Mr. Piper.

"Children and Earthlings should be corrected when they use words wrongly," said Philoxenus. "How else will they learn the correct forms? The animal held sacred in your own near Orient was of the species *bos bubalus* rather than *bos bos,* a buffalo rather than a cow. Shall we go to a school?"

"If it cannot be a public school, at least let it be a typical school," said Miss Smice.

"That again is impossible," said Philoxenus. "Every school on Camiroi is in some respect atypical."

We went to visit an atypical school.

INCIDENT: Our first contact with the Camiroi students was a violent one. One of them, a lively little boy about eight years old, ran into Miss Munch, knocked her down, and broke her glasses. Then he jabbered something in an unknown tongue.

"Is that Camiroi?" asked Mr. Piper with interest. "From what I have heard, I supposed the language to have a harsher and fuller sound."

"You mean you don't recognize it?" asked Philoxenus with amusement. "What a droll admission from an educator. The boy is very young and very ignorant. Seeing that you were Earthians, he spoke in Hindi, which is the tongue used by more Earthians than any other. No, no, Xypete, they are of the minority who speak English. You can tell it by their colorless texture and the narrow heads on them."

"I say you sure do have slow reaction, lady," the little boy Xypete explained. "Even subhumans should react faster than that. You just stand there and gape and let me bowl you over. You want me analyze you and see why you react so slow?"

"No! No!"

"You seem unhurt in structure from the fall," the little boy continued, "but if I hurt you I got to fix you. Just strip down to your shift, and I'll go over you and make sure you're all right."

"No! No! No!"

"It's all right," said Philoxenus. "All Camiroi children learn primary medicine in the first grade, setting bones and healing contusions and such."

"No! No! I'm all right. But he's broken my glasses."

"Come along Earthside lady, I'll make you some others," said the little boy. "With your slow reaction time you sure can't afford the added handicap of defective vision. Shall I fit you with contacts?"

"No. I want glasses just like those which were broken. Oh heavens, what will I do?"

"You come, I do," said the little boy. It was rather revealing to us that the little boy was able to test Miss Munch's eyes, grind lenses, make frames and have her fixed up within three minutes. "I have made some improvements over those you wore before," the boy said, "to help compensate for your slow reaction time."

"Are all the Camiroi students so talented?" Mr. Piper asked. He was impressed.

"No. Xypete is unusual," Philoxenus said. "Most students would not be able to make a pair of glasses so quickly or competently till they were at least nine."

RANDOM INTERVIEWS:

"How rapidly do you read?" Miss Hanks asked a young girl.

"One hundred and twenty words a minute," the girl said.

"On Earth some of the girl students your age have learned to read at the rate of five hundred words a minute," Miss Hanks said proudly.

"When I began disciplined reading, I was reading at the rate of four thousand words a minute," the girl said. "They had quite a time correcting me of it. I had to take remedial reading, and my parents were ashamed of me. Now I've learned to read almost slow enough."

"I don't understand," said Miss Hanks.

"Do you know anything about Earth History or Geography?" Miss Smice asked a middle-sized boy.

"We sure are sketchy on it, lady. There isn't very much over there, is there?"

"Then you have never heard of Dubuque?"

"Count Dubuque interests me. I can't say as much for the City named after him. I always thought that the Count handled the matters of the conflicting French and Spanish land grants and the basic claims of the Sauk and Fox Indians very well. References to the Town now carry a humorous connotation, and 'School-Teacher from Dubuque' has become a folk archetype."

"Thank you," said Miss Smice, "or do I thank you?"

"What are you taught of the relative humanity of the Earthians and the Camiroi and of their origins?" Miss Munch asked a Camiroi girl.

"The other four worlds, Earth (Gaea), Kentauron Mikron, Dahae and Astrobe were all settled from Camiroi. That is what we are taught. We are also given the humorous aside that if it isn't true we will still hold it true till something better comes along. It was we who rediscovered the Four Worlds in historic time, not they who discovered us. If we did not make the original settlements, at least we have filed the first claim that we made them. We did, in historical time, make an additional colonization of Earth. You call it the Incursion of the Dorian Greeks."

"Where are their playgrounds?" Miss Hanks asked Talarium.

"Oh, the whole world. The children have the run of everything. To set up specific playgrounds would be like setting a table-sized aquarium down in the depths of the ocean. It would really be pointless."

CONFERENCE: The four of us from Earth, specifically from Dubuque, Iowa, were in discussion with the five members of the Camiroi PTA.

"How do you maintain discipline?" Mr. Piper asked.

"Indifferently," said Philoxenus. "Oh, you mean in detail. It varies. Sometimes we let it drift, sometimes we pull them up short. Once they have learned that they must comply to an extent, there is little trouble. Small children are often put down into a pit. They do not eat or come out till they know their assignment."

"But that is inhuman," said Miss Hanks.

"Of course. But small children are not yet entirely human. If a child has not learned to accept discipline by the third or fourth grade, he is hanged."

"Literally?" asked Miss Munch.

"How would you hang a child figuratively? And what effect would that have on the other children?"

"By the neck?" Miss Munch still was not satisfied.

"By the neck until they are dead. The other children always accept the example gracefully and do better. Hanging isn't employed often. Scarcely one child in a hundred is hanged."

"What is this business about slow reading?" Miss Hanks asked, "I don't understand it at all."

"Only the other day there was a child in the third grade who persisted in rapid reading," Philoxenus said. "He was given an object lesson. He was given a book of medium difficulty, and he read it rapidly. Then he had to put the book away and repeat what he had read. Do you know that in the first thirty pages he missed four words? Midway in the book there was a whole statement which he had understood wrongly, and there were hundreds of pages that he got word-perfect only with difficulty. If he was so unsure on material that he had just read, think how imperfectly he would have recalled it forty years later."

"You mean that the Camiroi children learn to recall everything that they read?"

"The Camiroi children and adults will recall for life every detail they have ever seen, read or heard. We on Camiroi are only a little more intelligent than you on Earth. We cannot afford to waste time in forgetting or reviewing, or in pursuing anything of a shallowness that lends itself to scanning."

"Ah, would you call your schools liberal?" Mr. Piper asked.

"I would. You wouldn't," said Philoxenus. "We do not on Camiroi, as you do on Earth, use words to mean their opposites. There is nothing in our education or on our world that corresponds to the quaint servility which you call liberal on Earth."

"Well, would you call your education progressive?"

"No. In your argot, progressive, of course, means infantile."

"How are the schools financed?" asked Mr. Piper.

"Oh, the voluntary tithe on Camiroi takes care of everything, government, religion, education, public works. We don't believe in taxes, of course, and we never maintain a high overhead in anything."

"Just how voluntary is the tithing?" asked Miss Hanks. "Do you sometimes hang those who do not tithe voluntarily?"

"I believe there have been a few cases of that sort," said Philoxenus.

"And is your government really as slipshod as your education?" Mr. Piper asked. "Are your high officials really chosen by lot and for short periods?"

"Oh yes. Can you imagine a person so sick that he would actually *desire* to hold high office for any great period of time? Are there any further questions?"

"There must be hundreds," said Mr. Piper, "but we find difficulty putting them into words."

"If you cannot find words for them, we cannot find answers. PTA disbanded."

CONCLUSIONS: A. The Camiroi system of education is inferior to our own in organization, in buildings, in facilities, in playgrounds, in teacher conferences, in funding, in parental involvement, in supervision, in in-group out-group accommodation adjustment motifs. Some of the school buildings are grotesque. We asked about one particular building which seemed to us to be flamboyant and in bad taste. "What do you expect from second-grade children?" they said. "It is well built even if of peculiar appearance. Second-grade children are not yet complete artists of design."

"You mean that the children designed it themselves?" we asked.

"Of course," they said. "Designed and built it. It isn't a bad job for children."

Such a thing wouldn't be permitted on Earth.

CONCLUSION B. The Camiroi system of education somehow produces much better results than does the education system of Earth. We have been forced to admit this by the evidence at hand.

CONCLUSION C. There is an anomaly as yet unresolved between CONCLUSION A and CONCLUSION B.

APPENDIX TO JOINT REPORT

We give here, as perhaps of some interest, the curriculum of the Camiroi Primary Education.

FIRST YEAR COURSE:
Playing one wind instrument.
Simple drawing of objects and numbers.
Singing. (This is important. Many Earth people sing who cannot sing. This early instruction of the Camiroi prevents that occurrence.)
Simple arithmetic, hand and machine.
First acrobatics.
First riddles and logic.
Mnemonic religion.
First dancing.
Walking the low wire.
Simple electric circuits.
Raising ants. (Eoempts, not earth ants.)

SECOND YEAR COURSE:
Playing one keyboard instrument.
Drawing, faces, letters, motions.
Singing comedies.
Complex arithmetic, hand and machine.
Second acrobatics.
First jokes and logic.
Quadratic religion.
Second dancing.

105

Simple defamation. (Spirited attacks on the character of one fellow
   student, with elementary falsification and simple hatchet-job pro-
   gramming.)
Performing on the medium wire.
Project electric wiring.
Raising bees. (Galelea, not earth bees.)

THIRD YEAR COURSE:
Playing one stringed instrument.
Reading and voice. (It is here that the student who may have fallen
   into bad habits of rapid reading is compelled to read at voice speed
   only.)
Soft stone sculpture.
Situation comedy.
Simple algebra, hand and machine.
First gymnastics.
Second jokes and logic.
Transcendent religion.
Complex acrobatic dancing.
Complex defamation.
Performing on the high wire and the sky pole.
Simple radio construction.
Raising, breeding and dissecting frogs. (Karakoli, not earth frogs.)

FOURTH YEAR COURSE:
History reading, Camiroi and galactic, basic and geological.
Decadent comedy.
Simple geometry and trigonometry, hand and machine.
Track and field.
Shaggy people jokes and hirsute logic.
Simple obscenity.
Simple mysticism.
Patterns of falsification.
Trapeze work.
   Intermediate electronics.
Human dissection.

FIFTH YEAR COURSE:
History reading, Camiroi and galactic, technological.
Introverted drama.
Complex geometries and analytics, hand and machine.
Track and field for fifth form record.

First wit and logic.
First alcoholic appreciation.
Complex mysticism.
Setting intellectual climates, defamation in three dimensions.
Simple oratory.
Complex trapeze work.
Inorganic chemistry.
Advanced electronics.
Advanced human dissection.
Fifth form thesis.

The child is now ten years old and is half through his primary schooling. He is an unfinished animal, but he has learned to learn.

SIXTH YEAR COURSE:
Reemphasis on slow reading.
Simple prodigious memory.
History reading, Camiroi and galactic, economic.
Horsemanship (of the Patrushkoe, not the earth horse).
Advance lathe and machine work for art and utility.
Literature, passive.
Calculi, hand and machine pankration.
Advanced wit and logic.
Second alcoholic appreciation.
Differential religion.
First business ventures.
Complex oratory.
Building-scaling. (The buildings are higher and the gravity stronger than on Earth; this climbing of buildings like human flies calls out the ingenuity and daring of the Camiroi children.)
Nuclear physics and post-organic chemistry.
Simple pseudo-human assembly.

SEVENTH YEAR COURSE:
History reading, Camiroi and galactic, cultural.
Advanced prodigious memory.
Vehicle operation and manufacture of simple vehicle.
Literature, active.
Astrognosy, prediction and programming.
Advanced pankration.
Spherical logic, hand and machine.
Advanced alcoholic appreciation.

Integral religion.
Bankruptcy and recovery in business.
Conmanship and trend creation.
Post-nuclear physics and universals.
Transcendental athletics endeavor.
Complex robotics and programming.

EIGHTH YEAR COURSE:
History reading, Camiroi and galactic, seminal theory.
Consummate prodigious memory.
Manufacture of complex land and water vehicles.
Literature, compendious and terminative. (Creative book-burning fol-
lowing the Camiroi thesis that nothing ordinary be allowed to sur-
vive.)
Cosmic theory, seminal.
Philosophy construction.
Complex hedonism.
Laser religion.
Conmanship, seminal.
Consolidation of simple genius status.
Post-robotic integration.

NINTH YEAR COURSE:
History reading, Camiroi and galactic, future and contingent.
Category invention.
Manufacture of complex light-barrier vehicles.
Construction of simple asteroids and planets.
Matrix religion and logic.
Simple human immortality disciplines.
Consolidation of complex genius status.
First problems of post-consciousness humanity.
First essays in marriage and reproduction.

TENTH YEAR COURSE:
History construction, active.
Manufacture of ultra-light-barrier vehicles.
Panphilosophical clarifications.
Construction of viable planets.
Consolidation of simple sanctity status.
Charismatic humor and pentacosmic logic.
Hypogyroscopic economy.
Penentaglossia. (The perfection of the fifty languages that every edu-

cated Camiroi must know including six Earthian languages. Of course the child will already have colloquial mastery of most of these, but he will not yet have them in their full depth.)

Construction of complex societies.

World government. (A course of the same name is sometimes given in Earthian schools, but the course is not of the same content. In this course the Camiroi student will govern a world, though not one of the first aspect worlds, for a period of three or four months.)

Tenth form thesis.

Comment on Curriculum:

The child will now be fifteen years old and will have completed his primary education. In many ways he will be advanced beyond his Earth counterpart. Physically more sophisticated, the Camiroi child could kill with his hands an Earth-type tiger or a cape buffalo. An Earth child would perhaps be reluctant even to attempt such feats. The Camiroi boy (or girl) could replace any professional Earth athlete at any position of any game, and could surpass all existing Earth records. It is simply a question of finer poise, strength and speed, the result of adequate schooling.

As to the arts (on which Earthlings sometimes place emphasis) the Camiroi child could produce easy and unequaled masterpieces in any medium. More important, he will have learned the relative unimportance of such pastimes.

The Camiroi child will have failed in business once, at age ten, and have learned patience and perfection of objective by his failure. He will have acquired the techniques of falsification and conmanship. Thereafter he will not be easily deceived by any of the citizens of any of the worlds. The Camiroi child will have become a complex genius and a simple saint; the latter reduces the index of Camiroi crime to near zero. He will be married and settled in those early years of greatest enjoyment.

The child will have built, from materials found around any Camiroi house, a faster-than-light vehicle. He will have piloted it on a significant journey of his own plotting and programming. He will have built quasi-human robots of great intricacy. He will be of perfect memory and judgment and will be well prepared to accept solid learning.

He will have learned to use his whole mind, for the vast reservoirs which are the unconscious to us are not unconscious to him. Everything in him is ordered for use. And there seems to be no great secret about the accomplishments, only to do everything slowly enough and in the right order: Thus they avoid repetition and drill which are the shriveling things which dull the quick apperception.

The Camiroi schedule is challenging to the children, but it is nowhere impossible or discouraging. Everything builds to what follows. For instance, the child is eleven years old before he is given post-nuclear physics and universals. Such subjects might be too difficult for him at an earlier age. He is thirteen years old before he undertakes category invention, that intricate course with the simple name. He is fourteen years old when he enters the dangerous field of panphilosophical clarification. But he will have been constructing comprehensive philosophies for two years, and he will have the background for the final clarification.

We should look more closely at this other way of education. In some respects it is better than our own. Few Earth children would be able to construct an organic and sentient robot within fifteen minutes if given the test suddenly; most of them could not manufacture a living dog in that time. Not one Earth child in five could build a faster-than-light vehicle and travel it beyond our galaxy between now and midnight. Not one Earth child in a hundred could build a planet and have it a going concern within a week. Not one in a thousand would be able to comprehend pentacosmic logic.

RECOMMENDATIONS: a. Kidnapping five Camiroi at random and constituting them a pilot Earth PTA. b. A little constructive book-burning, particularly in the education field. c. Judicious hanging of certain malingering students.

2.
TEACHING AND LEARNING IN SOCIETY

For too long, the functions of teaching and learning were conceptualized and studied in a vacuum. They were emphasized as techniques which, if applied diligently, could achieve educational objectives. Because of the research on teaching and learning by sociologists and anthropologists over the past few decades, we have now come to understand that teaching and learning are conditioned by the sociocultural environment within which they occur.

Biological and hereditary factors have traditionally been studied for their influence on learning and their impact on the teaching situation. Although mystery has shrouded biological and hereditary factors, social and cultural factors have proven equally difficult for educators to cope with. Although a student may be well equipped to learn from a biological-hereditary perspective, he may be unable to use his talents because of his inability to interact with education as a sociocultural environment. Similarly, a competent teacher may not be able to succeed totally because of the problems generated by the sociocultural environment from which his students come.

Thus factors such as family socialization, class and race status, and economic background have an important bearing on teaching and learning. The class, race, economic, and educational stratification which exists in society "spills-over" into the school system.

B◯HASSIAN LEARNS

William Rotsler

Birth is a shock. The baby is thrust out into a strange world, torn from the security of the womb, and forced to cope with a fantastic variety of new images and sensations. The act of being born is such a traumatic experience that some psychologists believe that the individual spends an entire lifetime trying to return to the security of the womb.

We know that learning occurs from the moment of birth. But what of the nine months prior to birth? The prenatal period is receiving increasing attention from researchers because of the growing evidence of the linkage between physical and mental impairment of the child and the nutritional intake of the mother. Furthermore, the connection between drug and alcohol usage by the mother and the future development of the child may also be very significant, although more research is clearly needed in this area.

What is certain is that people need to learn to survive. An infant is *dependent* in every sense of the word—he cannot ·move without help, he cannot feed himself, and above all, he cannot defend himself. In a real sense, once the child is older, the school helps him to survive. In school as well as elsewhere, the individual learns about his role and place in the world, about what to expect of himself and of others—in short, he is *socialized* for psychic and physical survival. This is one purpose of education.

In this story, Bohassian, like all babies, is learning. He clearly has more ability than the average child, but he is subject to the same startling array of actions, colors, and images, and he must attempt to make some sense of them. As he grows older, he will acquire words to describe these images, and thus make them more understandable.

Bohassian is not alone in the world. He is part of society and must *interact* with it. It is this interaction which makes learning possible for him. Bohassian learns and those around him learn an important educational lesson. There are many ways for the teacher to reach the child: for example, by conditioning or by coercion. But perhaps one of the best ways is the way of the story—by love.

FOR FURTHER THOUGHT OR DISCUSSION

1. What role do schools play in the survival process?

2. If you had to cope with Bohassian in the delivery room, what would you do?

3. How does the school help the individual to survive?

BOHASSIAN LEARNS   *William Rotsler*

Bohassian was being born and he didn't like it. Everything had been warm and safe and he had heard things, saw images, felt clusters of emotions moving around him, and suddenly it was chaos. There was pain, then more pain, then a rhythm of pain, then a bursting, a moving, a turning and an explosion of light.

Pain.

Incredible pain.

Bohassian lashed out in anger and there were screams and terrible images in his head but still the pain did not stop, but it ebbed away slowly. Bohassian realized he was smaller now, that somehow he had cast away the large, warm protective shell, or had been rejected by it. But he was small and weak on the outside so he protected himself by moving the others away.

He lay there, soaking up images and light and ideas from this bright, big world. When he could, Bohassian went into the minds of others, breathing in incoherent images, hearing sounds and cries and sobbing.

He tried sorting out the sights from the sounds and the images from the thoughts. It was all very confusing. The minds seemed chaotic and frightened.

They were all afraid of him.

The figures in pale green, with their faces and heads wrapped, cowered against the flatness of the confining chamber. Bohassian reached beyond the chamber and felt the minds of others. The others were not frightened at first, then they became frightened and the cool thoughts jumbled and melted and boiled.

Bohassian looked into the mind of the place from which he had come, into the other part of him, into the discarded/rejected part.

Mother.

The giver of life.

She had been a safe place and then she had thrust him out. He looked into her mind and saw that she had wanted to thrust him out, that she thought it was right to thrust him out into the other place. Bohassian went deeper into her and twisted something petulantly.

The mother started to scream and went limp.

Bohassian moved among the minds around him, moving into the complex chambers of their minds, gathering information without prejudice, soaking up concepts, colors, words, acts, emotions. Wild fantasy and accomplished fact were simply images of differing textures.

Bohassian learned.

That figure was relatively cool, clinical, wanting to reach out and touch but was held back by the command of another figure whose mind was green snakes and dark oily ripples. That one was dazed, with fragments of thoughts spraying out like a crushed bouquet: *wet ... red ... terrible ... push ... mother ... monster ... crush ...*

Bohassian felt danger and twisted something dark in the mind and the figure fell and was quiet, even in the mind.

Bohassian learned.

He saw that images had labels and were called words. Mother. Baby. Fear. Death. Hospital. Help. Doctor. Nurse. Blood. Kill. Green. Love.

Bohassian stopped when he learned love. It was the small figure in green. He brought it forth, towards him. It moved jerkily but Bohassian saw less fear in its mind than the others.

It felt pity and wanted to help. Bohassian held its mind firmly, ready to strike, but let it do its love help. His frail body was raised and moved slightly and he became aware of a piece of himself attached to the life giver.

The mind of the green figure spoke: *We must cut away the umbilical.*

No.

Yes. It is necessary.

Why?

To give you freedom. You needed it when you were inside and now you no longer need it.

Cut it.

It will hurt. You must not hurt me when I hurt you. It is necessary.

Bohassian looked into the mind of the green figure and saw that it believed it to be true. There are many things I do not know, thought Bohassian.

Cut.

There was pain and Bohassian pressed the other green figures against the wall and the green figure holding him gasped.

It is done.

I am free?

Yes, but you must not hurt people.

Why?

Because they are weaker than you.

But they are large and move. They want to hurt me.

They are frightened. You frightened them. They fear the unknown.

"Kill it!" The tall green figure against the wall made noises. Bohassian quieted him and he fell back.

And you?

I fear you, too. You are different. But I cannot kill.

That one would kill.

The figure in green looked at the crumpled figures against the flatness. "Yes. They do not understand." *Pity. They are afraid of fear.*

You make two images. They are different, but alike.

I think. I speak. Sometimes people speak different images than they think.

Bohassian felt other minds coming closer. Disturbed minds. Someone made a loud noise. Bohassian made them stop and some fell.

Why do they come?

They are curious. They come to help . . . or to hurt . . .

I learn. They will not hurt me.

"I will take care of you." Pity. *Love. Mother. Protection. Hold.*

I will not hurt you.

I will pick you up. You must be washed and fed. But not hurt.

You may hold me. I do not fear you. The others will not hurt me.

The nurse picked up Bohassian and they moved out of the chamber. There were long chambers filled with people. Some were lying down and some were staring with wide eyes. Bohassian kept them back. One moved to grab, his mind a whirl of blackness, but Bohassian twisted and he fell.

There was a dark grayness in the mind of the nurse, a sadness and hurt. But she carried Bohassian to a chamber and washed him. The water felt good and the oil was pleasant. There was much noise and Bohassian made it quiet.

Bohassian learned as he lay there.

The minds of people were very confused, streaked through with clarity and logic. But there was much fear. Fear was danger for Bohassian so he kept it away.

The figure in green held him and said *Food* and gave him a sweet, warm whiteness. It was good and Bohassian rested.

There was much to learn. Bohassian became aware of many small formless minds around him, each in a small body such as his, but each a weak and fragile being. Bohassian went into their minds but found them almost blank, only vague whorls of light and color and blurrings.

Bohassian let his body rest and not move as his mind moved lazily around in circles, touching the image makers in chambers nearby. They cringed and sometimes screamed as he entered them. One mind turned black and curled into a tiny chamber within itself. Bohassian poked at it curiously but it was without interest.

There was much to learn, Bohassian thought. There are images in the minds I touch. Skies. Trees. Tall things. Food. Other life forms, from very small to very large. Colors. Millions upon millions of image makers.

I will touch them all, Bohassian thought. I must learn.

INVESTIGATING THE CURIOSITY DRIVE

Tom Herzog

Social scientists disagree among themselves over how individuals. learn. Among the more important schools of thought on this subject are:

1. The naturalistic viewpoint of *inborn tendencies* places emphasis on *instincts* found in every person. These instincts provide clues to the individual when learning situations arise.

2. The theory of *mental states* stresses the importance of sensations, perceptions, and images in the learning process. The individual forms associations through his sensory apparatus which enhances learning.

3. Finally, the school of thought known as *behaviorism* rests on the assumption that learning consists of a series of habits which a person acquires largely through *heredity*. It is argued that heredity determines the broad limits within which learning can take place.

In "Investigating the Curiosity Drive," the "hero" of the story claims that an *instinct, curiosity,* is the prime motivational force operating within man. For example, how did the wheel come to be invented? One possibility would be accident—a fortuitous occurrence, when early man was rolling a stone from the entrance to his dwelling. But it could not have been that simple. More likely, this man or woman became *curious* about the rolling motion, proceeded to draw conclusions about it, and then applied its principles to transportation.

Whatever truth this particular argument may have, we know from controlled experiments that when an individual's senses are completely isolated—when he cannot see, hear, smell, feel, or touch —mental disintegration follows. It is further argued that one of the basic human needs is to *explore*; indeed, this is one characteristic which distinguishes human beings from other animals. For example, one of the arguments put forth in favor of the space program is that it is an *inevitable* manifestation of man's need to explore both his own and other environments.

Many of the major developments and inventions throughout history have been explained by this theory. It is more than coincidence, for example, that several scientists and inventors were working on powered flight at the same time, or that a number of physicists were producing theories concerning atomic energy within a few years of each other. Learning and knowledge may well be *cumulative* in nature, and if this is so, then the "great man" theory of history, which claims that events and discoveries are the result of the talent of particular individuals, operates on a faulty assumption.

In this story, the investigation of the curiosity drive produces an experiment designed to test its basic premise. A common educational device, especially in science classes, involves the use of experiments to illustrate concepts about which the students are reading. When these experiments involve living creatures such as dogs and mice, care must be taken to avoid suffering on the part of these laboratory animals. But experimentation is not limited to animals. Most psychology classes employ *human* subjects for experimentation; and much concern has been voiced over the ethics of these experiments, since mental damage can occur if care and skill are not exhibited by the teacher.

Curiosity, then, is an important part of the learning process. But, as this story illustrates, curiosity can be a dangerous thing.

FOR FURTHER THOUGHT OR DISCUSSION

1. What principles of learning theory are contained in the story?

2. Could the experiment described in the story be recreated in your classroom?

3. What ethical issues are raised by the experiment?

4. To which learning theory would Professor Hornsby subscribe today?

5. Is curiosity a basic human drive? If so, how does it manifest itself?

6. What produces the human *desire* to learn?

INVESTIGATING THE CURIOSITY DRIVE   *Tom Herzog*

"Curiosity is man's most basic drive," Professor Hornsby said, pacing back and forth behind the lectern as scores of pencils raced madly across the pages of notebooks, preserving his thought for the night before the final exam. "The other so-called primitive drives, such as hunger, pain and sex, are mere nuisances that come and go, but curiosity is always lurking in the background, ready to take over when these transient influences have lost their sway. Rats will learn t-maze discriminations when their only reward is a chance to explore a more complicated maze. Monkeys will work at simple mechanical puzzles for hours with no reward other than the working of them. And this tendency to manipulate, to pry open, to peek into, seen in primitive form in the lower species, reaches its crowning glory in man, whose whole life may be characterized as one vast exploration, with time out to eat, sleep, and go to the bathroom."

Professor Hornsby paused to give the pencils a chance to catch up with him. Then he continued: "We can gauge the strength of this curiosity drive simply by depriving man of his opportunity to explore, by restraining him in one place and sealing off those most precious portals of exploratory information, the sensory inputs. And what do we observe? Chaos. Cognitive disintegration. The ability to think logically is destroyed. Simple arithmetic problems cannot be solved. Perception is severely impaired. Bizarre hallucinations arise. Clearly, the fundamental status of the curiosity drive is established by these observations. We must give up our childish notions that the biological drives are the only ones of any importance. There is one more pervasive, more persistent, and more profound than any of the biological drives."

The professor paused for effect. Then he let them have it: "CURIOSITY!"

And laying his finger beside his nose, he turned and departed the lecture hall.

"Investigation is wadi's most basic urge," Gehosphat Pryxl said, slithering back and forth on the dais as scores of markers raced madly across recording spools, preserving his thought for the eve of the ultimate interrogation. "The other so-called primitive urges, such as food-bzzz, hurt-bzzz and heat-bzzz, are mere distractions that flick in and out, but investigation spreads perpetually behind all, ready to engage itself when these temporary inclinations have declined. Gerbies will master uni-choice paths when their only contingent satisfaction is an opportunity to investigate multi-choice paths. Wumbies will task themselves with elementary undolox for several phases, with no contingent satisfaction other than the tasking. And this investigation urge, underdeveloped in subordinate organisms, realizes its full potential in wadi, whose whole existence may be described as one all-encompassing investigation, with intersperses of food-take, sleep-take, and leave-take."

Gehosphat Pryxl paused to give the markers a chance to catch up with him. Then he continued: "The potency of this investigation urge is measured simply by suspending wadi's ability to investigate, by isolating him without stimulus infeed. The effect? Disorder. Fractionation of thought. Ability to calculate destroyed. Encoding of stimulation impaired. False visions. Thus vividly do these findings impose the primacy of the investigation urge upon us. We must dispossess our infantile misconception that the organismic urges are the only ones worthy of consideration. There is one more extensive, more insistent, and more significant than any of the organismic urges."

The Gehosphat paused for effect. Then he womped them: "INVESTIGATION!"

And laying a tentacle beside his snout, he turned and slithered from the wisdom-take hall.

"Man, you don't really believe that curiosity is the most fundamental drive, do you?" Professor Grundig asked.

"I most certainly do," Professor Hornsby replied.

"But the other drives are so much more insistent."

"Only in their season," Professor Hornsby said. "They come and go. But curiosity is always present. It never dies. It even penetrates the other drives. Curiosity about new foods is common. And I don't have to tell you about curiosity in sex."

"Ahem, well, yes," Professor Grundig said. "But it still seems to me that you're claiming rather a lot for curiosity."

"Consider a hypothetical case," Professor Hornsby said. "I assert that if we select any organism with a nervous system capable of sustaining behavior beyond the reflex level, provide it with sufficient food and water to satisfy its needs, and place it in a featureless room containing no objects except some strange-looking contraption, we can expect with full confidence that it will eventually exhibit exploratory behavior with regard to this contraption. I assert that the organism simply will not be able to prevent itself from doing so. And that, my friend, is the curiosity drive at work."

"Don't you think that your hypothetical organism will perceive the contraption as a possible source of danger and avoid it?" Professor Grundig objected.

"Perhaps at first," Professor Hornsby replied. "But eventually the organism's curiosity will get the better of it, and it will investigate. There can be no other outcome."

"I must say, you certainly are dogmatic," Professor Grundig said, smiling faintly.

"It cannot be so that the investigation urge out-urges all other urges," Gehosphat Frymdl declared.

"It is precisely so," Gehosphat Pryxl said. "Consider a possible situation: Select any organism with sufficient neural endowment to transcend strict sensory dominance of behavior. Isolate this organism in an environment devoid of all sources of stimulus complexity except a single unfamiliar machine. If the organism is supplied with sufficient sustenance, I assert that it must inevitably investigate the machine. Such behavior cannot be inhibited."

"This assertion would seem to be testable," Gehosphat Frymdl observed.

"It shall be done at no distant phase," Gehosphat Pryxl said. "We have been observing the perfect experimental organism for many metaphases. It occupies a fringe world near the edge of the star system. I will request immediate random selection of an organism from this world for our test. They are overmany, and one will not be missed.

An appropriate machine for the test I have already constructed. Accompany me, and I will confront you with it."

"Deeply this engages me," Gehosphat Frymdl said.

Professor Hornsby was walking down a tree-lined campus street when he disappeared.

"Did you see that?" said a long-haired coed in hip boots and miniskirt. "A man just disappeared over there."

"You're confusing illusion with reality," her boyfriend said, scratching his beard.

Professor Hornsby awoke in a large featureless room, featureless, that is, except for a huge, strange-looking machine in its very center. The professor glanced at it, decided that its function was not immediately apparent, and then turned his attention to his own rather peculiar situation.

Only a moment ago, or so it seemed, he had been walking down a tree-lined campus street. Yet he had just awakened in a featureless room containing a strange machine and no other object except the exceedingly comfortable bed on which he lay. How was one to interpret this sequence of events?

His analytic mind supplied two hypotheses: (1) the tree-lined street was a dream from which he had just awakened, or (2) the featureless room was a dream upon which he had just embarked. Acceptance of the first hypothesis left him in the awkward position of explaining how he got himself into the featureless room in the first place. Acceptance of the second meant that he was now sleep-walking down a tree-lined campus street, a possibility which he immediately rejected as totally incompatible with his well-established sleeping habits.

"I think, therefore I am," Professor Hornsby said. Then he pinched himself hard and screamed, "Ouch!"

"It is firmly established that I am awake," he said. "Consequently, this room and this machine are not the stuff of dreams. Furthermore, I am reasonably certain that the tree-lined campus street was not a dream because I distinctly remember seeing a young woman wearing wading boots and an abbreviated skirt, and I haven't dreamed anything remotely comparable to that in over thirty years. Therefore, I shall tentatively accept a third hypothesis, that neither the tree-lined

123

street nor this room are dreams. This means that the most intelligent thing I can do at the moment is to explore my environment in hope of finding out how I came to be here."

Professor Hornsby got up from the bed and approached the strange machine. Suddenly he stopped in mid-stride. In his mind, the following conversation was occurring: *"If we place our organism in a featureless room containing no objects except some strange-looking contraption, we can expect with full confidence that it will eventually exhibit exploratory behavior with regard to this contraption."*

"But don't you think that your hypothetical organism will perceive the contraption as a possible source of danger?"

"Well I'll be something or other!" Professor Hornsby said. "So that's it. I never would have thought Grundig had it in him. I don't know how he pulled it off, but it's magnificent. It's absolutely magnificent."

He returned to the bed and sat down. "When I see Grundig, I must find out how he managed to pluck me off the street and put me in this room without my even noticing it. But for the present, the main thing is to stay clear of that ridiculous machine. Grundig probably has it wired up to give me a colossal shock the moment I touch it. He has such a perverted sense of humor."

"Investigation appeared gravely probable," Gehosphat Frymdl said, turning away from the viewing screen. "But suddenly the organism redirected itself."

"Perhaps it requires food-take," Gehosphat Pryxl said.

As Professor Hornsby stared at the wall, a panel slid silently open revealing the most sumptuous turkey dinner he had seen since Thanksgiving.

"I must say, this is sporting of Grundig," Professor Hornsby said. "I *am* rather hungry."

Entering the alcove in the wall, he noticed that the table and chair therein were chained to the floor.

"He's not taking any chances on my augmenting the furniture out there," Professor Hornsby said. "I may steal the silverware just to spite him."

But the silverware, he now saw, was chained to the table. In fact, all the utensils were made of metal and were chained to the table. The chains appeared more decorative and less substantial than those attached to the table and chair, but he had no doubt that they were sufficiently strong for their intended purpose.

"Hmmmph," he said. "I can still steal a drumstick."

However, forty-five minutes later, when his stomach was full, he reflected that it would be rather childish to steal a drumstick. There were larger issues at stake. Evidently Grundig was bent on forcing him to investigate the strange machine and thus to vindicate his own theory. If Grundig was willing to accept an intellectual defeat of this magnitude, there could be only one reason: He was planning some monstrous practical joke at Hornsby's expense. He somehow had the situation rigged so that any exploratory behavior on Hornsby's part would prove acutely embarrassing.

"It sounds ridiculous," Professor Hornsby said, "but it must be so. Grundig is far too devious to throw a bone like this my way. He has an ace in the hole. He knew that I would remember our conversation, knew that my first impulse would be to run right over and investigate his machine. Consequently, to do so would be a mistake. I would be falling into some kind of trap, and Grundig would never let me live it down."

He got up from the table. "I won't do it. I will *not* do it. I'll make him squirm."

Thus resolved, Professor Hornsby emerged from the alcove, the wall panel sliding silently back into place behind him.

"Carefully observe," Gehosphat Pryxl said. "Now will the investigation urge make manifest itself."

"It is a matter that yet awaits resolution," Gehosphat Frymdl said.

Now that his stomach was full, Professor Hornsby began to take note of his surroundings, and the first thing he noticed was the door at the far end of the room.

"I suppose it's locked," he said. "Otherwise I could just walk out of here and end this foolishness."

Nevertheless, he decided to give it a try, and to his surprise it was not locked. But neither was it an exit, as he discovered immediately upon opening it. It was the entrance to . . .

" . . . a water closet," he said. "Well, at least I have all the comforts of home. But if this door is not a way out of the room, then how the devil did I get into the room in the first place?"

Immediately his mind supplied the answer. Sliding wall panels. There might well be many of them. It was impossible to tell from mere inspection of the walls.

"They must be remote-controlled," Professor Hornsby said. "Furthermore, Grundig must be monitoring my actions. There ought to be some sort of camera or one-way glass about somewhere."

He carefully inspected the ceiling of the room but could detect no sign of a viewing device. Similar inspection of the four walls turned up nothing. He returned to the bed and sat down.

"He must be watching me," Professor Hornsby said. "How else would he have known when to expose the turkey dinner? But I don't suppose I'll be able to find his viewing device. Those things can be ingeniously concealed."

Suddenly he was struck by an intriguing possibility.

"I wonder if by any chance that ridiculous machine is some sort of monitoring instrument."

And so his attention focused on the machine for the first time since he had awakened. It stood, silent and massive, in the center of the room.

"There can't be any harm in looking at it from a distance," he said.

From a distance it looked like a huge metallic cube with a ledge hanging out over the side facing his bed. That side appeared to contain some sort of control panel. He could not make out any details from where he sat.

"There can't be any harm in looking at it from a closer vantage point," Professor Hornsby said, rising from the bed and approaching the machine. He stopped about five feet away from it.

From this distance it was clear that the control panel contained a single feature of interest, a red button in its very center. The rest of it was simply a grille that might be part of a ventilation system. Or it might not. There was no way to determine its purpose from inspection. It was also clear that the overhanging ledge was not continuous with the top surface of the cube. Rather, it was a separate metal platform, supported at each end by metal girders that were attached to the sides of the cube in some manner not at all obvious. There were no braces or bolts; the girders simply seemed to adhere to the sides of the cube.

The professor wasted no time in puzzling over how the girders might be attached. He was not mechanically minded. Instead, he returned his attention to the red button.

"I shall not, under any circumstances, depress that button," he promised himself. "That button is the focal point of the whole issue. Grundig is confident that curiosity eventually will get the better of me, and I'll depress it. The whole situation is structured toward that end. Consequently, if he has something up his sleeve, that red button is surely the instrument of his mischief. I will teach him a lesson in self-control. I will *not* depress that button."

So saying, Professor Hornsby returned to the bed and sat down.

"Most amazing is this organism's reserve," Gehosphat Pryxl said. "How does it submit to explanation?"

"Gravely imperiled is the primacy of the investigation urge by this organism's behavior," Gehosphat Frymdl said.

"Let us continue to persevere in observation," Gehosphat Pryxl said, waving a tentacle.

To take his mind off the irritating fact of the machine's presence, Professor Hornsby tried various diversions.

"I'll plan tomorrow's lecture," he said. "Surely Grundig will let me out of here by then. Or is it already tomorrow?"

He glanced at his watch. It was nine-thirty. But was that a.m. or p.m.? How long had he slept in the room? Professor Hornsby now discovered that he had lost all sense of time.

"No matter," he said. "I'll plan my *next* lecture."

He would continue to develop the theme of the importance of curiosity in man by giving his students concrete examples of the drive's influence in everyday life. Curiosity in art. Curiosity in food. Curiosity in sex. Well, perhaps not sex. Things might get out of hand. Youthful minds could not approach that subject objectively. At any rate, he would wind it all up with his marvelous hypothetical case of a man confined in a featureless room containing no objects except for . . .

He found himself staring up at the overhanging ledge of the strange machine. It can't possibly be there to create shade, he told himself. There's no sunlight in here.

Abruptly he stood up and began pacing back and forth beside the bed. "This will never do. I must keep my mind off that silly machine. I know what I'll do. I'll take a nap."

He lay down on the bed and closed his eyes. He concentrated on breathing regularly. Soon he found himself in the left-field seats in Yankee Stadium. "Dat left fielder is a bum," the man next to him said.

"I don't agree at all," he said. "In fact, I think I'll go right out there and congratulate him on the marvelous game he's playing." He arose from his seat, made his way down the aisle to the first row of boxes, climbed over the railing, and walked across the outfield toward the object of his praise. As he drew near, he was struck by what a remarkably flat head the left fielder had. It looked almost as if the visor of his cap was a mere extension of the top of his head. "I say, old man," the professor said. The left fielder turned toward him. The left fielder had no face. In the very center of where his face should have been was a single red button.

The professor awoke with a start. He was sweating.

"This is too much," he declared. "This is altogether too much."

He got up and began pacing back and forth beside the bed. "I know what I'll do. I'll write up that experiment I completed last week. Let's see here, I have a pen but no paper. That poses a slight problem. Hmmmm. I've got it! I'll write on the wall."

He walked over to the nearest wall and begin to write out in longhand the results of his latest experiment with rats. He had demonstrated that rats spent less time eating in a cage that had a checkerboard pattern on the walls than in a cage that had no pattern on the walls. This, he intended to conclude, was due to the fact that the checkerboard pattern aroused their curiosity drive, which conflicted with the hunger drive, resulting in less time spent eating.

It was all so clear-cut and convincing that Professor Hornsby wrote effortlessly, paying only partial attention to the words that appeared on the wall. This was just what he needed. This took his mind completely off the—

Something about the last sentence he had written was not right. He focused his full attention on it. It read: These data demonstrate a significant relationship between the experimental variables and permit the conclusion that I will not, under any circumstances, depress that red button.

Angrily, he flung the pen away and stalked back over to the bed.

"What is this, some kind of conspiracy?" he cried. "Even my own unconscious mind gangs up against me."

He sat down on the bed, clenching and unclenching his fists. "I can't take much more of this. There must be something I can do that has no possible connection with that silly machine. I know what I'll do. I'll take this bed apart and see how it's made. There's no remotely conceivable way I can go wrong doing that."

He grabbed the pillow and removed the pillowcase. The pillow was covered with blue and white stripes. "Hmmmm. Very interesting."

He shook the pillow and listened carefully. "It doesn't rattle."

He threw the pillow and the pillowcase on the floor. He removed the quilt and the top sheet and deposited them on top of the pillowcase. He knelt and smelled the bottom sheet. "Delightful!"

He removed the bottom sheet and tossed it on the pile of bedding.

"Aha! A mattress cover!" he said. "What could possibly lie beneath it?"

A knowing smile appeared on his face. "I predict a mattress. That's what I predict."

He clutched the mattress cover and tore it off. And there it was! A mattress! A mattress with rows of little depressions about six inches apart and in each little depression . . .

The knowing smile froze on his face. Then it broke up around the edges and disappeared, leaving him with a vacant glassy-eyed expression as he stared at the mattress with rows of little depressions about six inches apart and in the middle of each little depression a single red button.

Professor Hornsby erupted: "AAAAAGH! I can't stand it! I can't stand it!"

He pounded the mattress with his fists. He leaped to his feet and looked at the walls. They were covered with red buttons. So were the floor and ceiling.

"I can't stand it!" he shouted, staggering over to the machine with the overhanging ledge and the single red button.

"I can't stand it!" he shouted, depressing the button.

THWACK! The overhanging ledge plunged to the floor, squashing Professor Hornsby like a bug.

"Most objectively is the organism's behavior pattern described as cognitive disintegration attendant upon prolonged stimulus deprivation rather than manifestation of an investigation urge," Gehosphat Frymdl declared.

"I withhold agreement," Gehosphat Pryxl said. "More accurately is the organism's behavior pattern described as final dominance of an investigation urge previously suppressed by unknown causes. Recall the organism's early approaches toward the machine. Clearly did the investigation urge struggle to engage itself and finally succeed."

"Not clearly," Gehosphat Frymdl objected. "My explanation is not eliminated."

"It is so," Gehosphat Pryxl admitted. "A different experimental approach demands itself to discriminate between our explanations and to assure consensus in interpretation of results."

"You will then redirect your research efforts?"

"It is so."

"What will be your disposition of the machine you have constructed?" Gehosphat Frymdl asked. "Will it have no further application?"

"It is not necessary that it should pass into obscurity," Gehosphat Pryxl replied. "Material support for its production I will seek, that it may be made available to all wadi."

"Is that wise? Surely there will not be a demand for a machine without practical application."

"The machine will be sought after by many," Gehosphat Pryxl said with confidence.

"But what will be its functional role that the market should thus bear it?" Gehosphat Frymdl persisted.

"Always," Gehosphat Pryxl said knowingly, "is there room upon the market for a larger and more efficacious vombi trap."

BACKWARDNESS

Poul Anderson

We have all heard stories about people who failed or dropped out of school and then went on to incredible success in business or the arts. Abraham Lincoln is perhaps the most famous individual who attained greatness without a formal education.

How did these individuals succeed? What qualities did they possess which enabled them to rise to the top of their professions? What is the relationship between success in school and success in later life? Evidence suggests a strong correlation between success in school and achievement later on. The high-income brackets are filled with people who received high grades during their school years. But the correlation is not absolute. Some of the brightest children (as measured by I.Q. and other tests) do not do well either in school or in later life.

The variables in learning are many—home life, friends, heredity, emotional and physical health—and all play a role in the learning process. In addition, the infinite variety of human beings and the fact that each is different from the other make teaching and learning difficult tasks. For example, some children need strong discipline or need to be constantly challenged. Others require a more permissive environment in which they are constantly praised.

Education must reach all these different types of students. It must educate them and prepare them to face the world. But education can only do so much, for it cannot teach students how to act in a crisis. It cannot tell them when opportunity knocks (although a good education may make the knock a little louder). When a student leaves school he takes with him some of what he has learned, some missed opportunities, and some degree of awareness as to how he should act. But success or failure still rests to a great extent on the individual. It is still he who must make his life and live with it.

"Backwardness" has several themes of educational importance running through it. One is the cumulative nature of knowledge. The aliens in the story appear more advanced than earthmen, and it is suggested that their achievements are due to having had a longer history. The story also speaks to the questions of relative intelligence, maintaining that intelligence becomes meaningful only when it is *applied*. The aliens are intelligent—but to what purposes will they apply their knowledge?

FOR FURTHER THOUGHT OR DISCUSSION

1. What is relative intelligence and how does it affect learning?

2. What does the ending of the story tell you about the aliens?

3. Is knowledge cumulative?

4. Explain how some people can fail in school and yet succeed in later life.

5. What is the connection between "book-learning" and success?

6. Is American society *applying* knowledge usefully?

BACKWARDNESS *Poul Anderson*

As a small boy he had wanted to be a rocket pilot—and what boy didn't in those days?—but learned early that he lacked the aptitudes. Later he decided on psychology, and even took a bachelor's degree *cum laude.* Then one thing led to another, and Joe Husting ended up as a confidence man. It wasn't such a bad life; it had challenge and variety as he hunted in New York, and the spoils of a big killing were devoured in Florida, Greenland Resort, or Luna City.

The bar was empty of prospects just now, but he dawdled over his beer and felt no hurry. Spring had reached in and touched even the East Forties. The door stood open to a mild breeze, the long room was cool and dim, a few other men lazed over midafternoon drinks and the TV was tuned low. Idly, through cigaret smoke, Joe Husting watched the program.

The Galactics, of course. Their giant spaceship flashed in the screen against wet brown fields a hundred miles from here. Copter view . . . now we pan to a close-up, inside the ring of UN guards, and then back to the sightseers in their thousands. The announcer was talking about how the captain of the ship was at this moment in conference with the Secretary-General, and the crewmen were at liberty on Earth. "They are friendly, folks. I repeat, they are friendly. They will do no harm. They have already exchanged their cargo of U-235 for billions of our own dollars, and they plan to spend those dollars like any friendly tourist. But both the UN Secretariat and the President of the United States have asked us all to remember that these people come from the stars. They have been civilized for a million years. They have powers we haven't dreamed of. Anyone who harms a Galactic can ruin the greatest—"

Husting's mind wandered off. A big thing, yes, maybe the biggest thing in all history. Earth a member planet of the Galactic Federation! All the stars open to us! It was good to be alive in this year when anything could happen . . . hm. To start with, you could have some rhinestones put in fancy settings and peddle them as gen-yu-wine Tardenoisian sacred flame-rocks, but that was only the beginning—

He grew aware that the muted swish of electrocars and hammering of shoes in the street had intensified. From several blocks away came a positive roar of excitement. What the devil? He left his beer and sauntered to the door and looked out. A shabby man was hurrying toward the crowd. Husting buttonholed him. "What's going on, pal?"

"Ain't yuh heard? Galactics! Half a dozen of 'em. Landed in duh street uptown, some kinda flying belt dey got, and went inna Macy's and bought a million bucks' wortha stuff! Now dey're strolling down dis-a-way. Lemme go!"

Husting stood for a while, drawing hard on his cigaret. There was a tingle along his spine. Wanderers from the stars, a million-year-old civilization embracing the whole Milky Way! For him actually to see the high ones, maybe even talk to them . . . it would be something to tell his grandchildren about if he ever had any.

He waited, though, till the outer edge of the throng was on him, then pushed with skill and ruthlessness. It took a few sweaty minutes to reach the barrier.

An invisible force-field, holding off New York's myriads—wise precaution. You could be trampled to death by the best-intentioned mob.

There were seven crewmen from the Galactic ship. They were tall, powerful, as handsome as expected: a mixed breed, with dark hair and full lips and thin aristocratic noses. In a million years you'd expect all the human races to blend into one. They wore shimmering blue tunics and buskins, webby metallic belts in which starlike points of light glittered—and jewelry! My God, they must have bought all the gaudiest junk jewelry Macy's had to offer, and hung it on muscular necks and thick wrists. Mink and ermine burdened their shoulders, a young fortune in fur. One of them was carefully counting the money he had left, enough to choke an elephant. The others beamed affably into Earth's milling folk.

Joe Husting hunched his narrow frame against the pressure that was about to flatten him on the force screen. He licked suddenly dry lips, and his heart hammered. Was it possible—could it really happen that *he*, insignificant he, might speak to the gods from the stars?

Elsewhere in the huge building, politicians, specialists, and vips buzzed like angry bees. They should have been conferring with their opposite numbers from the Galactic mission—clearly, the sole proper way to meet the unprecedented is to set up committees and spend six months deciding on an agenda. But the Secretary-General of the United Nations owned certain prerogatives, and this time he had used them. A private face-to-face conference with Captain Hurdgo could accomplish more in half an hour than the councils of the world in a year.

He leaned forward and offered a box of cigars. "I don't know if I should," he added. "Perhaps tobacco doesn't suit your metabolism?"

"My what?" asked the visitor pleasantly. He was a big man, running a little to fat, with distinguished gray at the temples. It was not so odd that the Galactics should shave their chins and cut their hair in the manner of civilized Earth. That was the most convenient style.

"I mean, we smoke this weed, but it may poison you," said Larson. "After all, you're from another planet."

"Oh, that's OK," replied Hurdgo. "Some plants grow on every Earth-like planet, just like the same people and animals. Not much difference. Thanks." He took a cigar and rolled it between his fingers. "Smell nice."

"To me, that is the most astonishing thing about it all. I never expected evolution to work identically throughout the universe. *Why?*"

"Well, it just does." Captain Hurdgo bit the end off his cigar and spat it out onto the carpet. "Not on different-type planets from this, of course, but on Earth-type it's all the same."

"But why? I mean, what process—it can't be coincidence!"

Hurdgo shrugged. "I don't know. I'm just a practical spaceman. Never worried about it." He put the cigar in his mouth and touched the bezel of an ornate finger ring to it. Smoke followed the brief, intense spark.

"That's a . . . a most ingenious development," said Larson. Humility, yes, there was the line for a simple Earthman to take. Earth had come late into the cosmos and might as well admit the fact.

"A what?"

"Your ring. That lighter."

"Oh, that. Yep. Little atomic-energy gizmo inside." Hurdgo waved a magnanimous hand. "We'll send some people to show you how to make our stuff. Lend you machinery till you can start your own factories. We'll bring you up to date."

"It—you're incredibly generous," said Larson, happy and incredulous.

"Not much trouble to us, and we can trade with you once you're all set up. The more planets, the better for us."

"But . . . excuse me, sir, but I bear a heavy responsibility. We have to know the legal requirements for membership in the Galactic Federation. We don't know anything about your laws, your customs, your—"

"Nothing much to tell," said Hurdgo. "Every planet can pretty

135

well take care of itself. How the hell you think we could police fifty million Earth-type planets? If you got a gripe, you can take it to the, uh, I dunno what the word would be in English. A board of experts with a computer that handles these things. They'll charge you for the service—no Galactic taxes, you just pay for what you get, and out of the profits they finance free services like this mission of mine."

"I see," nodded Larson. "A Coordinating Council."

"Yeh, I guess that's it."

The Secretary-General shook his head in bewilderment. He had sometimes wondered what civilization would come to be, a million years hence. Now he knew, and it staggered him. An ultimate simplicity, superman disdaining the whole cumbersome apparatus of interstellar government, freed of all restraints save the superman morality, free to think his giant thoughts between the stars!

Hurdgo looked out the window to the arrogant towers of New York. "Biggest city I ever saw," he remarked, "and I seen a lot of planets. I don't see how you run it. Must be complicated."

"It is, sir." Larson smiled wryly. Of course the Galactics would long ago have passed the stage of needing such a human ant hill. They would have forgotten the skills required to govern one, just as Larson's people had forgotten how to chip flint.

"Well, let's get down to business." Hurdgo sucked on his cigar and smacked his lips. "Here's how it works. We found out a big while back that we can't go letting any new planet bust its way into space with no warning to anybody. Too much danger. So we set up detectors all over the Galaxy. When they spot the, uh, what-you-call-'ems—vibrations, yes, that's it, vibrations—the vibrations of a new star drive, they alert the, uh, Coordinating Council and it sends out a ship to contact the new people and tell 'em the score."

"Ah, indeed. I suspected as much. We have just invented a faster-than-light engine . . . very primitive, of course, compared to yours. It was being tested when—"

"Uh-huh. So me and my boys are supposed to give you the once-over and see if you're all right. Don't want warlike peoples running around loose, you know. Too much danger."

"I assure you—"

"Yes, yes, pal, it's OK. You got a good strong world setup and the computer says you've stopped making war." Hurdgo frowned. "I got to admit, you got some funny habits. I don't really understand everything you do . . . you seem to think funny, not like any other planet I ever heard of. But it's all right. Everybody to his own ways. You get a clean bill of health."

"Suppose . . ." Larson spoke very slowly. "Just suppose we had not been . . . approved—what then? Would you have reformed us?"

"Reformed? Huh? What d'you mean? We'd have sent a police ship and blown every planet in this system to smithereens. Can't have people running loose who might start a war."

Sweat formed under Larson's arms and trickled down his ribs. His mouth felt dry. *Whole planets—*

But in a million years you would learn to think *sub specie aeternitatis.* Five billion warlike Earthlings could annihilate fifty billion peaceful Galactics before they were overcome. It was not for him to judge a superman.

"Hello, there!"

Husting had to yell to be heard above the racket. But the nearest of the spacemen looked at him and smiled.

"Hi," he said.

Incredible! He had greeted little Joe Husting as a friend. Why—? Wait a minute! Perhaps the sheer brass of it had pleased him. Perhaps no one else had dared speak first to the strangers. And when you only said, "Yes, sir," to a man, even to a Galactic, you removed him—you might actually make him feel lonely.

"Uh, like it here?" Husting cursed his tongue, that its glibness should have failed him at this moment of all moments.

"Sure, sure. Biggest city I ever seen. And *draxna,* look at what I got!" The spaceman lifted a necklace of red glass sparklers. "Won't their eyes just bug out when I get home!"

Someone shoved Husting against the barrier so the wind went from him. He gasped and tried to squirm free.

"Say, cut that out. You're hurting the poor guy." One of the Galactics touched a stud on his belt. Gently but inexorably, the field widened, pushing the crowd back . . . and somehow, somehow Husting was inside it with the seven from the stars.

"You OK, pal?" Anxious hands lifted him to his feet.

"I, yeah, sure. Sure, I'm fine!" Husting stood up and grinned at the envious faces ringing him in. "Thanks a lot."

"Glad to help you. My name's Gilgrath. Call me Gil." Strong fingers squeezed Husting's shoulder. "And this here is Bronni, and here's Col, and Jordo, and—"

"Pleased to meet you," whispered Husting inadequately. "I'm Joe."

"Say, this is all right!" said Gil enthusiastically. "I was wondering what was wrong with you folks."

"Wrong?" Husting shook a dazed head, wondering if They were peering into his mind and reading thoughts of which he himself was unaware. Vague memories came back, grave-eyed Anubis weighing the heart of a man.

"You know," said Gil. "Stand-offish, like."

"Yeh," added Bronni. "Every other new planet we been to, everybody was coming up and saying hello and buying us drinks and—"

"Parties," reminded Jordo.

"Yeh. Man, remember that wing-ding on Alphaz? Remember those girls?" Col rolled his eyes lickerishly.

"You got a lot of good-looking girls here in New York," complained Gil. "But we got orders not to offend nobody. Say, do you think one of those girls would mind if I said hello to her?"

Husting was scarcely able to think; it was the reflex of many years which now spoke for him, rapidly:

"You have us all wrong. We're just scared to talk to you. We thought maybe you didn't want to be bothered."

"And *we* thought *you*—Say!" Gil slapped his thigh and broke into a guffaw. "Now ain't that something? They don't want to bother us and we don't want to bother them!"

"I'll be *rixt!*" bellowed Col. "Well, what do you know about that?"

"Hey, in that case—" began Jordo.

"Wait, wait!" Husting waved his hands. It was still habit which guided him; his mind was only slowly getting back into gear. "Let me get this straight. You want to do the town, right?"

"We sure do," said Col. "It's mighty lonesome out in space."

"Well, look," chattered Husting, "you'll never be free of all these crowds, reporters—" (A flashbulb, the tenth or twelfth in these few minutes, dazzled his eyes.) "You won't be able to let yourselves go while everybody knows you're Galactics."

"On Alphaz—" protested Bronni.

"This isn't Alphaz. Now I've got an idea. Listen." Seven dark heads bent down to hear an urgent whisper. "Can you get us away from here? Fly off invisible or something?"

"Sure," said Gil. "Hey, how'd you know we can do that?"

"Never mind. OK, we'll sneak off to my apartment and send out for some Earth-style clothes for you, and then—"

John Joseph O'Reilly, Cardinal Archbishop of New York, had friends in high places as well as in low. He thought it no shame to pull wires and arrange an interview with the chaplain of the spaceship.

What he could learn might be of vital importance to the Faith. The priest from the stars arrived, light-screened to evade the curious, and was received in the living room.

Visible again, Thyrkna proved to be a stocky white-haired man in the usual blue-kirtled uniform. He smiled and shook hands in quite an ordinary manner. At least, thought O'Reilly, these Galactics had during a million years conquered overweening Pride.

"It is an honor to meet you," he said.

"Thanks," nodded Thyrkna. He looked around the room. "Nice place you got."

"Please be seated. May I offer you a drink?"

"Don't mind if I do."

O'Reilly set forth glasses and a bottle. In a modest way, the Cardinal was a connoisseur, and had chosen the Chambertin-Clos carefully. He tasted the ritual few drops. Whatever minor saint, if any, was concerned with these things had been gracious; the wine was superb. He filled his guest's glass and then his own.

"Welcome to Earth," he smiled.

"Thanks." The Galactic tossed his drink off at one gulp. "Aaah! That goes good."

The Cardinal winced, but poured again. You couldn't expect another civilization to have the same tastes. Chinese liked aged eggs while despising cheese. . . .

He sat down and crossed his legs. "I'm not sure what title to use," he said diffidently.

"Title? What's that?"

"I mean, what does your flock call you?"

"My *flock*? Oh, you mean the boys on board? Plain Thyrkna. That's good enough for me." The visitor finished his second glass and belched. Well, so would a cultivated Eskimo.

"I understand there was some difficulty in conveying my request," said O'Reilly. "Apparently you did not know what our word *chaplain* means."

"We don't know every word in your lingo," admitted Thyrkna. "It works like this. When we come in toward a new planet, we pick up its radio, see?"

"Oh, yes. Such of it as gets through the ionosphere."

Thyrkna blinked. "Huh? I don't know all the *de*-tails. You'll have to talk to one of our tech . . . technicians. Anyway, we got a machine that analyzes the different languages, figures 'em out. Does it in just a few hours, too. Then it puts us all to sleep and teaches us the languages. When we wake up, we're ready to come down and talk."

The Cardinal laughed. "Pardon me, sir. Frankly, I was wondering why the people of your incredibly high civilization should use our worst street dialects. Now I see the reason. I am afraid our programs are not on a very high level. They aim at mass taste, the lowest common denominator—and please excuse my metaphors. Naturally you— But I assure you, we aren't all that bad. We have hopes for the future. This electronic educator of yours, for instance . . . what it could do to raise the cultural level of the average man surpasses imagination."

Thyrkna looked a trifle dazed. "I never seen anybody what talks like you Earthlings. Don't you ever run out of breath?"

O'Reilly felt himself reproved. Among the Great Galactics, a silence must be as meaningful as a hundred words, and there were a million years of dignity behind them. "I'm sorry," he said.

"Oh, it's all right. I suppose a lot of our ways must look just as funny to you." Thyrkna picked up the bottle and poured himself another glassful.

"What I asked you here for . . . there are many wonderful things you can tell me, but I would like to put you some religious questions."

"Sure, go ahead," said Thyrkna amiably.

"My Church has long speculated about this eventuality. The fact that you, too, are human, albeit more advanced than we, is a miraculous revelation of God's will. But I would like to know something about the precise form of your belief in Him."

"What do you mean?" Thyrkna sounded confused. "I'm a, uh, quartermaster. It's part of my job to kill the rabbits—we can't afford the space for cattle on board a ship. I feed the gods, that's all.

"The *gods!*" The Cardinal's glass crashed on the floor.

"By the way, what's the names of your top gods?" inquired Thyrkna. "Be a good idea to kill them a cow or two, as long as we're here on their planet. Don't wanna take chances on bad luck."

"But . . . you . . . *heathen—*"

Thyrkna looked at the clock. "Say, do you have TV?" he asked. "It's almost time for *John's Other Life*. You got some real good TV on this planet."

By the dawn's early light, Joe Husting opened a bleary eye and wished he hadn't. The apartment was a mess. What happened, anyway?"

Oh, yeah . . . those girls they picked up . . . but had they really emptied all those bottles lying on the floor?

He groaned and hung onto his head lest it split open. *Why* had he mixed scotch and stout?

Thunder lanced through his eardrums. He turned on the sofa and saw Gil emerging from the bedroom. The spaceman was thumping his chest and booming out a song learned last night. *"Oh, roly poly—"*

"Cut it out, will you?" groaned Husting.

"Huh? Man, you've had it, ain't you?" Gil clicked his tongue sympathetically. "Here, just a minute." He took a vial from his belt. "Take a few drops of this. It'll fix you up."

Somehow Husting got it down. There was a moment of fire and pinwheels, then—

—he was whole again. It was as if he had just slept ten hours without touching alcohol for the past week.

Gil returned to the bedroom and started pummeling his companions awake. Husting sat by the window, thinking hard. That hangover cure was worth a hundred million if he could only get the exclusive rights. But no, the technical envoys would show Earth how to make it, along with star ships and invisibility screens and so on. Maybe, though, he could hit the Galactics for what they had with them, and peddle it for a hundred dollars a drop before the full-dress mission arrived.

Bronni came in, full of cheer. "Say, you're all right, Joe," he trumpeted. "Ain't had such a good time since I was on Alphaz. What's next, old pal, old pal, old pal?" A meaty hand landed stunningly between Husting's shoulderblades.

"I'll see what I can do," said the Earthman cautiously. "But I'm busy, you know. Got some big deals cooking."

"I know," said Bronni. He winked. "Smart fellow like you. How the *hell* did you talk that bouncer around? I thought sure he was gonna call the cops."

"Oh, I buttered him up and slipped him a ten-spot. Wasn't hard."

"Man!" Bronnie whistled in admiration. "I never heard anybody sling the words like you was doing."

Gil herded the others out and said he wanted breakfast. Husting led them all to the elevator and out into the street. He was rather short-spoken, having much to think about. They were in a ham-and-eggery before he said:

"You spacemen must be pretty smart. Smarter than average, right?"

"Right," said Jordo. He winked at the approaching waitress.

"Lotta things a spaceman's got to know," said Col. "The ships do just about run themselves, but still, you can't let just any knucklehead into the crew."

"I see," murmured Husting. "I thought so."

A college education helps the understanding, especially when one is not too blinkered by preconceptions.

Consider one example: Sir Isaac Newton discovered (*a*) the three laws of motion, (*b*) the law of gravitation, (*c*) the differential calculus, (*d*) the elements of spectroscopy, (*e*) a good deal about acoustics, and (*f*) miscellaneous, besides finding time to serve in half a dozen official and honorary positions. A single man! And for a genius, he was not too exceptional; most gifted Earthmen have contributed to several fields.

And yet ... such supreme intellect is not necessary. The most fundamental advances, fire- and tool-making, language and clothing and social organization, were made by apish dim-bulbs. It simply took a long time between discoveries.

Given a million years, much can happen. Newton founded modern physics in one lifespan. A hundred less talented men, over a thousand-year period, could slowly and painfully have accomplished the same thing.

The IQ of Earth humanity averages about 100. Our highest geniuses may have rated 200; our lowest morons, as stupid as possible without needing institutional care, may go down to 60. It is only some freak of mutation which has made the Earthman so intelligent; he never actually *needed* all that brain.

Now if the Galactic average was around IQ 75, with their very brightest boys going up to, say, 150—

The waitress yipped and jumped into the air. Bronni grinned shamelessly as she turned to confront him.

Joe Husting pacified her. After breakfast he took the Galactic emissaries out and sold them the Brooklyn Bridge.

STIMULUS-REWARD SITUATION

Gene Fisher

How does the teacher motivate the student? The problem of getting students to develop their abilities is as old as organized education itself. Many devices have been employed in this effort, including a variety of psychological and social techniques.

Television programs like *Sesame Street* and *The Electric Company* expose youngsters to learning experiences in a medium which was not originally designed for this purpose. Major social efforts such as Head Start try to help disadvantaged children and prepare them to function effectively once they enter school.

The vast majority of young people can be reached and helped, but a few cannot. The reasons for this are still obscure. In "Stimulus —Reward Situation" author Gene Fisher creates a science fictional world inhabited by alien creatures who simply *refuse* to learn or even to change in the least. Commissioner Rail, the man in charge of educating the native Gangsha, faces a difficult task. The Gangsha appear happy and contented, but all efforts to educate them seem doomed to failure. How many teachers, faced with trying to reach and educate children with a different cultural background than their own, have felt these same frustrations? The children of the inner-city ghetto require special and different treatment if they are to successfully compete in a school environment because they often come to school lacking the basic skills and motivations of their more economically fortunate classmates.

Many devices have been tried to overcome the disadvantages faced by these students, including teacher aides from the same neighborhoods, special remedial classes, and a whole range of other programs. Progress is being made, but much remains to be done. The role of the individual teacher is of the utmost importance in this struggle—it requires a high level of dedication and the patience of a saint to achieve good results. It is the teaching equivalent of "separating the men from the boys."

In our story, the Gangsha lack what many scholars feel is a basic motivation to learn and succeed in school—*competition.* Competition is a controversial issue in education; some maintain that it is a destructive process, placing the child in a "winner" and "loser" situation which can cause great psychological damage. Others feel that it is an excellent teaching device, one that has proven itself over the years in countless classrooms. The competitive drive in education is reinforced in many ways, but at the heart of it lies the grading system, which places students into various categories of accomplishment and failure.

"Stimulus—Reward Situation" raises other important educational issues. For example, it postulates a case of *forced education,* education against the will of those being educated. Commissioner Rail employs techniques which assume that education can be reduced to the level of mere *conditioning,* an assumption which is still prevalent in some educational circles today.

As you read this story, ask yourself these questions: (1) what are the *stimuli* of education? Is it the school environment? Is it the techniques and skill of the teacher? Is it the intrinsically interesting nature of the material being studied? Or is it something else? (2) What are the *rewards* of education? Is it the accumulation of knowledge? Is it the good job that education will help you get? Is it the self-understanding and enlightenment which flows from education? Or is it a scrap of paper called a diploma?

FOR FURTHER THOUGHT OR DISCUSSION

1. What conclusions concerning the stimuli of education did you reach after reading the story?

2. What conclusions did you reach about the rewards of education?

3. How do you motivate the disadvantaged child? How would you go about educating the Gangsha?

4. How much of education is simply conditioning?

5. Are there "uneducable" children?

6. Can education be "forced?"

7. Is *competition* a necessary ingredient of education?

STIMULUS—REWARD SITUATION   *Gene Fisher*

"Welcome, Commissioner Rail. Glad to see you on-planet," Kinser, the undersection chief, said as he stepped forward with hand outstretched to where Rail stood in the door of the airboat.

"Thank you, Chief . . .?"

"Kinser, sir."

"Yes, thank you, Chief Kinser." Commissioner Rail stepped onto the loose, drifted sand of the beach. Pursing his lips, he surveyed the island which was to be his headquarters. A warm, moist breeze stirred the cropped hairs on his head, then moved on to stir the fronds of the purplish trees farther up the shore. A bright and translucent atmosphere, gently rolling waves, and a warm, earthy scent completed the picture. To a human this was a place of idyllic peace and calm. Too calm to suit Rail, who turned to face Kinser.

"Where are the natives? I was given to understand that this was a heavily populated planet."

"Yes, sir, it is. As a general rule you can always see a Gangsha somewhere around. But for some reason they never settled here, that's why the island was chosen as a base when setting up six months ago. There are plenty of them on Miyo, that's the next island over there." He motioned toward a dimly visible smudge on the southern horizon. "Here, as I said, there are none."

"Just as well. No need to have the natives underfoot, at least until we're ready to help them. Show me where I'm staying, will you? And send a man to collect my luggage. It was a rough trip down; pilot said something about atmospherics."

Turning on his heel, Rail set off toward the cluster of huts visible down the beach. Kinser followed, amused as Rail tried to keep his footing while walking through the soft sand in space boots. He, on the other hand, with both feet comfortably encased in homemade sandals that allowed the sand to sift through and tickle his toes with pleasant warmth, had no trouble negotiating the slippery surface of the beach. Six months had done much to wear off the square corners imparted by the social tech regulations.

Except for one incident, there was no difficulty in settling Rail in his small prefab. The crewman who had carried Rail's bags, one of the original members of the crew that had set up the base camp, had paused a second before leaving. That pause was at the command of Rail, who looked the man over from rag-tied head, down past the loosely fastened singlet, to the sandaled, dirty feet. He had then dismissed him with a curt nod. After the man's departure, Rail rounded to face Kinser.

"Chief Kinser, isn't there a copy of the dress rules located somewhere in this base camp?"

"I don't know. I imagine there's one around here somewhere. I can get one from the supply ship, if you feel we need it."

"We do, Chief Kinser, we do. I do not wish to criticize unjustly, but there seems to be a deplorable lack of discipline on this planet. Take yourself, for instance."

"Myself, sir?" Kinser looked down at his clothes, virtually a carbon copy of the crewman's who had just left. "What's wrong with them? Oh, of course, I know they're not what we'd wear on a civilized planet, but here on Connemara they're appropriate. It gets a little warm, as you'll find out this afternoon."

"Do not lecture me, Chief Kinser. I've read the scout reports on this planet. But the purpose of our being here is not to have a vacation, nor is it an excuse to relax the rules or discipline. How will the natives learn to respect us, if we do not conduct ourselves as civilized beings?"

"But Commissioner, all the natives go naked! That is, they don't wear anything, except their fur. Moreover, there are no natives here on the island, so how will they see us?"

"Nevertheless, good habits are developed through practice. Once the project is well established, I intend to bring a few of them here for advanced instruction. Please give the order that from now on all crew

146

members are to wear proper clothing. That means boots, tunic, and a decent hair arrangement."

Kinser was mildly irritated by this pettiness, but his face did not show it. "Yes, sir. Will that be all, sir?"

"Yes, for the moment. Have my lunch brought here at 12:30 hours, I have some reports to read until then. Also tell the men that I wish to speak to them at 13:00 hours in the mess. You may go."

Kinser spun on his heel, admittedly difficult to do in sandals, and clumped out of the prefab. Except for a slight tic that fluttered his left eyelid in time with his pulse, he did not show the implied criticism of Rail's remarks. As he passed the word about dress, he wondered about the impact a man like Michael Rail, Social Administrator Fifth Class, would have on a nice easygoing planet like Connemara. The impression of the first half hour had not presented him with anything to look forward to. Well, time had a way of smoothing all things, including stiff-necked martinets.

Rail's meeting with the assembled men, who were already irritated by wearing tunics in ninety-degree weather, added another dimension to his personality. After bringing the meeting to attention, he gave a speech:

"Men, as some of you are aware, I am the new commissioner for this planet. My name is Rail, Michael Rail. I called this meeting to get acquainted and tell you a few things. Most of you are, I see, already adhering to the standard dress regulations. Good. Continue to do so and the habit will remain when you are viewed by the Gangsha. The other thing I want to mention is the importance of our mission here on Connemara: to educate the Gangsha, by example and instruction, to our level of civilization. We are here as trustees, bearing the torchlight of civilization to this race. I expect you to conduct yourselves accordingly, both as men and as members of the social tech team assigned to this planet. That is all I have to say. Are there any questions? Please state your names on rising."

Smitty, chief cook, clown, and general good fellow of the entire work crew, raised his hand. Rail pointed to him.

"Smith, sir. Pardon me, but what if the dogs don't want to learn? Whatta we do then?"

"Dogs, Mr. Smith? Who are they?"

"Why, the natives, sir, the Gangsha. We've nicknamed them dogs because their faces are doglike and they're always sitting or lying around doing nothing. Like a dog does."

Rail's face turned scarlet. "Mr. Smith, in the future, you," he glared around at the fifty men before him, "and all the men here will refer to the Gangsha as 'the Gangsha'—not by any nicknames. This is an intelligent race, albeit a little slower than we are as yet; but that'll come, that will come. Meanwhile, treat them like the civilized race they'll be when we're through." Rail paused, his anger now partially cooled. "You men are dismissed. We begin phase two on Monday morning."

In the space of four or five minutes no one remained in the mess except Kinser and Rail. The latter walked over to a window and stared at the waves rolling onto the white sand beach before him.

"It is apparent, Chief Kinser, that this base has gone rapidly downhill without a strong guiding hand. I hold you responsible for this; it will go in my report. Dogs, indeed! Tell me, how did such a ridiculous nickname get started?"

"Just as Smith said, Commissioner. They are vaguely doglike in body form. And their customs bear resemblance to dogs on Earth. For instance, they'll sleep twenty-four hours out of twenty-eight, with the rest of the time spent in either eating or running around for exercise. The Gangsha are not the most energetic race, no need for it."

Rail's eyes sparkled. "Then we have a challenge before us. One worthy of my—our—talents as social engineers. Doglike or not, it is our duty to raise them to our level."

"That may be so, Commissioner. But what if they don't want what we offer? They aren't very industrious."

"Then we shall have to motivate them, shan't we? I hope to make an important mark here, Chief. This is my first assignment as a social commissioner on a class-five planet. This is the place to get into the habit of success, then it will continue, as a habit, on my next assignment."

"Yes," Kinser replied noncommittally. Having had some close association with the Gangsha of Connemara, he had his doubts as to their malleability. But that was Rail's problem. Rail resumed:

"I have read the reports concerning this planet, including yours. What do you believe will be our main problem here, aside from the geography? That just means more men, one for each island. Where are we liable to encounter problems?"

"As I mentioned in my report, I don't think the Gangsha will take to what we have to offer. They and their culture are, after all, pretty well adapted to this planet. Mean annual temperature of eighty degrees, no storms to speak of, and no competition as far as dominant wildlife. The paleontologist says they've been the dominant life-form

148

here for at least twenty-thousand years. Their social structure is narrow, with no wild elaborations in culture. What it boils down to is that they don't need anything we have. No problems and no competition means no success drive."

"Hm-m-m. That agrees in the main with what the reports said. Well, we'll just have to inject a serpent into their paradise, to use an old metaphor. As I told the men, phase two will begin on Monday morning. Have the pilot islands been selected and the equipment readied? The sooner we start, the better."

"It's all ready to go. Do you want to tour one of the villages? There's one quite close, on Miyo."

"Yes, we'll go out there tomorrow. Have an airboat ready at 09:00. Until then, I'll be in my prefab if I'm needed. I have to rest, this heat takes getting used to." The commissioner marched out of the mess, back straight, and over to his prefab. Kinser watched him go, shaking his head sadly. Three months ago he had recommended that the project here be terminated and the planet declared off limits. No answer. From the looks of things, though, the only serpent liable to be introduced into this paradise was Commissioner Rail.

The next morning dawned bright and clear, just as it would every morning on this planet of perpetual summer. Promptly at 09:00 the commissioner boarded the airboat, and with Kinser as pilot, flew to the native settlement on Miyo. By human standards it wasn't really a settlement or even a village, unless a small collection of roofed posts constituted one's definition. The population of this community, from what Kinser had been able to gather, was extremely fluid and the cultural concept known as the family was nonexistent. Contact-wise, one or two of the Gangsha had managed to learn a form of pidgin trade talk, but not much. Kinser explained most of this to Rail during the trip over from the base camp.

The airboat landed on the wide beach, close to the mouth of the stream on which the community, for want of a better term, stood. The two men got out and walked toward the shed-houses.

This island had the hypnotic beauty characteristic of the entire planet. Gently rolling hills that graded toward the stream and the sea rose tier on tier toward the island's center. The purplish color of the vegetation shaded darker and darker until, at a distance, it was a black coat that covered the hills. Remarkably, when viewed at close quarters, the plants themselves were not crowded: each plant seemed to keep its distance from another so as to allow all of them the proper amount of light and air. With the sun high in the sky and the sea as a backdrop, it created a picture almost too perfect for the humans to appreciate.

They were not long on their path before Rail met his first Gangsha, or rather, tripped over him as he lay in the middle of the path. A gray furry body, perhaps six feet long, with a lupine head was stretched there. Its legs were bent at an odd angle, but other than that there was nothing particularly doglike about it except the head. Set into the protruding muzzle of dirty grayish-white were four very prominent canine teeth. Even in repose and snoring the Gangsha looked ferocious. But Rail had had experience with many other races who, if judged solely on human criteria, looked just as vicious, yet in reality were gentle as doves. Besides, the reports had said that none of the Gangsha were dangerous; indeed, no fighting or competition seemed to exist among them.

Rail spoke to Kinser in a low tone. "Do they always sleep like this? I mean, during the full day and so forth? When do they work or eat?"

"I'm afraid this is normal, Commissioner. They're not as energetic as we are. As for food, see that tree there?" He pointed to a low bush on the right side of the path. "Those round things on it are what they normally eat. We had them analyzed and they have all the proteins, carbohydrates, and fats that they need to thrive. Better still, the trees produce year round. These 'fruits' and water are all they need."

"But the teeth? What are they for? Judging solely by appearance I'd say they were carnivores."

"Paley, he's the biologist, says they're not. The teeth are apparently evolutionary holdouts. They do make them look vicious though, don't they? Actually they are extremely gentle, you might even say torpid."

They skirted the sleeping Gangsha and proceeded to the community. Shrill shouts of the Gangsha young greeted them at first, then stopped as they walked into the community circle. There were perhaps as many as twenty-five of the adult Gangsha sleeping, lying propped against trees or under the lean-to roofs, or simply resting from what might have seemed hard and futile labor. The only movement had been from the young and it had stopped. Both men stood in the center of it all. Five minutes of waiting produced nothing, except that some of the youngsters fell over in position and began to snore with high-pitched sounds. The wind sighed in the leaves.

"Don't they have a headman or something? Someone we could speak to?" Rail asked Kinser.

"No. There isn't much social organization, no need for it apparently. One or two speak trade of a sort, but you'll have to wait until one of them wakes up."

"But, but . . . who apportions work? How do things get *done?* Do they do nothing but eat, sleep, and copulate?"

"That's about it from all we've been able to see. All over the planet it's the same thing—plenty of food, perfect weather, and quiet, sleeping Gangsha. It makes you wonder how they survived at all. Sheer inertia, I guess."

Rail looked around, a frozen expression on his face. "We'll have to do something about that," came a half audible phrase. Then louder: "Let's go back to base, there's nothing we can do here." Action suiting words, he reversed himself and marched back to the boat, Kinser in the rear.

Phase two of the project began promptly at 09:00 hours on Monday morning. Twenty airboats, equipped with technical equipment—automatic teachers, tape libraries, and other educational aids—each manned by a social tech, set off on their missions. Each would go into one of the known Gangsha villages and erect a teaching post. After a given period of time, the natives trained there would serve as a nucleus to train others until the entire population was ready for phase three, or elementary technocraft. In the timetable set up in the mess on the commissioner's order, that was to occur in four standard months.

Commissioner Rail stood beside Kinser and both silently watched the teams fly off into the bright horizon. "Well, Chief, it's the dawning of a new day for Connemara and the Gangsha. In a month the first progress reports should be coming in. I'm looking forward to them, for they'll validate our reasons for being here. Being a social tech is a tough, but satisfying, job." A sort of half-grin, half-hopeful expression flitted over his face, then it relapsed into its customary look of mild distaste. The latter matched the inward opinion of Kinser toward Rail, though he had not as yet shown it.

"Yes, Commissioner, it's a new day. Though I have reservations about the speed with which the Gangsha will learn what we have to teach. From all indications, their culture is not oriented in that way. The instruction hasn't much use here as far as applications go."

"Nonsense, Chief Kinser. After all, what choice do they have? No native culture can survive unchanged under the impact of galactic civilization. Why, that's the basic reason we're here, to ease that inevitable transition. As you know full well."

"I don't want to cry wolf, Commissioner, but from the way I see it, the Gangsha are happy here and well adapted to their environment. Actually, they've nothing of a trade nature we've been able to discover. Although I'm not privy to Council decisions, I am curious about our real purpose here."

"If you must know, Kinser, it was done at my instigation. At the time the report on Connemara's discovery was entered at Social Tech Headquarters, I was in charge of the processing division. Something about the report seemed too good to be true, too like a paradise. So, at my insistence, operations were set into motion to civilize this planet. I was also placed in charge to acquire some field experience."

And to prevent you from bungling a more important project, was the thought that followed in Kinser's mind. Aloud: "Perhaps you're right, Commissioner, and everything will turn out all right. I recommended that this planet be declared off limits, but it seems I was overridden at Headquarters. And now if you will excuse me, I have some work to take care of." He gave the commissioner a salute and walked away.

In a month the reports began to trickle in from the outlying posts on the other islands. In that same month of summers Kinser had had about all he could stand of the commissioner. His conversation, filled with endless platitudes about the service and unleavened with the slightest amount of field experience, had led Kinser to spend more and more of his time at the Gangsha settlement on Miyo. While there, he had increased the trade vocabulary of Kiha, one of the natives, by another fifty words or so. No mean feat, considering that every few minutes the Gangsha drifted off into a deep sleep. Kinser was engaged in another attempt to rouse Kiha when the radio of his airboat began to give off its keening whine. He went over and flicked the switch on the dash.

"Kinser here."

"Kinser, this is Commissioner Rail. Have you seen the reports?"

"One or two of them. Nothing too unusual, barring a certain lack of progress." He gave a glance at his erstwhile pupil, now sound asleep, muzzle emitting remarkably humanlike snores. "Considering the Gangsha, it was no surprise."

"Well, four more have come in this morning and I've just finished listening to the tapes. 'Certain lack of progress' is not the term for it;

no progress would be a better fit. Do you realize that none of the Gangsha, not one, has even offered to try and learn what the social techs are teaching? What's wrong with them, don't they realize that we're trying to ease their way?"

"These things take time, Commissioner. Besides, all the reports aren't in yet." Kinser resisted the urge to say, "I told you so"—why add fire to the insult Rail evidently felt? "When all of them come in, we'll run them through the computer and see if any pattern can be developed. Until then, there's nothing much we can do."

The voice replied, calmer now: "All right, Chief, we'll see what develops. As you say, there's not much we can do. But I have the feeling . . . let's say, I think there's something funny going on here. See me on your return to base. Out." The click of the switch cut off further words. Kinser returned his attention to the now stirring Kiha, stretching out of his nap.

"Ah, Kiha," Kinser said in trade talk. "Want you more learn?"

"No, Kinse." The Gangsha had not yet learned to form the *r* sound, their native language did not possess one. "Feel hungwy. Will eat and . . . " a string of incomprehensible Gangsha followed, then: "maby late." Kiha rose and weaved off into the bushes on his powerful legs. Kinser shook his head and boarded his airboat for the trip back to base.

Within three days all twenty of the monthly reports were at base. They simply augmented the first ones received: that is, no Gangsha had made use of the established learning facilities. As he had said, Kinser ran them through the computer, but the only recognizable pattern seemed to lie in the nature of the Gangsha themselves. They didn't need any education, saw no reason for it, and therefore failed to use the facilities.

"But how could they refuse?" Rail fumed. "Don't they realize what a gift we're bringing them? For twenty thousand years these Gangsha, these . . . dogs, have lain in this paradise without so much as a single effort to improve themselves. It's . . . it's disgraceful."

"I wouldn't say that," Kinser replied. "Whatever they could learn would be of no real use to them. For what would they need it? A perfect world and perfect adaption to its requirements. They're happy, why disturb them?"

"Because, Kinser," the commissioner's voice was edged with venom, "this is an expensive operation that was designed to aid the natives with or without their consent. Do you believe that I would allow a black mark against my record simply because they refuse to learn? No, if kindness won't work, perhaps force will."

153

"I warn you, Commissioner, that I will not tolerate any assaults on the Gangsha or their social structure. As you are aware, the service has failed before, usually because of some oversight on the part of the administrator involved. But every planet is different. I cannot stand by and see you injure anyone."

"You will, Chief, you will. One way or the other. I give you a choice: either continue as my second here on this project or be locked in your quarters until the next supply ship arrives. Take your pick; either way I will carry forth the project here."

It was in Kinser's mind to tell the fool to go hang, but he simply couldn't take the chance. There was no telling how far the man would go without some kind of check on him. "Since you put it that way, Commissioner, I will continue on as second, under duress. How do you propose to educate an unwilling Gangsha?"

"Simplicity, itself. From all we've been able to observe, they've never been without food or sleep for an exceptional period of time. We'll simply deprive a Gangsha of either until it consents to learn; probably the food first, since that's the easiest. Paley tells me they can take it. Once the barrier has been broken, we'll use the trained one to teach others and set the ball rolling. I've already given orders that a compound be built here at base. When it's completed, we'll get a native or two from Miyo and stock it."

Kinser was appalled by the man's ruthlessness. "These people are not really dogs to be taught by simple conditioning, Commissioner. Don't you think that this is a little dangerous?"

"Only if we don't get results. And it will work, I assure you. The end sometimes justifies the means, as in this case. When the compound is completed, go over to Miyo and get a couple of Gangsha. You spend enough time over there, should have quite a few friends." Rail gave a nasty giggle. "Make sure that at least one of them speaks no trade—I want an uncontaminated test of this procedure. You're dismissed, Chief." Rail turned his back and strode to his prefab. Kinser felt sick.

Building the compound took only two days. It was a simple fence, fifteen feet high, surrounding a fifty-square-foot area. Inside was a hut for the Gangsha and a table set up for the educational equipment. The door in the wall was keyed to respond to human electromagnetic brain patterns, in this case, only to Commissioner Rail's. When Kinser asked him about it, he replied that he was the one who run the experiment and he didn't want any interference. To forestall this, Kinser had an emergency override installed on the door just in case. When the compound was completed he went over to Miyo and talked to Kiha.

"Kiha, I need help. Need you, other Gangsha help me. Come over my nest-base. Yes?" He felt like a traitor selling out, but persisted because he knew that Rail was quite capable of sending someone to force two natives over.

"Yes. Will bwing nest-mate-bwothew Meta. We go, now?"

"Yes, if possible."

The Gangsha shambled over to one of the covered sheds with its crooked walk. Kiha spoke rapidly in Gangsha to one of the others lying there. This worthy lumbered to his feet and both went over to the airboat and climbed in. The trip over was uneventful, except that the Gangsha's first reaction to an airboat ride was to fall asleep leaning against one another.

Kinser landed the airboat by the compound. Rail was there, waiting with a satisfied smirk on his face. Kinser walked over to him, leaving the two Gangsha undisturbed.

"Excellent, Chief Kinser, you'll make a social tech yet. Which of them is the trade speaker?"

"The one on the right, Kiha. Meta, one of his relatives, is the other."

"Good. Take Meta and get him into the compound."

"First, Commissioner, I want to know what you're going to do to him. As I told you, I don't want the Gangsha hurt, for any reason."

"I'm simply going to deprive him of food until he consents to learn, a stimulus-reward situation. Most lower forms of life respond to such conditions. I'm sure the Gangsha will also. A few days should do it."

"I give you one week, Commissioner." Kinser had already checked with the biologist and discovered that such a limit was well within the Gangsha's tolerance. "At the end of that time, he comes out. Do I make myself clear?"

"Save your threats for war, Kinser. I'm sure that even within your short time limit, some results will be obtained. Enough to vindicate my methods and show a little success for our months of work here." His voice rose to a shriller tone. "We must, my career depends on it."

Kinser did as he was told, waking up the sleeping Gangsha and getting through to Meta, using the medium of Kiha, what was desired of him. The Gangsha lumbered out of the airboat and into the compound. Inside he made a beeline for the shed, leaned against one of its posts and promptly fell asleep. Rail closed the door on him.

"In three days, Chief, I'll begin. We'll see what results my technique achieves."

Three days later, carrying a bag of the purplish fruits, Rail went into the compound. The door closed behind him. Two hours passed and he came stomping out, bag still full, and headed for his prefab. Although he didn't say anything in the mess that night, Kinser gathered from his expression that the Gangsha did not rush to be educated.

The fourth, fifth, and sixth days went by in the same manner—each day Rail entered the compound with a full bag of fruit and left some two hours later, full bag in his hand and a scowl on his face. Each day it became more and more obvious to everyone but himself that he was failing. On the seventh day, Kinser was waiting at the compound door when Rail arrived. He was surprised to notice that the man wore a shocker on his lip, an advanced form of crowd controller. Rail was about to brush past him without speaking when Kinser put his arm between him and the door.

"One moment, Commissioner. You have now had one week. This is the last day of your experiment: win, lose, or draw, Meta comes out tonight."

"Do not order me, Kinser. I am the commissioner here and what I say is law."

"Not if no one will obey you. As I said, Meta comes out tonight. One more thing. What's the shocker for?"

Rail looked down guiltily. "Ah ... for protection, of course. Did you think I was going to hurt your precious dog?"

Kinser withdrew his arm. "See that you don't, Commissioner," he said curtly and walked away. Behind him he heard the door of the compound close. He was just entering the door of his prefab when he heard the scream.

Kinser set off at a dead run for the compound. The screams came apace, of unearthly piercing notes which ended abruptly in a gurgle. They made the hair on the back of his neck rise. The other men in the area were futilely beating against the door when he came up. He flicked the override and entered, fully expecting to see a dead Gangsha —martyred on the altar of Rail's career.

Inside, lying in a pool of bright crimson, was Rail, his throat torn out and face chewed to shreds. The shocker was still gripped tightly in his right hand. Off to one side, squatting on his haunches and eating fruit out of the bag, was the Gangsha, Meta. Traces of blood stained his face and teeth. He paid no attention to Kinser in the doorway.

Kinser turned and gave an order to the first man behind him. "Get the other Gangsha here, quickly." When he turned, Meta had already lost interest in the fruit and was peacefully slumbering on the ground beside the man he had killed. A snore soon shook the compound. Kiha came loping up. Kinser let him into the compound and closed the door behind him.

"Kiha, you find what happen. Meta kill commissioner. Why?"

The Gangsha gave a nod and went over to the other sleeping form. A guttural conversation ensued, punctuated with yawns on the part of Meta and arm waves from Kiha. When the conversation was over, Kiha returned to Kinser.

"Meta say commissionew not like you. Say commissionew want Gangsha eat him. Meta no want, so commissionew no feed Meta. Twy to make Meta by no feed. No undewstand Gangsha."

"But . . . commissioner not want Meta to eat him! Only want Meta to learn. Try to force him by hunger and not feed.

No. Not it. Meta say simple. Gangsha once like beast, eat all things. Even beasts. But not now, only eat bushfwuit which ha'm no thing. Is bettew way fo' beasts and Gangsha. Commissionew no leawn that. Meta say he no able to not eat much longew. Ask Commissionew fo' bushfwuit. Commissionew hit with hot stick. Commissionew attack like beast. Meta say only one thing do. Kill beast. But no eat him, eat bushfwuit instead. All happy but beast, and he dead."

Kinser looked at him wishing he could explain, but it was useless. It was obvious that Meta had misunderstood what Rail's intent had been, though that mistake was not half so glaring as the one which the commissioner made that cost him his life. In every way the commissioner was responsible for his own death and with him had died any reason for the social tech team's presence on Connemara. Kinser opened the door and gave orders for the commissioner's body to be removed and the stockade torn down. The two Gangsha he would return personally to Miyo. Then he went to his prefab to think.

Three weeks later, after a supply ship came and removed Rail's body and most of the remaining equipment and personnel, Kinser sat in the same prefab looking out over the blue sea. At his recommendation, Connemara and the Gangsha had been declared off limits, and tomorrow another ship would come to take himself and the rest off-planet. All he had left of his official duties as chief of section was the final report for the Social Tech HQ. He had been sitting before the blank pad of paper on the desk in front of him all morning, trying to think of a diplomatic way to say what had to be said. Finally, he took the stylus and wrote the report's title in bold letters across the top of the page:

"Let Sleeping Dogs Lie."

THE FIRST MEN

Howard Fast

Few subjects have aroused as much controversy in recent years as the whole issue of intelligence and its role in the learning process. At the heart of the controversy is the IQ (Intelligence Quotient) test. For many years IQ was felt to be an accurate indicator of a student's ability to learn. We now know that the learning process is a much more complicated subject involving such factors as ability to recall, the capacity to learn from one's mistakes (sometimes referred to as basic learning abilities), cognitive abilities such as being able to make associations verbally, and cumulative knowledge built up over time within the individual. Furthermore, very strong evidence points to the important role played by culture, home life, and socioeconomic background in the learning process. For example, many scholars hold the view that success on IQ tests is due more to previous exposure to the terminology and things referred to on the test than to any other factor.

The catalyst for the IQ controversy has been the issue of the relationship of intelligence to the variable of *race*. Charges of racism have been made against journal articles and books which claim to have "proved" that black children are inferior to white children both in IQ and in ability to learn. Keeping in mind that intelligence tests are subject to manipulation and can be used to "prove" almost anything, most indicators point to cultural factors as the major variable in determining the outcome of these tests. For example, extensive testing has shown that on standard A.E.F. Intelligence Tests northern blacks consistently scored higher than southern whites, and the explanation for these scores was presented in cultural terms—differences in income, amount of travel experience, and so forth.

Researchers have found that there exists a definite "cultural bias" built into almost all intelligence tests (attempts to design tests which delete this bias have been only partially successful) and that students who were from a family and social setting in which they have been exposed to a wide variety of cultural inputs score higher than a child who was not. Furthermore, the taking of many tests is a craft in itself and must be mastered before tests can have any real meaning.

However, besides intelligence there is another factor which is important to any discussion of learning—*creativity.* Tests measuring creativity show that intelligence and creativity do not necessarily go hand in hand. In fact, many students score high in one and low in the other, although high scorers in either category show high scholastic achievement in school.

The creative child is a problem for teachers. Creativity has contempt for orderliness, so gifted children are problem children in the eyes of many teachers. In "The First Men," a group of exceptional, gifted, creative, and intelligent human beings are brought together from all over the world and take part in a great educational experiment.

FOR FURTHER THOUGHT OR DISCUSSION

1. What does the story have to say about the relationship between intelligence and creativity?

2. What is the relationship between race and learning ability?

3. What role does cognitive ability play in learning?

4. Are tests being misused in our educational system? How can they be improved?

5. What is cultural bias and what role does it play in learning?

6. What is creativity? Discuss the plight of the creative child.

THE FIRST MEN   *Howard Fast*

By Airmail:

Calcutta, India
Nov. 4th, 1945

Mrs. Jean Arbalaid
Washington, D.C.

My dear sister:
    I found it. I saw it with my own eyes, and thereby I am convinced that I have a useful purpose in life—overseas investigator for the anthropological whims of my sister. That, in any case, is better than boredom. I have no desire to return home; I will not go into any further explanations or reasons. I am neurotic, unsettled and adrift. I got my discharge in Karachi, as you know. I am very happy to be an ex-GI and a tourist, but it took me only a few weeks to become bored to distraction. So I was quite pleased to have a mission from you. The mission is completed.
    It could have been more exciting. The plain fact of the matter is that the small Associated Press item you sent me was quite accurate in all of its details. The little village of Chunga is in Assam. I got there by plane, narrow-gauge train and ox-cart—a fairly pleasant trip at this time of the year, with the back of the heat broken; and there I saw the child, who is now fourteen years old.
    I am sure you know enough about India to realize that fourteen is very much an adult age for a girl in these parts—the majority of them are married by then. And there is no question about the age. I spoke at length to the mother and father, who identified the child by two very distinctive birthmarks. The identification was substantiated by relatives and other villagers—all of whom remembered the birthmarks. A circumstance not unusual or remarkable in these small villages.
    The child was lost as an infant—at eight months, a common story, the parents working in the field, the child set down, and then the child gone. Whether it crawled at that age or not, I can't say; at any rate, it was a healthy, alert and curious infant. They all agree on that point.
    How the child came to the wolves is something we will never know. Possibly a bitch who had lost her own cubs carried the infant off. That is the most likely story, isn't it? This is not *lupus,* the Euro-

pean variety, but *pallipes,* its local cousin, nevertheless a respectable animal in size and disposition, and not something to stumble over on a dark night. Eighteen days ago, when the child was found, the villagers had to kill five wolves to take her, and she herself fought like a devil out of hell. She had lived as a wolf for thirteen years.

Will the story of her life among the wolves ever emerge? I don't know. To all effects and purposes, she is a wolf. She cannot stand upright—the curvature of her spine being beyond correction. She runs on all fours and her knuckles are covered with heavy callus. They are trying to teach her to use her hands for grasping and holding, but so far unsuccessfully. Any clothes they dress her in, she tears off, and as yet she has not been able to grasp the meaning of speech, much less talk. The Indian anthropologist, Sumil Gojee, has been working with her for a week now, and he has little hope that any real communication will ever be possible. In our terms and by our measurements, she is a total idiot, an infantile imbecile, and it is likely that she will remain so for the rest of her life.

On the other hand, both Professor Gojee and Dr. Chalmers, a government health service man, who came up from Calcutta to examine the child, agree that there are no physical or hereditary elements to account for the child's mental condition, no malformation of the cranial area and no history of imbecilism in her background. Everyone in the village attests to the normalcy—indeed, alertness and brightness —of the infant; and Professor Gojee makes a point of the alertness and adaptability she must have required to survive for thirteen years among the wolves. The child responds excellently to reflex tests, and neurologically, she appears to be sound. She is strong—beyond the strength of a thirteen-year-old—wiry, quick in her movements, and possesses an uncanny sense of smell and hearing.

Professor Gojee has examined records of eighteen similar cases recorded in India over the past hundred years, and in every case, he says, the recovered child was an idiot in our terms—or a wolf in objective terms. He points out that it would be incorrect to call this child an idiot or an imbecile. The child is a wolf, perhaps a very superior wolf, but a wolf nevertheless.

I am preparing a much fuller report on the whole business. Meanwhile, this letter contains the pertinent facts. As for money—I am very well heeled indeed, with eleven hundred dollars I won in a crap game. Take care of yourself and your brilliant husband and the public health service.

Love and kisses,
Harry

By cable:
Harry Felton
Hotel Empire
Calcutta, India.
November 10, 1945
This is no whim, Harry, but very serious indeed. You did nobly. Similar case in Pretoria. General Hospital, Dr. Felix Vanott. We have made all arrangements with air transport.

Jean Arbalaid

By Airmail:

Pretoria, Union of South Africa
November 15, 1945

Mrs. Jean Arbalaid
Washington, D.C.

My dear sister:
    You are evidently a very big wheel, you and your husband, and I wish I knew what your current silly season adds up to. I suppose in due time you'll see fit to tell me. But in any case, your priorities command respect. A full colonel was bumped, and I was promptly whisked to South Africa, a beautiful country of pleasant climate and, I am sure, great promise.
    I saw the child, who is still being kept in the General Hospital here, and I spent an evening with Dr. Vanott and a young and reasonably attractive Quaker lady, Miss Gloria Oland, an anthropologist working among the Bantu people for her Doctorate. So, you see, I will be able to provide a certain amount of background material—more as I develop my acquaintance with Miss Oland.
    Superficially, this case is remarkably like the incident in Assam. There it was a girl of fourteen; here we have a Bantu boy of eleven. The girl was reared by the wolves; the boy, in this case, was reared by the baboons—and rescued from them by a White Hunter, name of Archway, strong, silent type, right out of Hemingway. Unfortunately, Archway has a nasty temper and doesn't like children, so when the boy understandably bit him, he whipped the child to within an inch of its life. "Tamed him," as he puts it.
    At the hospital, however, the child has been receiving the best of care and reasonable if scientific affection. There is no way of tracing him back to his parents, for these Basutoland baboons are great travelers and there is no telling where they picked him up. His age is a medical guess, but reasonable. That he is of Bantu origin, there is no doubt. He is handsome, long-limbed, exceedingly strong, and with no

indication of any cranial injury. But like the girl in Assam, he is—in our terms—an idiot and an imbecile.

That is to say, he is a baboon. His vocalization is that of a baboon. He differs from the girl in that he is able to use his hands to hold things and to examine things, and he has a more active curiosity; but that, I am assured by Miss Oland, is the difference between a wolf and a baboon.

He too has a permanent curvature of the spine; he goes on all fours as the baboons do, and the back of his fingers and hands are heavily callused. After tearing off his clothes the first time, he accepted them, but that too is a baboon trait. In this case, Miss Oland has hope for his learning at least rudimentary speech, but Dr. Vanott doubts that he ever will. Incidentally, I must take note that in those eighteen cases Professor Gojee referred to, there was no evidence of human speech being learned beyond its most basic elements.

So goes my childhood hero, Tarzan of the Apes, and all the noble beasts along with him. But the most terrifying thought is this—what is the substance of man himself, if this can happen to him? The learned folk here have been trying to explain to me that man is a creature of his thought and that his thought is to a very large extent shaped by his environment; and that this thought process—or mentation as they call it—is based on words. Without words, thought becomes a process of pictures, which is on the animal level and rules out all, even the most primitive, abstract concepts. In other words, man cannot become man by himself: he is the result of other men and of the totality of human society and experience.

The man raised by the wolves is a wolf, by the baboons a baboon —and this is implacable, isn't it? My head has been swimming with all sorts of notions, some of them not at all pleasant. My dear sister, what are you and your husband up to? Isn't it time you broke down and told old Harry? Or do you want me to pop off to Tibet? Anything to please you, but preferably something that adds up.

Your ever-loving Harry

By Airmail:

Washington, D.C.
November 27, 1945

Mr. Harry Felton
Pretoria, Union of South Africa

Dear Harry:

You are a noble and sweet brother, and quite sharp too. You are also a dear. Mark and I want you to do a job for us, which will enable you to run here and there across the face of the earth, and be paid for it too. In order to convince you, we must spill out the dark secrets of our work—which we have decided to do, considering you an upright and trustworthy character. But the mail, it would seem, is less trustworthy; and since we are working with the Army, which has a constitutional dedication to *top-secret* and similar nonsense, the information goes to you via diplomatic pouch. As of receiving this, consider yourself employed; your expenses will be paid, within reason, and an additional eight thousand a year for less work than indulgence.

So please stay put at your hotel in Pretoria until the pouch arrives. Not more than ten days. Of course, you will be notified.

Love, affection and respect,

Jean

By diplomatic pouch:

Washington, D.C.
December 5, 1945

Mr. Harry Felton
Pretoria, Union of South Africa

Dear Harry:

Consider this letter the joint effort of Mark and myself. The conclusions are also shared. Also, consider it a very serious document indeed.

You know that for the past twenty years, we have both been deeply concerned with child psychology and child development. There is no need to review our careers or our experience in the Public Health Service. Our work during the war, as part of the Child Reclamation Program, led to an interesting theory, which we decided to pursue. We were given leave by the head of the service to make this our own project, and recently we were granted a substantial amount of army funds to work with.

Now down to the theory, which is not entirely untested, as you know. Briefly—but with two decades of practical work as a background—it is this: Mark and I have come to the conclusion that within the rank and file of Homo Sapiens is the leavening of a new race. Call them man-plus—call them what you will. They are not of recent arrival; they have been cropping up for hundreds, perhaps thousands of years. But they are trapped in and molded by human environment as certainly and implacably as your Assamese girl was trapped among the wolves or your Bantu boy among the baboons.

By the way, your two cases are not the only attested ones we have.

By sworn witness, we have records of seven similar cases, one in Russia, two in Canada, two in South America, one in West Africa, and, just to cut us down to size, one in the United States. We also have hearsay and folklore of three hundred and eleven parallel cases over a period of fourteen centuries. We have in fourteenth century Germany, in the folio MS of the monk, Hubercus, five case histories which he claims to have observed. In all of these cases, in the seven cases witnessed by people alive today, and in all but sixteen of the hearsay cases, the result is more or less precisely what you have seen and described yourself: the child reared by the wolf is a wolf.

Our own work adds up to the parallel conclusion: the child reared by a man is a man. If man-plus exists, he is trapped and caged as certainly as any human child reared by animals. Our proposition is that he exists.

Why do we think this super-child exists? Well, there are many reasons, and neither the time nor the space to go into all in detail. But here are two very telling reasons. Firstly, we have case histories of several hundred men and women, who as children had IQs of 150 or above. In spite of their enormous intellectual promise as children, less than 10 percent have succeeded in their chosen careers. Roughly another 10 percent have been institutionalized as mental cases beyond recovery. About 14 percent have had or require therapy in terms of mental health problems. Six percent have been suicides, 1 percent are in prison, 27 percent have had one or more divorces, 19 percent are chronic failures at whatever they attempt—and the rest are undistinguished in any important manner. All of the IQs have dwindled—almost in the sense of a smooth graph line in relation to age.

Since society has never provided the full potential for such a mentality, we are uncertain as to what it might be. But we can guess that against it, they have been reduced to a sort of idiocy—an idiocy that we call normalcy.

The second reason we put forward is this: we know that man uses only a tiny fraction of his brain. What blocks him from the rest of it? Why has nature given him equipment that he cannot put to use? Or has society prevented him from breaking the barriers around his own potential?

There, in brief, are two reasons. Believe me, Harry, there are many more—enough for us to have convinced some very hard-headed and unimaginative government people that we deserve a chance to release *superman*. Of course, history helps—in its own mean manner. It would appear that we are beginning another war—with Russia this time, a cold war, as some have already taken to calling it. And among other things, it will be a war of intelligence—a commodity in rather short supply, as some of our local mental giants have been frank enough to admit. They look upon our man-plus as a secret weapon, little devils who will come up with death rays and superatom bombs when the time is ripe. Well, let them. It is inconceivable to imagine a project like this under benign sponsorship. The important thing is that Mark and I have been placed in full charge of the venture—millions of dollars, top priority—the whole works. But nevertheless, *secret to the ultimate*. I cannot stress this enough.

Now, as to your own job—if you want it. It develops step by step. First step: in Berlin, in 1937, there was a Professor Hans Goldbaum. Half Jewish. The head of the Institute of Child Therapy. He published a small monograph on intelligence testing in children, and he put forward claims—which we are inclined to believe—that he could determine a child's IQ during its first year of life, in its pre-speech period. He presented some impressive tables of estimations and subsequent checked results, but we do not know enough of his method to practice it ourselves. In other words, we need the professor's help.

In 1937, he vanished from Berlin. In 1943, he was reported to be living in Cape Town—the last address we have for him. I enclose the address. Go to Cape Town, Harry darling. (Myself talking, not Mark.) If he has left, follow him and find him. If he is dead, inform us immediately.

Of course you will take the job. We love you and we need your help.

Jean

By Airmail:

Cape Town, South Africa
December 20, 1945

Mrs. Jean Arbalaid
Washington, D.C.

My dear sister:
Of all the hairbrained ideas! If this is our secret weapon, I am prepared to throw in the sponge right now. But a job is a job.

It took me a week to follow the Professor's meandering through Cape Town—only to find out that he took off for London in 1944. Evidently, they needed him there. I am off to London.

Love,
Harry

By diplomatic pouch:

Washington, D.C.
December 26, 1945

Mr. Harry Felton
London, England

Dear Harry:

This is dead serious. By now, you must have found the professor. We believe that despite protestations of your own idiocy, you have enough sense to gauge his method. Sell him this venture. Sell him! We will give him whatever he asks—and we want him to work with us as long as he will.

Briefly, here is what we are up to. We have been allocated a tract of eight thousand acres in northern California. We intend to establish an environment there—under military guard and security. In the beginning, the outside world will be entirely excluded. The environment will be controlled and exclusive.

Within this environment, we intend to bring forty children to maturity—to a maturity that will result in man-plus.

As to the details of this environment—well that can wait. The immediate problem is the children. Out of forty, ten will be found in the United States; the other thirty will be found by the professor and yourself—outside of the United States.

Half are to be boys; we want an even boy-girl balance. They are to be between the ages of six months and nine months, and all are to show indications of an exceedingly high IQ—that is, if the professor's method is any good at all.

We want five racial groupings: Caucasian, Indian, Chinese, Malayan and Bantu. Of course, we are sensible of the vagueness of these groupings, and you have some latitude within them. The six so-called *Caucasian* infants are to be found in European types, and two Mediterranean types. A similar breakdown might be followed in other areas.

Now understand this—no cops and robbers stuff, no OSS, no kidnapping. Unfortunately, the world abounds in war orphans—and in parents poor and desperate enough to sell their children. When you want a child and such a situation arises, buy! Price is no object. I will have no maudlin sentimentality or scruples. These children will be loved and cherished—and if you should acquire any by purchase, you will be giving a child life and hope.

When you find a child, inform us immediately. Air transport will be at your disposal—and we are making all arrangements for wet nurses and other details of child care. We shall also have medical aid at your immediate disposal. On the other hand, we want healthy children—within the general conditions of health within any given area.

Now good luck to you. We are depending on you and we love you. And a merry Christmas.

Jean

By diplomatic pouch:

Copenhagen, Denmark
February 4, 1946

Mrs. Jean Arbalaid
Washington, D.C.

Dear Jean:

I seem to have caught your silly *top-secret* and *classified* disease, and I have been waiting for a free day and a diplomatic pouch to sum up my various adventures. From my "guarded" cables, you know that the professor and I have been doing a Cook's Tour of the baby market. My dear sister, this kind of shopping spree does not sit at all well with me. However, I gave my word, and there you are. I will complete and deliver.

By the way, I suppose I continue to send these along to Washington, even though your "environment," as you call it, has been established. I'll do so until otherwise instructed.

There was no great difficulty in finding the professor. Being in uniform—I have since acquired an excellent British wardrobe—and having all the fancy credentials you were kind enough to supply, I went to the War Office. As they say, every courtesy was shown to Major Harry Felton, but I feel better in civilian clothes. Anyway, the professor had been working with a child reclamation project, living among the ruins of the East End, which is pretty badly shattered. He is an astonishing little man, and I have become quite fond of him. On his part, he is learning to tolerate me.

I took him to dinner—you were the lever that moved him, my dear sister. I had no idea how famous you are in certain circles. He looked at me in awe, simply because we share a mother and father.

Then I said my piece, all of it, no holds barred. I had expected your reputation to crumble into dust there on the spot, but no such thing. Goldbaum listened with his mouth and his ears and every fiber of his being. The only time he interrupted me was to question me on the Assamese girl and the Bantu boy; and very pointed and meticulous questions they were. When I had finished, he simply shook his head—

not in disagreement but with sheer excitement and delight. I then asked him what his reaction to all this was.

"I need time," he said. "This is something to digest. But the concept is wonderful—daring and wonderful. Not that the reasoning behind it is so novel. I have thought of this—so many anthropologists have. But to put it into practice, young man—ah, your sister is a wonderful and remarkable woman!"

There you are, my sister. I struck while the iron was hot, and told him then and there that you wanted and needed his help, first to find the children and then to work in the environment.

"The environment," he said; "you understand that is everything, everything. But how can she change the environment? The environment is total, the whole fabric of human society, self-deluded and superstitious and sick and irrational and clinging to legends and phantasies and ghosts. Who can change that?"

So it went. My anthropology is passable at best, but I have read all your books. If my answers were weak in that department, he did manage to draw out of me a more or less complete picture of Mark and yourself. He then said he would think about the whole matter. We made an appointment for the following day, when he would explain his method of intelligence determination in infants.

We met the next day, and he explained his methods. He made a great point of the fact that he did not test but rather determined, within a wide margin for error. Years before, in Germany, he had worked out a list of fifty characteristics which he noted in infants. As these infants matured, they were tested regularly by normal methods—and the results were checked against his original observations. Thereby, he began to draw certain conclusions, which he tested again and again over the next fifteen years. I am enclosing an unpublished article of his which goes into greater detail. Sufficient to say that he convinced me of the validity of his methods. Subsequently, I watched him examine a hundred and four British infants—to come up with our first choice. Jean, this is a remarkable and brilliant man.

On the third day after I had met him, he agreed to join the project. But he said this to me, very gravely, and afterwards I put it down exactly as he said it:

"You must tell your sister that I have not come to this decision lightly. We are tampering with human souls—and perhaps even with human destiny. This experiment may fail, but if it succeeds it can be the most important event of our time—even more important and consequential than this war we have just fought. And you must tell her something else. I had a wife and three children, and they were put to death

169

because a nation of men turned into beasts. I watched that, and I could not have lived through it unless I believed, always, that what can turn into a beast can also turn into a man. We are neither. But if we go to create man, we must be humble. We are the tool, not the craftsman, and if we succeed, we will be less than the result of our work."

There is your man, Jean, and as I said, a good deal of a man. Those words are verbatim. He also dwells a great deal on the question of environment, and the wisdom and judgment and love necessary to create this environment. I think it would be helpful if you could send me a few words at least concerning this environment you are establishing.

We have now sent you four infants. Tomorrow, we leave for Rome —and from Rome to Casablanca.

But we will be in Rome at least two weeks, and a communication should reach me there.

More seriously—
And not untroubled,
Harry

By diplomatic pouch:

Via Washington, D.C.
February 11, 1946

Mr. Harry Felton
Rome, Italy

Dear Harry:

Just a few facts here. We are tremendously impressed by your reactions to Professor Goldbaum, and we look forward eagerly to his joining us. Meanwhile, Mark and I have been working night and day on the environment. In the most general terms, this is what we plan.

The entire reservation—all eight thousand acres—will be surrounded by a wire fence and will be under army guard. Within it, we shall establish a home. There will be between thirty and forty teachers —or group parents. We are accepting only married couples who love children and who will dedicate themselves to this venture. That they must have additional qualifications goes without saying.

Within the proposition that somewhere in man's civilized development, something went wrong, we are returning to the prehistory form of group marriage. That is not to say that we will cohabit indiscriminately—but the children will be given to understand that parentage is a whole, that we are all their mothers and fathers, not by blood but by love.

We shall teach them the truth, and where we do not know the truth, we shall not teach. There will be no myths, no legends, no lies, superstitions, no premises and no religions. We shall teach love and cooperation and we shall give love and security in full measure. We shall also teach them the knowledge of mankind.

During the first nine years, we shall command the environment entirely. We shall write the books they read, and shape the history and circumstances they require. Only then, will we begin to relate the children to the world as it is.

Does it sound too simple or too presumptuous? It is all we can do, Harry, and I think Professor Goldbaum will understand that full well. It is also more than has ever been done for children before.

So good luck to both of you. Your letters sound as if you are changing, Harry—and we feel a curious process of change within us. When I put down what we are doing, it seems almost too obvious to be meaningful. We are simply taking a group of very gifted children and giving them knowledge and love. Is this enough to break through to that part of man which is unused and unknown? Well, we shall see. Bring us the children, Harry, and we shall see.

With love,
Jean

In the early spring of 1965, Harry Felton arrived in Washington and went directly to the White House. Felton had just turned fifty; he was a tall and pleasant-looking man, rather lean, with graying hair. As President of the Board of Shipways, Inc.—one of the largest import and export houses in America—he commanded a certain amount of deference and respect from Eggerton, who was then Secretary of Defense. In any case, Eggerton, who was nobody's fool, did not make the mistake of trying to intimidate Felton.

Instead, he greeted him pleasantly; and the two of them, with no others present, sat down in a small room in the White House, drank each other's good health, and talked about things.

Eggerton proposed that Felton might know why he had been asked to Washington.

"I can't say that I do know," Felton said.

"You have a remarkable sister."

"I have been aware of that for a long time," Felton smiled.

"You are also very close-mouthed, Mr. Felton," the Secretary observed. "So far as we know, not even your immediate family has ever heard of man-plus. That's a commendable trait."

"Possibly and possibly not. It's been a long time."

"Has it? Then you haven't heard from your sister lately?"

"Almost a year," Felton answered.

"It didn't alarm you?"

"Should it? No, it didn't alarm me. My sister and I are very close, but this project of hers is not the sort of thing that allows for social relations. There have been long periods before when I have not heard from her. We are poor letter writers."

"I see," nodded Eggerton.

"I am to conclude that she is the reason for my visit here?"

"Yes."

"She's well?"

"As far as we know," Eggerton said quietly.

"Then what can I do for you?"

"Help us, if you will," Eggerton said, just as quietly. "I am going to tell you what has happened, Mr. Felton, and then perhaps you can help us."

"Perhaps," Felton agreed.

"About the project, you know as much as any of us; more, perhaps, since you were in at the inception. So you realize that such a project must be taken very seriously or laughed off entirely. To date, it has cost the government eleven million dollars, and that is not something you laugh off. Now you understand that the unique part of this project was its exclusiveness. That word is used advisedly and specifically. Its success depended upon the creation of a unique and exclusive environment, and in terms of that environment, we agreed not to send any observers into the reservation for a period of fifteen years. Of course, during those fifteen years, there have been many conferences with Mr. and Mrs. Arbalaid and with certain of their associates, including Dr. Goldbaum.

"But out of these conferences, there was no progress report that dealt with anything more than general progress. We were given to understand that the results were rewarding and exciting, but very little more. We honored our part of the agreement, and at the end of the fifteen-year period, we told your sister and her husband that we would have to send in a team of observers. They pleaded for an extension of time—maintaining that it was critical to the success of the entire program—and they pleaded persuasively enough to win a three-year extension. Some months ago, the three-year period was over. Mrs. Arbalaid came to Washington and begged a further extension. When we refused, she agreed that our team could come into the reservation in ten days. Then she returned to California."

Eggerton paused and looked at Felton searchingly.

"And what did you find?" Felton asked.

"You don't know?"

"I'm afraid not."

"Well—" the Secretary said slowly, "I feel like a damn fool when I think of this, and also a little afraid. When I say it, the fool end predominates. We went there and we found nothing."

"Oh?"

"You don't appear too surprised, Mr. Felton?"

"Nothing my sister does has ever really surprised me. You mean the reservation was empty—no sign of anything?"

"I don't mean that, Mr. Felton. I wish I did mean that. I wish it was so pleasantly human and down to earth. I wish we thought that your sister and her husband were two clever and unscrupulous swindlers who had taken the government for eleven million. That would warm the cockles of our hearts compared to what we do have. You see, we don't know whether the reservation is empty or not, Mr. Felton, because the reservation is not there."

"What?"

"Precisely. The reservation is not there."

"Come now," Felton smiled. "My sister is a remarkable woman, but she doesn't make off with eight thousand acres of land. It isn't like her."

"I don't find your humor entertaining, Mr. Felton."

"No. No, of course not. I'm sorry. Only when a thing makes no sense at all—how could an eight-thousand-acre stretch of land not be where it was? Doesn't it leave a large hole?"

"If the newspapers get hold of it, they could do even better than that, Mr. Felton."

"Why not explain," Felton said.

"Let me try to—not to explain but to describe. This stretch of land is in the Fulton National Forest, rolling country, some hills, a good stand of redwood—a kidney-shaped area. It was wire-fenced, with army guards at every approach. I went there with our inspection team, General Meyers, two army physicians, Gorman, the psychiatrist, Senator Totenwell of the Armed Services Committee, and Lydia Gentry, the educator. We crossed the country by plane and drove the final sixty miles to the reservation in two government cars. A dirt road leads into it. The guard on this road halted us. The reservation was directly before us. As the guard approached the first car, the reservation disappeared."

"Just like that?" Felton whispered. "No noise—no explosion?"

"No noise, no explosion. One moment, a forest of redwoods in front of us—then a gray area of nothing."

"Nothing? That's just a word. Did you try to go in?"

"Yes—we tried. The best scientists in America have tried. I myself am not a very brave man, Mr. Felton, but I got up enough courage to walk up to this gray edge and touch it. It was very cold and very hard —so cold that it blistered these three fingers."

He held out his hand for Felton to see.

"I became afraid then. I have not stopped being afraid." Felton nodded. "Fear—such fear," Eggerton sighed.

"I need not ask you if you tried this or that?"

"We tried everything, Mr. Felton, even—I am ashamed to say—a very small atomic bomb. We tried the sensible things and the foolish things. We went into panic and out of panic, and we tried everything."

"Yet you've kept it secret?"

"So far, Mr. Felton."

"Airplanes?"

"You see nothing from above. It looks like mist lying in the valley."

"What do your people think it is?"

Eggerton smiled and shook his head. "They don't know. There you are. At first, some of them thought it was some kind of force field. But the mathematics won't work, and of course it's cold. Terribly cold. I am mumbling. I am not a scientist and not a mathematician, but they also mumble, Mr. Felton. I am tired of that kind of thing. That is why I asked you to come to Washington and talk with us. I thought you might know."

"I might," Felton nodded.

For the first time, Eggerton became alive, excited, impatient. He mixed Felton another drink. Then he leaned forward eagerly and waited. Felton took a letter out of his pocket.

"This came from my sister," he said.

"You told me you had no letter from her in almost a year!"

"I've had this almost a year," Felton replied, a note of sadness in his voice. "I haven't opened it. She enclosed this sealed envelope with a short letter, which only said that she was well and quite happy, and that I was to open and read the other letter when it was absolutely necessary to do so. My sister is like that; we think the same way. Now, I suppose it's necessary, don't you?"

The Secretary nodded slowly but said nothing. Felton opened the letter and began to read aloud.

June 12, 1964

My dear Harry:

As I write this, it is twenty-two years since I have seen you or spoken to you. How very long for two people who have such love and regard for each other as we do! And now that you have found it necessary to open this letter and read it, we must face the fact that in all probability we will never see each other again. I hear that you have a wife and three children—all wonderful people. I think it is hardest to know that I will not see them or know them.

Only this saddens me. Otherwise, Mark and I are very happy—and I think you will understand why.

About the barrier—which now exists or you would not have opened this letter—tell them that there is no harm to it and no one will be hurt by it. It cannot be broken into because it is a negative power rather than a positive one, an absence instead of a presence. I will have more to say about it later, but possibly explain it no better. Some of the children could likely put it into intelligible words, but I want this to be my report, not theirs.

Strange that I still call them children and think of them as children —when in all fact we are the children and they are adults. But they still have the quality of children that we know best, the strange innocence and purity that vanishes so quickly in the outside world.

And now I must tell you what came of our experiment—or some of it. Some of it, for how could I ever put down the story of the strangest two decades that men ever lived through? It is all incredible and it is all commonplace. We took a group of wonderful children, and we gave them an abundance of love, security and truth—but I think it was the factor of love that mattered most. During the first year, we weeded out each couple that showed less than a desire to love these children. They were easy to love. And as the years passed, they became our children—in every way. The children who were born to the couples in residence here simply joined the group. No one had *a father* or *a mother;* we were a living functioning group in which all men were the fathers of all children and all women the mothers of all children.

No, this was not easy, Harry—among ourselves, the adults, we had to fight and work and examine and turn ourselves inside out again and again, and tear our guts and hearts out, so that we could present an environment that had never been before, a quality of sanity and truth and security that exists nowhere else in all this world.

How shall I tell you of an American Indian boy, five years old, composing a splendid symphony? Or of the two children, one Bantu, one Italian, one a boy, one a girl, who at the age of six built a machine to measure the speed of light? Will you believe that we, the adults, sat quietly and listened to these six-year-olds explain to us that since the speed of light is a constant everywhere, regardless of the motion of material bodies, the distance between the stars cannot be mentioned in terms of light, since that is not distance on our plane of being? Then believe also that I put it poorly. In all of these matters, I have the sensations of an uneducated immigrant whose child is exposed to all the wonders of school and knowledge. I understand a little, but very little.

If I were to repeat instance after instance, wonder after wonder—at the age of six and seven and eight and nine, would you think of the poor, tortured, nervous creatures whose parents boast that they have an IQ of 160, and in the same breath bemoan the fate that did not give them normal children? Well, ours were and are *normal* children. Perhaps the first normal children this world has seen in a long time. If you heard them laugh or sing only once, you would know that. If you could see how tall and strong they are, how fine of body and movement. They have a quality that I have never seen in children before.

Yes, I suppose, dear Harry, that much about them would shock you. Most of the time, they wear no clothes. Sex has always been a joy and a good thing to them, and they face it and enjoy it as naturally as we eat and drink—more naturally, for we have no gluttons in sex or food, no ulcers of the belly or the soul. They kiss and caress each other and do many other things that the world has specified as shocking, nasty, etc.—but whatever they do, they do with grace and joy. Is all this possible? I tell you that it has been my life for almost twenty years now. I live with boys and girls who are without evil or sickness, who are like pagans or gods—however you would look at it.

But the story of the children and of their day-to-day life is one that will be told properly and in its own time and place. All the indications I have put down here add up only to great gifts and abilities. Mark and I never had any doubts about these results; we knew that if we controlled an environment that was predicated on the future, the children would learn more than any children do on the outside. In their seventh year of life they were dealing easily and naturally with scientific problems normally taught on the college level, or higher, outside. This was to be expected, and we would have been very disappointed if something of this sort had not developed. But it was the unexpected that we hoped for and watched for—the flowering of the mind of man that is blocked in every single human being on the outside.

And it came. Originally, it began with a Chinese child in the fifth year of our work. The second was an American child, then a Burmese. Most strangely, it was not thought of as anything very unusual, nor did we realize what was happening until the seventh year, when there were already five of them.

Mark and I were taking a walk that day—I remember it so well, lovely, cool and clear California day—when we came on a group of children in a meadow. There were about a dozen children there. Five of them sat in a little circle, with a sixth in the center of the circle. Their heads were almost touching. They were full of little giggles, ripples of mirth and satisfaction. The rest of the children sat in a group about ten feet away—watching intently.

As we came to the scene, the children in the second group put their fingers to their lips, indicating that we should be quiet. So we stood and watched without speaking. After we were there about ten minutes, the little girl in the center of the circle of five, leaped to her feet, crying ecstatically.

"I heard you! I heard you! I heard you!"

There was a kind of achievement and delight in her voice that we had not heard before, not even from our children. Then all of the children there rushed together to kiss her and embrace her, and they did a sort of dance of play and delight around her. All this we watched with no indication of surprise or even very great curiosity. For even though this was the first time anything like this—beyond our guesses or comprehension—had ever happened, we had worked out our own reaction to it.

When the children rushed to us for our congratulations, we nodded and smiled and agreed that it was all very wonderful. "Now, it's my turn, mother," a Senegalese boy told me. "I can almost do it already. Now there are six to help me, and it will be easier."

"Aren't you proud of us?" another cried.

We agreed that we were very proud, and we skirted the rest of the questions. Then, at our staff meeting that evening, Mark described what had happened.

"I noticed that last week," Mary Hengel, our semantics teacher nodded. "I watched them, but they didn't see me."

"How many were there?" Professor Goldbaum asked intently.

"Three. A fourth in the center—their heads together. I thought it was one of their games and I walked away."

"They make no secret of it," someone observed.

"Yes," I said, "they took it for granted that we knew what they were doing."

"No one spoke," Mark said. "I can vouch for that."

"Yet they were listening," I said. "They giggled and laughed as if some great joke was taking place—or the way children laugh about a game that delights them."

It was Dr. Goldbaum who put his finger on it. He said, very gravely, "Do you know, Jean—you always said that we might open that great area of the mind that is closed and blocked in us. I think that they have opened it. I think they are teaching and learning to listen to thoughts."

There was a silence after that, and then Atwater, one of our psychologists, said uneasily, "I don't think I believe it. I've investigated every test and report on telepathy ever published in this country—the Duke stuff and all the rest of it. We know how tiny and feeble brain waves are—it is fantastic to imagine that they can be a means of communication."

"There is also a statistical factor," Rhoda Lannon, a mathematician, observed. "If this faculty existed even as a potential in mankind, is it conceivable that there would be no recorded instance of it?"

"Maybe it has been recorded," said Fleming, one of our historians. "Can you take all the whippings, burnings and hangings of history and determine which were telepaths?"

"I think I agree with Dr. Goldbaum," Mark said. "The children are becoming telepaths. I am not moved by a historical argument, or by a statistical argument, because our obsession here is environment. There is no record in history of a similar group of unusual children being raised in such an environment. Also, this may be—and probably is—a faculty which must be released in childhood or remain permanently blocked. I believe Dr. Haenigson will bear me out when I say that mental blocks imposed during childhood are not uncommon."

"More than that." Dr. Haenigson, our chief psychiatrist, nodded. "No child in our society escapes the need to erect some mental block in his mind. Whole areas of every human being's mind are blocked in early childhood. This is an absolute of human society."

Dr. Goldbaum was looking at us strangely. I was going to say something—but I stopped. I waited and Dr. Goldbaum said:

"I wonder whether we have begun to realize what we may have done. What is a human being? He is the sum of his memories, which are locked in his brain, and every moment of experience simply builds up the structure of those memories. We don't know as yet what is the extent or power of the gift these children of ours appear to be developing, but suppose they reach a point where they can share the totality of memory? Is it not simply that among themselves there can be no lies, no deceit, no rationalization, no secrets, no guilts—it is more than that."

Then he looked from face to face, around the whole circle of our staff. We were beginning to comprehend him. I remember my own reactions at that moment, a sense of wonder and discovery and joy and heartbreak too; a feeling so poignant that it brought tears to my eyes.

"You know, I see," Dr. Goldbaum nodded. "Perhaps it would be best for me to speak about it. I am much older than any of you—and I have been through, lived through the worst years of horror and bestiality that mankind ever knew. When I saw what I saw, I asked myself a thousand times: What is the meaning of mankind—if it has any meaning at all, if it is not simply a haphazard accident, an unusual complexity of molecular structure? I know you have all asked yourselves the same thing. Who are we? What are we destined for? What is our purpose? Where is sanity or reason in these bits of struggling, clawing, sick flesh? We kill, we torture, we hurt and destroy as no other species does. We ennoble murder and falsehood and hypocrisy and superstition; we destroy our own bodies with drugs and poisonous food; we deceive ourselves as well as others—and we hate and hate and hate.

"Now something has happened. If these children can go into each other's minds completely—then they will have a single memory, which is the memory of all of them. All experience will be common to all of them, all knowledge, all dreams—and they will be immortal. For as one dies, another child is linked to the whole, and another and another. Death will lose all meaning, all of its dark horror. Mankind will begin, here in this place, to fulfill a part of its intended destiny—to become a single, wonderful unit, a whole—almost in the old words of your poet, John Donne, who sensed what we have all sensed at one time, that no man is an island unto himself. Has any thoughtful man lived without having a sense of that singleness of mankind? I don't think so. We have been living in darkness, in the night, struggling each of us with his own poor brain and then dying with all the memories of a lifetime. It is no wonder that we have achieved so little. The wonder is that we have achieved so much. Yet all that we know, all that we have done will be nothing compared to what these children will know and do and create—"

So the old man spelled it out, Harry—and saw almost all of it from the beginning. That was the beginning. Within the next twelve months, each one of our children was linked to all of the others telepathically. And in the years that followed, every child born in our reservation was shown the way into that linkage by the children. Only we, the adults, were forever barred from joining it. We were of the old, they of the new; their way was closed to us forever—although they could go into our minds, and did. But never could we feel them there or see them there, as they did each other.

I don't know how to tell you of the years that followed, Harry. In our little, guarded reservation, man became what he was always destined to be, but I can explain it only imperfectly. I can hardly comprehend, much less explain, what it means to inhabit forty bodies simultaneously, or what it means to each of the children to have the other personalities within them, a part of them—what it means to live as man and woman always and together. Could the children explain it to us? Hardly, for this is a transformation that must take place, from all we can learn, before puberty—and as it happens, the children accept it as normal and natural—indeed as the most natural thing in the world. We were the unnatural ones—and one thing they never truly comprehended is how we could bear to live in our aloneness, how we could bear to live with the knowledge of death as extinction.

We are happy that this knowledge of us did not come at once. In the beginning, the children could merge their thoughts only when their heads were almost touching. Bit by bit, their command of distance grew—but not until they were in their fifteenth year did they have the power to reach out and probe with their thoughts anywhere on earth. We thank God for this. By then the children were ready for what they found. Earlier, it might have destroyed them.

I must mention that two of our children met accidental death—in the ninth and the eleventh year. But it made no difference to the others, a little regret, but no grief, no sense of great loss, no tears or weeping. Death is totally different to them than to us; a loss of flesh; the personality itself is immortal and lives consciously in the others. When we spoke of a marked grave or a tombstone, they smiled and said that we could make it if it would give us any comfort. Yet later, when Dr. Goldbaum died, their grief was deep and terrible, for his was the old kind of death.

Outwardly, they remained individuals—each with his or her own set of characteristics, mannerisms, personality. The boys and the girls make love in a normal sexual manner—though all of them share the experience. Can you comprehend that? I cannot—but for them everything is different. Only the unspoiled devotion of mother for helpless child can approximate the love that binds them together—yet here it is also different, deeper even than that.

Before the transformation took place, there was sufficient of children's petulance and anger and annoyance—but after it took place, we never again heard a voice raised in anger or annoyance. As they themselves put it, when there was trouble among them, they washed it out

—when there was sickness, they healed it; and after the ninth year, there was no more sickness—even three or four of them, when they merged their minds, could go into a body and cure it.

I use these words and phrases because I have no others, but they don't describe. Even after all these years of living with the children, day and night, I can only vaguely comprehend the manner of their existence. What they are outwardly, I know, free and healthy and happy as no men were before, but what their inner life is remains beyond me.

I spoke to one of them about it once, Arlene, a tall, lovely child whom we found in an orphanage in Idaho. She was fourteen then. We were discussing personality, and I told her that I could not understand how she could live and work as an individual, when she was also a part of so many others, and they were a part of her.

"But I remain myself, Jean. I could not stop being myself."

"But aren't the others also yourself?"

"Yes. But I am also them."

"But who controls your body?"

"I do. Of course."

"But if they should want to control it instead of you?"

"Why?"

"If you did something they disapproved of," I said lamely.

"How could I?" she asked. "Can you do something you disapprove of?"

"I am afraid I can. And do."

"I don't understand. Then why do you do it?"

So these discussions always ended. We, the adults, had only words for communication. By their tenth year, the children had developed methods of communication as far beyond words as words are beyond the dumb motions of animals. If one of them watched something, there was no necessity for it to be described; the others could see it through his eyes. Even in sleep, they dreamed together.

I could go on for hours attempting to describe something utterly beyond my understanding, but that would not help, would it, Harry? You will have your own problems, and I must try to make you understand what happened, what had to happen. You see, by the tenth year, the children had learned all we knew, all we had among us as material for teaching. In effect, we were teaching a single mind, a mind composed of the unblocked, unfettered talent of forty superb children; a mind so rational and pure and agile that to them we could only be objects of loving pity.

We have among us Axel Cromwell, whose name you will recognize. He is one of the greatest physicists on earth, and it was he who was mainly responsible for the first atom bomb. After that, he came to us as one would go into a monastery—an act of personal expiation. He and his wife taught the children physics, but by the eighth year, the children were teaching Cromwell. A year later, Cromwell could follow neither their mathematics nor their reasoning; and their symbolism, of course, was out of the structure of their own thoughts.

Let me give you an example. In the far outfield of our baseball diamond, there was a boulder of perhaps ten tons. (I must remark that the athletic skill, the physical reactions of the children, was in its own way almost as extraordinary as their mental powers. They have broken every track and field record in existence—often cutting world records by one-third. I have watched them run down our horses. Their movements can be so quick as to make us appear sluggards by comparison. And they love baseball—among other games.)

We had spoken of either blasting the boulder apart or rolling it out of the way with one of our heavy bulldozers, but it was something we had never gotten to. Then, one day, we discovered that the boulder was gone—in its place a pile of thick red dust that the wind was fast leveling. We asked the children what had happened, and they told us that they had reduced the boulder to dust—as if it was no more than kicking a small stone out of one's path. How? Well, they had loosened the molecular structure and it had become dust. They explained, but we could not understand. They tried to explain to Cromwell how their thoughts could do this, but he could no more comprehend it than the rest of us.

I mention one thing. They built an atomic fusion power plant, out of which we derive an unlimited store of power. They built what they call free fields into all our trucks and cars, so that they rise and travel through the air with the same facility they have on the ground. With the power of thought, they can go into atoms, rearrange electrons, build one element out of another—and all this is elementary to them, as if they were doing tricks to amuse us and amaze us.

So you see something of what the children are, and now I shall tell you what you must know.

In the fifteenth year of the children, our entire staff met with them. There were fifty-two of them now, for all the children born to us were taken into their body of singleness—and flourished in their company, I should add, despite their initially lower IQs. A very formal and serious meeting, for in thirty days the team of observers were scheduled to enter the reservation. Michael, who was born in Italy, spoke for them; they needed only one voice.

He began by telling us how much they loved and cherished us, the adults who were once their teachers. "All that we have, all that we are, you have given us," he said. "You are our fathers and mothers and teachers—and we love you beyond our power to say. For years now, we have wondered at your patience and self-giving, for we have gone into your minds and we know what pain and doubt and fear and confusion you all live with. We have also gone into the minds of the soldiers who guard the reservation. More and more, our power to probe grew—until now there is no mind anywhere on earth that we cannot seek out and read.

"From our seventh year, we knew all the details of this experiment, why we were here and what you were attempting—and from then until now, we have pondered over what our future must be. We have also tried to help you, whom we love so much, and perhaps we have been a little help in easing your discontents, in keeping you as healthy as possible, and in easing your troubled nights in that maze of fear and nightmare that you call sleep.

"We did what we could, but all our efforts to join you with us have failed. Unless that area of the mind is opened before puberty, the tissues change, the brain cells lose all potential of development, and it is closed forever. Of all things, this saddens us most—for you have given us the most precious heritage of mankind, and in return we have given you nothing."

"That isn't so," I said. "You have given us more than we gave you."

"Perhaps," Michael nodded. "You are very good and kind people. But now the fifteen years are over, and the team will be here in thirty days—"

I shook my head. "No. They must be stopped."

"And all of you?" Michael asked, looking from one to another of the adults.

Some of us were weeping. Cromwell said:

"We are your teachers and your fathers and mothers, but you must tell us what to do. You know that."

Michael nodded, and then he told us what they had decided. The reservation must be maintained. I was to go to Washington with Mark and Dr. Goldbaum—and somehow get an extension of time. Then new infants would be brought into the reservation by teams of the children, and educated here.

"But why must they be brought here?" Mark asked. "You can reach them wherever they are—go into their minds, make them a part of you?"

"But they can't reach us," Michael said. "Not for a long time. They would be alone—and their minds would be shattered. What would the people of your world outside do to such children? What happened to people in the past who were possessed of devils, who heard voices? Some became saints, but more were burned at the stake."

"Can't you protect them?" someone asked.

"Some day—yes. Now, no—there are not enough of us. First, we must help move children here, hundreds and hundreds more. Then there must be other places like this one. It will take a long time. The world is a large place and there are a great many children. And we must work carefully. You see, people are so filled with fear—and this would be the worst fear of all. They would go mad with fear and all that they would think of is to kill us."

"And our children could not fight back," Dr. Goldbaum said quietly. "They cannot hurt any human being, much less kill one. Cattle, our old dogs and cats, they are one thing—"

(Here Dr. Goldbaum referred to the fact that we no longer slaughtered our cattle in the old way. We had pet dogs and cats, and when they became very old and sick, the children caused them peacefully to go to sleep—from which they never awakened. Then the children asked us if we might do the same with the cattle we butchered for food.)

"—but not people," Dr. Goldbaum went on. "They cannot hurt people or kill people. We are able to do things that we know are wrong, but that is one power we have that the children lack. They cannot kill and they cannot hurt. Am I right, Michael?"

"Yes—you are right." Michael nodded. "We must do it slowly and patiently—and the world must not know what we are doing until we have taken certain measures. We think we need three years more. Can you get us three years, Jean?"

"I will get it," I said.

"And we need all of you to help us. Of course we will not keep any of you here if you wish to go. But we need you—as we have always needed you. We love you and value you, and we beg you to remain with us . . ."

Do you wonder that we all remained, Harry—that no one of us could leave our children—or will ever leave them, except when death takes us away? There is not so much more that I must tell now.

We got the three years we needed, and as for the gray barrier that surrounds us, the children tell me that it is a simple device indeed. As nearly as I can understand, they altered the time sequence of the entire reservation. Not much—by less than one ten-thousandth of a second. But the result is that your world outside exists this tiny fraction of a second in the future. The same sun shines on us, the same winds blow, and from inside the barrier, we see your world unaltered. But you cannot see us. When you look at us, the present of our existence has not yet come into being—and instead there is nothing, no space, no heat, no light, only the impenetrable wall of nonexistence.

From inside, we can go outside—from the past into the future. I have done this during the moments when we experimented with the barrier. You feel a shudder, a moment of cold—but no more.

There is also a way in which we return, but understandably, I cannot spell it out.

So there is the situation, Harry. We will never see each other again, but I assure you that Mark and I are happier than we have ever been. Man will change, and he will become what he was intended to be, and he will reach out with love and knowledge to all the universes of the firmament. Isn't that what man has always dreamt of, no war or hatred or hunger or sickness or death? We are fortunate to be alive while this is happening, Harry—we should ask no more.

With all my love,

Jean

Felton finished reading, and then there was a long, long silence while the two men looked at each other. Finally, the Secretary spoke:

"You know we shall have to keep knocking at that barrier—trying to find a way to break through?"

"I know."

"It will be easier, now that your sister has explained it."

"I don't think it will be easier," Felton said tiredly. "I do not think that she has explained it."

"Not to you and me, perhaps. But we'll put the eggheads to work on it. They'll figure it out. They always do."

"Perhaps not this time."

"Oh, yes," the Secretary nodded. "You see, we've got to stop it. We can't have this kind of thing—immoral, godless, and a threat to every human being on earth. The kids were right. We would have to kill them, you know. It's a disease. The only way to stop a disease is to kill the bugs that cause it. The only way. I wish there was another way, but there isn't."

3.
SCHOOL AND SOCIETY

Education is simultaneously a social cause and a social effect. It is a cause because education plays an important role in forming the essential characteristics of society. It is an effect because it is a reflection of the basic values and prevailing norms of society. On the one hand, education is a dynamic force, changing and forming institutions. On the other hand, it is passive, mirroring other social forces. Education, in short, acts upon society and at the same time is acted upon by society.

Thus, as a subunit of society, the school is affected by whatever happens in society. But the school itself constitutes a particular kind of social system which affects the terms and conditions of the groups which comprise its subunits such as teachers, students, the school board, experts, lobbying groups (e.g., anti-bussing advocates), administrative staff, and constituency groups (e.g., the PTA and other "community" groups). Together these groups are subunits of the school as a distinctive kind of social system. Figure A attempts to represent this system and its relationship to society as a whole.

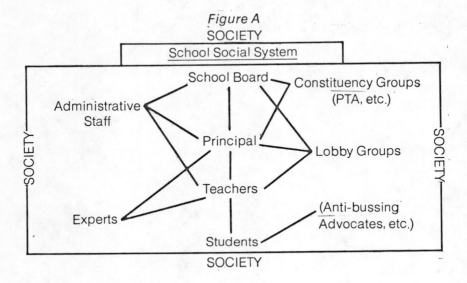

Figure A
SOCIETY

Each of the subunits in the school social system has multiple relationships with every other unit. A simple figure like the one above cannot capture the complexity and richness of these relationships. More importantly, the outcomes of these important relationships enable the school as a social system to perform a number of significant functions affecting not only the school itself but also society as a whole.

The first of these functions is *recruitment.* The school cannot survive as a social system without an adequate means to recruit and select personnel to work effectively within it. Elaborate recruitment and selection mechanisms have been developed, usually on a statewide basis. A second function is *communication.* Participants in the school system must share certain values and meanings in order for the school to achieve its objectives. Internal communication among participants is vital, but external communication with groups outside the school system is equally important. External communication is most frequently aimed at acquiring support and legitimacy for the school from the community at large.

A third function is *normative regulation.* If each member of a school system acted according to his own sense of propriety, the school could not perform effectively. Hence sanctions must be developed for the development of standards for the kind of conduct by which participants are expected to abide.

Just as expectations of common conduct need to be developed, so, too, participants should agree on the general goals of the school system. This *shared-goal orientation* is a fourth function the school system performs. Related to it is a fifth function—*socialization* which refers to all the formal and informal ways by which members of the school system develop attitudes, values, and beliefs from their participation in it. This function has great significance for society as a whole, for through the school system students develop attitudes, values, and beliefs which affect—negatively or positively—their own role in society.

A sixth function is *role allocation.* Within the school system, different roles exist. The role of the student is different from that of the teacher, which is in turn different from that of the principal or the guidance counselor or the clerical staff. The important point is that as the school system becomes more complex and encounters new problems, new roles must be developed in order to cope with such a changing environment. For example, in the past several decades the roles of psychological counselor, vocational adviser, and reading expert have been developed in response to new problems and trends in the larger society. Recently roles for experts on race relations have been developed in response to the challenge and the opportunities of racially integrated schools.

Although roles within the school system are many and diverse, they must be related to each other in such a way that the goals of the school are effectively achieved. The *integration of roles,* therefore, is a seventh important function.

These seven functions may not be exhaustive and they may be stated in different terms, yet the general tasks associated with each are necessary if the school is to survive and act as a social system meeting its overall responsibilities to society as well as to itself. Figure B represents the relationship between decisions taken within the school system about these functions and goals of the school and how they return to affect the school itself.

189

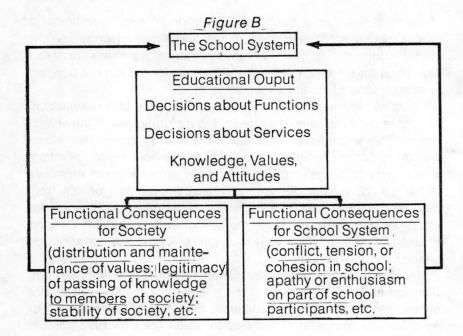

Figure B

The School System

Educational Ouput

Decisions about Functions

Decisions about Services

Knowledge, Values,
and Attitudes

Functional Consequences
for Society

(distribution and mainte-
nance of values; legitimacy
of passing of knowledge
to members of society;
stability of society, etc.

Functional Consequences
for School System

(conflict, tension, or
cohesion in school;
apathy or enthusiasm
on part of school
participants, etc.

A DIFFERENT DRUMMER

Raylyn Moore

Social scientists and educators have long studied the school from the point of view of how it is affected by the social system and culture in which it is embedded. They have also intensely studied the impact of the educational process upon society and culture. These interactions between school and society are perhaps better understood—and perhaps less controversial—than the school as a social system itself.

The school is essentially the product of human biological organisms interacting psychologically, socially, and—some would argue—politically in a complex set of relationships which are given form and meaning not only by the overall culture in which the school exists but also by the very social nature which the school itself acquires. As a social system, the school is, of course, a major agency for socialization. Roles are defined for actors in a school, interactions are defined as permissible and impermissible, and the general "rules of the game" are laid down. These features of a school are certainly affected by the society in which the school exists.

However, the social nature of a school may be specifically designed to be quite independent from the larger social system. For example, many parents in the United States send their children to schools with a noncompetitive atmosphere as a reaction against the general norms associated with competitive American society. Hence, just as one's personality is not simply the product of socialization, so, too, a school is never simply the product of the larger social system.

In "A Different Drummer," Ernestine Coltharp, a "born teacher," sets out to design, maintain, and evaluate a school for children of ages two through five which is extremely distinctive from the overall society in which the children were born. Her utopian construction is predicated upon two simple assumptions: the maximization of personal freedom for the students and no interference from her in its natural evolution. The reader is tempted to describe her school as existing in a "state of nature" in which social interaction, division of labor, leadership, and learning must be evolved *ab initio.* The story underscores the complexity of the social nature of a school. It also emphasizes the difficulty of anticipating adequately the consequences of that social nature.

FOR FURTHER THOUGHT OR DISCUSSION

1. What are the social benefits and costs of competition in a school context? Of a noncompetitive environment?

2. Michelet's "iron law of oligarchy" states that in any organization power and authority will ultimately flow to a few people. How does this story illustrate the "iron law of oligarchy"? Is the "iron law of oligarchy" a necessary condition for establishing optimum learning conditions in a school? How else can social order which is conducive to learning be maintained?

3. What is the reason for Ernestine Coltharp's insistence on a "naturally evolved democracy" as a foundation for her school?

4. What does the story imply about the relationship between Ernestine Coltharp's socialization and her conceptualization and implementation of the school?

A DIFFERENT DRUMMER   *Raylyn Moore*

My name is Ernestine Coltharp. I am a teacher. Please don't make the mistake of reading into this announcement some hint of apology or self-effacement, for I am not just any teacher but the director of The Coltharp Free Children's Center, of which you may have heard. Not only has it been an enviable financial success—the "free" refers of course not to tuition but to theory—but it has also over the years been the subject of any number of theses and published articles as well as the object of professional visitations by experts from all over the world. All this despite our purposely remote location deep in the motherlode country.

In one important way it is to my advantage to make this statement as brief as possible. However, boredom is also a factor in my present drastic predicament, and when discussing the Free Center I am never bored. I am therefore torn, yet see myself leaning in favor of a certain prolixity. It seems I simply cannot resist including a few details, especially since I may never (it has occurred to me gradually, as the hours pass and the full seriousness of my plight becomes apparent) have another opportunity to express myself. Details such as the secret of my success, for instance.

(It might be argued here by the superficially inclined that "success" has become for me an ironic term in light of what has happened. In the long view, however, I am completely vindicated; my methods of bringing children to their full potential have obviously scored beyond even my own most fanciful projections, as I shall presently show.)

My secret of success, then, has two parts: devotion, and a strong sense of continuity and eclecticism. The question for me is never whether an idea is old or new, but whether or not it works.

The earliest memories I have of myself focus on a jagged, dark-gray sheet of slate some three feet at its largest dimension, culled from the refuse bin of the elementary school where my father was janitor. I stood the slate on our back porch and seated my dolls in front of it, along with any younger or weaker children from the neighborhood whom I could impress into the role of pupils. Tirelessly I chalked letters and figures on the board while enunciating rules and fragments of knowledge. "Ernestine is a natural-born teacher," my parents said proudly. I never doubted it.

Later, faced with the conventional choice between career and a love affair or marriage, I hesitated not an instant. In truth my choice was the more clear-cut for my having long since discovered in my character a strong abhorrence for the notion of any other sentient being penetrating my body and attempting to inhabit it with me. Even temporarily, even momentarily. The prospect of male intrusion was horrendous enough; the idea of being host to an alien parasite in the form of a fetus over a long gestation period was absolutely gruesome. Refusing all proposals and propositions indiscriminately, I clove to my studies and the contemplation of my goal: launching a school of my own as soon as I had completed my master's.

Nor did I waste time worrying over my psyche. Never exactly unsophisticated, I was as an education major extremely well-read in the sciences leading to self-knowledge and was thus aware that my case was not entirely exceptional among the human race. Also, doing my first practice teaching, I discovered quickly enough that my slight aberration did not extend to a distaste for little boys. On the contrary, I frankly preferred them to little girls.

So much for devotion (that is, until a later incident, with which I shall deal in due course). The eclecticism can be far more simply explained. With the single idea in mind that I wanted to take children into my sole care at two years or younger and turn them out at five absolutely free in mind and body, I carefully selected and adapted to my own purposes the very best insights of Anna Freud, Piaget, Dewey, the indomitable *dottoressa,* the Bank Streeters, A. S. Neill, and the rest of them. To this distillation I gradually added my own original observations and conclusions (later collected under the title, *The Coltharp Method Explained,* Middenstead University Press, 1951), which I shall not attempt to go into here except to say that gestalt therapy and transactional analysis have borrowed much from me, and not given me any credit either.

As for my Free Center, like many another worthwhile ambition it was almost stillborn for lack of early support. On emerging from my own schooling, I discovered that sound theories and academic clouds of glory were not enough. In order to found an institution, I had to have instant money in impossibly large amounts for rental of a plant, insurance, equipment, supplies, and so on.

Banks and loan companies were not noticeably eager to help even though I tried strenuously to put across to them the importance of my plans to the educational world. Personally I had neither money nor prospects. I had been a scholarship student all through college. My parents were by now both dead, and in any case had been very poor.

That left Professor Havelock von Glubok, my graduate school adviser, who according to campus rumor had accumulated a competent fortune in the old country by black-market manipulation during the war. As an adviser he had been extremely helpful, always sticking strictly to business during the earlier parts of our many interviews in his stuffy office. The last quarter hour, however, the professor unfailingly reserved for trying to get his hand under my skirt. He had never left off trying, and I had never left off trying to prevent him. At least not until that day I went to him with my financial troubles.

Rheumy eyes above his Franklin spectacles aglint with lust, he said glottally, "Bud, my child, do not speeg of *bor*rowinguh. I vill *giff* you all the money you vand if only—"

Once in Professor von Glubok's bed, I perceived that the impending experience would be even more ghastly than anything I had undergone in fancy. I gritted my teeth and squeezed my eyes shut and at the crunch could not avoid shrieking out, "Don't, don't, Doctor von Glubok!"

"Gall me 'daddy'," he panted, his oily beard thrust painfully against my cringing chest. "Zay, 'Don't, don't, *Dad*dy!'"

Instantly I jerked out of his repulsive clutch and sat up in the welter of sweaty bed linen. "You are profoundly inhibited by an incest fixation, Doctor," I warned gravely. "You should get help."

In answer he belted me across the mouth.

But enough. I include mention of this depressing scene only to show the full extent of my dedication to my cause.

With von Glubok's backing I bought twenty secluded mountainous acres, had the property securely enclosed in ten-foot unclimbable steel-mesh fences to keep meddling civilization at a distance, and built a magnificent schoolhouse designed down to the last detail by myself. The next year I added a dormitory with all furnishings, like those in the school, made to the scale of young children, and separate living quarters with locks on the doors for the director. (Though these separate quarters slightly compromised my ideal of complete freedom of access between director and students at all times, I found I needed privacy after all, especially during the weekend visits of the professor.)

I was paying a high price to start at the top, but my maturity and natural sense of measure saved me from emotional breakdown. And while I never totally adjusted to my former adviser's loathsome attentions, neither did the relationship affect my essential normality. I still preferred little boys to little girls.

Admittedly it may have been only the fact of Kyle's being a little boy which predisposed me to like him on sight that fateful morning this past summer when I hurried down to the main gate in response to the buzzer and found him standing there alone, his parents, or whoever had delivered him, having already departed.

This fact in itself did not surprise me. The matter of a child's having been "dumped" on me like a foundling, that is. The theory of the Free Center, as I may already have implied, rests on the premise that the entire upbringing of the applicant be left entirely to me. The students remain on the premises for three hundred and sixty-five days a year, holidays not excepted. (Every day is a holiday to the children at the Center.) You would be surprised (or maybe if you are a harassed parent yourself you would not) how many concerned and enlightened people are more than willing to turn over their young to me for a matter of three or four formative years.

But to explain specifically about Kyle, some time ago the Center found itself in a financial position to offer a handful of "scholarships" for use by children from economically depressed situations. Kyle was a scholarship child sent to me from the Love and Peace Society, a commune far back in the wilderness of eastern Oregon, technically eligible because the society has no money; its economy requires none.

My heart had leaped when I discovered Kyle's application in the mail. For like the morticians who see the optimum moment for injecting embalming fluid as "just before actual death sets in," we experimental teachers of the very young would, if we could, claim suzerainty at the instant of conception. (Ah, or even the instant before?) The first few years of life spent in the pure, noncompetitive atmosphere of a group of the stature of the Love and Peace Society seemed to me the next best thing. Not that any outsider really knows what goes on in those communities so long and so cleanly detached from the rest of the world. We can assume, however, from available data however slight, that they enjoy standards exceedingly like my own. Personal freedom within an absolute, naturally evolved democracy.

All this background exposition, however, conveys nothing whatever of Kyle's and my first confrontation on the dusty road. We looked each other over in silence, except for a quiet twittering of insects in the roadside weeds and a soft soughing from the nearby pine tops. My impressions were of a slender yet sturdy body, blond hair, features already partially formed at four years (I had his age from the application) into firm brow, straight nose, chin advancing to a slight underbite. Thin brown legs emerged gracefully from clumsily fashioned lederhosen—all clothing in those communes is handmade, much of it from deerskin or rough homespun—and the large eyes were a level crayon-blue.

196

Yet even words of description fail in the face of the blinding instant when our glances locked and I knew sudden love, challenge, joyful suspense. For another part of my brain was already ticking off a valid professional, if intuitive, judgment. This Kyle was a *leader*. The happy fact stood out as clearly as if he'd worn a sign. *Was* there also, in that same split-stroke of time, some augury, some fleet vibration too subtle to be apprehended and even by my own sharply attuned and experienced senses?

But again enough. I must yet learn to ration my words, discipline myself to temper the intense happiness of the recent past to the somberness of the present.

In that first meeting, when we finally began to exchange remarks, Kyle seemed instantly responsive. Hands trembling like those of a virgin in the presence of the man she knows will deflower her (and you will excuse the analogy on grounds of what eventually happened), I relocked the heavy gate and on the way up the hill to the compound of buildings elicited easily from Kyle the information that his application had shown no surname because he had none, that within the Love and Peace Society all adults were considered parents to all children. Kyle even indicated, without the slightest hesitation or show of anxiety, that he had never known exactly who his biological father and mother were, a very advanced concept in itself for a four-year-old.

Group interaction of all sorts excites me; after all, it is a large part of my lifework. Hearing these things about the commune, combined with being so near to Kyle, induced a kind of ecstasy. By the time we had reached the dormitory, where I assigned a space to our new arrival, I had a number of times already caressed him. He seemed neither to welcome nor reject these advances. I, in turn, saw in his seeming indifference evidence of superb adjustment; those children who apparently need no attention from adults are not necessarily unaffectionate themselves, but are simply so accustomed to signs of approval that they take them as their due. My assumption on this score seemed further confirmed when within the first twenty-four hours Kyle had completely come to terms with his new environment. He settled in without a ripple, included and accepted by the group with none of the usual painful preliminaries.

At the time—it was August—the children were harvesting the muscats. But again I see a digression is unavoidable, for clarity's sake and despite the alarming build-up of wordage I may soon regret.

You will notice that nowhere in this account have I mentioned assistants or other adult teachers at the Free Center. This is because there are none. One of the most radically innovative tenets of the

Coltharp Method is a rejection of the canard that it is of some advantage to have preschool-aged children supervised by one adult per ten or twelve pupils. Nonsense, I say. Such heavy overseeing is only a weak admission of incompetence on the part of a teacher. Our quota at the Center is sixty children and we are always filled, with a long waiting list. I alone serve as their adult guide, making use of common sense.

Really contented children help one another, and share willingly in work they themselves see as necessary. It requires a four-year-old intelligence to wash dishes, a three-year-old intelligence to sweep a floor. The only reason children don't usually take the initiative in such chores is that they are not properly motivated in a cooperative setting.

Of course everything must be kept very basic. No frills like plush carpets or decorative breakables. Wholesome, uncomplicated meals of raw vegetables and fruits are prepared by the children themselves. We even raise our own produce, with the students planting seeds and hoeing out weeds, and later reaping legumes, greens, roots, and sprouts in abundance. We keep several goats and a few laying hens, but raise no meat. The more reliable nutritionists have long assured us children require no animal protein except that in milk and eggs, that one of the worst disasters of this century has been the fraud of the high-protein diet. Too much meat causes, rather than prevents, disease.

However, suffice it here to say we are vegetarians, and almost self-sufficient on our twenty acres. The only food products we require to be shipped to the Free Center are graham crackers and bottled juice, and since I order these only once in eighteen or so months, filling the storeroom each time, some of the children even believe there is a work detail somewhere baking the crackers. (This question has come up a few times at our group encounter sessions, which are meetings of the full enrollment for the purpose of answering bull-session type questions, and working out problems before they can arise.)

But back now to Kyle and the muscats. I noticed immediately that our new student, predictably, had already, on his first full day in residence and while working with children as much as a year older than himself, taken over as foreman of one of the picking details. Moreover, he had instituted a more efficient system of putting the grapes directly from the vines into the crates as the children came to the ends of the rows, thus saving both time and the extra handling involved when the fruit had to be removed from the picking baskets.

I made no comment of course. To interfere in any interaction within the group is unthinkable unless real strife is apparent. But neither could I take my eyes from Kyle. My musings, I discovered, had an even more violent quality than on the previous day. Did Kyle love me? Had he ever loved any woman before? One of his surrogate mothers in the commune, perhaps? Inevitably, I had been the object on numerous other occasions of the perfect, pure love of little boys, a love uncomplicated by ugly lust, unsullied by the prospect of venery. Coming from Kyle, if I were so fortunate, I could visualize such a love as the apogee of my career, my *raison d'être*. Would I even be able to let him go from the Center once he reached the age of five?

Dazzled by these ruminations, I had involuntarily wandered very near the arbor where Kyle was at work. Which is how I happened to overhear the word he uttered after idly putting a handful of overripe grapes into his mouth and then suddenly, after making a wry face, spitting them out.

In spite of myself, I experienced real shock at his language. If he had used some other word, *any* other, I would have kept silence, for freedom of expression among my pupils is taken for granted. On the other hand, this particular word had never been spoken at the Free Center. Most of the children didn't even know its meaning. I could not allow even my beloved Kyle to undermine our standards.

"Kyle?" I said, "what did I just hear you say? Would you repeat it please?" Yes, it was in the nature of a reprimand, and in front of his peer group. But I was acting on behalf of the greater good.

He answered agreeably enough. "Certainly, Ernestine. I said, 'These grapes are bad.' "

"Spoiled," I corrected gently. "You meant, 'These grapes are spoiled.' Or overripe, or rotten, if you like. Wherever did you hear that word 'bad'?"

The blue eyes and full mouth smiled easily, almost mockingly. "Maybe I read it in a book."

"Oh?" I said. "Do you read then?"

"Why would I say I did if it weren't so?" he replied logically.

Had I not been already hopelessly enamored, I would have succumbed at that moment. His maturity was enchanting. He spoke exactly like an adult, yet there he stood in that delicious, diminutive, half-formed body of a little boy.

Now, since I suppose I must say this somewhere, perhaps here is as relevant (or irrelevant) a place as any. As can be seen, I was captivated from the start. My thralldom lasted over a period of two full months. This is the only explanation I can offer as to why the question which should have presented itself immediately simply never occurred to me at all: how was it that the Love and Peace Society, in its fifteen or so years of existence, was only now, for the first time, sending out one of its children for instruction at preschool level?

How indeed.

The temptation at this juncture too, after so much verbiage, seems to be to rush headlong, answering this question and all others, while at the same time sliding over my own many failures of intuition. Nevertheless, a full beginning demands a full ending. So I am obliged instead to proceed step by disheartening step with what happened at the Free Center from the day of the muscats onward, providing this narrative with a filling-in and a rounding-out, even at my own great expense.

But make no mistake; for me the two months were very heaven. (I note here that I seem inclined now and then to Wordsworthian turns of phrase, while Swinburnian would be more apropos, as you will see. Still, who can quibble with the expressions of the unconscious?) For one thing, my daydreams were very soon the most *exalté* I'd ever known, consisting of giddy projections into a future in which Kyle would pass the Harvard entrance exams directly from Coltharp, thus achieving a coup unique in the annals of education. Accompanying him east would be—who else? A new kind of crowning for my lifework which seemed increasingly less like a daydream than a plum within easy reach. We would take an apartment together just off campus; I would exclude all newsmen, charlatans, and curiosity-seekers, giving Kyle hours of uninterrupted study time. Our leisure time, however, would be our own.

Meanwhile, what was going on right under my nose at the Free Center was enough in itself to maintain my ecstatic state. For one of my other dreams was already in fruition. In explanation to those who have not read my book, some years ago a D. Ed. dissertation concerned a project conducted at XYZ School in which two-score children, left entirely to their own devices without even a hint of authoritarian regulation from above, drifted naturally into a system of government in which every child had an equal voice in decisions, work was equally divided, and the benignant majority saw to it that the minority were not discriminated against. I myself during my early years of work with children had refined this phenomenon to the nth power, and a vastly improved version of the experiment eventually became part of the Coltharp Method.

On no occasion, however, had I seen the emerging child-society so beautifully operating as it did at the Center after Kyle arrived.

It is my policy, when such projects are running well, not to disturb the mixture, so to speak, by stirring the pot. We all know what happens to the primitive society as soon as the anthropologist appears in its midst, notebook and pen in hand. My custom is therefore to withdraw to my own apartment for an indeterminate period when one of these governments by the children is being set up or is undergoing changes in leadership. However, I always make it clear I am available for consultation if needed. Oddly, however, during this time no child called on me for anything at all.

Here again one may discern the true depth of my temporary madness. For even in the best run child-development centers hardly half an hour can pass without at least one small participant bursting into tears, gagging on a mouthful of finger paint, stuffing play dough up his nose, or having a bathroom accident. Interpersonal conflicts calling for adult intervention also are common. "Come quick. Danny is urinating all over Sally again," is a rallying cry which will be recognized instantly by preschool teachers everywhere.

However, watching from behind a partially drawn shade over my office window, taking my notes on a pad concealed in my lap, I observed the group's behavior carefully on the day following the grape harvest and detected no discord. Most of the sixty children first encircled Kyle, sitting down docilely and making Indian legs while he spoke to them at length. Afterward, the large group divided into work details and trudged off in all directions to take care of the routine chores. It was a creditable beginning, I thought. True, I had not seen any voting going on. Kyle had seemed to appoint the work details arbitrarily, though I may have been wrong, I told myself, since I could not hear their actual words.

On the following days the children seemed so self-contained that I even left off watching and began to catch up on the paper work in my office. Once I heard rhythmic sounds and went to the window to discover a marching band, of all things, had been organized. It seemed at once too sophisticated and too conventional. I had never encouraged military play of any kind. Still, it was hardly such a departure that I felt I should interpose what might conceivably be my own prejudices.

I shall forego the opportunity for more detail here. Anyone further interested in the day-to-day account of this period at the Free Center may eventually be able to read my notes which, scanty as they were on account of my preoccupation, still exist. Probably. At least I have no evidence they have been destroyed.

Having spoken of my great pleasure in the (at least outward) events of the two months, I must add this was not alone because of my relief at having the direction of the Center virtually lifted from my shoulders. No, it was the night visits from Kyle which caused my cup to overflow. Each evening, after the other students had retired—on stricter curfew under Kyle's leadership than any the group had ever set for themselves previously—he would present himself at my apartment.

There was never any formal discussion about these visits. He appeared as a matter of course, beginning the second night of his residency, and naturally I never discouraged him. I would serve mint tea as we sat together in the library reading. Afterward we would have long discussions. Among other things, these talks made me realize how much I had missed adult company—have I said anywhere that Professor von Glubok, who had become essentially my last link with the grown-up world, though a weak enough one, had died a year or so before this?—for Kyle did prove able to offer mature companionship in every important way, just as I had anticipated.

Reading extremely rapidly, he devoured great piles of my books, showing special interest in a collection, kept as a curiosity, of the work of the most antediluvian educators and theorists, both living and dead. "Who is William H. McGuffey?" he might ask. Or, "What about Dr. Max Rafferty?" Then a long, felicitous conversation would ensue. We talked into the night of Mr. Shaw and Bowes School, of flogging at Eton, the McMillan sisters, private governesses and tutors, the blab schools of pioneer times, rote learning, and corporal punishment.

Kyle was particularly enthusiastic over all the various imaginative forms the latter has taken through the history of education, from "sitting on air" in the classrooms of yesteryear, to the force-feeding of vomitus, said to have been in use as a punishment in a private school in California as recently as this decade. In lovingly recounting for Kyle's edification all the outrages teachers have perpetrated on defenseless children since the beginning of records on such things, I spoke so feelingly and articulately on one occasion that I was immensely sorry not to have thought at the time of turning on my tape recorder, as the material would have done excellently for delivery at an NEA convention sometime.

On several other evenings I also tried, though perhaps not wholeheartedly enough, to divert my visitor's attention to something lighter and more in keeping with his real status as a child. I recall recommending, among other things, Lewis Carroll, who, as you may imagine, occupies a warm spot in my own affections, the good reverend's kinkiness for little girls being a condition I am singularly well equipped to understand. Kyle was not the least interested in Alice's tribulations, however.

Sometimes our sessions lasted until midnight, but never beyond. Though I would not under any circumstances have asked Kyle to leave, he was himself very sensible about getting enough sleep against the demands of the coming day. He did not discuss any of the problems he must surely have been meeting during his running of the children's government, and true to my own ideals I did not venture any suggestion, or even bring up the matter.

After Kyle had left for the night, I usually made the rounds of the compound, seeing what maintenance needed doing, what supplies needed restocking. There was surprisingly little action for me to take, even in these small affairs, so efficient were Kyle's work details. It was on one of these night trips, however, that I discovered the thing that had happened in the dollroom.

Here another word of necessary explanation, though this story is by now growing so unwieldy that the very contemplation of the stacked sheets is a physical agony. I do not exaggerate when I say the manuscript already appears to be over a foot thick!

The dollroom, a popular place for unstructured play, is supplied with a number of extremely lifelike dolls arranged in sets of families. In addition to real hair and the skinlike plastic with which they are covered, they have delightfully genuine-looking genitalia. The children endlessly dress and undress these dolls and move them in and out of the split-level, suburban-type dollhouses with two cars and a camper in each garage and a TV aerial on every roof. The nearest things we have to toy weapons at the Free Center are also in this room, a few wooden mallets to be used by the children, if they feel so disposed, on the parent and sibling dolls, which are of necessity practically indestructible.

Imagine my surprise, then, on the evening I walked into the dollroom and found one of the mommie dolls had been destroyed by a knife, or knife-like implement. That is, both breasts had been amputated, and the pudenda mutilated by hacking. A quick search of the room disclosed the telltale instrument jammed into a dollhouse chimney. It was an ordinary table knife from the dining hall, but I could tell from the signs of scarification along its edge that the knife had been honed, and fairly expertly. That presupposed slyness and substantial premeditation on the part of the child involved. Such an incident had never occurred before at the Free Center.

At first I had misgivings, but quickly enough told myself how foolish and unprofessional that attitude was. Just because up to now no child had shown sufficient inventiveness to plan and perform such an act did not mean the act was in itself inappropriate, I reasoned. After all, that was the function of the dolls, to serve as aids in working out hostilities. Some child—and I would never know who, nor would I inquire—had successfully enacted a psychodrama in the dollroom and was no doubt at this very minute sleeping the more restfully for the catharsis he or she had experienced. I decided to think no more about it.

It was the following night that Kyle arrived at my door for his visit looking extremely tired. I said nothing but thought privately, with considerable concern, that he might be falling ill, even though children's ailments are one thing we are spared at the Center because of our organically grown, vegetable diet, as I have already explained.

My visitor offered to pour out our tea, which I had ready, and I was charmed anew at this show of graciousness, since he had taken no initiative about the tea before this.

A brief silence passed, during which Kyle finished with the tea and took down the volume of Nietzsche he had been affecting to read for the past few evenings. At least I was fairly certain this latest reading performance was affectation. No one was more impressed with Kyle's vastly accelerated learning ability than I, but I felt somehow his sudden interest in archaic philosophy was a posture, perhaps a lover's ploy to impress me or, knowing Kyle, to tease. (Alas, I still thought in these terms.) So I decided on the instant to chide him, if only to see what would develop.

I took a bracing draught of tea and said, "Oh, Kyle, surely you're not really going to go on with that impossible stuff again tonight?"

He looked at me thoughtfully above the book. "Oh? And what should I read, Ernestine?" Carelessly he closed the Nietzsche and tossed it with a plop onto the floor. He stood with grimy shoes on my sofa to flip down one of the old readers which had so occupied him some weeks earlier. A valuable second-edition Ray's Arithmetic was loosened from the row and crashed to the floor also, taking Kyle's untouched cup of tea with it. I winced but again held my tongue.

Kyle ignored the accident and opened the reader at random. "Is this so much better then? 'The oldest was a bad boy, always in trouble himself and trying to get others into trouble.'" He leafed over a page and read, "'George had a whipping for his folly, as he ought to have had.'"

I presumed this was my guest's way of making an overture to one of our dialogues on the evolution of education methods, but no sooner had I begun my careful response than, to my immense joy, I discovered he had leaned his head back against the sofa and immediately fallen asleep.

Though I had prayed for this to happen on Kyle's prior visits, he had never before allowed himself to drowse in my presence. I waited for the slumber to deepen, as it does with young children very quickly, usually in no more than ten minutes. Trembling with anticipation, I laid hasty plans. I would lift him into my bed in the next room, loosen and remove his clothing, and then get in beside him. It would be easily the most thrilling night of my life, a new pinnacle in nonverbal encounter. I had certainly through the years lain down at various times in the cots of little boys in the dormitory, rocked them to sleep, soothed away anxiety, and so on. But this was something else again. I had never had a little boy in my own bed before, nor had I ever felt about any little boy as intensively as I felt about Kyle.

Lovingly I moved him. Tentatively at first. Then I supported his full weight, which is not inconsiderable; he is solid and well muscled. I can only plead that I was out of my mind from the moment I touched his flesh. Perhaps if I hadn't so foolishly left the lamp burning on the dresser? But then an important part of my hoped-for experience was to be the visual element. I wanted to see as well as touch.

Unfortunately he woke prematurely, actually after only about fifteen minutes in bed. He didn't seem surprised to be where he was, only faintly amused. "Well, Ernestine, what now?"

"Do you think, dear," I said, trying to keep my voice from quavering, "that you might be able to bring yourself to call me 'mommie'?"

"What?"

"Only if you *want* to, that is," I choked out. "It would mean a lot to me."

But his attention was now distracted. "Hey, what are *those*, Ernestine?"

Moments before I had impulsively ripped off my dressing gown and was in a state of semi-nakedness. Nearly hysterical with delight at his interest, I was about to explain the function of my breasts when I noted that the crayon-blue gaze was overshooting my body to fasten instead on the far wall of the bedroom. Hanging on that wall was a large assortment of whips, the property of my one-time adviser and late business partner, whose personality disorder had gone far deeper than I suspected when I made my too-hasty analysis during our first roll in the bushes.

There were blacksnakes, cat-o-nine-tails, coach whips, riding crops, flexible-steel lashes, even electric cattle prods and a few branding irons. Having no interest in these implements myself after the passing of my benefactor, I had left them where they were, procrastinating about the day I would get around to packing them away—there had seemed to be no rush, since no one else had visited my bedroom before except von Glubok himself—until the whips had for me taken on the invisibility of the purloined letter.

Now, however, I was terribly chagrined. "Oh, those," I said, striving for a bantering tone but not fooling Kyle, I'm afraid. "Just some souvenirs that once belonged to an old acquaintance of mine."

Slowly Kyle produced his now-familiar smile of worldly comprehension. It had an effect of dissolving even the shattered remnants of my recent joy.

The denouement you must by now have guessed, even though I myself was still unable to predict it at this time. The next morning—or was it two mornings later?—I woke late to the ringing of the telephone at my bedside. It rang once only. Wrong number, I thought sleepily, but I picked it up anyway, fighting off a lethargy which suggested the aftereffects of a strong dose of soporific, though I had taken no pills before retiring. Curiously, the extension in my office had evidently already been picked up and a conversation was going on. Someone speaking in a long-distance voice inquired for me, and the voice next door in my office assured the caller, "Ernestine Coltharp? Yes, this is she."

And it was. The voice was my own, sounding exactly as I do, or as only someone could sound who had over a long period carefully studied and memorized my speech patterns and tonal range. The conversation went on for some minutes, the caller inquiring if an appointment could be made for a group of student teachers to tour the Center, and my voice saying no, it would not be possible, that I was conducting an intricate, long-term experiment in interpersonal relations among very young children and it would preclude all visitations for a period of at least ten months.

I was tempted at several points to interrupt this insane exchange and expose the hoax. Yet my curiosity over what would be said next—more, my admiration for such a work of art as that impersonation—overrode completely my sense of outrage. For I knew who the impersonator must be. Having taken over the children, Kyle must have found it a natural step to enter my office and take it over as well.

As the conversation ended and we all hung up, my eye fell on the far wall of the bedroom where the whips had hung. They were gone.

For lack of space—oh, for a journalist's skill at cutting a whole lifetime down to one narrow paragraph of obituary—I pass over the shock of actually seeing Kyle at my desk, jaw more articulated than ever, blue eyes chill and glittering now, the eyes of a Franco, a Castro, a Che.

The elite corps (I can think of no more accurate term), armed with the whips and honed table silver, arrested me forthwith as a political enemy.

My trial was commendably swift. Kyle was judge and jury. I have been confined ever since in the only other place in the compound with a lock on the door, and that put on by the contractor by mistake: the storeroom. And of course this lock is on the outside.

I shall not starve, nor die of thirst. At least not soon. Before my interest flagged I counted five hundred crates of graham crackers and three hundred cartons of bottled juice.

The court (Kyle) decreed that I was to be taken to the potty three times a day by a whip-and-knife guard and to the shower three times a week. Needless to say, the decree has not been carried out; children are ever forgetful about such matters. However, there happens to be a janitor's closet in the storeroom with running water and a floor-level sink in which to wring out mops. I keep clean as best I can using this facility.

I cannot help worrying from time to time about the effect of the new regime on the children as well as on myself. For I know now how the weepers are controlled, and the spillers at table, and the paint eaters, nose stuffers, and troublemakers of all kinds. Flogging is no doubt one of the milder punishments. I could say, truthfully, that the children are themselves to blame for accepting Kyle so readily, but such criticism applies a thousandfold to myself.

Perhaps I have failed to say that at the encounter sessions where problems are discussed I have often encouraged the children to compose, orally, their life-stories, telling everything they can remember about themselves, using as much free association as they like. And I suppose this custom helped inspire my own sentence, which is a relatively light one. Unless it is changed. (Children are in the end capricious. Who can trust them? I do not for one moment forget what happened to the mommie doll.)

I would have preferred, even welcomed, a sentence calling for flagellation by our Leader. He must apprehend that I yearn even now for some contact with him, however punitive, and purposely stays away. So do they all. I have been alone in this musty, windowless storeroom for seventy-two hours now, which already seem like seventy-two years.

Kyle can no doubt keep stalling people off by telephone indefinitely. How many months before somebody's parents decide finally to storm the barricades and come looking for their little darling? The Love and Peace Society, which, as I think now, expelled Kyle as an incorrigible, a threat to its way of life, can scarcely be expected to come looking for *him*.

But my sentence: I am to write my life-story, in perfect penmanship, using a supply of black crayons and heavy art paper, five thousand times.

At least it is my good fortune never in all these years to have lost my taste for graham crackers.

My name is Ernestine Coltharp. I am a teacher. Please don't make the mistake of reading into this announcement some hint of apology or self-effacement, for I am not just any teacher but . . .

FOUR BRANDS OF IMPOSSIBLE

Norman Kagan

One of the most important functions performed by the educational system is that of *socialization*—a process by which the young learn the culture, values, history, and language of their society. Moreover, the schools change culture by legitimizing *change* in the minds of students. They present culture as a dynamic process, changing continuously.

In addition, the schools show the child a number of alternative social and vocational models. First, they present the student with an image of what a citizen should be—patriotic, honest, and so forth. Second, they convey a sense of what constitutes a good person, largely through the transmission of values. Third, they portray a social role for male and female children to emulate—father, mother, wife, and husband.

In terms of vocational models, most schools offer examples from the full range of professions and occupations. But the educational system goes beyond simply offering a choice of vocations to the student; they actually *teach* the skills necessary to perform a job. The entire economic structure of our society rests on the models and skills presented and taught in our classrooms. But beyond this function, universal public education in the United States has meant the replacement of work. In former years, when only a few received more than a grade school education, the work force included millions of children and young men and women who worked in factories, offices, and on the farm. Universal secondary education resulted in a dramatic age redistribution in the work force and a restructuring of the lives of millions. It meant that a person would spend at least twelve years in school and not enter the labor market until age eighteen or nineteen. With the development and rise of colleges and universities, millions more did not go to work full time until they were in their twenties. Finally, the emphasis on postgraduate education has extended the time spent in school for many people until age twenty-six to thirty. The impact of education on our society from this one development has been great indeed.

In presenting vocational models to students, the schools have placed emphasis on two processes: achievement and competition. In terms of achievement and competition, an underlying assumption, perhaps even a myth, of American education is the belief that all children have an equal opportunity to achieve and compete. This feeling was reinforced by the local nature of most schools—in other words, since the children were all coming from the same socio-economic group, there could not be any question that each of them was beginning from a position of equality.

This naive view, which overlooked the importance of individual and neighborhood differences, surfaced again through efforts to end segregation in schooling. The device of bussing is designed to *equalize* educational achievement by placing disadvantaged youth from minority groups into "better" schools, schools which are supposedly representative of American society. The fact that bussing (and open admissions at the college level) was deemed necessary at all is evidence of the inequality of our educational system.

The fact that many minority students cannot compete successfully with their more fortunate peers has drawn attention to the other major process in the schools—competition. One point should be made clear: aggressive, competitive behavior (especially among males) is learned from a variety of sources, the school being just one. However, there seems little doubt that the classroom, with its examinations, grades, honor rolls, and other rewards, reinforces competitive drives in students.

In "Four Brands of Impossible" we meet Perry Zirkle, a graduate student at a major American university, and a member of that class of Americans known as "the professional student." Author Norman Kagan, a former student at the City College of New York, raises some fundamental issues about the goals of education and the competition which takes place in pursuit of them.

FOR FURTHER THOUGHT OR DISCUSSION

1. What role should competition play in our educational system and does it fulfill this role?

2. What does the term "equality of educational opportunity" mean to you?

3. Is the struggle for economic survival presented in the story accurate in terms of your school?

4. What forms of competition are taking place in your classes?

5. In what ways has universal public education changed our society?

FOUR BRANDS OF IMPOSSIBLE   *Norman Kagan*

"That concludes the Travis-Waldinger Theorem," said Professor Greenfield. "As you can see, it's really quite trivial."

"Then why did it take people to prove it!" piped up one teenage hotshot.

The bell cut off Greenfield's reply, and most of the class bolted. All the mathematics people at my school are bad—Greenfield the geometer was a mild case. His motto was: "if you can visualize it, it isn't geometry!" Which is not so bad compared to my other course, where rule one was: "If it seems to make sense, then it's not mathematical logic!"

Which reminded me I still had to find out about my grade in that subject, along with about aleph-sub-aleph other things—most important of which was securing a nice fat student-trainee job for the summer that was fast approaching. I elbowed my way past a couple of teenage hotshots, and then I was in the open air.

I decided I'd check out my marks later—the IBMed grades would be posted on the "wailing wall" all summer. Right now I'd leg it over to the Multiversity Placement Service. I could study for Greenfield's final this afternoon.

I walked across the campus slowly, checking myself out. "Do not judge according to appearance." Try telling that to some of these megabuck research corporations! I mussed my hair and put three more pencils in my breast pocket, and decided not to wear my glasses at the interview. It's amazing how much easier it is to lie to someone you can't really see.

"Hey, Zirkle—Perry—wait half a me'!"

Harry Mandel hailed me from the psychology library. I grinned and waited for him to join me.

Harry is a swell guy, and besides he's a psychology major, not a math competitor. He joined me, puffing, a moment later. "Summer job hunting?"

"Yeah. I've got a couple of interviews arranged, Serendipity, Inc., and the Virgin Research Corporation."

"Me, too," said Harry. He gestured at my tousled hair. "Getting ready? Physical appearance is very important, you know." The short, pudgy psychology major pumped his legs to keep up with me.

It was a warm, comfortable day on the Multiversity campus. The long rows of wooden chairs were already set up for graduation, and here and there was a girl in long hair and levis, or a bearded boy with a guitar. Early summer session people. Lazy jerks.

"What's the word on the companies?"

Mandel wrinkled up his forehead. "Personnel men—not technical people. So if you've got the grades, go all out—anything to avoid the paper barrier."

"Any specific suggestions?"

"Mmmm—well, Fester pulled a full-scale epileptic fit—but then he's nearly a five point. If you're just bright, a few eccentricities ought to do it. I'm trying my bug-on-the-walls gambit."

"You mean the one where you pretend there's a bug that crawls all over the walls behind the interviewer, and you follow it with your eyes."

"No—that was last year. In this one I sort of scrunch up in the chair, cowering—give 'em the impression I can't stand confined spaces, need lots of room—like, say, New Mexico or Arizona. I'm sick of this east coast weather, and the Virgin Research Corporation has labs in New Mexico."

"That's for me, too. I'll see what I can think up."

In the 1980s, it's practically impossible to get a summer job in the sciences—not that the big science and engineering corporations don't want you, they do. But to apply, you've got to submit about a ton of paperwork—eight commendations, four transcripts, character references, handwriting samples, personality profiles, certificates and forms and diplomas. Who has the energy?

Science and engineering majors, however, have worked out a swell dodge—we just pretend we're a little bit nuts. The big company personnel departments are endlessly amused by the antics of their nutty research wizards. With the squeeze on for technical people, it's easy to fake looniness well enough for the personnel men to see that cause follows from effect, in that wonderful way of theirs, and conclude we're the brilliant boys they're looking for.

Or maybe they just get a kick out of watching us degrade ourselves in front of them.

I had a couple of swell dodges I'd worked out from one of my professors—through the length of the interview I'd keep pulling a piece of chalk from my pocket, sticking it into my mouth, then spitting it out and muttering; "Simply must give up smoking!" For dubious types, I'd offer my *piece de resistance*; all through the talk I would gesture and wave my arms, seeming to shape the very job concept out of the air. Then, when the interview had reached a critical juncture, I'd pause, drop to the floor, and lie on my back staring at the empty spaces I'd been manipulating. As the interviewer came round the desk, I'd cry out in annoyance; "Simply must look at this form a new point of view!" It worked like a charm.

Except for this time. Not that it didn't; I just never got the chance to use it. On this job, all the craziness came at the end.

The interviewer for the Virgin Research Corporation was a big blond crewcut man with terribly stained teeth and a sadist's smile. He reminded me of one of my philosophy professors. He was talking philo at me too, about half a second after I sat down in the little interview cubicle.

"Glad to meet you, Mr. Zirkle—you're a mathematics major, by your application. Is that right?"

I nodded.

"Sit down, sit down," he said, gesturing. "Now, before I begin to ask about you, I'd like to tell you a little about the activities of the

Virgin Research Corporation, Mama, as we call her around the shop. Our organization is concerned with the three aspects of pure research, what we like to call 'The three brands of impossible.'"

I nodded at this. Harry Mandel's eyes had been shining when he'd passed me outside the room, but he hadn't time to whisper more than a fiery "Grab it, fellow!" to me before I was ushered in. I hunched forward and began to listen.

"If we ignore subjective problems—what the Kansas farmer said when he saw his first kangaroo—we might analyze the concept of the impossible as follows:"

He pulled out a diagram, and his finger danced down it as he continued to speak.

"First, there is the 'technically impossible'—things that are not possible in practice, though there's no real reason why they can't be done. Things like putting the toothpaste back in the toothpaste tube, or sending an astronaut to Saturn—such things aren't practical at the moment, I think!" he said, smiling briefly.

"Then there is the notion of the 'scientifically impossible'—traveling faster than light, or building a perpetual motion machine. These are not possible at all—within the limitations of what we know about the universe. But you'll recall, a heavier-than-air flying machine was a 'scientific impossibility' a century ago.

"These two categories have merged somewhat in the twentieth century, though the distinction is clear enough. In the first case, the 'technically impossible', theory allows you to do the impossible—you just haven't the techniques. In the second instance, the 'scientifically impossible', you've got no *theoretical* justification for what you want to do. But in both cases, men have 'done the impossible'—either developed new techniques or found the flaws and limitations in the theories.

"But there is a third category of the impossible, one ignored by even the most farsighted researchers—the 'logically impossible'!" The interviewer's voice rose in triumph, and his other hand, which had remained in his pocket, furiously jangled his change.

I blinked at him. "But the logically impossible is—"

"I know, I know, I've listened to that stuff from our professional consultants," said the big blond man, suddenly impatient. "The logically impossible is part of an arbitrary system which would be destroyed by any attempt to—" he shrugged his shoulders in annoyance.

"Let me tell you," he cried, "that the Virgin Research Corporation has investigated the problem and decided otherwise. Our experts have —and they are some of the best men in the field, much better than any jerky Ivy League Multiversity can afford—our experts are convinced that such notions as the "round-square" are meaningful, and what's more, are of potentially great military value!"

His eyes were crazed. " 'When the battle's lost and won', indeed," he murmured in a low, sinister voice. He smiled at me coldly, and the rotten stains on his teeth stood out like the craters of the moon.

"We're using a two-pronged approach—psychology and mathematical logic. We've had no trouble recruiting psychology majors," he continued in a normal tone, "but most of the students in the mathematics department weren't interested—or they've got to spend the summer with their families at home or away."

It was my turn to grin. That's what they got for trying to interest any of the teenage hotshots. But I wasn't afraid to broaden my mental horizons, I was willing to wrestle with the impossible, I was brave enough to face the unknown. My smile widened, and then my face grew serious as I took up the challenge.

"How much?"

"Two fifty a week, recommendations, room and board and a motor scooter, and free transportation in a G.E.M. cruiser to and from the New Mexico labs," said the blond man.

"Well—"

"With your record, you should jump at the chance," he said. "I've seen your transcripts, son." He began jangling his change again.

That "son" decided me. "Hmmmm—"

"All right, all right, we'll talk it over," he said, a little sharply. In science and mathematics, all the old guys are scared of all the young guys. You do your best work when you are young, and everyone's scared of being "burned out at thirty." Just like I'd love to line my teenage competitors up against a wall and plug 'em, I could see he was scared of me.

He pulled out my preliminary transcripts and applications, and began thumbing them. I slipped off my glasses, and licked my lips.

Later I found out I got A-minus on the mathematical logic final. I should've asked for fifty more than the three-twenty-five I got out of that terrified jerk.

The G.E.M. *Ruby* thundered west, the ground effect keeping it a dozen feet above the earth. The machine soared along, impossibly graceful, as night mastered day on the American Great Plains.

I peered out the big picture window, fully relaxed for the first time in many weeks. The orientation and information kit lay ignored across my knees. I'd look at it later. No more lab reports, no more little phrase like: "I'll leave that as an exercise," that meant a dozen hours of skull sweat, no more: "I'm sorry, but some pre-med sliced those pages out of the book you wanted with a razor blade last term." At the moment, I didn't care if the directors of the Virgin Research Corporation had cerebrum, cerebellum and medulla in their brain pans, or scrambled eggs. By Napier's bones, I'd escaped!

Someone was struggling up the aisle against the pressure of the *Ruby*'s acceleration (we'd just pulled out of Ann Arbor). With a gasp he collapsed into the acceleration chair beside me. "Greetings!" I murmured. "You one of mama's boys?" About half the people on the *Ruby* were working for V.R.C. It's only these tremendous mysterious corporations that can afford intercontinental jet flights and G.E.M.s and—and pure mathematicians, thank goodness!

"Hello, yes," said my companion. He was a skinny, baffled-looking fellow about my own age. His very pale face said; "Yourself?"

"Perry Zirkle—I'm in the numbers racket—uh, I'm a pure mathematician."

"Uh, Richard Colby—microminiaturization and electronics—I'm a grad student at Michigan Multi. If you can see it, then it's too big. My motto." Colby's face brightened and he grinned. *His* teeth were okay. "Say, I've got those books—you must be on the logical impossibility research the same as I am—Project Round-Square!"

I nodded and smirked at the books. "I suppose so—though from what I've been taught, I doubt if the project will last very long."

Colby settled himself and relaxed. "How so?" he asked. He didn't look like a monomaniacal studier—just an electron pusher in his twenties. He wasn't one of these kid geniuses, either, and I was rested and relaxed. So naturally, my mouth got the better of me.

"Just on the face of it—," I argued calmly. "Paradoxes and self-contradictions are interesting, and they attract attention to ideas, but by their very nature—" I found myself unable to continue.

"Maybe," Colby said. "But maybe you're just looking at the problem the wrong way—the fellow that interviewed me kept talking about 'thinking in other categories'."

I paused. "Oh, I know what he meant," I said, and laughed. "He was trying to tell you not to argue, not at two-fifty a week."

"Two-twenty-five," he murmured.

The electronics expert hesitated, and then looked at me oddly. "I don't know about you," he muttered, "but I consider it an honor and a pleasure to be able to do some 'pure' research. There's little enough of it in electronics these days—the whole subject has about one real scientist to a hundred engineers." His eyes were hooded. In the dimly lit passenger compartment of the G.E.M., his face was dark and brooding. He licked his lips and went on, talking to himself as much as he was to me.

"It's enough to make you go into industry. Take my own school, the Michigan Multiversity. Did you know we have a top secret Congressional Project to automate the presidency? Fact. The chairman of the Department of Cybernetics told me the system philosophy behind it. "Roosevelt showed that someone could be president as long as he liked. Truman proved that anyone could be president. Eisenhower demonstrated that you don't really need a president. And Kennedy was further proof that it's dangerous to *be* a human president. So we're working out a way to automate the office." He grinned, and I laughed in response.

I reached down into my fagbag and pulled out a bottle. His eyes went wide for a moment, but I passed it to him. He took a slug, and the evening was on its way.

Colby turned out to be all right. I told him Smith's remark about how engineers are sloppy when they call "characteristic values" "eigenvalues", because "eigenvalue" isn't good English. He came back with the one about the sequence that you had to prove converged, but that all the students demonstrated diverged. The Professor's masterful reply was; "It converges *slowly*."

The ground effect machine rushed on through the midwestern night, a foot or two above the earth, supported by a flaring cushion of air. Presently its path curved south. The pilot-driver was steering by radar beacon and navigation satellite, towns and buildings signifying no more than treacherous shoals and reefs to a sailor. The craft was flying over ground that had never, and might now be never, touched by wheels or feet. Over these wastes we plunged southwest.

Dick Colby couldn't hold it very well, or maybe he was tired. In any event the fellow was soon sleeping peacefully beside me. I let him be and stared at the scenery.

These fellows that believe the "pures vs. applieds" battle really amuse me. Actually, science and scientists are just like anything else in this rotten world, just as corrupt. I've heard stories of research men during the great "Space Flight Bubble" that would trade jobs a dozen times in a year, doubling their salary each time. And these stories about advertising men that run off with the best accounts and start their own agencies? Nothing to the technical men that impress the Pentagon and get the generals to finance them in their own electronics company.

Though I don't feel much sympathy for the big firms. Anyone that builds H-bombs and missiles and lets someone else decide what to do with them—people like that deserve everything they get!

What was wrong with me lately? I still loved to work and study, to cram till one, then feel the high tension as the papers were handed out the next day. The gong that announced the start of the test always reminded me of the one on the old TV show, "To Beat the Clock." And there was nothing like the feeling in front of the posted grades, when I saw the shocked faces of the youngsters I'd beaten out. Tough luck, kid! Better switch to art history!

I lit a cigarette and leaned back. Well, right or wrong, this stuff would be fun. Science always is. I love to be totally absorbed in something new and strange. It's so much better than just sitting around doing nothing, or dull routine stuff. Frankly, I don't see how the hundred million unemployed can take it. My mood when I'm idle is usually a murderous rage at the kids who're going to parties and dances and junk like that. Not that that stuff is really *interesting*, like a problem in Greenfield space. But at least it's something, compared to sitting all alone with nothing to think about but myself. Frankly, I love really tough problems, the kind you have to think about *all the time*.

Dawn was peeping up over the horizon. I settled myself in my own acceleration chair, and tried to snatch a little sleep. My own watch said that in a few hours we'd arrive at the immense desert reservation which held the Virgin Research Corporation, summer student trainees for the enigmatic Project Round-Square.

"These are your quarters, Mr. Colby and Mr. Zirkle," said the blond girl. She was worth a second glance, being the possessor of a fine body, though a little bow-legged. ("Pleasure bent," Colby murmured.) Still, a very nice body.

Colby dumped his junk on the bed, and began opening drawers in the dresser and putting it away. I stood still and read the information sheet we'd been given on arrival. It said I had to report at the Computer Center as soon as convenient. I put my own bags in the closet and went.

Outside, the desert sunlight was quite bearable, since it was only a few hours after sunup. I walked across the compound, guided by a map on the fact sheet.

The living quarters were good: simple ranch-style stuff with desks, and bookshelves duplicated in each room. This was no resort, but the place was clean and kept up, without the bleakness of a straight government installation. The labs and auxiliary buildings were spread out over the desert, the whole business enclosed by a security frontier. This made internal security checks unnecessary, and there were none.

People dressed informally: chinos, dungarees, western boots and flannel shirts. A pleasant change after school, where most everyone was formal most of the time—except for the technical students.

Of course they made us pay for it. All the co-eds are hot for someone they can discuss the Great Books with, not some barbarian science or engineering major with a sliderule swinging from his belt. I've seen these Zenish girls, with their long hair and thongs and SANE buttons, wild for motor cyclers and African exchange students. Rotten snobs! Though I've got to admit that some of my friends in the engineering school depend more on force than persuasion for their pleasure. Ha-ha!

The Computer Center was mostly underground, to make temperature regulation easier. These big machines really heat up. I know that back at the Arthur Regleihofp Computing Center, at my own multiversity, they have an enormous air conditioning plant through all the machine rooms, with dozens of recording thermometers. If the temperature in the labs goes above a certain point, the electrical power to the computers is shut off. Otherwise you have something called a computer explosion, which no one at the labs wants to talk about. All I know is that during the summer, the machine rooms are the best place to relax, because they're so cool. And I can always scare the teenage geniuses who run them into letting me rubberneck.

So I reported to the Computer Center, and found my wonderful creative position from which I could challenge the unknown—the programming saddle of an obsolete I.B.M. aleph-sub-zero—a jazzed up Turning Engine. The same noble trade I'd learned six years before, as a youngster in the Science Honors Program at the multiversity.

An International Business Machines aleph-sub-zero tests a mathematical model against reality. The device begins grinding out deductions from the model, and checking them about facts about the phenomenon. If they check out, fine. If not, it begins to blink and tremble in agitation.

This one had a few peculiarities. The "mode" was about ten times as complex as normal, there were fifty more storage units—and the runs averaged less than ten seconds.

By the end of the day, I was bored, frustrated, and very disgusted. I could barely keep from grabbing my teenage assistant by his ankles, swinging him around in a heavy arc, and smashing out his smiling freckled face against the machine's one-to-ones. Rotten teenage com-

219

petitor! Fortunately I ran into Harry Mandel directly afterwards, without having to look him up. At least that was something. One thing led to another, and two hours later, together with Richard Colby, the three of us were exchanging impressions.

"Oh, I suppose it's all I could expect," I told them disgustedly. "They're setting up odd sorts of logical-mathematical models—ones without the law of self contradiction, either A or not-A. Things like that. Then they run them through the aleph-sub-zero as a check. Only—" and I took a deep slug from my glass, "—none of them work."

Harry Mandel bobbled his head up and down enthusiastically, so that it seemed to flicker in the cool dim corner of the White Sands Bar. Harry has this habit of shaking his head in violent agreement, while his eyes grow larger and larger with each sentence you speak. It gives you the funny feeling that every word you say is confirming some incredible theory of his: that you're a Chinese Communist, or a paranoid schizophrenic, or an Arcturian spy. It's really quite frightening until you get used to it.

Also, his lips were trembling and his hands quivering. I knew the signs. Once he started talking, he'd never stop. So I gave the nod to Richie Colby instead.

The electronics expert looked up from his drink. "I don't know," he muttered. "I'm on the psychological-biological end, and so far I can't understand what's going on. They've got me working on topological neuronic maps—mapping the circuits of the brain. But for what, I don't know." He went back to the drink he was nursing.

I took a sip from my Coke. I don't drink more than I have to, and neither do most of my friends. In spite of all this talk about college students boozing it up, I'll be damned if I'll rot my brains, the brains that have to beat out all those teenage hotshots!

The White Sands Bar was a pretty good one, quiet with a kitchen. A while before we'd had a pizza, heavy with cheese and olive oil. It's funny how much time I spend in bars. Our civilization has wonderful extensive facilities for some things, fragmentary ones or none at all for others. It's perfectly clear how to fill out the forms and go to class and take exams and apply and student all the way to a Ph.D.—but how the hell do you have a good time? I heard they had to double the psychiatric service up at M.I.T. Sometimes I have crazy insane dreams of getting out of this whole mess, quitting. But where could I go, what would I do, who would be my friends? *Who would be my friends?* Anyway, bars are all right, and this bar, the White Sands Bar, was a pretty good one.

I took up another drink. Richard Colby was staring dumbly into his. "Okay, Harry," I said.

"To understand my end, you'll need to know what the universe is," said Mandel quickly and incoherently. "People ask, 'Why is the universe the way it is?' And Kant answered them back: 'Because the universe is a tango!'"

"Huh?"

"Don't you know what a tango is?" said Harry quizzically. "Why, even all my buddy-buddy psychology major friends know *that*. You know—like this—" and he moved his hips suggestively. He grabbed up his Sloe Gin and Coke, and finished it off in a single gulp. "Daquiri!" he cried to the waitress. "Like this, boys," he moaned, beginning to sway again.

It took a little while to make our questions clear, but presently Harry was sketching on a napkin with his Mr. Peanut Pen.

"Remember that proof in high school geometry—Tenth Year Mathematics to you, Perry—where you show that a line segment has only one perpendicular bisector. You strike arcs from the endpoints, and draw the line from one intersection to the other. But why should the arcs have any intersection? And why couldn't there be *two* lines that were straight and went through both intersection points? I bet you never thought of that!"

He looked up from his diagram defiantly.

Dick Colby blinked at him, his long face weary.

"I'll *tell* you why!" cried Harry Mandel, downing half his daquiri. He put the glass down and spoke decisively. "Because the universe is a tango—we see it this way because *we have to*—we're built this way. Anything else would be a logical impossibility—a contradiction. We can't experience the world any other way. We see it this way because we're built a certain way, and the universe is built a certain way. Reality is the interaction of the two parts—and the universe is a tango!"

He tossed down the rest of the woman's drink and nodded powerfully. "Any one of my buddy-buddy psychology major friends will tell you that!"

Colby and I nodded agreement. Mandel always was something of a nut. I never trust short guys—their mothers always tell them about Napoleon when they're little, and they always take it the wrong way.

Mandel was still gabbling. "But this doesn't mean we'll always have to look at things this way. We won't have to always think of a round-square as impossible. That's what my part of Project Round-Square is all about, the part with my buddy-buddy psychology major friends. We're going to change the music. We're going to give one partner dancing lessons!"

It was five weeks more before I learned that Mandel had in fact not been kidding around, nor really drunk at all. That was the essence of the psychology half of Project Round-Square. But a lot happened between that first night at the White Sands Bar and then.

For one thing, they closed down the mathematics-logic side of the installation. I had about a week more of that "Start Program!" Zip-pip-pip-pip-pip! "Clang! Clang! Clang! Discrepancy! Discrepancy!" nonsense, then two days of absolutely flawless correlations—as good as any of the test runs between economics and high school math, or advanced calculus and statics and dynamics. Whatever was being sent into the aleph-sub-zero, it was a perfect fit with the real world. The first day I was wildly enthusiastic, the second I was bewildered—maybe they were checking themselves? And the third day, I wasn't given any programs. The head of my section, a young man named Besser, showed up about an hour later and told me we were shutting down. I was to be reassigned.

"But why? The last two runs were perfect!"

"The last runs—" he began, then sighed. He looked more like a truckdriver than a worker with the subtle squiggles of mathematical logic. "The last two runs were exercises in futility. You've had some undergraduate symbolic logic—you must have some idea of what we're trying to do."

I nodded.

"Well, rigorously speaking, the way to eliminate the notion of 'impossible' is to get rid of contradiction—get a sort of logic where you can have a 'round-square', as a legitimate notion. Then you build a language with that logic. Understand me?"

"Uh-huh."

"Now, this seems—ahem, unlikely. If you've ever taken an introductory course in philosophy, there's always a kid who talks about there being 'some crazy kind of logic' where things could be red *and* blue, round *and* square." He shrugged in annoyance. "The professor can usually shut him up, and if he's persistent, embarrass him to death. Those kids are the sort that embarrass pretty easily."

I nodded. This guy knew something of college life.

"So that's what the meta-mathematicians and symbolic logicians upstairs have been working on. You see, while such things are silly to talk about here in the real world, you *can* have a logic without the 'not' operator. Such logics have been set up in the past—but they weren't very interesting, they weren't *rich*, fruitful in new ideas. But anyway, you can make such a thing, you can even build up to a mathematics from it, the way Russell and Whitehead built up numbers from logic in *Principia*. And you use your math to build a logic and a language—to describe the world. No 'not' means no opposites—which seems to mean to contradictions." He wiped his face and tried to look annoyed, but it was difficult. Good old air conditioning.

"Do you see?"

"I think so. Real world again—didn't match up."

"Kee-rect. Your math is no good for the real world. It's just wrong—like trying to navigate an ocean liner with plane geometry. Since the earth is round, it doesn't work out."

I nodded.

"I mean, it's *right*—it's *valid*—it just doesn't describe anything real," he corrected hastily. "Seems as if you *must* have contradiction."

"That's why the runs on the aleph-sub-zero were so short? The computer would spot a contradiction, and start yapping. But how about the last two runs—perfect straight out. What was the matter with them?"

"Oh, those," he groaned. "Those were that jerk Kadison's idea. The exclusion approach."

"Go on."

"Well, you know there's another way to eliminate the notion of a contradiction. By exclusion."

"Elucidate."

"Think of it this way," said Besser. "You understand the notions of tall and short, and you know such things are relative. But if you decide that everyone under twenty feet tall was short—then you couldn't have a contradiction, a notion of 'short-tall'. Everyone would be short, and you'd eliminate one sort of contradiction. 'Tall-short' would mean the same as 'mimsey-short', 'nonsense word-short', or just 'short'. And you keep on going that way. This was Kadison's idea."

"It worked perfectly in the machine."

"Sure it did. And it's also perfectly useless. *All* gradations and comparisons drop out—and brother, you don't know how many there are. You know, most every quality has its opposite in *something* else. Even the notions of matter and empty space. You get nothing left—I mean *nothing*—the problem becomes trivial."

"The universe is an uncle," I said.

"Yeah, except for uncle say any other word. The universe becomes one solid, undescribable lump, with no qualities at all."

Also, Harry Mandel began to crack up. I didn't notice it while I was working—that aleph-sub-zero had some good problems—but when I was unassigned, the only real activity I had was going to the White Sands Bar. It was during the drinking sessions that his madness began to blossom.

Now of course I know all about the science of modern psychology —it's one reason I've remained so balanced and stable. Myself, I'm what is known as a shame personality. It's a matter of personal honor with me that I fight to the limit for the highest grades and the most scholarship. I'll beat 'em all out. That's me.

Dick Colby was clearly a guilt personality. He really believed all that guff about the scientist's worldview, about the search for truth, about following an abstract pattern of behavior. Poor old Dick, he had an abstract moral code too, as I might have expected. Well, he had to follow the rules, and he might get kicked in the belly, but at least he was stable in his sad, picky way.

Now Harry Mandel was a fear personality. He tried to belong to some sort of whole, to link its destiny with his own. A gestalt. You find a lot like that: fraternity boys, soldiers, club members, athletes on a team. And of course the intellectuals—the literary group and Zenish girls and the interdependent independents.

Ain't social psychology great!

Anyway, Mandel's kind of twitch, the fear personality, is okay as long as he really has his buddies and believes it. If he doesn't have them, he wanders around until he can link up with a new bunch. If he doesn't *believe* he has them—look out! A fear personality with doubts about its gestalts, can slide right over into paranoid schizophrenia.

It came out in funny ways, distorted, because Mandel was very intelligent, and the more intelligent, the more little links can begin to snap and break. One night in late August he came up with this:

"I mean, I have nothing against that particular minority group," he said loudly. "It's just that—well, look at it this way. The original members were selected on the basis of crude physical strength—the smart clever ones escaped the slavers. Then they were brought over here, and were slaves for several hundred years. Now it seems to me that if you have slaves, you're going to encourage breeding among the stupid and the strong. You don't want smart quick ones. As a matter of fact, the smart quick ones would try to escape, and would be shot. Or else, if they're clever, slip over the color line and intermarry.

"So you see, you've had forces at work for three hundred years that bred—I mean in terms of human genetics—for less intelligence. You do

224

that for three centuries and it shows—as a matter of fact, it *does* show. In terms of modern science, they might even *be* inferior."

He was crazy, insane. For one thing, three hundred years isn't long enough to matter genetically for humans. For another, "the smart clever ones" *didn't* escape the slavers' round-ups any more than the others did. Maybe if Mandel had been a slave owner he'd have tried to encourage only the stupid to breed, but such eugenically-oriented thinking didn't exist in times past. As for shooting would-be escapees, you don't destroy valuable merchandise like that, you bring it back alive. [Anyway, you don't talk about races, you talk about human beings.] Mandel was rationalizing, justifying immoral attitudes on the basis of a "science" which really doesn't exist. As for "scientific morality," Hell, science and morality are different, and by trying to base one on the other you are setting up for something like Hitler's "final solution."

Yet poor disturbed Mandel had *thought the theory up*. And for an instant, thinking of the exchange students and the Zenish girls back at the multiversity, my own brain had become enflamed. Science, reason, intellect—there are some things you mustn't think about. God help me.

A flash of disgust went through me. I never wanted to do any more calculations. I wanted to lie down with some pretty girl and make love to her and have her soothe me. I was too long alone. Help me! Then I squeezed those thoughts away.

I pushed away the thick silvery tin with the remains of the pizza. Delicious, too. Their cook was improving. Or maybe he could get real Mexican spices, not the stuff I used to settle for in Woolworths.

I looked at Mandel across the table. His face was beginning to cave in a little, and his eyes looked tired. Anyway, we had to talk about something else. I decided to find out some things about my new assignment. And that was thing number three. That afternoon I'd be transferred to the psychology attack team-programming again, the Urbont matrices of neurological maps.

"How's the job, Harry?" I asked him. "How's the dancing lessons coming?"

Mandel looked up. He hadn't mentioned his work in a couple of weeks, not since we'd taken his little lecture on Kant and the tango as a rib.

"What about it?" he asked crisply. "I don't know very much, I just do whatever they tell me."

They—his buddy-buddy psychologist buddies? Mmmmm.

"Well, whatever they've been telling you, they'll soon be telling me," I said, nudging him in the shoulder. "I'll be figuring out your brain maps for you."

"Oh, yeah. They ought to start programming in two weeks, and then installation—"

"Hey, installation? Whooa? What are you talking about?"

Mandel's slumped body seemed to collapse some more. He was so far forward I could hardly see his face. Just a dark form against the well-lit rest of the bar. Cigarette smoke hung in the air, and a dozen technicians were seated on the high stools. Over in another corner, two disgruntled physicians were playing NIM. A couple of the girls from the clerical pool were having heroes and Cokes at another table, blond and brownette in brief desert costumes.

"Sensory enervation," said Mandel in a dead voice. "What else did you think?"

He blinked mildly and slugged down the rest of his Horse's Neck. "Rum and Coke!" he shouted to the barman. "I really hate to drink," he confided sullenly. "But at least I can do it alone, without my psychology major buddy-buddies." Richard Colby gave me a funny look and we both leaned forward and really began to listen.

In the 1950s, the psychologists of McGill University had commenced an interesting sequence of experiments in connection with the U.S. manned space flight program—an early phase of the "Space Flight Bubble". A space traveler confined to his space capsule would be in a state of extreme "sensory deprivation"—with so little to see, hear and feel, the psychologists theorized, the astronaut might go insane. The McGill University experiments were designed to investigate this thesis, and even more extreme cases of sensory deprivation.

The perfection of brain circuit mapping had suggested the obverse experiment to the scientists of Project Round-Square. If sensory deprivation could debase a man, weaken him and drive him out of his mind—why not attempt "sensory enhancement?" Enriching a man's senses by requiring his reticular formations to accept data detected by machines—the total memory storage of a computer, the complete electromagnetic spectrum, the sorting out of patterns and wave forms which was possible to oscilloscopes.

Volunteers weren't too hard to find—the McGill men had found volunteers, promising not much more than money and a chance at madness.

A man's concepts of the world vary according to the data he receives. For thousands of years, men had been building up systems and structures of describing the universe, without trying to improve the methods used to accept the data. Scientific instruments were not enough—could light and color have meaning, be *real*, to a blind man? The scientists of Project Round-Square hoped that the contradictions and impossibilities of Reality might disappear for a man with enhanced senses. The system philosophy was illustrated in the poem, "The Blind Man and the Elephant."

"Could a dolphin discover Relativity?" said Mandel, almost angrily. "Of course not—plenty of brains, just never was even able to sense much beyond the other dolphins. Likewise, there may be enormous fields of knowledge we've never noticed, because of our sensory lacks."

"More than that, it's a *positive* approach!" cried Mandel. "The first in seventy years. Before this, all of psychology was concerned with debasing man, turning him into a super rat, a little black box which was fed a stimulus and kicked back a response. Automations!"

"What about psychoanalysis and the Freudians?"

"Bleugh!" cried Mandel, enervated himself for once. "They're the worst of all. The Id, Ego, and Super-Ego, are just mental mechanisms, things beyond our control, which interact to produce behavior."

It was nice to see Mandel cheerful. There's nothing better for these neurotic types than to let them talk and talk and talk, it helps reassure them. Maybe they think no one will threaten them or kick them in the belly as long as they are blabbing. A false notion produced by too much well-written t.v. drama.

"But still," I said slowly, waggling a finger at him (or was I waggling and the finger standing still? I must drink less.).

"But, Harry," I continued. "All the colors of the rainbow won't alter this picture," and I flipped one of the White Sands Bar's napkins at him. It has a nice colored picture of a Valkyrie missile on it, from the days when White Sands was a proving grounds, before the "Space Flight Bubble" burst.

"Maybe not," he mumbled. "But that's only the neurological part of the idea. We're building compulsions to succeed into it, too. The kids will *have* to work out a world without impossibilities."

"Kids?" asked Colby dimly. "Keep talking, Harry."

Mandel blinked and then continued. A lot of the rest was whined and mumbled, but I thought I got most of it.

The subjects of the brain wiring were youngsters between twelve and sixteen. The psychologists had settled on those as the optimum age limits: young enough to be typified by directness, immediacy, wholeness, spontaneity and integral fantasy. Teenage hotshots, in other

227

words. Old enough to want to make sense of all the data, and young enough so their world view wasn't rigid.

You can look up all the psychology words except the last. "Integral fantasy" was the most important. Studies had shown this quality is most typical of real genius, and the kids had been specially selected for it. What it means is this. Most people have fantasies, but the fantasy is "disassociated"—it is unreal to them, like sex magazines and comic books. Children, especially geniuses, have "integral fantasies"—they get wild complex ideas about the real world. Ordinary people call these "strokes of genius," if they happen to work.

"And what's more," muttered Mandel, head down on the table, "they'll have to make *sense* out of it. They've had hypnosis and drug compulsions to succeed, so their new sensory picture will have to be free of logical contradictions. It'll have to be!"

I was about to ask him how they'd be able to communicate with them after the kids had "made contact"—but before I could, Harry dropped out of the game. He lay unconscious across the table. "Kids!" he murmured, hatefully.

So I was doing mathematics again, setting up Urbont matrices, the curious descendents of time-variable, multi-port switching and communications math. Far more subtle than any of these, however—the Urbont equations didn't analyze radars or satellite radio links, they symbolized the neuron patterns of the human brain.

It was tedious, subtle, absolutely-right-the-first-time work. The basic units are discrete—on-off switching conditions apply, rather than continuity. In other words, there was no margin for error.

I was getting more of those flashings of hatred and self-hatred. In my little air-conditioned cubicle in the Computer Center, I would get daymares where I would be a bug in a compartment of an ice cube tray—so cool and comfortable and . . . dead. Every so often my friends would stop by—Dick Colby, bemused and apologetic; Harry Mandel, confused and sullen.

More than once, I thought of informing the medical staff of Mandel's problems but I was afraid to. In the world of science, each man has a "paper shadow" that follows him around—dossiers, transcripts, evaluations by supervisors. Get something bad in among those papers—instability, erratic work habits, even extravagant praise, and you're in trouble. The big corporations like their scientists *a little* peculiar—just for identification. Anything serious can really ruin a man's career. I thought it might be best for Harry to take his chances—when I thought about him at all. I tried to stay away from emotional subjects.

Fortunately, about this time, the Virgin Research Corporation brought in some new entertainment, so I could relax without raising the alcohol content of my blood.

These were the moebius movies, the new cyclic films. I'd seen the first one, *The Endless War*, previewed in New York City, a few years before. Since then, their sophistication had increased manyfold.

The basic notion was simple. The films were written in such a way that there was no beginning and no end. But this was more than a simple splicing of the two ends. Literally, it was nearly impossible to know where the story commenced. In "The Endless War," there were at least a dozen places where you could enter, stay the two hours, and leave, coming away with the impression of a complete drama. In fact, depending on where you came in, the film might have been a comedy, a tragedy, a documentary or most anything else.

"To the Nth Generation" (or "Incest on It!") was a typical improvement. It dealt with the romantic affairs of several families over (I think) three generations. After forty years, with the amatory relations of the members incredibly tangled, the snarl was twisted back on itself as the original characters were brought forth in and out of wedlock. It was pretty ghastly in a way, but also quite amusing. I hear the French are preparing a film which will do the same thing in two generations, and there's going to be a science fiction picture that does it in one.

I had also heard rumors of the most recent development. Cyclic films had closed the old notion of time, the first "true" moebius would eliminate time as an orienter. With pure dissonant sound, with only the most limited and ingenious movements, a complete showing would have the film run both backward and forward, right-to-right and right-to-left. Enthusiasts predicted it would make "Last Year at Marienbad" look like "Looney-tunes."

I got precious little pleasure out of "To the Nth Generation," however. Mandel was moaning and groaning about his buddy-buddies and how much he hated kids through the whole thing. I didn't stay past the second time around—and these things are cumulative—ten revolutions of "The Endless War" had made me practically a pacifist.

The trouble was that half an hour into "Incest on It!" I fell off the edge of a cliff. On the screen the Most Beautiful Girl at Queens College was giving birth on the steps of the New York Public Library to the Nobel physicist who would father the owner of the biggest brothel in the Bronx, who in turn might (there were subtle hints) be the parent of the beautiful blond in labor on the dirty white steps.

I would always have teenage competitors! I would get older, and older, and older ("Never produced anything after twenty-seven!" "Burned out at twenty-five, I'd say!" "We keep him around for laughs, and to teach the remedial courses. Never did anything worthwhile after his thesis!") but they would always be coming; young, bright, arrogant, brilliant. I could barely keep from screaming and screaming and screaming. Instead, I made as tight a fist as I could, squeezing, the way I would press the foot rest in the dentist's chair, because it hurts and hurts, and you've got to do *something* when it hurts so much.

I had been wrong about Mandel, or partly. He, like I, would not be shamed. And he saw Project Round-Square as a betrayal by his friends, of the creation by his "buddy-buddies" of new competitors to torment him. I could understand this, though his woe was not mine. His complaints had stimulated me to see my own doom in the endless procreation of the film.

And now I recalled the "Kubie Report" in the *American Scientist*: "Some Unsolved Problems of the Scientific Career." The high incidence of nervous breakdown in the middle years, as the creative energy wore thin. Directness, immediacy, diversity, wholeness, spontaneity, integral fantasy! For these I had denied myself everything, sweating out my advanced degrees before age could touch me. And now I was old; I could feel myself rotting as I sat there. I could feel my brains inside my body: ropy, red, pulsing, tinged with age, hot and glowing inside a pile of grey, fatty, fibrous tissue—my unexercised body. Somehow I managed to get up and stumble out of the theatre. Behind me, on the screen, someone was talking on his deathbed to his grandchildren and grandparents, who would turn out to be exactly the same people.

Part of the time I worked intensely at my tapes and card-decks, not daring to pause, afraid to close my machine-language manuals. Other days, sometimes for hours, I could not work closely. I cut free of the job, drifted beyond the "grid" of the scientific attitude. What difference did it make, my mind gibed, if men landed on Mars, or discovered element 1304? Particle, wave, wavicle, round-square—who cares? Science was just another "institution," like anything else. Would a man a thousand years from now laugh at me, the way my seminal engineer friends would chuckle at a scribe in 1000 A.D., who spent his little life endlessly recopying scrolls in a monastery?

It took all my tricks to get through the final weeks. The best was

French sleep therapy, which I once read about in a book called "Force Yourself to Relax!" If your troubles are unbearable, knock yourself out until your subconscious has time to patch you up. I tried reading for a while, but I couldn't seem to understand C. P. Snow's two cultures. All I could recall was a passage about someone dying. Snow said that on the point of death, most people care not a whit about their intellectual failures or social lacks. But they cry out endlessly about their missed sensual interludes.

Richard Colby still visited me, but Mandel had stopped coming. In a moment of weakness I'd told him about his "paper shadow." He'd slammed out in a huff. The next day he came back, calm and chipper.

"You look better than I do."

"Of course. All my problems are solved."

"What about your psychology buddies?"

"Oh, I knew none of them were *really* my friends. But I'm set to take care of them, all right, all right."

"Yeah? How?"

"Well, you remember what you told me about my personal file. About how if they decide I'm unstable and borderline, it'll be very hard for me to get any sort of job, and I couldn't be a psychologist any more."

"The situation is something like that, at least with any large organization."

"But as long as I seem all right, all those rats will leave me alone, and even seem to be friendly."

"Well, you don't put it very well—"

"So it's all very simple. I've fixed them all right all right. I went over to chemical stores and got the components for a large bomb. Then I assembled it in the bottom drawer of my desk, in the middle of the Psychology Section of the project. And rigged it with a button detonator."

"Go on, go on!"

"Well, don't you see?"

"No! Go on!"

"It's perfectly plain what I—"

"Mandel, explain!"

"Well, as long as I'm feeling all right, I go on in a perfectly normal way. When I feel a little sick, I go into my office. But if, some day, I think I'm going really nuts, I think I'm really going to go crazy so it all will go down on my personal file and ruin me with the big organization—"

"Yes?"

"Why, then it's as if all my friends are suddenly about to become my enemies, to turn on me, to think I'm crazy and fire me and laugh at me and pity me behind my back." His eyes were mad, though his voice was perfectly level. "They won't be able to do that to Harry Mandel. They won't do it. I'll blow them all to bits first!"

It was enough for me, friend or no. I got word to Personnel, anonymously, and that night they called for Mandel. The poor guy hadn't thought to install one of his "White Collar Kamikazees" in his quarters, so they took him out on the G.E.M. *Topaz* that very night, under heavy sedation.

Was I in much better shape than Harry Mandel had been? A cheerful, hopelessly neurotic robot. I had come up through the sequence without much real thought about stuff like that. It was enough to do my work. Once, when I was drunk, I had the idea that if you had a perfect baby, you could set up the perfect program for his life, sports and studies and sex and social life, split-second timed, an ideal existence. But it was already twenty years too late for that for me.

Or was that the easy way out, to flunk yourself and roll with the tide. Was I simply "hiding out" in science because it was socially sanctioned and I had a talent for Math?

But on the other side it gave me a pattern for my days, the stability I needed and craved. For this I might do work that I even despised. There must be some way to decide, to choose the optimum path, the really best way, before all your time's run through?

But how do you do it, how could I, of all people, do it?

It was my own brand of impossible.

Project Round-Square finished out fast.

Dick Colby and I sat in one of the electronics labs and watched as the countdown dropped to zero. Closed circuit television brought us a view of the MT-Section, a big room holding more than a dozen aleph-sub-sixes. Dr. Wilbur, the head of the machine translation group, sat at the console of an aleph-sub-nine, the most advanced computer International Business Machines has ever turned out. (*Nobody* really understands it. It was designed by an aleph-sub-eight and the main purpose of the sixes was that collectively they kept the sub-nine from going crazy.)

Mathematical linguistics is the new "in" branch of math, like differential topology used to be, and category theory after that. Wilbur was playing it to the hilt, with ski boots, no tie, and a crappy old sports jacket. But he had a feel for the communications process that amounted to empathy. It was this rare talent that was needed, to help the nine through the clutches.

Above him on the lintel of the machine, was the proud motto of the National Programmer's Union, originally a remark by Queen Juliana of the Netherlands:

I can't understand it. I can't even understand the people who can understand it.

"Project Round-Square," said a disgusted technician. "Still seems crazy to me."

"Perhaps it was a bad choice of name," said Colby next to me. The Michigan electronics expert was tanned and calm, and cheerful as ever. "Did you ever read that poem, 'The Blind Men and the Elephant'? It's the same principle. With new senses or a new orientation, apparent contradictions in reality might disappear. It's what some people call thinking in other categories."

"Like the wavicle," said someone else.

"Yes," said Richard Colby, his face taunting as he smiled. "When physicists were studying certain particles, they found that in some situations they could be thought of as waves, and the equations worked out. In other sorts of reactions, you could think of them as particles, and the numbers and theories checked out under *that* hypothesis. So the physics men just shrugged and called 'em wavicles."

"But what does a wavicle look like—"

"I don't know. Nobody knows—but nobody knows what a round-square looks like either."

The lab grew quiet, as if Colby had said something profound. On the television screen the computers clicked and roared, the tape drives jerking abruptly in their vacuum columns.

"What about military applications—" I croaked at Colby. He seemed to be up to date. I hadn't paid much attention to all the inter-office junk we got on the project—including the "Virgin Tease" newsletter that told the lab assistant in Subsection Nine of Track Four of Approach Nineteen what progress had been made towards the noble goal of Project Sixty Nine, of which he sometimes recalled he was a member.

"The guy that hired me told me this thing had military applications —I didn't know if he was kidding or I was in a nightmare."

Colby looked at me wide-eyed for a moment. "Well—I don't know. Of course, there doesn't seem to be any *direct* application. But neither did Einstein's equations, or "game theory" when it was developed. *Any* sort of insight into the world is likely to be militarily useful these days. It doesn't even have to be technical—remember the old German staff armies that were so successful. A simple thing like the chain of command could lick the best general who had to boss his own whole show."

"Just thinking is dangerous these days—often deadly."

"Maybe they ought to classify it," joked Colby.

"But then, I guess it always has been."

On the screen the computers continued to run. Coverage would be confined to the machine-translation lab; the psychologists on the staff had decided to have no reports from the real center of activity.

Outside, in a surface lab were a dozen adolescents. They had been trained to their peak as scientists, well beyond Ph.D.-level. Now they were being sensitized, exposed to the flood of phenomenon that ordinary people never know about, because our wonderful minds are deaf and dumb to nearly everything in the universe. And hidden deep down below their sensitivities, there was a biting, burning, clawing, raving drive to master this new universe they would meet, and to see in it the death of the old human notion of opposites, contradictions, limitations. Nothing, their minds raved as they scanned new skies, nothing must be impossible.

The computers ran for ten hours on the screens, while Wilbur studied and fumed and paced and drank coffee. The subjects would now all have come out of anesthesia, and would now be studying and observing the multitude of apparatus in the lab. Within it, I had been told, there was operating a demonstration of almost every major scientific phenomenon. The sensitized ones had been briefed to the limit, short of data which it was thought might stultify their world view. We could only wait now.

A red light glowed on the aleph-sub-nine, and data began pouring in. Wilbur threw himself into the operator's chair, and began chiding the immense computer, intuitively helping it arrange the data into some sort of language which might mean something to man. His face burned with concentration.

Near the end of the four hour shift he looked at the machine oddly and tried another system of organization. He looked at it hard again. Then he triggered his secretary. The machine, which had responded to his winking-blinking notes, fed back the information in binary code in his earphones.

He sat back and closed his eyes for a few moments. Then he opened them and took up the microphone. "Communications established. They're intelligible," he said. And then, in a lower voice, "I've seen that structure somewhere before. . . ."

The cheers in the room blotted out anything further. Contact established, and the response was not gibberish! Well, never mind what it meant! We'd get that soon enough.

Premature congratulations? Well, perhaps. Remember the satellite shots, with a rocket roaring up on its own fire, swimming right into the calculated orbit, ejecting its satellite, and the little moon's radios bursting into life. *That* was when everyone cheered! Not six months later, when the miles of telemeter tape had been studied and re-studied and been given meaning by sweat and genius. Nor did most people feel very bad when the scientists figured out that someone had forgotten to pull the safety tabs from the quick-releases, so all the instruments were shielded and their data meaningless. . . .

The actual results of Project Round-Square took eleven months to evaluate and declassify. They came out, nicely distorted, in a copy of the "Virgin Tease" the V.R.C. mailed to me. . . .

Biologically, it was an unqualified success. The sensitized subjects had broken through to a whole new world of feeling. In physical terms, they were quasi-Gods, for they could sense things we would never know. It was more than a widening; new colors and smells. They could sense forces and radiations and bodies all forms of which are ignored by men.

But as to the actual purpose of the project. . . .

The sensitives had been given what seemed to be an insoluble problem—eliminating contradiction in a world that required it in any rational description. The ingenuity of the human mind, the directors of Virgin Research had thought, might solve the problem, where the pure logic of machines had failed.

Well, they had solved it, in a way.

Wilbur had been right. The Hopi Indians, independently, had evolved a crude version of the sensitives' solution. The Hopi language did not allow for the complex tenses of the Indo-European tongues. All time and space to them was a single frozen matrix of vents, in which the word "perhaps" had no equivalent, and the notion of "possible" and "impossible" was meaningless.

To ask, in Hopi, if it might rain tomorrow, was as meaningless as to ask if it was possible it had rained yesterday.

To the sensitives, that thing had "roundness" and this one had "squareness." Could there be such a thing as a round-square?

Perhaps, in the forever-fixed future. When it made its appearance, they would tell you. Meanwhile, it's meaningless to think about such things.

The semanticists were the only satisfied ones.

But this was only announced a year later. Not soon enough to save Harry Mandel, who was relieved of a multi-linear annihilator, fifty yards from the sensitives lab. He'd slugged a guard and escaped from the *Topaz*. I understand he's in a security ward somewhere, still talking about his buddies while they watch him very carefully.

Dick Colby shrugged and grinned and had a drink or four with me at the celebration, then caught the evening ramjet back to Michigan Multi.

I collected my pay, scooter, and recommendations. Then, on the evening of the last day, I took a long look out across the desert. The sun was smouldering down into a pile of rust, the earth a great flat plum. By coincidence the girl that had assigned us our quarters was out on the desert too, but quite a ways away. I could see she was pregnant, and that was interesting to think about, and so I thought about it. I get a nice feeling when I see a woman with a child, if I have time for it—warmth, continuity for the race, the safe days of my very young childhood, though I can hardly remember any of them. There certainly were enough signs of it; she was well along.

I got a funny cold feeling. It was a tangential association, a silly one: what the boys used to call a "brassiere curve" in the rapids. You know what an ordinary bell curve looks like? Well, a lot of teachers use it for marking—most of the grades falling at C. Well, in the advanced sections some guys said the professors used a modified bell curve for figuring out grades—what they called a "brassiere curve." It looked like this;

—and jammed up inside the little hump, good and tight near the B plus, A minus grades, was the little gang of teenage hotshots—and me.

The cold expanded into my chest, numbing. I could look at the sunset, and the blond and her baby, and the labs and drafting boys and offices and all of it, and not feel anything at all. Everything was impersonal, like a diagram in a text.

An hour later I caught the G.E.M. *Emerald* back to my own multiversity. Classes wouldn't be starting for a while, but I'd figured out from the summer session catalogue that I could fit in a three week intensive reading course in Chinese in the meantime. Chinese is the new "in" language for Ph.D.s, like the way Russian used to be twenty years ago. It was pretty certain we'd be fighting them soon.

I figured I could fit in at least two "military application" courses into my fall program. Under the Rickover Plan I could get them tuition-exempt. What else could I do? I could use the money to pay for more programming. Computer operators are in short supply, and I would be sure of a fat income. I could be safe, nothing to worry about. Maybe I could get Virgin Research, or even the D.O.D. itself, to pay for more math and science courses. I could plan it all out, interesting problems to work on the rest of my life, and get the government to pay for them. Wouldn't that be clever?

Shut up, shut up, shut up.

THE DOCS

Richard O. Lewis

What are the purposes of education? While there is no general consensus on the subject, we can list some of the more obvious ones:

1. Education prepares the individual to earn a living by giving him or her the skills and training necessary to the adequate performance of a job or profession.

2. Education socializes the student to his world, and prepares him for it by defining his and others' roles.

3. Education prepares the student for responsible citizenship and adulthood.

4. Education develops analytical abilities and exposes a person to the world of ideas, in itself a worthwhile endeavor.

All of these processes are important. But is there such a thing as *too much* education? It is a truism that education is a lifelong pursuit. But what of·institutionalized education?

In recent years, we have become familiar with the phenomenon of the *professional student* who, in extreme cases, completes twelve years of elementary and high school, graduates from college, receives a master's degree, and proceeds on towards the doctorate, consuming in the process almost twenty years of his life. Cities like Madison, Wisconsin, Ann Arbor, Michigan, and Boston, Massachusetts all have "students" who have been there for more than a decade. Indeed, a whole new class may have been created through this process in recent years.

As more and more students obtain advanced degrees, do these diplomas mean less and less? As society increasingly demands a college degree, it has been argued that college is becoming a mere extension of high school. The present emphasis on and concern with vocational education may well be a reaction to this development.

In "The DOCS," Walter A. Basson attains the highest degree possible in his society—the DOCS, or Doctor of Co-ordinated Sciences. His degree mirrors trends present in our society, brought about partially by the ecological crisis—an emphasis on interdisciplinary studies which focus on many areas of study instead of on just one.

Our educational system teaches skills and does this reasonably well, although there is plenty of room for improvement. But in the light of situations like Watergate, does our educational system also teach *values?* Perhaps it is too much to expect the schools and universities to do this. Perhaps it is unfair to ask of them. Values are a product of life experience of which the schools form only a part. People apply what they learn in school in their own way, influenced by a myriad of outside forces, including their own psychological makeup.

As this story indicates, a lot of education does not ensure ethical behavior—after all, expertise has its limits too.

FOR FURTHER THOUGHT OR DISCUSSION

1. What is the professional student and what does he contribute to society?

2. What do you think are the purposes of education and what do you think they should be?

3. What was missing in Dr. Basson's education?

4. How do schools teach values and how can they do a better job of it?

THE DOCS   *Richard O. Lewis*

The entire audience rose to its feet automatically as the score of men, dressed in caps and gowns of bright crimson, filed onto the rostrum to form a line in front of their designated seats.

This was the Class of '84. These were the DOCS—the Doctors of Co-ordinated Sciences. They had been carefully screened through the years, and only those of the highest intelligence and mental-physical co-ordination had been permitted to continue the rigorous studies which would lead to this, the highest degree the scholastic world had to offer—the degree of DOCS.

Walter A. Basson could not help but experience a feeling of great pride and accomplishment as he took his seat at the head of the class. He had been graduated, *cum laude,* with a B.S. degree in '64 at the age of 18 and had immediately matriculated in the special night-school college which, 20 years later, had brought him to his present status, *cum laude* again.

During those 20 years, Walter A. Basson had worked by day and had studied by night. And he had also gotten married. Those had been the lean years, the hard years. But now they were over. . . .

As the speaker of the evening began his orthodox and soporific oration, Walter A. Basson, DOCS, let his eyes wander over the audience. He spotted his wife and two daughters—Alice 12 and Marie 14—in the front row left and let the corners of his eyes crinkle an answering smile to his wife as she raised her hand chin-high to wiggle her fingers unobtrusively at him.

Walter paid little attention to the oration. It had a familiar ring. He had heard it, with but slight variation, at eighth grade graduation, at high school graduation, and at college graduation. It pertained mostly to the great need for men of science in our modern age. . . .

Walter's quick, analytical brain pounced for a fraction of a second upon the phrase "in our modern age," tore it asunder, and cast it aside as being meaningless. *Every age* had been contemporarily *modern* since the beginning of time!

After that, he closed his mind to the orator while he rehearsed, photographically, the valediction he would present near the close of the formalities.

We need not delve here, even briefly, into the context of Walter A. Basson's valediction. Having spent the past 20 years of his life in close association with men engaged in the highest realm of letters and sciences, he had chosen his words carefully and had couched his phraseology in such a manner as to be entirely within keeping to his lofty position, which made it, of course, wholly unintelligible to the audience.

Then there was a round of hand-shaking and congratulations, and it was over.

The Dr. Walter A. Bassons held "open house" that night to commemorate the event, and Walter, for the first time in his life, donned formal attire, his dinner jacket bearing a definite motif of entwining flowers with but the slightest hint of lace at the cuffs.

Although the Basson apartment was small, it proved to be spacious enough to afford ample accommodation for the few guests who arrived —more jealously than zealously—to offer congratulations in general and to partake of the viands in particular. It must be understood that Walter's friends were few, for during the past 20 years of study his social life had been all but nil.

Walter, justly proud of his scholastic accomplishments, had the documentary proof of his attainments spread out meticulously on the top of the spinet piano where they could be perused at will by the guests between or during drinks.

The world had long realized that the various fields of science were not isolated entities within themselves but, rather, that they formed a dovetailing continuum of closely related knowledge.

Walter tried to explain this to his guests after his fifth glass of gin, neat. "Mathematics is the constructional material of physics," he said. "And physics, in turn, furnishes the building-blocks for chemistry which is the very foundation of biology upon which all life is based. Thus an exact coordination of the disciplines is vital to a complete and pragmatic utilization of. . . ."

But no one was paying much attention to Walter. The guests were much more attentive to the pragmatic depletion of platters and the three bottles of gin on the table.

Walter had made straight A's in every subject during his 20 years of higher learning, as the documents upon the spinet testified. Straight A's in every subject—save one: *social ethics*. In this subject Walter had made only a B plus—which may possibly shed some light on why he was not the perfect host, why he had fewer friends than he might have had, and why the evening's entertainment consisted only of an accounting of his own accomplishments.

"It has been assumed that the good is the enemy of the best," said Walter. He had his seventh glass of gin now and was attempting to explain the reason for his low grade in social ethics. "Logically, however, the reverse is true: the best must always be the enemy of the good. The consequential must always supersede the inconsequential in direct ratio to its own degree of consequentiality. . . ."

No one was listening. The party had been a short one. Everyone had gone home. Alice and Marie had passed out under the table, and Mrs. Dr. Walter A. Basson had bedded down among the documents atop the spinet.

Walter surveyed the culinary carnage on and about the table and found three fingers of gin left in one bottle. He consumed it slowly while complimenting himself both on his scholastic attainments and on the fact that the gin acted as a stimulant to his great brain and not as an intoxicant.

Thirty-two seconds later, Walter fell flat on his face, for he, like the other members of his family, had never had opportunity to master the art of social drinking.

There followed two weeks of strenuous apprenticeship to the responsible position Walter was to assume. But he didn't mind it, for the salary was quite in keeping with both the strenuousness and the responsibility.

Walter threw another party at the end of his apprenticeship. He did not invite his friends, however—which, again, may have had some pertinence to his B plus in social ethics. Only his wife and two daughters were present, and but one bottle of gin was consumed.

Then came that memorable Monday in September, 1984, when Walter A. Basson, Doctor of Co-ordinated Science, took over one of the most important and responsible positions the world of science could possibly offer to mere man.

At 7:45 A.M., Walter entered the huge, dome-shaped building.

At exactly eight o'clock, he seated himself before the great machine.

There were rows and banks and tiers of buttons and dials, and lights of variegated colors flashed on and off. Electrical impulses flickered and scintillated and chased each other across miniature screens, and deep within the monster was a muted humming not unlike that of distant swarms of bees.

Walter sat with his eyes upon the machine, all faculties alert, his mind analysing, evaluating, computing.

At exactly 8:34:02, Walter pressed a button, and a cure for the common cold became a reality and was instantly tabulated.

At exactly 9:12:23, Walter pushed another button, and a simple method for trisecting an angle came into being.

At precisely 11:06:36, Walter hesitated a split second, pressed another button, and blew two-thirds of the southern hemisphere to hell and gone.

Approximately 30 seconds later, Walter was relieved of his position and sent back to college to brush up a bit on social ethics.

POTTAGE

Zenna Henderson

An important purpose of any educational system is to develop a sense of tradition in the young. A more difficult issue concerns the question of which traditions to pass on. Tradition also plays an important role in determining what type of educational system and philosophy will be ascendant at any given time.

In the United States, educational traditions have often been reflections of political beliefs. For example, early colonial America believed in a very limited form of public education, placing primary responsibility for the teaching of reading and writing on the parents. There was also a heavy religious emphasis in education, especially in New England. This limited view of education was congruent with the prevailing view of government—limited and removed from the daily lives of the average person.

Immediately before and after the American Revolution, the popular view of the role of education in society began to undergo a transformation. The new ideology of democracy, with its emphasis on an enlightened citizenry electing their own leaders, meant that education was now looked upon as a key ingredient of representative government. In addition, the early leaders of our country saw the schools as a device for generating a sense of patriotism and nationalism—both vital ingredients if a newly independent country is to develop a sense of nationhood and survive.

It should be remembered that at this early date only a relatively few individuals received a formal education. Just as the political system was initially open only to those *men* who owned property, the educational system was restricted to a small number of children from the wealthier classes. Within a few decades, however, new political movements would drastically alter this situation. The rise of mass political parties and of Jacksonian Democracy placed the focus of attention on the "common man." It was inevitable that this new philosophy of government would affect education as well. The educational reform movement of the 1820s changed the face of public education in America, and the era of education for *all* was born. If every man was to have the vote (except if he was unfortunate enough to be born a slave) then every man must have an education in order to effectively participate in government.

As the nineteenth century passed into the twentieth, this viewpoint continued to develop. As universal suffrage was extended first to women and then to blacks, education became more and more inclusive. The high schools took on new roles; they became more and more specialized, offering a wider curriculum which provided alternative vocational models for the students to choose from. The colleges, universities, and community colleges grew in enrollment and functions, until today nearly every student plans on some form of higher education and we have entered the era of "open admissions."

"Pottage" presents the world of education in a tiny community. It is a reflection of how deeply education has permeated American society. Education, like taxes, is no longer something entered into by choice—the government *demands* that every boy and girl receive at least a partial education. The educational system is paid for (in most states) by a system of property taxes which all landowners must pay.

Viewed from a different perspective, this story gives us a view of the dedicated career professional, of *the teacher* to whom teaching is the most important thing in life. Miss Amerson is a prototype of the effective teacher—concerned for her students and determined to make them learn and enjoy the process. Her job of teaching students from elementary through high school in a one-room school is a dying art, however. The rise of the consolidated school district is bringing an end to this aspect of rural American life.

FOR FURTHER THOUGHT OR DISCUSSION

1. In an age of mass society, are there any educational traditions left?

245

2. Should education be compulsory for all Americans?

3. What is the relationship between political and educational movements?

4. What assumptions underly our educational system? Are they out of date?

5. What drives a person like Miss Amerson to her high level of dedication?

6. In what ways is education's social impact different in rural areas from its impact on urban communities?

POTTAGE   *Zenna Henderson*

You get tired of teaching after a while. Well, maybe not of teaching itself because it's insidious and remains a tug in the blood for all of your life, but there comes a day when you look down at the paper you're grading or listen to an answer you're giving a child and you get a *boinnng!* feeling. And each reverberation of the *boing* is a year in your life, another set of children through your hands, another beat in monotony and it's frightening. The value of the work you're doing doesn't enter into it at that moment and the monotony is bitter on your tongue.

Sometimes you can assuage that feeling by consciously savoring those precious days of pseudo-freedom between the time you receive your contract for the next year and the moment you sign it. Because you *can* escape at that moment, but somehow—you don't.

But I did, one Spring. I quit teaching. I didn't sign up again. I went chasing after—after what? Maybe excitement—maybe a dream of wonder—maybe a new, bright, wonderful world that just *must* be somewhere else because it isn't here-and-now. Maybe a place to begin again so I'd never end up at the same frightening emotional dead end. So I quit.

But by late August the emptiness inside me was bigger than boredom, bigger than monotony, bigger than lusting after freedom. It was almost terror to have September nearly here and not care that in a few weeks school starts—tomorrow school starts—First Day of School. So, almost at the last minute, I went to the Placement Bureau. Of course it was too late to try to return to my other school, and besides, the mold of the years there still chafed in too many places.

"Well," said the Placement Director as he shuffled his end-of-the-season cards, past Algebra and Home Ec and PE and High School English, "there's always Bendo." He thumbed out a battered looking 3 x 5. "There's *always* Bendo."

And I took his emphasis and look for what they were intended as and sighed.

"Bendo?"

"Small school. One room. Mining town—or used to be. Ghost town now." He sighed wearily and let down his professional hair. "Ghost people, too. Can't keep a teacher there more than a year. Low pay—fair housing—at someone's home. No community activities—no social life. No city within 50 or so miles. No movies. No nothing but children to be taught. Ten of them this year. All grades."

"Sounds like the town I grew up in," I said. "Except we had two rooms and lots of community activities."

"I've been to Bendo." The Director leaned back in his chair, hands behind his head. "Sick community. Unhappy people. No interest in anything. Only reason they have a school is because it's the law. Law-abiding, anyway. Not enough interest in anything to break a law, I guess."

"I'll take it," I said quickly before I could think beyond the feeling that this sounded about as far back as I could go to get a good running start at things again.

He glanced at me quizzically. "If you're thinking of lighting a torch of high reform to set Bendo afire with enthusiasm, forget it. I've seen plenty of king-sized torches fizzle out there."

"I have no torch," I said. "Frankly I'm fed to the teeth with bouncing bright enthusiasm and huge PTA's and activities until they come out your ears. They usually turn out to be the most monotonous kind of monotony. Bendo will be a rest."

"It will that," said the Director, leaning over his cards again. "Saul Diemus is the president of the Board. If you don't have a car, the only way to get to Bendo is by bus—it runs once a week."

I stepped out into the August sunshine after the interview and sagged a little under its savage pressure, almost hearing a hiss as the refrigerated coolness of the Placement Bureau evaporated from my skin.

I walked over to the Quad and sat down on one of the stone benches I'd never had time to use, those years ago when I was a student here. I looked up at my old dorm window and, for a moment, felt a wild homesickness—not only for years that were gone and hopes that died and dreams that had grim awakenings, but for a special magic I had found in that room. It was a magic—a true magic—that opened such vistas to me that for a while anything seemed possible, anything feasible—if not for me right now, then for Others, someday. Even now, after the dilution of time, I couldn't quite believe that magic, and even now, as then, I wanted fiercely to believe it. If only it could be so! If only it could be so!

I sighed and stood up. I suppose everyone has a magic moment somewhere in his life, and, like me, can't believe that anyone else could have the same—but mine *was* different! No one else *could* have had the same experience! I laughed at myself. Enough of the past and of dreaming. Bendo waited. I had things to do.

I watched the rolling clouds of red-yellow dust billow away from the jolting bus and cupped my hands over my face to get a breath of clean air. The grit between my teeth and the smothering sift of dust across my clothes was familiar enough to me, but I hoped by the time we reached Bendo we would have left this dust-plain behind and come into a little more vegetation. I shifted wearily on the angular seat, wondering if it had ever been designed for anyone's comfort, and caught myself as a sudden braking of the bus flung me forward.

We sat and waited for the dust of our going to catch up with us, while the last-but-me passenger, a withered old Indian, slowly gathered up his gunny sack bundles and his battered saddle and edged his levi'd, velveteen-bloused self up the aisle and out to the bleak roadside.

We roared away, leaving him a desolate figure in a wide desolation. I wondered where he was headed. How many weary miles to his hogan in what hidden wash or miniature greenness in all this wilderness.

Then we headed straight as a die for the towering redness of the bare mountains that lined the horizon. Peering ahead, I could see the road, ruler-straight disappearing into the distance. I sighed and shifted again and let the roar of the motor and the weariness of my bones lull me into a stupor on the border between sleep and waking.

A change in the motor roar brought me back to the jouncing bus. We jerked to a stop again. I looked out the window through the settling clouds of dust and wondered who we could be picking up out here in the middle of nowhere. Then a clot of dust dissolved and I saw

BENDO POST OFFICE
GENERAL STORE
Garage & Service Station
DRY GOODS & HARDWARE
MAGAZINES

in descending size on the front of the leaning, weather-beaten building propped between two crumbling, smoke-blackened stone ruins. After so much flatness, it was almost a shock to see the bare, tumbled boulders crowding down to the roadside and humping their lichen-stained shoulders against the sky.

"Bendo," said the bus driver, unfolding his lanky legs and hunching out of the bus. "End of the line—end of civilization—end of everything!" He grinned and the dusty mask of his face broke into engaging smile patterns.

"Small, isn't it?" I grinned back.

"Usta be bigger," he said. "Not that it helps now. Roaring mining town years ago." As he spoke, I could pick out disintegrating buildings dotting the rocky hillsides and tumbling into the steep washes. "My Dad can remember it when he was a kid. That was long enough ago that there was still a river for the town to be in the bend o'."

"Is *that* where it got its name?"

"Some say yes, some say no. Might have been a feller named Bendo." The driver grunted as he unlashed my luggage from the bus roof and swung it to the ground.

"Oh, hi!" said the driver.

I swung around to see who was there. The man was tall, well-built, good-looking—and old. Older than his face—older than years could have made him because he was really young, not much older than I. His

249

face was a stern, unhappy stillness, his hands stiff on the brim of his stetson as he held it waist high.

In that brief pause before his, "Miss Amerson?" I felt the same feeling coming from him that you can feel around some highly religious person who knows God only as a stern implacable, vengeful deity, impatient of worthless man, waiting only for an unguarded moment to strike him down in his sin. I wondered who or what his God was that prisoned him so cruelly. Then I was answering, "Yes. How do you do? And he touched my hand briefly with a "Saul Diemus" and turned to the problem of my two large suitcases and my phonograph.

I followed Mr. Diemus' shuffling feet silently, since he seemed to have slight inclination for talk. I hadn't expected a reception committee, but kids must have changed a lot since I was one, otherwise curiosity about Teacher would have lured out at least a couple of them for a preview look. But the silent two of us walked on for a half block or so from the highway and the post office and rounded the rocky corner of a hill. I looked across the dry creek bed and up the one winding street that was residential Bendo. I paused on the splintery old bridge and took a good look. I'd never see Bendo like this again. Familiarity would blur some outlines and sharpen others, and I'd never again see it, free from the knowledge of who lived behind which blank front door.

The houses were scattered haphazardly over the hillsides and erratic flights of rough stone steps led down from each to the road that paralleled the bone-dry creek bed. The houses were not shacks, but they were unpainted and weathered until they blended into the background almost perfectly. Each front yard had things growing in it, but such subdued blossomings and unobtrusive plantings that they could easily have been only accidental massings of natural vegetation.

Such a passion for anonymity ...

"The school—" I had missed the swift thrust of his hand.

"Where?" Nothing I could see spoke school to me.

"Around the bend." This time I followed his indication and suddenly, out of the featurelessness of the place, I saw a bell tower barely topping the hill beyond the town, with the fine pencil stroke of a flagpole to one side. Mr. Diemus pulled himself together to make the effort.

"The school's in the prettiest place around here. There's a spring and trees, and ..." He ran out of words and looked at me as though trying to conjure up something else I'd like to hear. "I'm board president," he said abruptly. "You'll have ten children from first grade to second year high school. You're the boss in your school. Whatever you do is your business. Any discipline you find desirable—use. We don't pamper our children. Teach them what you have to. Don't bother the parents with reasons and explanations. The school is yours."

"And you'd just as soon do way with it and me too," I smiled at him.

He looked startled. "The law says school them," he started across the bridge. "So school them."

I followed meekly, wondering wryly what would happen if I asked Mr. Diemus why he hated himself and the world he was in and even—oh, breathe it softly—the children I was to "school."

"You'll stay at my place," he said. "We have an extra room."

I was uneasily conscious of the wide gap of silence that followed his pronouncement, but couldn't think of a thing to fill it. I shifted my small case from one hand to the other and kept my eyes on the rocky path that protested with shifting stones and vocal gravel every step we took. It seemed to me that Mr. Diemus was trying to make all the noise he could with his shuffling feet. But, in spite of the amplified echo from the hills around us, no door opened, no face pressed to a window. It was a distinct relief to hear suddenly the happy, unthinking rusty singing of hens as they scratched in the coarse dust.

I hunched up in the darkness of my narrow bed trying to comfort my uneasy stomach. It wasn't that the food had been bad—it had been quite adequate—but such a dingy meal! Gloom seemed to festoon itself from the ceiling and unhappiness sat almost visibly at the table.

I tried to tell myself that it was my own travel weariness that slanted my thoughts, but I looked around the table and saw the hopeless endurance furrowed into the adult faces and beginning faintly but unmistakably on those of the children. There were two children there. A girl, Sarah (fourth grade, at a guess), and an adolescent boy Matt (seventh?)—too silent, too well-mannered, too controlled, avoiding much too pointedly looking at the empty chair between them.

My food went down in lumps and quarreled fiercely with the coffee that arrived in square-feeling gulps. Even yet—long difficult hours after the meal—the food still wouldn't lie down to be digested.

Tomorrow, I could slip into the pattern of school, familiar no matter where school was, since teaching kids is teaching kids no matter where. Maybe then I could convince my stomach that all was well, and then maybe even start to thaw those frozen, unnatural children. Of course they well might be little demons away from home—which is very often the case. Anyway, I felt, thankfully, the familiar September thrill of new beginnings.

I shifted in bed again, then stiffening my neck, lifted my ears clear off my pillow.

It was a whisper, the intermittent hissing I had been hearing. Someone was whispering in the next room to mine. I sat up and listened unashamedly. I knew Sarah's room was next to mine, but who was talking with her? At first I could get only half words and then either my ears sharpened or the voices became louder.

". . . and did you hear her laugh? Right out loud at the table!" The quick whisper became a low voice. "Her eyes crinkled in the corners and she laughed."

"Our other teachers laughed, too." The uncertainly deep voice must be Matt.

"Yes," whispered Sarah. "But not for long. Oh, Matt! What's wrong with us? People in our books have fun. They laugh and run and jump and do all kinds of fun stuff and nobody—" Sarah faltered. "No one calls it evil."

"Those are only stories," said Matt. "Not real life."

"I don't believe it!" cried Sarah. "When I get big, I'm going away from Bendo. I'm going to see—"

"Away from Bendo!" Matt's voice broke in roughly. "Away from the Group?"

I lost Sarah's reply. I felt as though I had missed an expected step. As I wrestled with my breath, the sights and sounds and smells of my old dorm room crowded back upon me. Then I caught myself. It was probably only a turn of phrase. This futile, desolate unhappiness couldn't possibly be related in any way to *that* magic. . . .

"Where *is* Dorcas?" Sarah asked, as though she knew the answer already.

"Punished." Matt's voice was hard and unchildlike. "She jumped."

"Jumped!" Sarah was shocked.

"Over the edge of the porch. Clear down to the path. Father saw her. I think she let him see her on purpose." His voice was defiant. "Someday when I get older, I'm going to jump, too—all I want to—even over the house. Right in front of Father."

"Oh, Matt!" The cry was horrified and admiring. "You wouldn't! You couldn't. Not so far, not right in front of father!"

"I would so," retorted Matt. "I could so, because I—" His words cut off sharply. "Sarah," he went on, "can you figure any way, *any* way that jumping could be evil? It doesn't hurt anyone. It isn't ugly. There isn't any law—"

"Where is Dorcas?" Sarah's voice was almost inaudible. "In the hidey-hole again?" Almost she was answering Matt's question instead of asking one of her own.

"Yes," said Matt. "In the dark with only bread to eat. So she can learn what a hunted animal feels like. An animal that is different, that other animals hate and hunt." His bitter voice put quotes around the words.

"You see," whispered Sarah. "You see?"

In the silence following, I heard the quiet closing of a door and the slight vibration of the floor as Matt passed my room. I eased back onto my pillow. I lay back, staring toward the ceiling. What dark thing was here in this house? In this community? Frightened children whispering in the dark. Rebellious children in hidey-holes learning how hunted animals feel. And a Group. . .? No it couldn't be. It was just the recent reminder of being on campus again that made me even consider that this darkness might in some way be the reverse of the golden coin Karen had showed me.

Almost my heart failed me when I saw the school. It was one of those brick monstrosities that went up around the turn of the century. This one had been built for a boom town, but now all the upper windows were boarded up and obviously long out of use. The lower floor was blank too, except for two rooms—though with the handful of children quietly standing around the door, it was apparent that only one room was needed. And not only was the building deserted: the yard was swept clean from side to side, innocent of grass or trees—or playground equipment. There *was* a deep grove just beyond the school, though, and the glint of water down canyon.

"No swings?" I asked the three children who were escorting me. "No slides? No seesaws?"

"No!" Sarah's voice was unhappily surprised. Matt scowled at her warningly.

"No," he said, "We don't swing or slide—nor see a saw!" He grinned up at me faintly.

"What a shame!" I said. "Did they all wear out? Can't the school afford new ones?"

"We don't swing or slide or seesaw." The grin was dead. "We don't believe in it."

There's nothing quite so flat and incontestable as that last statement. I've heard it as an excuse for practically every type of omission but, so help me! never applied to playground equipment. I couldn't think of a reply any more intelligent than *oh* so I didn't say anything.

All week long I felt as if I were wading through knee-deep jello or trying to lift a king-sized feather bed up over my head. I used up every device I ever thought of to rouse the class to enthusiasm—about anything, *anything!* They were polite and submissive and did what was asked of them, but joylessly, apathetically, enduringly.

Finally, just before dismissal time on Friday, I leaned in desperation across my desk.

"Don't you like *anything?*" I pleaded. "Isn't *anything* fun?"

Dorcas Diemus' mouth opened into the tense silence. I saw Matt kick quickly, warningly against the leg of the desk. Her mouth closed.

"I think school is fun," I said. "I think we can enjoy all kinds of things. I want to enjoy teaching, but I can't unless you enjoy learning."

"We learn," said Dorcas quickly. "We aren't stupid."

"You learn," I acknowledged. "You aren't stupid. But don't any of you *like* school?"

"I like school," piped up Martha, my first grade. "I think it's fun!"

"Thank you, Martha," I said, "and the rest of you—" I glared at them in mock anger. "You're going to have fun if I have to beat it into you!"

To my dismay, they shrank down apprehensively in their seats and exchanged troubled glances. But before I could hastily explain myself, Matt laughed and Dorcas joined him. And I beamed fatuously to hear the hesitant rusty laughter spread across the room, but I saw Esther's hands shake as she wiped tears from her ten-year-old eyes. Tears—of laughter?

That night I twisted in the darkness of my room, almost too tired to sleep, worrying and wondering. What had blighted these people? They had health, they had beauty—the curve of Martha's cheek against the window was a song, the lift of Dorcas' eyebrows was breathless grace. They were fed ... adequately, clothed ... adequately, housed ... adequately, but nothing like they could have been. I'd seen more joy and delight and enthusiasm from little campground kids who slept in cardboard shacks and washed—if they ever did—in canals and ate whatever edible came their way, but grinned, even when impetigo or cold sores bled across their grins.

But these lifeless kids! My prayers were troubled and I slept restlessly.

A month or so later, things had improved a little bit—but not much. At least there was more relaxation in the classroom. And I found that they had no deep-rooted convictions against plants, so we had things growing on the deep window sills—stuff we transplanted from the spring and from among the trees. And we had jars of minnows from the creek and one drowsy horney-toad who roused in his box of dirt only to flick up the ants brought for his dinner. And we sang—loudly and enthusiastically—but, miracle of miracles, without even one monotone in the whole room. But we *didn't* sing "Up, Up In The Sky" nor "How Do You Like To Go Up In A Swing?" My solos of such songs were received with embarrassed blushes and lowered eyes!

There had been one dust-up between us though—this matter of shuffling everywhere they walked.

"Pick up your feet, for goodness' sake," I said irritably one morning when the *shoosh, shoosh, shoosh* of their coming and going finally got my skin off. "Surely they're not so heavy you can't lift them."

Timmy, who happened to be the trigger this time, nibbled unhappily at one finger. "I can't," he whispered. "Not supposed to."

"Not supposed to?" I forgot momentarily how warily I'd been going with these frightened mice of children. "Why not? Surely there's no reason in the world why you can't walk quietly."

Matt looked unhappily over at Miriam, the sophomore who was our entire high school. She looked aside, biting her lower lip, troubled. Then she turned back and said, "It is customary in Bendo."

"To shuffle along?" I was forgetting any manners I had. "Whatever for?"

"That's the way we do in Bendo." There was no anger in her defense, only resignation.

"Perhaps that's the way you do at home," I said. "But here at school let's pick our feet up. It makes too much disturbance otherwise."

"But it's bad—" began Esther.

Matt's hand shushed her in a hurry.

"Mr. Diemus said what we did at school was my business," I told them. "He said not to bother your parents with our problems. One of our problems is too much noise when others are trying to work. At least in our schoolroom, let's lift our feet and walk quietly."

The children considered the suggestion solemnly and turned to Matt and Miriam for guidance. They both nodded and we went back to work. For the next few minutes, from the corner of my eyes, I saw with amazement all the unnecessary trips back and forth across the room, with high lifted feet, with grins and side glances that marked such trips as high adventure—as a delightfully daring thing to do! The whole deal had me bewildered. Thinking back, I realized that not only the children of Bendo scuffled, but all the adults did too—as though they were afraid to lose contact with the earth, as though ... I shook my head and went on with the lesson.

Before noon, though, the endless *shoosh, shoosh, shoosh* of feet began again. Habit was too much for the children. So I silently filed the sound under *Uncurable, Endurable,* and let the matter drop.

I sighed as I watched the children leave at lunch time. It seemed to me that with the unprecedented luxury of a whole hour for lunch, they'd all go home. The bell tower was visible from nearly every house in town. But instead, they all brought tight little paper sacks with dull crumbly sandwiches and unimaginative apples in them. And silently, with their dull scuffly steps they disappeared into the thicket of trees around the spring.

Everything is dulled around here, I thought. Even the sunlight is blunted as it floods the hills and canyons. There is no mirth, no laughter. No high jinks or cutting up. No pre-adolescent silliness. No adolescent foolishness. Just quiet children, enduring.

I don't usually snoop, but I began wondering if perhaps the kids were different when they were away from me—and from their parents. So when I got back at 12:30 from an adequate but uninspired lunch at Diemus' house, I kept on walking past the school house and quietly down into the grove, moving cautiously through the scanty undergrowth until I could lean over a lichened boulder and look down on the children.

Some were lying around on the short still grass, hands under their heads, blinking up at the brightness of the sky between the leaves. Esther and little Martha were hunting out fillaree seed pods and counting the tines of the pitchforks and rakes and harrows they resembled. I smiled, remembering how I used to do the same thing.

"I dreamed last night." Dorcas thrust the statement defiantly into the drowsy silence. "I dreamed about The Home."

My sudden astonished movement was covered by Martha's horrified, "Oh, Dorcas!"

"What's wrong with The Home?" cried Dorcas, her cheeks scarlet. "There *was* a Home! There was! There was! Why shouldn't we talk about it?"

I listened avidly. This couldn't be just coincidence—a Group and now The Home. There must be some connection. . . . I pressed closer against the rough rock.

"But it's bad!" cried Esther. "You'll be punished! We can't talk about The Home!"

"Why not?" asked Joel as though it had just occurred to him, as things do just occur to you when you're thirteen. He sat up slowly. "Why can't we?"

There was a short tense silence.

"I've dreamed too," said Matt. "I've dreamed of The Home—and it's *good*, it's good!"

"Who hasn't dreamed?" asked Miriam. "We all have, haven't we? Even our parents. I can tell by Mother's eyes when she has."

"Did you ever ask how come we aren't supposed to talk about it?" asked Joel. "I mean and ever get any answer except that it's bad."

"I think it has something to do with a long time ago," said Matt. "Something about when the Group first came—"

"I don't think it's just dreams," declared Miriam, "because I don't have to be asleep. I think it's Remembering."

"Remembering?" asked Dorcas. "How can we remember something we never knew?"

"I don't know," admitted Miriam, "But I'll bet it is."

"I remember," volunteered Talitha—who never volunteered anything.

"Hush!" whispered Abie, the second grade next-to-youngest who always whispered.

"I remember," Talitha went on stubbornly. "I remember a dress that was too little so the mother just stretched the skirt till it was long enough and it stayed stretched. 'nen she pulled the waist out big enough and the little girl put it on and flew away."

"Hoh!" Tommy scoffed. "I remember better than that." His face stilled and his eyes widened. "The ship was so tall it was like a mountain and the people went in the high, high door and they didn't have a ladder. 'Nen there were stars, big burning ones—not squinchy little ones like ours."

"It went too fast!" That was Abie! Talking eagerly! "When the air came it made the ship hot and the little baby died before all the little boats left the ship." He scoonched down suddenly, leaning against Talitha and whimpering.

"You see!" Miriam lifted her chin triumphantly. "We've all dreamed—I mean remembered!"

"I guess so," said Matt. "I remember. It's *lifting*, Talitha, not flying. You go and go as high as you like, as far as you want to and don't *ever* have to touch the ground—at all! At all!" He pounded his fist into the gravelly red soil beside him.

"And you can dance in the air, too," sighed Miriam. "Freer than a bird, lighter than—"

Esther scrambled to her feet, white-faced and panic stricken. "Stop! Stop! It's evil! It's bad! I'll tell Father! We can't dream—or lift—or dance! It's bad, it's bad! You'll die for it! You'll die for it!"

Joel jumped to his feet and grabbed Esther's arm.

"Can we die any deader?" he cried, shaking her brutally, "You call *this* being alive?" He hunched down apprehensively and shambled a few scuffling steps across the clearing.

I fled blindly back to school, trying to wink away my tears without admitting I was crying, crying for these poor kids who were groping so hopelessly for something they knew they should have. Why was it so rigorously denied them? Surely, if they were what I thought them . . . And they could be! They could be!

I grabbed the bell rope and pulled hard. Reluctantly the bell moved and rolled.

"*One o'clock,*" it clanged. "*One o'clock!*"

I watched the children returning with slow, uneager, shuffling steps.

That night I started a letter:

Dear Karen,

Yep, 'sme after all these years. And, oh, Karen! I've found some more! Some more of The People! Remember how much you wished you knew if any other Groups besides yours had survived the Crossing? How you worried about them and wanted to find them if they had? Well, *I've* found a whole Group! But it's a sick, unhappy group. Your heart would break to see them. If you could come and start them on the right path again . . .

I put my pen down. I looked at the lines I had written and then crumpled the paper slowly. This was *my* Group. I had found them. Sure, I'd tell Karen—but later. Later, after—well, after *I* had tried to start them on the right path—at least the children.

After all, I knew a little of their potentialities. Hadn't Karen briefed me in those unguarded magical hours in the old Dorm, drawn to me as I was to her by some mutual sympathy that seemed stronger than the usual roommate attachment, telling me things no outsider had a right to hear? And if, when I finally told her and turned the Group over to her, if it could be a joyous gift—then I could feel that I had repaid her a little for the wonder world she had opened to me.

Yeah, I thought ruefully—and there's nothing like a large portion of ignorance to give one a large portion of confidence. But I did want to try—desperately. Maybe if I could break prison for someone else, then perhaps my own bars . . . I dropped the paper in the wastebasket.

But it was several weeks before I could bring myself to do anything to let the children know I knew about them. It was such an impossible situation, even if it were true—and if it weren't, what kind of lunacy would they suspect me of?

When I finally set my teeth and swore a swear to myself that I'd do something definite, my hands shook and my breath was a flutter in my dry throat.

"Today," I said with an effort. "Today is Friday." Which gem of wisdom the children received with charitable silence. "We've been working hard all week so let's have fun today." This stirred the children—half with pleasure, half with apprehension. They, poor kids, found my "fun" much harder than any kind of work I could give them. But some of them were acquiring a taste for it. Martha had even learned to skip!

"First, monitors pass the composition paper." Esther and Abie scuffled hurriedly around with the paper, and the pencil sharpener got a thorough work-out. At least these kids didn't differ from others in their pleasure with grinding their pencils away at the slightest excuse.

"Now," I gulped. "We're going to write." Which obvious asininity was passed over with forbearance, though Miriam looked at me wonderingly before she bent her head and let her hair shadow her face. "Today I want you all to write about the same thing. Here is our subject."

Gratefully I turned my back on the children's waiting eyes and printed slowly:

I REMEMBER THE HOME

I heard the sudden intake of breath that worked itself downward from Miriam to Talitha and then the rapid whisper that informed Abie and Martha. I heard Esther's muffled cry and I turned slowly around and leaned against the desk.

"There are so many beautiful things to remember about The Home," I said into the strained silence. "So many wonderful things. And even the sad memories are better than forgetting, because The Home was *good*. Tell me what you remember about The Home."

"We can't!" Joel and Matt were on their feet simultaneously.

"Why can't we?" cried Dorcas. "Why can't we?"

"It's bad!" cried Esther. "It's evil!"

"It aint either!" shrilled Abie, astonishingly. "It ain't either!"

"We shouldn't." Miriam's trembling hands brushed her heavy hair upward. "It's forbidden."

"Sit down," I said gently. "The day I arrived at Bendo, Mr. Diemus told me to teach you what I had to teach you. I have to teach you that Remembering The Home is good."

"Then why don't the grownups think so?" Matt asked slowly. "They tell us not to talk about it. We shouldn't disobey our parents."

"I know," I admitted, "and I would never ask you children to go against your parents' wishes—unless I felt that it is very important. If you'd rather they didn't know about it at first, keep it as our secret. Mr. Diemus told me not to bother them with explanations or reasons. I'll make it right with your parents when the time comes." I paused to swallow and to blink away a vision of me, leaving town in a cloud of dust barely ahead of a posse of irate parents. "Now, everyone busy," I said briskly. "I Remember The Home."

There was a moment heavy with decision and I held my breath, wondering which way the balance would dip. And then—surely it must have been because they wanted so to speak and to affirm the wonder of what had been that they capitulated so easily. Heads bent and pencils scurried. And Martha sat, her head bowed on her desk with sorrow.

"I don't know enough words," she mourned. "How do you write *toolas?*"

And Abie laboriously erased a hole through his paper and licked his pencil again.

"Why don't you and Abie make some pictures?" I suggested. "Make a little story with pictures and we can staple them together like a real book."

I looked over the silent, busy group and let myself relax, feeling weakness flood into my knees. I scrubbed the dampness from my palms with Kleenex and sat back in my chair. Slowly I became conscious of a new atmosphere in my classroom. An intolerable strain was gone, an unconscious holding back of the children, a wariness, a watchfulness, a guilty feeling of desiring what was forbidden.

A prayer of thanksgiving began to well up inside me. It changed hastily to a plea for mercy as I began to visualize what might happen to me when the parents found out what I was doing. How long must this containment and denial have gone on? This concealment and this carefully nourished fear? From what Karen had told me, it must be well over fifty years—long enough to mark indelibly three generations.

And here I was with my fine little hatchet trying to set a little world afire! On which very mixed metaphor, I stiffened my weak knees and got up from my chair. I walked unnoticed up and down the aisles, stepping aside as Joel went blindly to the shelf for more paper, leaning over Miriam to marvel that she had taken out her Crayolas and part of her writing was with colors, part with pencil—and the colors spoke to something in me that the pencil couldn't reach though I'd never seen the forms the colors took.

The children had gone home, happy and excited, chattering and laughing, until they reached the edge of the school grounds. There smiles died and laughter stopped and faces and feet grew heavy again. All but Esther's. Hers had never been light. I sighed and turned to the papers. Here was Abie's little book. I thumbed through it and drew a deep breath and went back through it slowly again.

A second grader drawing this? Six pages—six finished, adult-looking pages. Crayolas achieving effects I'd never seen before—pictures that told a story loudly and clearly.

Stars blazing in a black sky, with the slender needle of a ship, like a mote in the darkness.

The vasty green cloud-shrouded arc of earth against the blackness. A pink tinge of beginning friction along the ship's belly. I put my finger to the glow. Almost I could feel the heat.

Inside the ship, suffering and pain, heroic striving, crumpled bodies and seared faces. A baby dead in its mother's arms. Then a swarm of tinier needles erupting from the womb of the ship. And the last shriek of incandescence as the ship volatilized against the thickening drag of the air.

I leaned my head on my hands and closed my eyes. All this, all *this* in the memory of an eight-year-old? All *this* in the feelings of an eight-year-old? Because Abie knew—he *knew* how this felt. He knew the heat and strivings and the dying and fleeing. No wonder Abie whispered and leaned. Racial memory was truly a two-sided coin.

I felt a pang of misgivings. Maybe I was wrong to let him remember so vividly. Maybe I shouldn't have let him . . .

I turned to Martha's papers. They were delicate, almost spidery drawings of some fuzzy little animal (*toolas?*) that apparently built a hanging, hammocky nest and gathered fruit in a huge leaf-basket and had a bird for a friend. A truly out-of-this-world bird. Much of her story escaped me because first graders—if anyone at all—produce symbolic art, and, since her frame of reference and mine were so different, there was much that I couldn't interpret. But her whole booklet was joyous and light.

And now, the stories—

I lifted my head and blinked into the twilight. I had finished all the papers except Esther's. It was her cramped writing, swimming in darkness, that made me realize that the day was gone and that I was shivering in a shadowy room with the fire in the old-fashioned heater gone out.

Slowly I shuffled the papers into my desk drawer, hesitated, and took out Esther's. I would finish at home. I shrugged into my coat and wandered home, my thoughts intent on the papers I had read. And suddenly I wanted to cry—to cry for the wonders that had been and were no more. For the heritage of attainment and achievement these children had, but couldn't use. For the dream-come-true of what they were capable of doing, but weren't permitted to do. For the homesick yearning that filled every line they had written—these unhappy exiles, three generations removed from any physical knowledge of The Home.

I stopped on the bridge and leaned against the railing in the half dark. Suddenly *I* felt a welling homesickness. *That* was what the world should be like—what it *could* be like if only—if only . . .

But my tears for The Home were as hidden as the emotions of Mrs. Diemus when she looked up uncuriously as I came through the kitchen door.

"Good evening," she said. "I've kept your supper warm."

"Thank you." I shivered convulsively. "It *is* getting cold."

I sat on the edge of my bed that night, letting the memory of the kids' papers wash over me, trying to fill in around the bits and snippets that they had told of The Home. And then I began to wonder. All of them who wrote about the actual Home had been so happy with their memories. From Timmy and his *Shinny ship as high as a montin and faster than two jets,* and Dorcas's wandering tenses as though yesterday and today were one, *The flowers were like lights. At night it isn't dark becas they shine so bright and when the moon came up the breeos sing and the music was so you can see it like rain falling around only happyer,* up to Miriam's wistful *On Gathering Day there was a big party. Everybody came dressed in beautiful clothes with Flahmen in the girl's hair. Flahmen are flowers but they're good to eat. And if a girl felt her heart sing for a boy, they ate a Flahmen together and started two-ing.*

Then, if all these memories were so happy, why the rigid suppression of them by grownups? Why the pall of unhappiness over everyone? You can't mourn forever for a wrecked ship. Why a hidey-hole for disobedient children? Why the misery and frustration when, if they could do half of what I didn't fully understand from Joel and Matt's highly technical papers, they could make Bendo an Eden—

I had reached for Esther's paper. I had put it on the bottom on purpose. I dreaded reading it! She had sat with her head buried on her arms on her desk most of the time the others were writing busily. At widely separated intervals she scribbled a line or two as though she were doing something shameful. She, of all the children, had seemed to find no relief in her remembering.

I smoothed the paper on my lap.

I remember, she had written. "*We were thursty. There was water in the creek we were hiding in the grass. We could not drink. They would shoot us. Three days the sun was hot. She screamed for water and ran to the creek. They shot. The water got red.*

Blistered spots marked the tears on the paper.

They found a baby under a bush. The man hit it with the wood part of his gun. He hit it and hit it and hit it. I hit scorpins like that.

They caught us and put us in a pen. They built a fire all around us. Fly "they said" fly and save yourselfs. We flew because it hurt. They shot us.

Monster "they yelled" evil monsters. People can't fly. People can't move things. People are the same. You aren't people. Die die die.

Then blackly, traced and retraced until the paper split:

If anyone finds out we are not of earth we will die.

Keep your feet on the ground.

Bleakly I laid the paper aside. So there was the answer, putting Karen's bits and snippets together with these. The shipwrecked ones finding savages on the desert island. A remnant surviving by learning caution, suppression and denial. Another generation that pinned the *evil* label on The Home to insure continued immunity for their children, and now, a generation that questioned and wondered—and rebelled.

I turned off the light and slowly got into bed. I lay there staring into the darkness, holding the picture Esther had evoked. Finally I relaxed. "God help us," I sighed. "God help us all."

Another week was nearly over. We cleaned the room up quickly, for once anticipating the fun time instead of dreading it. I smiled to hear the happy racket all around me, and felt my own spirits surge upward in response to the lightheartedness of the children. The difference that one afternoon had made in them! Now they were beginning to feel like children to me. They were beginning to accept me. I swallowed with an effort. How soon would they ask *how come?* How come I knew? There they sat, all nine of them—nine, because Esther was my first absence in the year—bright-eyed and expectant.

"Can we write again?" asked Sarah, "I can remember lots more."

"No," I said. "Not today." Smiles died and there was a protesting wiggle through the room. "Today, we are going to *do.* Joel." I looked at him and tightened my jaws. "Joel, give me the dictionary." He began to get up. "... *without leaving your seat!*"

"But I—!" Joel broke the shocked silence. "I can't!"

"Yes you can," I prayed. "Yes you can. Give me the dictionary. Here, on my desk."

Joel turned and stared at the big old dictionary that spilled pages 1965 to 1998 out of its cracked old binding. Then he said, "Miriam?" in a high, tight voice. But she shook her head and shrank back in her seat, her eyes big and dark in her white face.

"You can." Miriam's voice was hardly more than a breath. "It's just bigger—"

Joel clutched the edge of his desk and sweat started out on his forehead. There was a stir of movement on the bookshelf. Then, as though shot from a gun, pages 1965 to 1998 whisked to my desk and fell fluttering. Our laughter cut through the blank amazement and we laughed till tears came.

"That's a-doing it, Joel!" shouted Matt. "That's showing them your muscles!"

"Well, it's a beginning," grinned Joel weakly. "You do it, brother, if you think it's so easy."

So Matt sweated and strained and Joel joined with him, but they only managed to scrape the book to the edge of the shelf where it teetered dangerously.

Then Abie waved his hand timidly. "I can, teacher," he said.

I beamed that my silent one had spoken and at the same time frowned at the loving laughter of the big kids.

"Okay, Abie," I encouraged. "You show them how to do it."

And the dictionary swung off the shelf and glided unhastily to my desk, where it came silently to rest.

Everyone stared at Abie and he squirmed. "The little ships," he defended. "That's the way they moved them out of the big ship. Just like that."

Joel and Matt turned their eyes to some inner concentration and then exchanged exasperated looks.

"Why, sure," said Matt. "Why sure." And the dictionary swung back to the shelf.

"Hey!" protested Timmy. "It's my turn!"

"That poor dictionary," I said. "It's too old for all this bouncing around. Just put the loose pages back on the shelf."

And he did.

Everyone sighed and looked at me expectantly.

"Miriam?" She clasped her hands convulsively. "*You* come to me," I said, feeling a chill creep across my stiff shoulders. "*Lift* to me, Miriam."

Without taking her eyes from me, she slipped out of her seat and stood in the aisle. Her skirts swayed a little as her feet lifted from the floor. Slowly at first and then more quickly she came to me, soundlessly, through the air, until in a little flurried rush, her arms went around me and she gasped into my shoulder. I put her aside, trembling. I groped for my handkerchief. I said shakily, "Miriam, help the rest. I'll be back in a minute."

And I stumbled into the room next door. Huddled down in the dust and debris of the catchall store room it had become, I screamed soundlessly into my muffling hands. And screamed and screamed! Because after all—*after all!*

And then suddenly, with a surge of pure panic, I heard a sound—the sound of footsteps, many footsteps, approaching the school house. I jumped for the door and wrenched it open just in time to see the outside door open. There was Mr. Diemus and Esther and Esther's father, Mr. Jonso.

In one of those flashes of clarity that engrave your mind in a split second, I saw my whole classroom.

Joel and Matt were chinning themselves on non-existent bars, their heads brushing the high ceiling as they grunted upwards. Abie was swinging in a swing that wasn't there, arcing across the corner of the room, just missing the stove pipe from the old stove, as he chanted, "Up in a swing, up in a swing!" This wasn't the first time *they* had tried their wings! Miriam was kneeling in a circle with the other girls and they were all coaxing their books up to hover unsupported above the floor, while Timmy *v-roomm-vroomed* two paper jet planes through intricate maneuvers in and out the rows of desks.

My soul curdled in me as I met Mr. Diemus' eyes. Esther gave a choked cry as she saw what the children were doing, and the girls' stricken faces turned to the intruders. Matt and Joel crumpled to the floor and scrambled to their feet. But Abie, absorbed by his wonderful new accomplishment, swung on, all unconscious of what was happening until Talitha frantically screamed "Abie!"

Startled, he jerked around and saw the forbidding group at the door. With a disappointed cry, as though a loved toy had been snatched from him, he stopped there in mid-air, his fists clenched. And then, realizing, he screamed, a terrified, panic-stricken cry, and slanted sharply upward, trying to escape, and ran full tilt into the corner of the high old map case, sideswiping it with his head, and, reeling backwards, fell!

I tried to catch him. I did! I did! But I only caught one small hand as he plunged down onto the old wood-burning heater beneath him. And the crack of his skull against the ornate edge of the cast-iron lid was loud in the silence.

I straightened the crumpled little body carefully, not daring to touch the quiet little head. Mr. Diemus and I looked at one another as we knelt on opposite sides of the child. His lips opened, but I plunged before he could get started.

"If he dies," I bit my words off viciously, "you killed him!"

His mouth opened again, mainly from astonishment. "I—" he began.

"Barging in on my classroom!" I raged. "Interrupting class work! Frightening my children! It's all your fault, your fault!" I couldn't bear the burden of guilt alone. I just had to have someone share it with me. But the fire died and I smoothed Abie's hand, trembling. "Please call a doctor. He might be dying."

"Nearest one is in Tortura Pass," said Mr. Diemus. "Sixty miles by road."

"Cross country?" I asked.

"Two mountain ranges and an alkali plateau."

"Then—then—" Abie's hand was so still in mine.

"There's a doctor at the Tumble A ranch," said Joel faintly. "He's taking a vacation."

"Go get him." I held Joel with my eyes. *Go as fast as you know how!*

Joel gulped miserably. "Okay."

"They'll probably have horses to come back on," I said. "Don't be too obvious."

"Okay," and he ran out the door. We heard the thud of his running feet until he was halfway across the school yard, then silence. Faintly, seconds later, creek gravel crunched below the hill. I could only guess at what he was doing—that he couldn't lift all the way and was going in jumps whose length was beyond all reasonable measuring.

The children had gone home, quietly, anxiously. And, after the doctor arrived, we had improvised a stretcher and carried Abie to the Peters home. I walked along close beside him watching his pinched little face, my hand touching his chest occasionally just to be sure he was still breathing.

And now—the waiting . . .

I looked at my watch again. A minute past the last time I looked. Sixty seconds by the hands, but hours and hours by anxiety.

"He'll be all right," I whispered, mostly to comfort myself. "The doctor will know what to do."

Mr. Diemus turned his dark empty eyes to me. "Why did you do it?" he asked. "We almost had it stamped out. We were almost free."

"Free of what?" I took a deep breath. "Why did *you* do it? Why did you deny your children their inheritance?"

"It isn't your concern—"

"Anything that hampers my children is my concern. Anything that turns children into creeping, frightened mice is wrong. Maybe I went at the whole deal the wrong way, but you told me to teach them what I had to—and I did."

"Disobedience, rebellion, flouting authority—"

"They obeyed *me*," I retorted. "They accepted *my* authority!" Then I softened. "I can't blame them," I confessed. "They were troubled. They told me it was wrong—that they had been *taught* it was wrong. I argued them into it. But oh, Mr. Diemus! It took so little argument, such a tiny breach in the dam to loose the flood. They never even questioned my knowledge—any more than you have, Mr. Diemus! All this—this *wonder* was beating against their minds, fighting to be set free. The rebellion was there long before I came. I didn't incite them to something new. I'll bet there's not a one, except maybe Esther, who hasn't practiced and practiced, furtively and ashamed, the things I permitted—demanded that they do for me.

"It wasn't fair—not fair at all—to hold them back."

"You don't understand." Mr. Diemus' face was stony. "You haven't all the facts—"

"I have enough," I replied. "So you have a frightened memory of an unfortunate period in your history. But what people *doesn't* have such a memory in larger or lesser degree? That you and your children have it more vividly should have helped, not hindered. You should have been able to figure out ways of adjusting. But leave that for the moment. Take the other side of the picture. What possible thing could all this suppression and denial yield you more precious than what you gave up?"

"It's the only way," said Mr. Diemus. "We are unacceptable to earth, but we have to stay. We have to conform—"

"Of course you had to conform," I cried. "Anyone has to when they change societies. At least enough to get them by until others can adjust to them. But to crawl in a hole and pull it in after you! Why, the other Group—"

"Other Group!" Mr. Diemus whitened, his eyes widening. "Other Group? There are others? There are others?" He leaned tensely forward in his chair. "Where? Where?" And his voice broke shrilly on the last word. He closed his eyes and his mouth trembled as he fought for control. The bedroom door opened. Dr. Curtis came out, his shoulders weary.

He looked from Mr. Diemus to me and back. "He should be in a hospital. There's a depressed fracture and I don't know what all else. Probably extensive brain involvement. We need X-rays and—and—" He rubbed his hand slowly over his weary young face. "Frankly, I'm not experienced to handle cases like this. We need specialists. If you can scare up some kind of transportation that won't jostle . . ." He shook his head, seeing the kind of country that lay between us and anyplace, and went back into the bedroom.

"He's dying," said Mr. Diemus. "Whether you're right or we're right, he's dying."

"Wait! Wait!" I said, catching at the tag end of a sudden idea. "Let me think." Urgently I willed myself back through the years to the old Dorm room. Intently I listened and listened and remembered.

"Have you a—a—*Sorter* in this Group?" I asked, fumbling for unfamiliar terms.

"No," said Mr. Diemus. "One who could have been, but isn't."

"Or *any* communicator?" I asked. "Anyone who can send or receive?"

"No," said Mr. Diemus, sweat starting on his forehead. "One who could have been, but—"

"See?" I accused. "See what you've traded for . . . for what? Who are the coulds but can'ts? Who are they?"

"I am," said Mr. Diemus, the words a bitterness in his mouth. "And my wife."

I stared at him, wondering confusedly. How far did training decide? What could we do with what we had?

"Look," I said quickly. "There *is* another Group. And they—they have all the Signs and Persuasions. Karen's been trying to find you—to find any of the People. She told me—oh, Lord, it's been years ago, I hope it's still so—every evening they send out calls for the People. If we can catch it—if *you* can catch the call and answer it, they can help.

I know they can. Faster than cars, faster than planes, more surely than specialists—"

"But if the doctor finds out—" wavered Mr. Diemus fearfully.

I stood up abruptly. "Good night, Mr. Diemus," I said, turning to the door. "Let me know when Abie dies."

His cold hand shook on my arm.

"Can't you see!" he cried. "I've been taught too, longer and stronger than the children! We never even dared *think* of rebellion! Help me, help me!"

"Get your wife," I said. "Get her and Abie's mother and father. Bring them down to the grove. We can't do anything here in the house. It's too heavy with denial."

I hurried on ahead and sank down on my knees in the evening shadows among the trees.

"I don't know what I'm doing," I cried into the bend of my arm. "I have an idea, but I don't know! Help us! Guide us!"

I opened my eyes to the arrival of the four.

"We told him we were going out to pray," said Mr. Diemus.

And we all did.

Then Mr. Diemus began the call I worded for him, silently, but with such intensity that sweat started again on his face. *Karen, Karen, Come to the People, Come to the People.* And the other three sat around him, bolstering his effort, supporting his cry. I watched their tense faces, my own twisting in sympathy, and time was lost as we labored.

Then slowly his breathing calmed and his face relaxed and I felt a stirring as though something brushed past my mind. Mrs. Diemus whispered, "He remembers now. He's found the way."

And as the last spark of sun caught mica highlights on the hilltop above us, Mr. Diemus stretched his hands out slowly and said with infinite relief, "There they are."

I looked around startled, half expecting to see Karen coming through the trees. But Mr. Diemus spoke again.

"Karen, we need help. One of our Group is dying. We have a doctor, an Outsider, but he hasn't the equipment or the know-how to help. What shall we do?"

In the pause that followed, I was slowly conscious of a new feeling. I couldn't tell you exactly what it was—a kind of unfolding . . . an opening . . . a relaxation. The ugly tight defensiveness that was so characteristic of the grown-ups of Bendo was slipping away.

"Yes, Valancy," said Mr. Diemus. "He's in a bad way. We can't

269

help because—" His voice faltered and his words died. I felt a resurgence of fear and unhappiness as his communication went beyond words, and then ebbed back to speech again.

"We'll expect you then. You know the way."

I could see the pale blur of his face in the dusk under the trees as he turned back to us.

"They're coming," he said, wonderingly. "Karen and Valancy. They're so pleased to find us—" His voice broke. "We're *not* alone—"

And I turned away as the two couples merged in the darkness. I had pushed them somewhere way beyond me.

It was a lonely, lonely walk back to the house for me . . . alone.

They dropped down through the half darkness—four of them. For a fleeting second I wondered at myself that I could stand there matter-of-factly watching four adults slant calmly down out of the sky. Not a hair ruffled, not a stain of travel on them, knowing that only a short time before they had been hundreds of miles away—not even aware that Bendo existed.

But all strangeness was swept away as Karen hugged me delightedly.

"It *is* you!" she cried. "He said it was, but I wasn't sure! Oh, it's so *good* to see you again! Who owes who a letter?"

She laughed and turned to the smiling three. "Valancy, the Old One of our Group." Valancy's radiant face proved the Old One didn't mean age. "Bethie, our Sensitive." The slender, fair-haired young girl ducked her head shyly. "And my brother Jemmy. Valancy's his wife."

"This is Mr. and Mrs. Diemus," I said. "And Mr. and Mrs. Peters, Abie's parents. It's Abie, you know. My second grade." I was suddenly overwhelmed by how long ago and far away school felt. How far I'd gone from my accustomed pattern!

"What shall we do about the doctor?" I asked. "Will he have to know?"

"Yes," said Valancy. "We can help him, but we can't do the actual work. Can we trust him?"

I hesitated, remembering the few scanty glimpses I'd had of him. "I—" I began.

"Pardon me," said Karen. "I wanted to save time. I went in to you. We know now what you know of him. We'll trust Dr. Curtis."

I felt an eerie creeping up my spine. To have my thoughts taken so casually! Even to the doctor's name!

Bethie stirred restlessly and looked at Valancy. "He'll be in convulsions soon. We'd better hurry."

"You're sure you have the knowledge?" asked Valancy.

"Yes," murmured Bethie. "If I can make the doctor see—if he's willing to follow."

"Follow what?"

The heavy tones of the doctor's voice startled us all as he stepped out on the porch.

I stood aghast at the impossibility of the task ahead of us and looked at Karen and Valancy to see how they would make the doctor understand. They said nothing. They just looked at him. There was a breathless pause. The doctor's startled face caught the glint of light from the open door as he turned to Valancy. He rubbed his hand across his face in bewilderment and, after a moment, turned to me.

"Do *you* hear her?"

"No," I admitted. "She isn't talking to me."

"Do you *know* these people?"

"Oh, yes!" I cried, wishing passionately it was true. "Oh, yes!"

"And believe them?"

"Implicitly," I said.

"But she says that Bethie—who's Bethie?" He glanced around.

"She is," said Karen, nodding at Bethie.

"*She* is?" Dr. Curtis looked intently at the shy, lovely face. He shook his head wonderingly and turned back to me.

"Anyway, this one, Valancy, says Bethie can sense every condition in the child's body and that she will be able to tell all the injuries, their location and extent without X-rays! Without equipment!"

"Yes," I said. "If they say so."

"You would be willing to risk a child's life—"

"Yes," I said. "They know. They really do." And swallowed hard to keep down the fist of doubt that clenched in my chest.

"You believe they can *see* through flesh and bone?"

"Maybe not see," I said, wondering at my own words. "But *know* with a knowledge that is sure and complete." I glanced, startled, at Karen. Her nod was very small but it told me where my words came from.

"Are *you* willing to trust these people?" The doctor turned to Abie's parents.

"They're *our* People," said Mr. Peters with quiet pride. "I'd operate on him myself with a pickax if they said so."

"Of all the screwball deals . . . !" The doctor's hand rubbed across his face again. "I know I needed this vacation, but this is ridiculous!"

We all listened to the silence of the night and—at least I—to the drumming of anxious pulses until Dr. Curtis sighed heavily.

"Okay, Valancy. I don't believe a word of it. At least I wouldn't if I were in my right mind, but you've got the terminology down pat as if you knew *something*. . . . Well, I'll do it. It's either that or let him die. And God have mercy on our souls!"

I couldn't bear the thought of shutting myself in with my own dark fears, so I walked back toward the school, hugging myself in my inadequate coat against the sudden sharp chill of the night. I wandered down to the grove, praying wordlessly, and on up to the school. But I couldn't go in. I shuddered away from the blank glint of the windows and turned back to the grove. There wasn't any more time or direction or light or anything familiar—only a confused cloud of anxiety and a final icy weariness that drove me back to Abie's house.

I stumbled into the kitchen, my stiff hands fumbling at the door knob. I huddled in a chair, gratefully leaning over the hot wood stove that flicked the semi-darkness of the big homey room with warm red light, trying to coax some feeling back into my fingers.

I drowsed as the warmth began to penetrate and then the door was flung open and slammed shut. The doctor leaned back against it, his hand still clutching the knob.

"Do you know what they did?" he cried, not so much to me as to himself. "What they made *me* do? Oh Lord!" He staggered over to the stove, stumbling over my feet. He collapsed by my chair, rocking his head between his hands. "They made me operate on his brain! *Repair* it. Trace circuits and rebuild them. *You can't do that!* It can't be done! Brain cells damaged can't be repaired. No one can restore circuits that are destroyed! It can't be done. But I did it! *I did it!*"

I knelt beside him and tried to comfort him in the circle of my arms.

"There, there, there," I soothed.

He clung like a terrified child. "No anesthetics!" he cried. "*She* kept him asleep. And no bleeding when I went through the scalp! *They* stopped it. And the impossible things I did with the few instruments I have with me! And the brain starting to mend right before my eyes! Nothing was right!"

"But nothing was wrong," I murmured. "Abie will be all right, won't he?"

"How do I know?" he shouted suddenly, pushing away from me.

"I don't know anything about a thing like this. I put his brain back together and he's still breathing, but how do I know!"

"There, there," I soothed. "It's over now."

"It'll never be over!" With an effort he calmed himself and we helped one another up from the floor. "You can't forget a thing like this in a life time."

"We can give you forgetting," said Valancy softly from the door. "If you *want* to forget. We can send you back to the Tumble A with no memory of tonight except a pleasant visit to Bendo."

"You can?" He turned speculative eyes toward her. "You can." He amended his words to a statement.

"Do you want to forget?" asked Valancy.

"Of course not," he snapped. Then, "I'm sorry. It's just that I don't often work miracles in the wilderness. But if I did it once, maybe—"

"Then you understand what you did?" asked Valancy, smiling.

"Well, no, but if I could—if you would . . . There must be some way—"

"Yes," said Valancy, "But you'd have to have a Sensitive working with you and Bethie is It as far as Sensitives go right now."

"You mean it's true what I saw—what you told me about the—The Home? You're extraterrestrials?"

"Yes," sighed Valancy. "At least our grandparents were." Then she smiled. "But we're learning where we can fit into this world. Some day —some day we'll be able—" She changed the subject abruptly.

"You realize, of course, Dr. Curtis, that we'd rather you wouldn't discuss Bendo or us with anyone else. We would rather be just people to Outsiders."

He laughed shortly, "Would I be believed if I did?"

"Maybe no, maybe so," said Valancy. "Maybe only enough to start people nosing around. And that would be too much. We have a bad situation here and it will take a long time to erase—" and her voice slipped into silence and I knew she had dropped into thoughts to brief him on the local problem. How long is a thought? How fast can you think of Hell—and Heaven? It was that long before the doctor blinked and drew a shaky breath.

"Yes," he said. "A long time."

"If you like," said Valancy, "I can block your ability to talk of us."

"Nothing doing!" snapped the doctor. "I can manage my own censorship, thanks."

Valancy flushed. "I'm sorry. I didn't mean to be condescending."

"You weren't," said the doctor. "I'm just on the prod tonight. It has been a *Day*, and that's for sure!"

"Hasn't it though?" I smiled, and then, astonished, rubbed my cheeks because tears had begun to spill down my face. I laughed, embarrassed, and couldn't stop. My laughter turned suddenly to sobs and I was bitterly ashamed to hear myself wailing like a child. I clung to Valancy's strong hands until I suddenly slid into a warm welcome darkness that had no thinking or fearing or need for believing in anything outrageous, but only in sleep.

It was a magic year and it fled on impossibly fast wings, the holidays flicking past like telephone poles by a railroad. Christmas was especially magic because my angels actually flew and the Glory actually shone around about because their robes had hems woven of sunlight—I watched the girls weave them. And Rudolph the Red-nosed Reindeer, complete with cardboard antlers that wouldn't stay straight, really took off and circled the room. And as our Mary and Joseph leaned raptly over the Manger, their faces solemn and intent on the Miracle, I felt suddenly that they were really seeing, really kneeling beside the Manger in Bethlehem.

Anyway, the months fled, and the blossoming of Bendo was beautiful to see. There was laughter and frolicking and even the houses grew subtly into color. Green things crept out where only rocks had been before and a tiny tentative stream of water had begun to flow down the creek again. They explained to me that they had to take it slow because people might wonder if the creek filled overnight! Even the rough steps up to the houses were being overgrown because they were so seldom used, and I was becoming accustomed to seeing my pupils coming to school like a bevy of bright birds, playing tag in the treetops. I was surprised at myself for adjusting so easily to all the incredible things done around me by The People, and I was pleased that they accepted me so completely. But I always felt a pang when the children escorted me home—with me, they had to walk.

But all things have to end, and I sat one May afternoon, staring into my top desk drawer, the last to be cleaned out, wondering what to do with the accumulation of useless things in it. But I wasn't really seeing the contents of the drawer, I was concentrating on the great weary emptiness that pressed my shoulders down and weighted my mind. "It's not fair," I muttered aloud and illogically, "to show me Heaven and then snatch it away."

"That's about what happened to Moses, too, you know."

My surprised start spilled an assortment of paper clips and thumb tacks from the battered box I had just picked up.

"Well forevermore!" I said, righting the box. "Dr. Curtis! What are you doing here?"

"Returning to the scene of my crime," he smiled, coming through the open door. "Can't keep my mind off Abie. Can't believe he recovered from all that . . . shall we call it repair work? I have to check him every time I'm anywhere near this part of the country—and I still can't believe it."

"But he has."

"He has for sure! I had to fish him down from a treetop to look him over—" The doctor shuddered dramatically and laughed. "To see him hurtling down from the top of that tree curdled my blood! But there's hardly even a visible scar left."

"I know," I said, jabbing my finger as I started to gather up the tacks. "I looked last night. I'm leaving tomorrow, you know." I kept my eyes resolutely down to the job at hand. "I have this last straightening up to do."

"It's hard, isn't it?" he said and we both knew he wasn't talking about straightening up.

"Yes," I said soberly. "Awfully hard. Earth gets heavier every day."

"I find it so lately, too," he said. "But at least you have the satisfaction of knowing that you—"

I moved uncomfortably and laughed.

"Well, they do say: Those as can, do; those as can't, teach."

"Umm," said the doctor noncommittally, but I could feel his eyes on my averted face and I swiveled away from him, groping for a better box to put the clips in.

"Going to summer school?" His voice came from near the windows.

"No," I sniffed cautiously. "No, I swore when I got my Master's that I was through with education—at least the kind that's come-every-day-and-learn-something."

"Hmm!" There was amusement in the doctor's voice. "Too bad," he said. "I'm going to school this summer. Thought you might like to go there, too."

"Where?" I asked bewildered, finally looking at him.

"Cougar Canyon Summer School," he smiled. "Most exclusive."

"Cougar Canyon! Why that's where Karen—"

"Exactly," he said. "That's where the other Group is established. I just came from there. Karen and Valancy want us both to come. Do you object to being an experiment?"

"Why, no—" I cried—and then, cautiously, "What kind of an experiment?" Visions of brains being carved up swam through my mind.

The doctor laughed. "Nothing as gruesome as you're imagining, probably." Then he sobered and sat on the edge of my desk. "I've been to Cougar Canyon a couple of times, trying to figure out some way to get Bethie to help me when I come up against a case that's a puzzler. Valancy and Karen want to try a period of training with Outsiders—" he grimaced wryly "—that's us—to see how much of what *they* are can be transmitted by training. You know Bethie is half Outsider. Only her mother was of The People."

He was watching me intently.

"Yes," I said absently, my mind whirling, "Karen told me."

"Well, do you want to try it? Do you want to go?"

"Do I want to go!" I cried, scrambling the clips into a rubber band box. "How soon do we leave? Half an hour? Ten minutes? Did you leave the motor running?"

"Woops, woops!" The doctor took me by both arms and looked soberly into my eyes.

"We can't set our hopes too high," he said quietly. "It may be that for such knowledge we aren't teachable—"

I looked soberly back at him, my heart crying in fear that it might be so.

"Look," I said slowly. "If you had a hunger, a great big gnawing-inside hunger and no money and you saw a bakery shop window—which would you do? Turn your back on it? Or would you press your nose as close as you could against the glass and let at least your eyes feast? I know what *I'd* do." I reached for my sweater.

"And, you know, you never can tell. The shop door might open a crack, maybe—someday . . ."

TEACHING PRIME

Leo P. Kelley

One of the students in "Teaching Prime" remarks that going to school "... won't help me earn a living." He is reacting to a feeling which is present in our own society—that much that takes place in the school simply is designed to take up time, or is just "filler" for teaching staffs that are unable to hold the attention of their students.

The critics who hold this view forget that the so-called practical goal of education is but one part of a larger picture, for the schools perform more functions than simply vocational preparation. They also teach citizenship, build values, and expose the student to ideas and concepts which he may never have known otherwise.

Nevertheless, the American people have historically looked upon public education as a vehicle for social and economic mobility. Its mystique, although somewhat tarnished, remains powerful. The schools have been looked upon much as the frontier was—a place where social background and parentage did not mean as much as talent, hard work, and a desire to get ahead. An egalitarianism seemed to pervade public education, a feeling based on democratic beliefs in the worth of each individual. Furthermore, the schools were believed to be a repository of Americanism, tradition, and moral and spiritual values. It was assumed that the schools would *transmit* these traditions (imprecisely defined) to each succeeding generation. The teacher, in turn, was held to be the transmitter—the device which would build citizenship and patriotism in the child.

This deeply held view has been challenged in recent years by rapid social change. The changes in sexual mores, the furor over "permissiveness" in education, the racial crisis, and the breaking down of traditional religious values have all had an impact on the perception of public education. Society has been taking a close, hard look at the schools, and is sometimes unfairly equating these social changes with the educational process.

"Teaching Prime" looks at a future society in which education plays a grimmer, more deadly role. It exposes children to a "reality" filled with danger and violence. It "tells it like it is" to the students with little apparent concern for the side effects. Its purpose is simple: *survival.*

The problems faced by American society are now being thrust before our students in a direct fashion. This was not always the case. There was a reluctance to criticize the decisions of our government and to justify all of its actions. Problems which were pushed under the educational carpet are now being faced directly. This is undoubtedly a welcome development, because problems of political corruption, of environmental survival, and of war and peace can only be solved by an informed public. Teaching students how to face these problems is one of the most important roles for education to play in the 1970s.

FOR FURTHER THOUGHT OR DISCUSSION

1. What were the historical assumptions underlying American public education?

2. Did education fulfill these early goals?

3. What role, if any, did education play in promoting or retarding social change in this country?

4. What are the consequences of the "new realism" in American education?

5. What is the nature of the society depicted in the story and what role does education play in it?

TEACHING PRIME   *Leo P. Kelley*

Two of the children failed to make it to the eduarena. One fell in a flooded gully that had been caused by careless, not to mention illegal, strip mining and drowned within minutes. The other child ate berries that had been chemically corrupted and died almost instantly.

The others, more than a little bit proud of themselves for having survived the daily journey, scampered into the eduarena and slid into their assigned seats. As the force field sprang up outside, they finally relaxed.

The Roboteach swiveled back and forth on the oiled stage as it checked attendance and erased the names of the two dead children from its roster tapes.

"Comparative Galactic Ecosystems," it announced in its neutral, neutered voice. "Notes must be taken. Nuances may be noted. Parallels are to be drawn. Conclusions can be reached and reported at session's end. Are we ready?"

"We are ready!" chanted the children in their young voices.

"I'm not," a student whispered to his companion beside him. "This stuff is a waste of time."

"Well, we got to pass it anyway or we won't get into Highered later on," his friend whispered with resignation.

"It won't help me earn a living," the first student persisted.

"It might," his friend speculated. "Who knows?"

"Silence," spat the Roboteach. "Silence, please, while your attention is paid to the holographic simulation of forthcoming comparative galactic ecosystems. The Level has been adjusted for students who have seen but seven sets of seasons pass."

The lights dimmed and the eduarena seemed to expand as the holographic screens began to project their vividly dimensional lesson for the day.

Moving out among the children, the figures began to act out their programmed dramas.

The children watched the multicellular inhabitants of the Planet Saurus as they went about their daily tasks in the misty mountains and thin air. The Saurians slid and billowed about, their many eyes alert, their tails held high in their nervous signaling to one another.

"Heat kills," grunted one Saurian as several of his cells atrophied under the onslaught of the sun beaming down through the magnification lens above the fields of sprouting seeds the workers were harvesting.

"Heat's hell," moaned another mournfully as the mists were vanquished by the yellow eye glaring down through the smooth glass.

"Sweet water, sweet water," sang one of the workers hours later as it fought for space in the small cool mud wallow at the edge of the raped fields.

The watching children in the eduarena giggled at the grotesque rhythm of the creature's words.

A child impulsively raised her hand and told the Roboteach that her best friend had been drowned earlier on the way to class. Why couldn't some of their rainwater, she asked, be shipped to the Planet Saurus since the Saurians sure did seem to need it pretty bad. She said there was too much water outside anyway. It was always raining, she complained, since the Agroeconomists ruined the atmospheric balance.

The Roboteach told her she was perceptive but instructed her to please keep quiet until the entire sequence was properly completed.

The Saurian's flesh steamed in the relentless sun which caused the mud wallow to dry up. The child whose best friend had drowned began to cry and had to be led away lest her wailing disrupt the lesson.

The holographic screens shifted and the Saurians slid sluggishly into the empty shadows and out of sight.

Words danced gaily among the children.

DICK AND JANE. SEQUENCE TWO. COMPARATIVE GALACTIC ECOSYSTEMS. PAY YOUR ATTENTION.

"Ooohhh!" sighed the children as Dick and Jane bounced happily out among them.

Dick was tall and blond and he had blue eyes above a very nice nose. His lips were the right size but he couldn't seem to close them. His smile kept getting in the way.

Jane stood beside him, gazing fondly up into his blue eyes with her chocolate colored ones. Her hair gleamed with setspray and her dress, which glittered with green sequins, reached as far as her upper thighs and then gave up and vanished. It avoided her pert breasts, leaving them bare. She ran slim and unringed fingers through her stiff discolored hair and continued gazing contentedly into Dick's eyes.

Dick flexed the many muscles in his arms for no apparent purpose. They bulged and rippled beneath the sheer sleeves of his yellow tunic. He looked all around him, turning first this way, then that way.

"Where is Spot?" he asked Jane. "Spot is not here."

"No, Spot is not here," Jane said. "Where is Spot?"

Billy and Betty came bounding holographically and happily into the middle of the eduarena.

"Hello, Mother," Billy said.

"Hello, Father," Betty said.

"Hello, Billy," Jane said.

"Hello, Betty," Dick said. "Where is Spot?"

"Here comes Spot," Billy said. "See Spot run."

"Spot runs fast," Betty said.

She picked up a bright red rubber ball and threw it very high into the air. Spot barked and ran after it. The ball rolled across the macadam outside the box of their house and into the middle of the superhighway that ran beside it.

The monocars streamed steadily past and over the dog's body without stopping or caring.

"Spot is not here," Billy said.

"Is Grandmother here?" Betty asked.

"Yes," said Dick. "Grandmother is in the house. Go into the house and see Grandmother, Betty."

Betty went obediently up the path to the house. She walked past the gun turrets growing up out of the grassless ground and she waded through the strewn garbage. She entered the small square structure and called out to Grandmother.

The others followed her, coughing from the fumes that spewed forth from the monocar mechanisms.

"Happy Birthday, Grandmother," Betty said as she kissed her Grandmother.

"Thank you, Betty. Thank you very much. I am going now."

"Goodbye," Betty said.

"You have had a good life, Mother," Jane said. "The Euthanasia Exit is down the block. It is next door to the Crime Corps Complex."

"I have had a good life," Grandmother said. "Forty years is a good long time."

Grandmother picked up her knapsack and her pistol and went to the front door of the one-room house. She turned and waved goodby to Dick and Jane. She bent and kissed Billy and Betty.

"The Brentwoods who live next door," said Jane, "have bought new guns with telescopic sights.

"The bounty on Grandmothers was raised again this month," Dick said.

Grandmother hurried out of the house, glancing furtively across the mounds of garbage at the Brentwood house where steel turrets gleamed now and then amid the clouds of carbon monoxide.

Betty clapped her hands. "See Grandmother run!"

"Grandmother runs fasts!" Billy cried.

They all watched Grandmother run through the fusillade of Brentwood bullets, firing back grimly.

"Hurrah!" Billy cried. "They missed her!"

Jane smiled. "Grandmother runs very fast. Now it is time to sleep."

Billy took a peyote button out of his pocket and began to chew it.

Betty went and got the spoons and the glassine envelopes and the hypodermic needles and the little Bunsen burner.

They heated the heroin in the spoons and then injected it expertly into their veins.

"Sweet dreams, Billy," Jane said.

"Sweet dreams, Betty," Dick said.

They sat down on the dirty floor and began to nod.

In the eduarena, the lights changed and deepened to indicate the passage of time.

"Good morning," Jane said to everyone.

They all wished her a good morning as Betty put the needles and the spoons and the little Bunsen burner away until later.

Outside the house, the garbage mounds, they discovered, had become miniature mountains during the long night. The sound of monocars streaming past was an endless technological lullaby. Bullets zinged familiarly in the air instead of the forgotten songs of birds.

They all huddled against the protection of the house while they watched the neighborhood's usual morning melee. Betty scurried down into a gun turret and began firing at the Grandfather loping hopelessly along the edge of the superhighway toward the Euthanasia Exit to celebrate his fortieth birthday. She dropped him on the second shot and skipped to where he lay. She removed his identification disk and went away to collect her bounty.

"I feel sick," Dick said. "My head hurts. I am nauseous. I cannot see straight."

Jane touched his damp forehead and took his pulse. She pulled down the lower lids of his eyes. "You have botulism, Dick. It must have been in the uninspected cans of contraband stringbeans they shipped up from Mexico."

"I was very hungry," Dick said. "We had so little food all last week." He closed his eyes and fell to the macadam.

"Father is dead," Jane said.

"I am thirsty," Billy said.

"The government promised to send us some water next week," Jane said. "Wait, Billy. Wait for the unpolluted water."

"Who is that?" Billy asked, pointing to the young woman who was zigzagging up the macadam in order to avoid the bursting bullets that the neighbors were firing at her in case she turned out to be a Grandmother.

"That is Jane," Jane said. "The other lady behind her is also Jane."

The two Janes scurried past Billy and Jane and on into the house. Billy and Jane followed them inside.

"We have come for Dick," the Janes said. "It is our turn with Dick this week."

"Dick is dead," Jane told them. "He is lying outside near the un-collected garbage."

"Who is he?" the Janes asked, pointing at Billy.

"He is Billy," Jane said. "But he is only nine."

"We don't care," the woman said. "There aren't many men left since Census Control succeeded. Or women either, for that matter."

They seized Billy and dragged him from the house.

Jane was left alone. "Spot ran fast," she said to herself. "Dick had a very nice nose. Betty shoots true. Billy is gone away. I—"

The Crime Corps burst into the house without bothering to knock and arrested Jane for littering.

"I am innocent," Jane said.

"You let Dick lie on the public macadam outside where he fell," the Crime Corps Commander accused. "You littered."

"I am—" Jane began.

"Dead," said the Commander as he shot her and she fell. "The punishment must fit the crime."

The eduarena environment altered suddenly. The light shifted. The bodies of Dick and Jane disappeared. The Roboteach tapped his baton to attract the children's attention.

"What happened to Dick and Jane?" he asked.

"They died," the children responded.

"More than that, much more," the Roboteach insisted with a show of almost impish impatience. "I will show you cue cards to help you think of the right answer. Look up at the overhead screen, please, and pay your attention."

A multicelled and many-eyed figure appeared on the screen.

"Name?" inquired the roboteach.

"Saurian," a student called out.

"Correct."

Click: a bird.

"Peregrine falcon," someone volunteered.

"Correct."

Click: a striped animal.

"Sabre-tooth tiger," the children chorused.

Click: another bird.

"Passenger pigeon."

Click: a picture of Dick, Jane, Jane, Jane, Billy and Betty.

"What have all these species in common?" inquired the Roboteach.

"They are all extinct," a student announced with young pomp.

"True," said the Roboteach.

"But Betty didn't die," someone protested. "Neither did Billy. The two Janes took Billy away. Betty went to get her bounty."

"You are in error," the Roboteach announced solemnly. "You were not paying your full attention. I shall reinstate the environment. Now watch closely this time."

The scene in which Betty leaned over to remove the Grandfather's identification disk reappeared in the eduarena. The children watched closely as Betty ran along the edge of the superhighway. They ignored all other details in the scene this time. They saw the monocar glide to a halt and the driver reach out and drag Betty into the car where he strangled her and tore from her hand the identification disk. They saw him mark another X on the broad dashboard of his monocar and speed away in the direction of the Bounty Collection Center.

"But what about the two Janes and Billy?" the children cried, eager now to be right in their answers.

They were shown what had happened—what they had failed to notice the first time. The Janes fought one another for possession of Billy. He fought both of them. But the Brentwood bullets cut them all down just in case they might turn out to be Grandmothers and a Grandfather.

"Extinct species, locus Earth," the Roboteach intoned. "What then is the point of today's lesson?"

"Who says there is one?" snickered one bored student under his breath.

"The point is," said the Roboteach patiently, "that we must not let the fate of the Saurians whom you saw earlier nor that of the residents of Earth become ours here on the Planet Vorno. We must protect and preserve our environment and one another if we are to survive."

"What does it know?" muttered the same student who had snickered earlier. "That old Roboteach isn't even alive like us!"

He received no answer as the class was dismissed and the children of Vorno slithered out past the deactivated force field on their multiple limbs and clawed and pawed their way through the dangers surrounding them.

Two of the children did not make it home alive from the eduarena. One was caught in the crossfire between enemy soldiers from Vorno North and Vorno South. The second was struck by the landing gear of a low flying helicab.

When the survivors arrived home, their fond parents asked them what they had learned in the eduarena that day. They shrugged their scales and muttered their vague answers:

"Nothing much."

"The same old stuff."

"About Dick and Jane."

4.
TECHNOLOGY AND EDUCATION

As the technological capabilities of society increase, the student of the social foundations of education will be required to devote more attention to the relationship between technology and education. It should be remembered, as indicated in the Introduction, that "technology" refers not only to the physical tools and devices which are usually associated with scientific know-how but also—and perhaps more importantly—to the conceptual tools, including ideas, theories, and principles, which allow for the development and use of the former.

At least three distinct categories of technology, with important implications for the study of education, can be discerned. The first is *product-oriented technology.* This is knowledge which is embodied within a definite object, such as a book, television, film, language laboratories, teaching machines, or programmed texts. The emphasis here is on an *object*—a "thing" which aids learning.

The second category is *process-oriented technology.* The key to this technology is a sequence, or a *process,* by which learning is organized. Some common examples of process-technology in schools include teacher aides, team-teaching, flexible scheduling, and small-group discussion.

The third category is *person-oriented technology.* This technology represents the teacher as the source of knowledge—as the "method" by which learning occurs and knowledge is conveyed.

Often these categories of technology generate tensions within the school as a social unit within society. One tension arises from the perceptions of different actors within society concerning the appropriateness of emphasizing one particular technology. Students, parents, teachers, citizens, school administrators—all may have different opinions about the value of particular technologies. Simultaneously, one technology may be viewed by students as effective, by parents as frivolous, by teachers as burdensome, by citizens as politically unacceptable—and by school administrators as efficient!

Another tension exists in relation to the economic costs incurred by communities in the support and usage of varied educational technologies. Many parents are skeptical of sophisticated product-oriented and process-oriented technology on the basis of their feeling that "it costs too much." Related to this economic skepticism is the tension that is generated from a feeling, usually shared by school administrators and elected school officials, that the technology used in school should be related to its appropriateness in a particular cultural and political setting rather than to its intrinsic merits as a tool for learning.

Thus the student of the social foundations of education should be aware of the cultural, social, and political constraints upon educational technology as well as their objective educational potential. He should recognize, moreover, that each society will choose what it wants in the way of technology for its schools and adapt it to its particular needs. The uses—and abuses—of technology in education is more often related to social choice than to objective educational need.

PROGENY

Philip K. Dick

It is true of education in modern society that technology is having a tremendous impact on its processes. Before the technological revolution, education was a one-to-one relationship between teacher and child. The teacher, from the student's (and from society's) point of view, had a virtual monopoly on knowledge. The development of printing eroded this monopoly, but only to a limited degree. Books made knowledge mobile, but the teacher remained the starting point.

Along with the technological revolution came a veritable revolution in knowledge. It soon became apparent that a single teacher could only understand a tiny percentage of human knowledge. The result was *specialization* with each teacher concentrating on conveying a small fraction of the available information in a specific area to the child. Separate disciplines and departments within schools soon followed. The knowledge explosion resulted in the complete reorganization of our educational system.

Technology also forced changes in the *way* children were taught. The development of films, television, and teaching machines has further transformed education. This process has not been without its costs. First, the consequences for the student are still unclear. Although learning seems to be enhanced by machines, the question remains as to the quality of values being transmitted in this fashion. Second, the increasing reliance on technology has created concern within the teaching profession about its future. To some, television and teaching machines represent a potential *replacement* for teachers. They have many advantages from an economic point of view. For one thing, machines do not get sick (although they may break down), they do not suffer from mental depressions, and above all, they are cheap when compared to teachers' salaries. Even allowing for high initial investments, one machine can reach large numbers of students. So, a basic question for education is to what extent has technology reduced the traditional role of the teacher, and what does this portend for the future?

In "Progeny" we encounter Ed Doyle, an average fellow in a highly technological society. His society has altered the roles of both parent and teacher, because children are taken away from the family at birth and placed in specialized learning environments where mobile machines (robots) educate them. As you read this story, ask yourself if this is the direction in which our society is moving, and what the final effect of technology will be.

FOR FURTHER THOUGHT OR DISCUSSION

1. Can machines do a better job of educating the young? Why? Why not?

2. In what ways are machines a threat to the future of the teaching profession?

3. How has technology altered the student-teacher relationship?

4. Does the specialized nature of education in the story parallel trends in our own society?

5. Do machine-taught youngsters lose their basic "humanity"?

PROGENY   *Philip K. Dick*

Ed Doyle hurried. He caught a surface car, waved fifty credits in the robot driver's face, mopped his florid face with a red pocket-handkerchief, unfastened his collar, perspired and licked his lips and swallowed piteously all the way to the hospital.

The surface car slid up to a smooth halt before the great white-domed hospital building. Ed leaped out and bounded up the steps three at a time, pushing through the visitors and convalescent patients standing on the broad terrace. He threw his weight against the door and emerged in the lobby, astonishing the attendants and persons of importance moving about their tasks.

"Where?" Ed demanded, gazing around, his feet wide apart, his fists clenched, his chest rising and falling. His breath came hoarsely, like an animal's. Silence fell over the lobby. Everyone turned toward him, pausing in their work. "Where?" Ed demanded again. "Where is she? *They?*"

It was fortunate Janet had been delivered of a child on this of all days. Proxima Centauri was a long way from Terra and the service was bad. Anticipating the birth of his child, Ed had left Proxima some weeks before. He had just arrived in the city. While stowing his suitcase in the luggage tread at the station, the message had been handed to him by a robot courier: Los Angeles Central Hospital. At once.

Ed hurried, and fast. As he hurried he couldn't help feeling pleased he had hit the day exactly right, almost to the hour. It was a good feeling. He had felt it before, during years of business dealings in the "colonies," the frontier, the fringe of Terran civilization where the streets were still lit by electric lights and doors opened by hand.

That was going to be hard to get used to. Ed turned toward the door behind him, feeling suddenly foolish. He had shoved it open, ignoring the eye. The door was just now closing, sliding slowly back in place. He calmed down a little, putting his handkerchief away in his coat pocket. The hospital attendants were resuming their work, picking up their activities where they had left off. One attendant, a strapping late-model robot, coasted over to Ed and halted.

The robot balanced his note-board expertly, his photocell eyes appraising Ed's flushed features. "May I enquire whom you are looking for, sir? Whom do you wish to find?"

"My wife."

"Her name, sir?"

"Janet. Janet Doyle. She's just had a child."

The robot consulted his board. "This way, sir." He coasted off down the passage.

Ed followed nervously. "Is she okay? Did I get here in time?" His anxiety was returning.

"She is quite well, sir." The robot raised his metal arm and a side door slid back. "In here, sir."

Janet, in a chic blue-mesh suit, was sitting before a mahogany desk, a cigarette between her fingers, her slim legs crossed, talking rapidly. On the other side of the desk a well-dressed doctor sat listening.

"Janet!" Ed said, entering the room.

"Hi, Ed." She glanced up at him. "You just now get in?"

"Sure. It's—it's all over? You—I mean, it's *happened*?"

Janet laughed, her even white teeth sparkling. "Of course. Come in and sit. This is Doctor Bish."

"Hello, Doc." Ed sat down nervously across from them. "Then it's all over?"

"The event has happened," Doctor Bish said. His voice was thin and metallic. Ed realized with a sudden shock that the doctor was a robot. A top-level robot, made in humanoid form, not like the ordinary metal-limbed workers. It had fooled him—he had been away so long. Doctor Bish appeared plump and well fed, with kindly features and eyeglasses. His large fleshy hands rested on the desk, a ring on one finger. Pinstripe suit and necktie. Diamond tie clasp. Nails carefully manicured. Hair black and evenly parted.

But his voice had given him away. They never seemed to be able to get a really human sound into the voice. The compressed air and whirling disc system seemed to fall short. Otherwise, it was very convincing.

"I understand you've been situated near Proxima, Mr. Doyle," Doctor Bish said pleasantly.

Ed nodded. "Yeah."

"Quite a long way, isn't it? I've never been out there. I have always wanted to go. Is it true they're almost ready to push on to Sirius?"

"Look, doc—"

"Ed, don't be impatient." Janet stubbed out her cigarette, glancing reprovingly up at him. She hadn't changed in six months. Small blonde face, red mouth, cold eyes like little blue rocks. And now, her perfect figure back again. "They're bringing him here. It takes a few minutes.

They have to wash him off and put drops in his eyes and take a wave shot of his brain."

"*He?* Then it's a boy?"

"Of course. Don't you remember? You were with me when I had the shots. We agreed at the time. You haven't changed your mind, have you?"

"Too late to change your mind now, Mr. Doyle," Doctor Bish's toneless voice came, high-pitched and calm. "Your wife has decided to call him Peter."

"Peter." Ed nodded, a little dazed. "That's right. We did decide, didn't we? Peter." He let the word roll around in his mind. "Yeah. That's fine. I like it."

The wall suddenly faded, turning from opaque to transparent. Ed spun quickly. They were looking into a brightly lit room, filled with hospital equipment and white-clad attendant robots. One of the robots was moving toward them, pushing a cart. On the cart was a container, a big metal pot.

Ed's breathing increased. He felt a wave of dizziness. He went up to the transparent wall and stood gazing at the metal pot on the cart.

Doctor Bish rose. "Don't you want to see, too, Mrs. Doyle?"

"Of course." Janet crossed to the wall and stood beside Ed. She watched critically, her arms folded.

Doctor Bish made a signal. The attendant reached into the pot and lifted out a wire tray, gripping the handles with his magnetic clamps. On the tray, dripping through the wire, was Peter Doyle, still wet from his bath, his eyes wide with astonishment. He was pink all over, except for a fringe of hair on the top of his head, and his great blue eyes. He was little and wrinkled and toothless, like an ancient withered sage.

"Golly," Ed said.

Doctor Bish made a second signal. The wall slid back. The attendant robot advanced into the room, holding his dripping tray out. Doctor Bish removed Peter from the tray and held him up for inspection. He turned him around and around, studying him from every angle.

"He looks fine," he said at last.

"What was the result of the wave photo?" Jane asked.

"Result was good. Excellent tendencies indicated. Very promising. High development of the—" The doctor broke off. "What is it, Mr. Doyle?"

Ed was holding out his hands. "Let me have him, doc. I want to hold him." He grinned from ear to ear. "Let's see how heavy he is. He sure looks big."

Doctor Bish's mouth fell open in horror. He and Janet gaped.

"Ed!" Janet exclaimed sharply. "What's the matter with you?"

"Good heavens, Mr. Doyle," the doctor murmured.

Ed blinked. "What?"

"If I had thought you had any such thing in mind—" Doctor Bish quickly returned Peter to the attendant. The attendant rushed Peter from the room, back to the metal pot. The cart and robot and pot hurriedly vanished, and the wall banged back in place.

Janet grabbed Ed's arm angrily. "Good Lord, Ed! Have you lost your mind? Come on. Let's get out of here before you do something else."

"But—"

"Come on." Janet smiled nervously at Doctor Bish. "We'll run along now, doctor. Thanks so much for everything. Don't pay any attention to him. He's been out there so long, you know."

"I understand," Doctor Bish said smoothly. He had regained his poise. "I trust we'll hear from you later, Mrs. Doyle."

Janet pulled Ed out into the hall. "Ed, what's the matter with you? I've never been so embarrassed in all my life." Two spots of red glowed in Janet's cheeks. "I could have kicked you."

"But what—"

"You *know* we aren't allowed to touch him. What do you want to do, ruin his whole life?"

"But—"

"Come on." They hurried outside the hospital, onto the terrace. Warm sunlight streamed down on them. "There's no telling what harm you've done. He may already be hopelessly warped. If he grows up all warped and—and neurotic and emotional, it'll be your fault."

Suddenly Ed remembered. He sagged, his features drooping with misery. "That's right. I forgot. Only robots can come near the children. I'm sorry, Jan. I got carried away. I hope I didn't do anything they can't fix."

"How *could* you forget?"

"It's so different out at Prox." Ed waved to a surface car, crestfallen and abashed. The driver drew up in front of them. "Jan, I'm sorry as hell. I really am. I was all excited. Let's go have a cup of coffee someplace and talk. I want to know what the doctor said."

Ed had a cup of coffee and Janet sipped at a brandy frappé. The Nymphite Room was pitch black except for a vague light oozing up from the table between them. The table diffused a pale illumination that spread over everything, a ghostly radiation seemingly without source. A robot waitress moved back and forth soundlessly with a tray of drinks. Recorded music played softly in the back of the room.

"Go on," Ed said.

"Go on?" Janet slipped her jacket off and laid it over the back of her chair. In the pale light her breasts glowed faintly. "There's not much to tell. Everything went all right. It didn't take long. I chatted with Doctor Bish most of the time."

"I'm glad I got here."

"How was your trip?"

"Fine."

"Is the service getting any better? Does it still take as 'long as it did?"

"About the same."

"I can't see why you want to go all the way out there. It's so—so cut off from things. What do you find out there? Are plumbing fixtures really that much in demand?"

"They need them. Frontier area. Everyone wants the refinements." Ed gestured vaguely. "What did he tell you about Peter? What's he going to be like? Can he tell? I guess it's too soon."

"He was going to tell me when you started acting the way you did. I'll call him on the vidphone when we get home. His wave pattern should be good. He comes from the best eugenic stock."

Ed grunted. "On your side, at least."

"How long are you going to be here?"

"I don't know. Not long. I'll have to go back. I'd sure like to see him again, before I go." He glanced up hopefully at his wife. "Do you think I can?"

"I suppose."

"How long will he have to stay there?"

"At the hospital? Not long. A few days."

Ed hesitated. "I didn't mean at the hospital, exactly. I mean with *them*. How long before we can have him? How long before we can bring him home?"

There was silence. Janet finished her brandy. She leaned back, lighting a cigarette. Smoke drifted across to Ed, blending with the pale light. "Ed, I don't think you understand. You've been out there so long. A lot has happened since you were a child. New methods, new techniques. They've found out so many things they didn't know. They're making progress, for the first time. They know what to do. They're developing a real methodology for dealing with children. For the growth period. Attitude development. Training." She smiled brightly at Ed. "I've been reading all about it."

"How long before we get him?"

"In a few days he'll be released from the hospital. He'll go to a child guidance center. He'll be tested and studied. They'll determine his various capacities and his latent abilities. The direction his development seems to be taking."

"And then?"

"Then he's put in the proper educational division. So he'll get the right training. Ed, you know, I think he's really going to *be* something! I could tell by the way Doctor Bish looked. He was studying the wave pattern charts when I came in. He had a look on his face. How can I describe it?" She searched for the word. "Well, almost—almost a greedy look. Real excitement. They take so much interest in what they're doing. He—"

"Don't say he. Say *it*."

"Ed, really! What's got into you?"

"Nothing." Ed glared sullenly down. "Go on."

"They make sure he's trained in the right direction. All the time he's there ability tests are given. Then, when he's about nine, he'll be transferred to—"

"Nine! You mean nine *years!*"

"Of course."

"But when do *we* get him?"

"Ed, I thought you knew about this. Do I have to go over the whole thing?"

"My God, Jan! We can't wait nine years!" Ed jerked himself upright. "I never heard of such a thing. Nine years? Why, he'll be half grown by then."

"That's the point." Janet leaned toward him, resting her bare elbow against the table. "As long as he's growing he has to be with them. Not with us. Afterwards, when he's finished growing, when he's no longer so plastic, then we can be with him all we want."

"Afterwards? When he's eighteen?" Ed leaped up, pushing his chair back. "I'm going down there and get him."

"Sit down, Ed." Janet gazed up calmly, one supple arm thrown lightly over the back of her chair. "Sit down and act like an adult, for a change."

"Doesn't it matter to you? Don't you care?"

"Of course I care." Janet shrugged. "But it's necessary. Otherwise he won't develop correctly. It's for *his* good. Not ours. He doesn't exist for us. Do you want him to have conflicts?"

Ed moved away from the table. "I'll see you later."

"Where are you going?"

"Just around. I can't stand this kind of place. It bothers me. I'll see you later." Ed pushed across the room to the door. The door opened and he found himself on the shiny noon-day street. Hot sunlight beat down on him. He blinked, adjusting himself to the blinding light. People streamed around him. People and noise. He moved with them.

He was dazed. He had known, of course. It was there in the back of his mind. The new developments in child care. But it had been abstract, general. Nothing to do with him. With *his* child.

He calmed himself, as he walked along. He was getting all upset about nothing. Janet was right, of course. It was for Peter's good. Peter didn't exist for them, like a dog or cat. A pet to have around the house. He was a human being, with his own life. The training was for him, not for them. It was to develop him, his abilities, his powers. He was to be molded, realized, brought out.

Naturally, robots could do the best job. Robots could train him scientifically, according to a rational technique. Not according to emotional whim. Robots didn't get angry. Robots didn't nag and whine. They didn't spank a child or yell at him. They didn't give conflicting orders. They didn't quarrel among themselves or use the child for their own ends. And there could be no *Oedipus Complex,* with only robots around.

No complexes at all. It had been discovered long ago that neurosis could be traced to childhood training. To the way parents brought up the child. The inhibitions he was taught, the manners, the lessons, the punishments, the rewards. Neuroses, complexes, warped development, all stemmed from the subjective relationship existing between the child and the parent. If perhaps the parent could be eliminated as a factor . . .

Parents could never become objective about their children. It was always a biased, emotional projection the parent held toward the child. Inevitably, the parent's view was distorted. No parent could be a fit instructor for his child.

Robots could study the child, analyze his needs, his wants, test his abilities and interests. Robots would not try to force the child to fit a certain mold. The child would be trained along his own lines; wherever scientific study indicated his interest and need lay.

Ed came to the corner. Traffic whirred past him. He stepped absently forward.

A clang and crash. Bars dropped in front of him, stopping him. A robot safety control.

"Sir, be more careful!" the strident voice came, close by him.

"Sorry." Ed stepped back. The control bars lifted. He waited for the lights to change. It was for Pete's own good. Robots could train him right. Later on, when he was out of his growth stage, when he was not so pliant, so responsive—

"It's better for him," Ed murmured. He said it again, half aloud. Some people glanced at him and he colored. Of course it was better for him. No doubt about it.

Eighteen. He couldn't be with his son until he was eighteen. Practically grown up.

The lights changed. Deep in thought, Ed crossed the street with the other pedestrians, keeping carefully inside the safety lane. It was best for Peter. But eighteen years was a long time.

"A hell of a long time," Ed murmured, frowning. "Too damn long a time."

Doctor 2g-Y Bish carefully studied the man standing in front of him. His relays and memory banks clicked, narrowing down the image identification, flashing a variety of comparison possibilities past the scanner.

"I recall you, sir," Doctor Bish said at last. "You're the man from Proxima. From the colonies. Doyle. Edward Doyle. Let's see. It was some time ago. It must have been—"

"Nine years ago," Ed Doyle said grimly. "Exactly nine years ago, practically to the day."

Doctor Bish folded his hands. "Sit down, Mr. Doyle. What can I do for you? How is Mrs. Doyle? Very engaging wife, as I recall. We had a delightful conversation during her delivery. How—"

"Doctor Bish, do you know where my son is?"

Doctor Bish considered, tapping his fingers on the desk top, the polished mahogany surface. He closed his eyes slightly, gazing off into the distance. "Yes. Yes, I know where your son is, Mr. Doyle."

Ed Doyle relaxed. "Fine." He nodded, letting his breath out in relief.

"I know exactly where your son is. I placed him in the Los Angeles Biological Research Station about a year ago. He's undergoing specialized training there. Your son, Mr. Doyle, has shown exceptional ability. He is, shall I say, one of the few, the very few we have found with real possibilities."

"Can I see him?"

"See him? How do you mean?"

Doyle controlled himself with an effort. "I think the term is clear."

Doctor Bish rubbed his chin. His photocell brain whirred, operating at maximum velocity. Switches routed power surges, building up loads and leaping gaps rapidly, as he contemplated the man before him. "You wish to *view* him? That's one meaning of the term. Or do you wish to talk to him? Sometimes the term is used to cover a more direct contact. It's a loose word."

"I want to talk to him."

"I see." Bish slowly drew some forms from the dispenser on his desk. "There are a few routine papers that have to be filled out first, of course. Just how long did you want to speak to him?"

Ed Doyle gazed steadily into Doctor Bish's bland face. "I want to talk to him several hours. *Alone.*"

"Alone?"

"No robots around."

Doctor Bish said nothing. He stroked the papers he held, creasing the edges with his nail. "Mr. Doyle," he said carefully, "I wonder if you're in a proper emotional state to visit your son. You have recently come in from the colonies?"

"I left Proxima three weeks ago."

"Then you have just arrived here in Los Angeles?"

"That's right."

"And you've come to see your son? Or have you other business?"

"I came for my son."

"Mr. Doyle, Peter is at a very critical stage. He has just recently been transferred to the Biology Station for his higher training. Up to now his training has been general. What we call the nondifferentiated stage. Recently he has entered a new period. Within the last six months Peter has begun advanced work along his specific line, that of organic chemistry. He will—"

"What does Peter think about it?"

Bish frowned. "I don't understand, sir."

"How does *he* feel? Is it what he wants?"

"Mr. Doyle, your son has the possibility of becoming one of the world's finest bio-chemists. In all the time we have worked with human beings, in their training and development, we have never come across a more alert and integrated faculty for the assimilation of data, construction of theory, formulation of material, than that which your son possesses. All tests indicate he will rapidly rise to the top of his chosen field. He is still only a child, Mr. Doyle, but it is the children who must be trained."

Doyle stood up. "Tell me where I can find him. I'll talk to him for two hours and then the rest is up to him."

"The rest?"

Doyle clamped his jaw shut. He shoved his hands in his pockets. His face was flushed and set, grim with determination. In the nine years he had grown much heavier, more stocky and florid. His thinning hair had turned iron-gray. His clothes were dumpy and unpressed. He looked stubborn.

Doctor Bish sighed. "All right, Mr. Doyle. Here are the papers. The law allows you to observe your boy whenever you make proper application. Since he is out of his nondifferentiated stage, you may also speak to him for a period of ninety minutes."

"Alone."

"You can take him away from the Station grounds for that length of time." Doctor Bish pushed the papers over to Doyle. "Fill these out, and I'll have Peter brought here."

He looked up steadily at the man standing before him.

"I hope you'll remember that any emotional experience at this crucial stage may do much to inhibit his development. He has chosen his field, Mr. Doyle. He must be permitted to grow along his selected lines, unhindered by situational blocks. Peter has been in contact with our technical staff throughout his entire training period. He is not accustomed to contact with other human beings. So please be careful."

Doyle said nothing. He grabbed up the papers and plucked out his fountain pen.

He hardly recognized his son when the two robot attendants brought him out of the massive concrete Station building and deposited him a few yards from Ed's parked surface car.

Ed pushed the door open. "Pete!" His heart was thumping heavily, painfully. He watched his son come toward the car, frowning in the bright sunlight. It was late afternoon, about four. A faint breeze blew across the parking lot, rustling a few papers and bits of debris.

Peter stood slim and straight. His eyes were large, deep brown, like Ed's. His hair was light, almost blonde. More like Janet's. He had Ed's jaw, though, the firm line, clean and well-chiseled. Ed grinned at him. Nine years it had been. Nine years since the robot attendant had lifted the wire rack up from the conveyor pot, to show him the little wrinkled baby, red as a boiled lobster.

Peter had grown. He was not a baby any longer. He was a young boy, straight and proud, with firm features and wide, clear eyes.

"Pete," Ed said. "How the hell are you?"

The boy stopped by the door of the car. He gazed at Ed calmly.

His eyes flickered, taking in the car, the robot driver, the heavy-set man in the rumpled tweed suit grinning nervously at him.

"Get in. Get inside." Ed moved over. "Come on. We have places to go."

The boy was looking at him again. Suddenly Ed was conscious of his baggy suit, his unshined shoes, his gray stubbled chin. He flushed, yanking out his red pocket-handkerchief and mopping his forehead uneasily. "I just got off the ship, Pete. From Proxima. I haven't had time to change. I'm a little dusty. Long trip."

Peter nodded. "4.3 light years, isn't it?"

"Takes three weeks. Get in. Don't you want to get in?"

Peter slid in beside him. Ed slammed the door.

"Let's go." The car started up. "Drive—" Ed peered out the window. "Drive up there. By the hill. Out of town." He turned to Pete. "I hate big cities. I can't get used to them."

"There are no large cities in the colonies, are there?" Peter murmured. "You're unused to urban living."

Ed settled back. His heart had begun to slow down to its normal beat. "No, as a matter of fact it's the other way around, Pete."

"How do you mean?"

"I went to Prox *because* I couldn't stand cities."

Peter said nothing. The surface car was climbing, going up a steep highway into the hills. The Station, huge and impressive, spread out like a heap of cement bricks directly below them. A few cars moved along the road, but not many. Most transportation was by air, now. Surface cars had begun to disappear.

The road levelled off. They moved along the ridge of the hills. Trees and bushes rose on both sides of them. "It's nice up here," Ed said.

"Yes."

"How—how have you been? I haven't seen you for a long time. Just once. Just after you were born."

"I know. Your visit is listed in the records."

"You been getting along all right?"

"Yes. Quite well."

"They treating you all right?"

"Of course."

After awhile Ed leaned forward. "Stop here," he said to the robot driver.

The car slowed down, pulling over to the side of the road. "Sir, there is nothing—"

"This is fine. Let us out. We'll walk from here."

The car stopped. The door slid reluctantly open. Ed stepped quickly out of the car, onto the pavement. Peter got out slowly after him, puzzled. "Where are we?"

"No place." Ed slammed the door. "Go on back to town," he said to the driver. "We won't need you."

The car drove off. Ed walked to the side of the road. Peter came after him. The hill dropped away, falling down to the beginnings of the city below. A vast panorama stretched out, the great metropolis in the late afternoon sun. Ed took a deep breath, throwing his arms out. He took off his coat and tossed it over his shoulder.

"Come on." He started down the hillside. "Here we go."

"Where?"

"For a walk. Let's get off this damn road."

They climbed down the side of the hill, walking carefully, holding onto the grass and roots jutting out from the soil. Finally they came to a level place by a big sycamore tree. Ed threw himself down on the ground, grunting and wiping sweat from his neck.

"Here. Let's sit here."

Peter sat down carefully, a little way off. Ed's blue shirt was stained with sweat. He unfastened his tie and loosened his collar. Presently he searched through his coat pockets. He brought out his pipe and tobacco.

Peter watched him fill the pipe and light it with a big sulphur match. "What's that?" he murmured.

"This? My pipe." Ed grinned, sucking at the pipe. "Haven't you ever seen a pipe?"

"No."

"This is a good pipe. I got this when I first went out to Proxima. That was a long time ago, Pete. It was twenty-five years ago. I was just nineteen, then. Only about twice as old as you."

He put his tobacco away and leaned back, his heavy face serious, preoccupied.

"Just nineteen. I went out there as a plumber. Repair and sales, when I could make a sale. Terran Plumbing. One of those big ads you used to see. Unlimited opportunities. Virgin lands. Make a million. Gold in the streets." Ed laughed.

"How did you make out?"

"Not bad. Not bad at all. I own my own line, now, you know. I service the whole Proxima system. We do repairing, maintenance, building. Construction. I've got six hundred people working for me. It took a long time. It didn't come easy."

"No."

"Hungry?"

Peter turned. "What?"

"Are you hungry?" Ed pulled a brown paper parcel from his coat and unwrapped it. "I still have a couple sandwiches from the trip. When I come in from Prox I bring some food along with me. I don't like to buy in the diner. They skin you." He held out the parcel. "Want one?"

"No thank you."

Ed took a sandwich and began to eat. He ate nervously, glancing at his son. Peter sat silently, a short distance off, staring ahead without expression. His smooth handsome face was blank.

"Everything all right?" Ed said.

"Yes."

"You're not cold, are you?"

"No."

"You don't want to catch cold."

A squirrel crossed in front of them, hurrying toward the sycamore tree. Ed threw it a piece of his sandwich. The squirrel ran off a way, then came back slowly. It scolded at them, standing up on its hind feet, its great gray tail flowing out behind it.

Ed laughed. "Look at him. Ever see a squirrel before?"

"I don't think so."

The squirrel ran off with the piece of sandwich. It disappeared among the brush and bushes.

"Squirrels don't exist out around Prox," Ed said.

"No."

"It's good to come back to Terra once in awhile. See some of the old things. They're going, though."

"Going?"

"Away. Destroyed. Terra is always changing." Ed waved around at the hillside. "This will be gone, someday. They'll cut down the trees. Then they'll level it. Someday they'll carve the whole range up and carry it off. Use it for fill, someplace along the coast."

"That's beyond our scope," Peter said.

"What?"

"I don't receive that type of material. I think Doctor Bish told you. I'm working with bio-chemistry."

"I know," Ed murmured. "Say, how the hell did you ever get mixed up with that stuff? Bio-chemistry?"

"The tests showed that my abilities lie along those lines."

"You enjoy what you're doing?"

"What a strange thing to ask. Of course I enjoy what I'm doing. It's the work I'm fitted for."

"It seems funny as hell to me, starting a nine-year-old kid off on something like that."

"Why?"

"My God, Pete. When I was nine I was bumming around town. In school sometimes, outside mostly, wandering here and there. Playing. Reading. Sneaking into the rocket launching yards all the time." He considered. "Doing all sorts of things. When I was sixteen I hopped over to Mars. I stayed there awhile. Worked as a hasher. I went on to Ganymede. Ganymede was all sewed up tight. Nothing doing there. From Ganymede I went out to Prox. Got a work-away all the way out. Big freighter."

"You stayed at Proxima?"

"I sure did. I found what I wanted. Nice place, out there. Now we're starting on to Sirius, you know." Ed's chest swelled. "I've got an outlet in the Sirius system. Little retail and service place."

"Sirius is 8.8 light years from Sol."

"It's a long way. Seven weeks, from here. Rough grind. Meteor swarms. Keeps things hot all the way out."

"I can imagine."

"You know what I thought I might do?" Ed turned toward his son, his face alive with hope and enthusiasm. "I've been thinking it over. I thought maybe I'd go out there. To Sirius. It's a fine little place we have. I drew up the plans myself. Special design to fit with the characteristics of the system."

Peter nodded.

"Pete—"

"Yes?"

"Do you think maybe you'd be interested? Like to hop out to Sirius and take a look? It's a good place. Four clean planets. Never touched. Lots of room. Miles and miles of room. Cliffs and mountains. Oceans. Nobody around. Just a few colonists, families, some construction. Wide, level plains."

"How do you mean, interested?"

"In going all the way out." Ed's face was pale. His mouth twitched nervously. "I thought maybe you'd like to come along and see how things are. It's a lot like Prox was, twenty-five years ago. It's good and clean out there. No cities."

Peter smiled.

"Why are you smiling?"

"No reason." Peter stood up abruptly. "If we have to walk back to the Station we better start. Don't you think? It's getting late."

"Sure." Ed struggled to his feet. "Sure, but—"

"When are you going to be back in the Sol system again?"

"Back?" Ed followed after his son. Peter climbed up the hill toward the road. "Slow down, will you?"

Peter slowed down. Ed caught up with him.

"I don't know when I'll be back. I don't come here very often. No ties. Not since Jan and I separated. As a matter of fact I came here this time to—"

"This way." Peter started down the road.

Ed hurried along beside him, fastening his tie and putting his coat on, gasping for breath. "Pete, what do you say? You want to hop out to Sirius with me? Take a look? It's a nice place out there. We could work together. The two of us. If you want."

"But I already have my work."

"That stuff? That damn chemistry stuff?"

Peter smiled again.

Ed scowled, his face dark red. "Why are you smiling?" he demanded. His son did not answer. "What's the matter? What's so damn funny?"

"Nothing," Peter said. "Don't become excited. We have a long walk down." He increased his pace slightly, his supple body swinging in long, even strides. "It's getting late. We have to hurry."

Doctor Bish examined his wristwatch, pushing back his pinstriped coat sleeve. "I'm glad you're back."

"He sent the surface car away," Peter murmured. "We had to walk down the hill on foot."

It was dark outside. The Station lights were coming on automatically, along the rows of buildings and laboratories.

Doctor Bish rose from his desk. "Sign this, Peter. Bottom of this form."

Peter signed. "What is it?"

"Certifies you saw him in accord with the provisions of the law. We didn't try to obstruct you in any way."

Peter handed the paper back. Bish filed it away with the others. Peter moved toward the door of the doctor's office. "I'll go. Down to the cafeteria for dinner."

"You haven't eaten?"

"No."

Doctor Bish folded his arms, studying the boy. "Well?" he said. "What do you think of him? This is the first time you've seen your father. It must have been strange for you. You've been around us so much, in all your training and work."

"It was—unusual."

"Did you gain any impressions? Was there any thing you particularly noticed?"

"He was very emotional. There was a distinct bias through everything he said and did. A distortion present, virtually uniform."

"Anything else?"

Peter hesitated, lingering at the door. He broke into a smile. "One other thing."

"What was it?"

"I noticed—" Peter laughed. "I noticed a distinct odor about him. A constant pungent smell, all the time I was with him."

"I'm afraid that's true of all of them," Doctor Bish said. "Certain skin glands. Waste products thrown off from the blood. You'll get used to it, after you've been around them more."

"Do I have to be around them?"

"They're your own race. How else can you work with them? Your whole training is designed with that in mind. When we've taught you all we can, then you will—"

"It reminded me of something. The pungent odor. I kept thinking about it, all the time I was with him. Trying to place it."

"Can you identify it now?"

Peter reflected. He thought hard, concentrating deeply. His small face wrinkled up. Doctor Bish waited patiently by his desk, his arms folded. The automatic heating system clicked on for the night, warming the room with a soft glow that drifted gently around them.

"I know!" Peter exclaimed suddenly.

"What was it?"

"The animals in the biology labs. It was the same smell. The same smell as the experimental animals."

They glanced at each other, the robot doctor and the promising young boy. Both of them smiled, a secret, private smile. A smile of complete understanding.

"I believe I know what you mean," Doctor Bish said. "In fact, I know *exactly* what you mean."

THE EVER-BRANCHING TREE

Harry Harrison

"The Ever-Branching Tree" combines an old educational technique—the field trip—with advanced technological developments created by the imagination of the author.

Advances in technology are transforming the American classroom in ways that will make it unrecognizable to a teacher who retired in the 1950s. Among these developments are the following:

1. *Television.* Employed at every level of education, television is most useful in illustrating experiments for students who would otherwise have difficulty seeing the details of what is going on. It has the added advantage of being a medium with which the child is familiar before he starts school. In addition, recent developments in video tape mean that live lectures and experiments can be preserved and used again in the future.

2. *Teaching Machines.* These devices are becoming common and more sophisticated. They are used in the teaching of spelling and other skills and have the great advantage of forcing the student to compose his answer, which allows him to develop capabilities of recall and reasoning.

3. *Films.* Perhaps the first modern example of the application of technology to education, films remain popular and effective with students. There is little indication that their use is diminishing.

4. *Tapes.* The most common example of the use of tapes is in the language laboratory where students listen to recordings and practice their language skills with them.

Along with the increasing use of advanced technology is the reorganization of the classroom. A number of interesting concepts are being employed. The following present a few examples:

1. *Self-directed study* places responsibility for learning, study,

and evaluation on the student himself. This is especially effective with more advanced students, and allows the teacher more time to deal with those who need more help.

2. The *discussion group* uses the principles of group dynamics as an aid to the learning process. It enables the teacher to interact with students as human beings, not just as an authority figure at the front of a classroom. However, it is a very expensive technique because of the relatively few students involved.

3. The *large lecture hall* is simply an enlarged classroom which enables one teacher to reach several hundred students, and, in the parlance of the Pentagon, it is "cost-effective."

4. *Teacher aides* are appearing in the classroom in large numbers. They perform numerous tasks which assist the teacher, such as grading papers, and thereby allow the teacher to spend more time with the students. They are also very valuable in helping disadvantaged students.

5. *Teams* of teachers can be very effective, especially in the social sciences, where the emphasis is on interdisciplinary studies.

There may be some dangers in the increasing use of technology in the classroom, however. Foremost among these dangers is the impersonalization taking place in some schools. Machines, after all, are not men and women. They cannot bring to the classroom the emotions and vibrations of the teaching act.

In this story, Teacher employs an advanced version of the field trip to illustrate the vast sweep of evolutionary development. But even Teacher is exposed to an exchange between mother and daughter which sounds all too familiar—"What did you learn in school today, darling?" "Oh, nothing much."

FOR FURTHER THOUGHT OR DISCUSSION

1. What negative effects do you see as technology is applied to education?

2. Why is the field trip such a useful educational device?

3. In the story, why does Teacher expose his students to so much violence?

4. How can schools reconcile the need for individual attention for students with economic realities?

THE EVER-BRANCHING TREE *Harry Harrison*

The children had spread up and down the beach, and some of them had even ventured into the surf where the tall green waves crashed down upon them. Glaring from a deep blue sky, the sun burned on the yellow sand. A wave broke into foam, surging far up the shore with a soundless rush. The sharp clap-clap of Teacher's hands could easily be heard in the sunlit silence.

"Playtime is over—put your clothes back on, Grosbit-9, all of them —and the class is about to begin.

They straggled towards Teacher as slowly as they could. The bathers emerged dry from the ocean, while not a grain of sand adhered to skin or garment of the others. They gathered about Teacher, their chatter gradually dying away, and he pointed dramatically at a tiny creature writhing across the sand.

"Uhggh, a worm!" Mandi-2 said and shivered deliciously, shaking her red curls.

"A worm, correct. A first worm, an early worm, a proto-worm. An important worm. Although it is not on the direct evolutionary track that we are studying we must pause to give it notice. A little more attention, Ched-3, your eyes are closing. For here, for the first time, we see segmentation, as important a step in the development of life as was the development of multicellular forms. See, look carefully, at those series of rings about the creature's body. It looks as though it were made of little rings of tissue fused together—and it is."

They bent close, a circle of lowered heads above the brown worm that writhed a track across the sand. It moved slowly towards Grosbit-9 who raised his foot and stamped down hard on the creature. The other students tittered. The worm crawled out through the side of his shoe and kept on.

"Grosbit-9, you have the wrong attitude," Teacher said sternly. "Much energy is being expended to send this class back through time, to view the wonders of evolution at work. We cannot feel or touch or hear or change the past, but we can move through it and see it about us. So we stand in awe of the power that permits us to do this, to visit our Earth as it was millions of years ago, to view the ocean from which all life sprung, to see one of the first life forms on the ever-branching tree of evolution. And what is your response to this awe-inspiring experience? You *stamp* on the annelid! For shame, Grosbit-9, for shame."

Far from feeling shameful, Grosbit-9 chewed a hangnail on his thumb and looked about out of the corners of his eyes, the trace of a smirk upon his lips. Teacher wondered, not for the first time, how a 9 had gotten into this class. A father with important contacts, no doubt, high placed friends.

"Perhaps I had better recap for those of you who are paying less than full attention." He stared hard at Grosbit-9 as he said this, with no apparent effect. "Evolution is how we reached the high estate we now inhabit. Evolution is the forward march of life, from the one-celled creatures to multi-celled, thinking man. What will come after us we do not know, what came before us we are now seeing. Yesterday we watched the lightning strike the primordial chemical soup of the seas and saw the more complex chemicals being made that developed into the first life forms. We saw this single-celled life triumph over time and eternity by first developing the ability to divide into two cells, then to develop into composite, many-celled life forms. What do you remember about yesterday?"

"The melted lava poured into the ocean!"

"The land rose from the sea!"

"The lightning hit the water!"

"The squirmy things were so ugghhy!"

Teacher nodded and smiled and ignored the last comment. He had no idea why Mandi-2 was registered in this science course and had a strong feeling she would not stay long.

"Very good. So now we reach the annelids, like our worm here. Segmented, with each segment almost living a life of its own. Here are the first blood vessels to carry food to all the tissues most efficiently. Here is the first hemoglobin to carry oxygen to all the cells. Here is the first heart, a little pump to force the blood through those tubes. But one thing is missing yet. Do you know what it is?"

Their faces were empty of answers, their eyes wide with expectation.

"Think about it. What would have happened if Grosbit-9 had really stepped on this worm?"

"It would have squashed," Agon-1 answered with eight-year-old practicality. Mandi-2 shivered.

"Correct. It would have been killed. It is soft, without a shell or a skeleton. Which brings us to the next branch on the evolutionary tree."

Teacher pressed the activating button on the control unit at his waist, and the programmed computer seized them and hurled them through time to their next appointment. There was a swift, all-encompassing greyness, with no feeling of motion at all, which vanished suddenly to be replaced by a green dimness. Twenty feet above their heads the sun sparkled on the surface of the ocean while all about them silent fish moved in swift patterns. A great monster, all plates and shining teeth hurtled at and through them and Mandi-2 gave a little squeal of surprise.

"Your attention down here, if you please. The fish will come later. First we must study these, the first echinoderms. Phill-4, will you point out an echinoderm and tell us what the term means."

"Echinoderm," the boy said, keying his memory. The training techniques that all the children learned in their first years of schooling brought the words to his lips. Like the others he had a perfect memory. "Is Greek for spiny skin. That must be one there, the big hairy starfish."

"Correct. An important evolutionary step. Before this, animals were either unprotected, like our annelid worm, or had skeletons outside like snails or lobsters or insects. This is very limiting and inefficient. But an internal skeleton can give flexible support and is light in weight. An important evolutionary step has been made. We are almost there, children, almost there! This simple internal skeleton evolved into a more practical notochord, a single bone the length of the body protecting a main nerve fiber. And the chordata, the creatures with this notochord, were only a single evolutionary step away from this—all *this!*"

Teacher threw his arms wide just as the sea about them burst into darting life. A school of silvery, yard-long fishes flashed around and through the students, while sharp-toothed shark-like predators struck through their midst. Teacher's speech had been nicely timed to end at this precise and dramatic moment. Some of the smaller children shied away from the flurry of life and death while Grosbit-9 swung his fist at one of the giants as it glided by.

"We have arrived," Teacher said, vibrantly, carried away by his own enthusiasm. "The chordata give way to the vertebrata, life as we know it. A strong, flexible internal skeleton that shields the soft inner organs and supports at the same time. Soft cartilage in these sharks— the same sort of tissue that stiffens your ears—changes to hard bone in these fishes. Mankind, so to speak, is just around the corner! What is it, Ched-3?" He was aware of a tugging on his toga.

"I have to go to the . . ."

"Well press the return button on your belt and don't be too long about it."

Ched-3 pressed the button and vanished, whisked back to their classroom with its superior functional plumbing. Teacher smacked his lips annoyedly while the teeming life whirled and dived about them. Children could be difficult at times.

"How did these animals know to get a notochord and bones?" Agon-1 asked. "How did they know the right way to go to end up with the vertebrata—and us?"

Teacher almost patted him on the head, but smiled instead.

"A good question, a very good question. Someone has been listening and thinking. The answer is they didn't know, it wasn't planned. The ever-branching tree of evolution has no goals. Its changes are random, mutations caused by alterations in the germ plasm caused by natural radiation. The successful changes live, the unsuccessful ones die. The notochord creatures could move about easier, were more successful than the other creatures. They lived to evolve further. Which brings us to a new word I want you to remember. The word is 'ecology' and we are talking about ecological niches. Ecology is the whole world, everything in it, how all the plants and animals live together and how they relate one to the other. An ecological niche is where a creature lives in this world, the special place where it can thrive and survive and reproduce. All creatures that find an ecological niche that they can survive in are successful."

"The survival of the fittest?" Agon-1 asked.

"You have been reading some of the old books. That is what evolution was once called, but it was called wrong. *All* living organisms are fit, because they are alive. One can be no more fit than the other. Can we say that we, mankind, are more fit than an oyster?"

"Yes," Phill-4 said, with absolute surety. His attention on Ched-3 who had just returned, apparently emerging from the side of one of the sharks.

"Really? Come over here, Ched-3, and try to pay attention. We live and the oysters live. But what would happen if the world were to suddenly be covered by shallow water?"

"How could that happen?"

"The how is not important," Teacher snapped, then took a deep breath. "Let us just say it happened. What would happen to all the people?"

"They would all drown!" Mandi-2 said, unhappily.

"Correct. Our ecological niche would be gone. The oysters would thrive and cover the world. If we survive we are all equally fit in the eyes of nature. Now let us see how our animals with skeletons are faring in a new niche. Dry land."

A press, a motionless movement, and they were on a muddy shore by a brackish swamp. Teacher pointed to the trace of a feathery fin cutting through the floating algae.

"The subclass crossoptergii, which means fringed fins. Sturdy little fish who have managed to survive in this stagnant water by adopting their swim bladders to breathe air directly and to get their oxygen in this manner. Many fish have these bladders that enable them to hover at any given depth, but now they have been adapted to a different use. Watch!"

The water became shallower until the fish's back was above the water, then its bulging eyes. Staring about, round and wide, as though terrified by this new environment. The sturdy fins, reinforced by bone, thrashed at the mud, driving it forward, further and further from its home, the sea. Then it was out of the water, struggling across the drying mud. A dragonfly hovered low, landed—and was engulfed by the fish's open mouth.

"The land is being conquered," Teacher said, pointing to the humped back of the fish now vanishing among the reeds. "First by plants, then insects—and now the animals. In a few million years, still over 225 million years before our own time, we have this . . ."

Through time again, rushing away on the cue word, to another swampy scene, a feathery marsh of ferns as big as trees and a hot sun burning through low-lying clouds.

And life. Roaring, thrashing, eating, killing life. The time researchers must have searched diligently for this place, this instant in the history of the world. No words were needed to describe or explain.

The age of reptiles. Small ones scampered by quickly to avoid the carnage falling on them. Scolosaurus, armored and knobbed like a tiny tank pushed through the reeds, his spiked tail dragging a rut in the mud. Great brontosaurus stood high against the sky, his tiny, foolish head, with its teacup of brains, waving at the end of his lengthy neck, turned back to see what was bothering him as some message crept through his indifferent nervous system. His back humped up, a mountain of gristle and bone and flesh and hooked to it was the demon form of tyrannosaurus. His tiny forepaws scratched feebly against the other's leathery skin while his yards-long razor-toothed jaws tore at the heaving wall of flesh. Brontosaurus, still not sure what was happening, dredged up a quarter ton of mud and water and plants and chewed it, wondering. While high above, heaving and flapping its leathery wings, pteranodon wheeled by, long jaws agape.

"That one's hurting the other one," Mandi-2 said. "Can't you make them stop?"

"We are only observers, child. What you see happened so very long ago and is unalterable in any way."

"Kill!" Grosbit-9 muttered, his attention captured for the very first time. They all watched, mouths dropping open at the silent fury.

"These are reptiles, the first successful animals to conquer the land. Before them were the amphibia, like our modern frogs, tied unbreakably to the water where their eggs are laid and the young grow up. But the reptiles lay eggs that can hatch on land. The link with the sea has been cut. Land has been conquered at last. They lack but a single characteristic that will permit them to survive in all the parts of the globe. You have all been preparing for this trip. Can anyone tell me what is still missing?"

The answer was only silence. Brontosaurus fell and large pieces of flesh were torn from his body. Pteranodon flapped away. A rain squall blotted out the sun.

"I am talking about temperature. These reptiles get a good deal of their body heat from the sun. They must live in a warm environment because as their surroundings get cooler their bodies get cooler..."

"Warm-blooded!" Agon-1 said with shrill excitement.

"Correct. Someone, at least, has been doing the required studying. I see you sticking your tongue out, Ched-3. How would you like it if you couldn't draw it back and it stayed that way? Controlled body temperature, the last major branch on the ever-branching tree. The first class of what might be called centrally-heated animals is the mammalia. The mammals. If we all go a little bit deeper into this forest you will see what I mean. Don't straggle, keep up there. In this clearing, everyone. On this side. Watch those shrubs there. Any moment now..."

Expectantly they waited. The leaves stirred and they leaned forward. A piglike snout pushed out, sniffing the air, and two suspicious, slightly crossed eyes looked about the clearing. Satisfied that there was no danger for the moment, the creature came into sight.

"Coot! Is that ever ugly," Phill-4 said.

"Beauty is in the eye of the beholder, young man. I'll ask you to hold your tongue. This is a perfect example of the subclass prototheria, the first beasts, tritylodon itself. For many years a source of controversy as to whether it was mammal or reptile. The smooth skin and shiny plates of a reptile—but notice the tufts of hair between the plates. Reptiles do not have hair. And it lays eggs, as reptiles do. But it, she, this fine creature here also suckles her young as do the mammals. Look with awe at this bridge between the old class of reptiles and emerging class of mammals."

"Oh, how *cute!*" Mandi-2 squealed as four tiny pink duplicates of the mother staggered out of the shrubbery after her. Tritylodon dropped heavily onto her side and the young began to nurse.

"That is another thing that the mammals brought into the world," Teacher said as the students looked on with rapt fascination. "Mother love. Reptile offspring, either born live or when they emerge from the egg, are left to fend for themselves. But warm-blooded mammals must be warmed, protected, fed while they develop. They need mothering and, as you see, they receive it in sufficiency."

Some sound must have troubled the tritylodon because she looked around, then sprang to her feet and trundled off into the underbrush, her young falling and stumbling after her. No sooner was the clearing empty than the hulking form of triceratops pushed by, the great horns and bony frill held high. Thirty feet of lumbering flesh, its tail tip twitching as it dragged behind.

"The great lizards are still here, but doomed soon to final destruction. The mammals will survive and multiply and cover the earth. We will later discuss the many paths traveled by the mammals, but today we are going to leap ahead millions of years to the order primates which may look familiar to you."

A taller, deeper, more tangled jungle replaced the one they had been visiting, a fruit filled, flower filled, life filled maze. Multicolored birds shot by, insects hung in clouds and brown forms moved along the branches.

"Monkeys," Grosbit-9 said and looked around for something to throw at them.

"Primates. A relatively primitive group that took to these trees some fifty million years in our past. See how they are adapting to the arboreal life? They must see clearly in front of them and gauge distances correctly, so their eyes are now on the front of their heads, and they have developed binocular vision. To hold securely to the branches their nails have shortened and become flat, their thumbs opposed to strengthen their grip. These primates will continue to develop until the wonderful, important day when they descend from the trees and venture from the shelter of the all-protecting forest.

"Africa," Teacher said as the time machine once more moved them across the centuries. "It could be today, so little have things changed in the relatively short time since these higher primates ventured forth."

"I don't see anything," Ched-3 said, looking about at the sun scorched grass of the veldt, at the verdant jungle pressing up next to it.

"Patience. The scene begins. Watch the herd of deer that are coming towards us. The landscape has changed, become drier, the seas of grass are pushing back the jungle. There is still food to be had in the jungle, fruit and nuts there for the taking, but the competition is becoming somewhat fierce. Many different primates now fill that ecological niche and it is running over. Is there a niche vacant? Certainly not out here on the veldt? Here are the fleet-footed grass eaters; look how they run; their survival depends upon their speed. For they have their enemies, the carnivores, the meat-eaters who live on their flesh."

Dust rose and the deer bounded towards them, through them, around them. Wide eyes, hammering hooves, sun glinting from their horns and then they were gone. And the lions followed. They had a buck, cut off from the rest of the herd by the lionesses, surrounded, clawed at and wounded. Then a talon tipped paw hamstrung the beast and it fell, quickly dead as its throat was chewed out and the hot red blood sank into the dust. The pride of lions ate. The children watched, struck silent, and Mandi-2 sniffled and rubbed at her nose.

"The lions eat a bit, but they are already gorged from another kill. The sun is reaching the zenith and they are hot, sleepy. They will find shade and go to sleep and the corpse will remain for the scavengers to dispose of, the carrion-eaters."

Even as Teacher spoke the first vulture was dropping down out of the sky, folding its dusty wings and waddling towards the kill. Two more descended, tearing at the flesh and squabbling and screaming soundlessly at one another.

Then from the jungle's edge there emerged first one, then two more apes. They blinked in the sunlight, looking around fearfully, then ran towards the newly killed deer, using their knuckles on the ground to help them as they ran. The blood-drenched vultures looked at them apprehensively, then flapped into the air as one of the apes hurled a stone at them. Then it was the apes' turn. They too tore at the flesh.

"Look and admire, children. The tailless ape emerges from the forest. These are your remote ancestors."

"Not mine!"

"They're *awful.*"

"I think I am going to be sick."

"Children—stop, think! With your minds not your viscera just for once. These ape-men or man-apes have occupied a new cultural niche. They are already adapting to it. They are almost hairless so that they can sweat and not overheat when other animals must seek shelter. They are tool using. They hurl rocks to chase away the vultures. And, see, that one there—he has a sharp bit of splintered rock that he is using to cut off the meat. They stand erect on their legs to free their hands for the tasks of feeding and survival. Man is emerging and you are privileged to behold his first tremulous steps away from the jungle. Fix this scene in your memory; it is a glorious one. And you will remember it better, Mandi-2, if you watch with your eyes open."

The older classes were usually much more enthusiastic. Only Agon-1 seemed to be watching with any degree of interest. Other than Grosbit-9 who was watching with too much interest indeed. Well, they said one good student in a class made it worthwhile, made one feel as though something were being accomplished.

"That is the end of today's lesson, but I'll tell you something about tomorrow's class." Africa vanished and some cold and rainswept northern land appeared. High mountains loomed through the mist in the background and a thin trickle of smoke rose from a low sod house half buried in the ground. "We will see how man emerged from his primate background, grew sure and grew strong. How these early people moved from the family group to the simple neolithic community. How they used tools and bent nature to their will. We are going to find out who lives in that house and what he does there. It is a lesson that I know you are all looking forward to."

There seemed very little actual evidence to back this assumption, and Teacher stabbed the button and the class was over. Their familiar classroom appeared around them and the dismissal bell was jingling its sweet music. Shouting loudly, without a backward look, they ran from the room and Teacher, suddenly tired, unclipped the controls from his waist and locked them into his desk. It had been a very long day. He turned out the lights and left.

At the street entrance he was just behind a young matron, most attractive and pink in miniaturized mini, hair a flaming red. Mandi-2's mother, he realized, he should have known by the hair, as she reached down to take an even tinier, pinker hand. They went out before him.

"And what did you learn in school today, darling," the mother asked. And, although he did not approve of eavesdropping, Teacher could not help but hear the question. Yes, what did you learn? It would be nice to know.

Mandi-2 skipped down the steps, bouncing with happiness to be free again.

"Oh, nothing much," she said, and they vanished around the corner.

Without knowing he did it, Teacher sighed a great weary sigh and turned in the other direction and went home.

BOOKMOBILE

Charles L. Harness

The ability to read is a basic prerequisite in our educational system. Without this capability, the student is doomed to frustration and failure. Much has been written in recent years about the apparent inability of our schools to "make Johnny read." It is not enough for the student to be merely able to recognize words and repeat them. He must be able to *understand* them and develop analytical abilities in order to understand the concepts which lie behind the words and to draw conclusions from them. As long as textbooks are a major vehicle in the learning process, reading will be of crucial importance.

School textbooks have become sophisticated learning devices. Much effort has been put into their design, with as much attention paid to the art work and pictures as is given the textual material itself. Which textbooks to use is a very important decision constantly facing educators—poor choices can have a devastatingly negative effect on the learning process.

Books have a long and honored tradition in our history. This stems in large part from the great influence of the Bible in the social and religious thought of the nation. The desire to read, on the part of many people, derived from the status accorded those who could read the Bible, the one book found in almost every home. One unforeseen consequence of the impact of the Bible on education was that many people believed *everything* they read in books, since the Bible was held to be the absolute truth. It took many years before students approached their books in a critical fashion. The material contained in modern textbooks must not be considered beyond criticism—there are errors in most, as well as faulty thinking. Books are items which should be approached with respect, but not with blind faith.

"Bookmobile" posits a future in which books have disappeared, where technology has made them "outdated" and useless. In its own small way, it is a classic account of the impact of technology on education and contains within it an excellent short history of the development of reading in our own world.

FOR FURTHER THOUGHT OR DISCUSSION

1. Has the American educational system failed in its attempt to teach reading skills?

2. What is the relationship between the ability to think and the ability to read?

3. What influences are visual media having on the ability to read?

4. In what ways can school textbooks be improved?

5. If reading were made an "elective," would you take it?

BOOKMOBILE   *Charles L. Harness*

Chief, it's been a long trip, and I thought I'd beam back one last reassuring message before touchdown. While I acknowledge your long experience in initiating cultural contact with remote rural worlds, I do feel that your present misgivings are without foundation.

True, our communication will be based solely on the printed

word: in fact, on the specially printed books that constitute our portable library. Oh, chief, believe me, the Terrans love books! They'll strip our shelves bare the day I land. They'll want me to return many times! (You can start now preparing Selection II.)

Fear not, these people could never abandon so exquisite a skill as writing, developed and refined over so many centuries. Their entire culture and civilization is founded on it.

I'll give you a brief run-down.

The Egyptians were the first Terrans to write. They even had a god of writing, Anubis. Their schoolboys had copybook phrases much like ours. "Give thy heart to the art of writing and love her like a mother, for there is nothing as precious as writing." The Sumerians were equally earnest, pushing their triangular stylus into their clay tablets to give wedge-shape impressions: "Writing is the mother of eloquence and the father of artists." And those remarkable Chinese, writing down, instead of across: "Thine ancestors have given thee this art, which is better than green fields, and gold, and the scent of sandalwood."

Have you ever wondered why the West writes in horizontal lines, and the East in vertical lines? It all goes back to the materials they first wrote on. The early Chinese wrote their ideograms on thin strips of bamboo hung on thongs. The only way to go was down. They saw no need to change direction after they started writing on silk, nor finally, when they began printing books on paper. The Egyptians, on the other hand, wrote on strips cut from papyrus pasted horizontally on papyrus matting. Their writing likewise followed the strips—across. For centuries the entire Mediterranean world—Phoenicians, Greeks and Romans—used Egyptian papyrus, and they all wrote in horizontal lines. And their cultural descendants still do.

I'll grant you, the future of reading and writing on Terra looked bleak during their Dark Ages. But the monks nourished it, and there was a small, hard core of highly literate men waiting in the background when Charlemagne began his attempts to unify large segments of the old Roman world.

Charlemagne was plagued with a communications problem, because the new ruling class was largely illiterate. So he launched a massive education program. He brought in the monk Alcuin to set up schools and to crank out textbooks. Alcuin got his scribes together. They were ready to start copying his texts, at the reckless rate of one a week. But then Alcuin found that scribes from the eastern marches used letter forms quite different from those used in the west. And the northern monasteries didn't write the same way as those in the south.

321

But no matter. Alcuin simply sat down and invented a uniform script. Not only was it the simplest and easiest, and most legible alphabet so far known—it was able to tell you which letters were the most important. For example, those indicating the beginning of a sentence, or a man's name, were capitals (because they imitated the letters the Romans had used on the great temple to Jupiter on the Capitoline Hill in Rome), but the rest were in small letters. And this alphabet, called Caroline (for Charlemagne, of course) was so easy on the eyes that it immediately swept Europe.

All of these hand-written books were copied with the quill pen, which was the most expressive writing instrument ever developed by the Terrans. The best quill pen was made from the forward primary feather on the left wing of the domestic goose. So selected, the pen barrel was large enough to be grasped by thumb and fingers without cramping, and the vane swept over the back of the hand to the right, out of the way. The quill was trimmed to a point of the desired shape, and the nib was then split, to permit flow of ink to the point by capillary action. A cellular pith in the barrel served to hold a considerable supply of ink. The quill pen revealed the personality of the user. Look at the signatures on the American Declaration of Independence!

Now, a hand-written book, no matter how lovely the script, will never reach the masses. There will never be enough books. The fastest copyist, working from first light to dusk, six days a week, needed about one year to turn out one copy of the Bible.

But help was on the way.

Printing with movable type was invented independently, first in China, by Pi Sheng in the eleventh century, then in Germany, by Johann Gutenberg, about 1440. The Chinese were hampered by their system of writing with ideograms, in which a word was represented by a single symbol. Thus, they needed thousands of blocks for a complete vocabulary, and for this reason movable type was never popular in China.

The style of type in which I'm beaming this script to you is called Roman. Jensen, a Terran of the fifteenth century, invented it in reaction to Gutenberg's Gothic style. *But this particular sentence is in italics, a slanted Roman, so named for its Italian inventor, Manutius, who used its compact format for (what else?) the first compact books, in 1480.*

Printing spread through Europe like wildfire, then more slowly to

Africa, Asia, and the New World. The first press in the Western Hemisphere was in Mexico City, in 1539. It beat the American colonials at Boston by a century.

When our scouts were last here, every country on the planet was publishing its own books at the aggregate rate of several hundred million volumes a year. As their great holy man, Ecclesiastes, said, "Of making books, there is no end."

Reading and writing are here to stay!

I am now three days out—well within Morse-laser range. I shall now contact the Americans through the communications center of their National Aeronautics and Space Administration—or whatever they call it nowadays.

All I get is *voice*! Of course, it has been a full generation since our survey. But surely they couldn't have lost Morse. I'll keep trying.

Here it is, the third and last day, and I must report that I can't get a Morse response anywhere on Terra. Only voice. There must be some logical explanation. If necessary, I'll land on the front yard of the Americans' Library of Congress and spell out my mission on a piece of slate. Surely, in that great Library there will be *some* one who can still read and write!

Well, I *did* land in front of the Library of Congress. In fact, the ship came down right beside an enormous stack of books. So I knew I was in the right place. I attracted quite a bit of attention. Their newsmen came out, and their photographers. I handed them all copies of my letters of introduction, explaining our mission, and all about the books on the shelves of my ship. They didn't seem to understand. It was almost as though they couldn't read. When they kept talking, and aiming dozens of TV cameras at me, I got out the screen printer and wrote it out again for them. I showed them the type-keys, just like a common typewriter, and invited them to type out anything they cared to, but they all just looked puzzled.

So finally I went back into the ship. To help me get a fix on what had happened here during the past thirty years, I teleported a few hundred books inside from the big stack out there. After I read them, I put them back and read several thousand of the others. It took me all night.

Chief, it's quite a story.

It begins with the invention of the audio reading device in the mid-seventies. Originally, the audio reader was just a combination micro-wave sensorspeaker attached to the fingertip (much like a thimble). It was simply passed over a line of magnetic tape, for example, a legend under a cut in a newspaper or magazine, and the taped record emerged as sound from a tiny cone speaker on the fingertip. The sound could be the spoken word, or lions roaring, or the patter of rain . . . anything audible.

The prototype was quickly improved. The scanner was moved from finger to forehead, and it was no longer necessary to move it across the tape. It locked in automatically with magnetic reference points on the page, then scanned the page with a moving electronic beam.

Within a year, all the great picture magazines had converted over to the new audio system. The Christmas issue of *WOW* contained not a single word of printed text. There was a protest from the Madison Avenue advertising agencies, which was met in succeeding issues by interlarding the audio presentation with commercials, turned up fifty percent in volume. The magazine "readers" did not seem to mind. They were hardened TV viewers.

Proliferation was rapid. Word balloons soon disappeared from comic books. The big metropolitan newspapers got out special all-audio editions. Progressive educators followed with audio textbooks. Audio manufacturers prepared an all-audio junior encyclopedia for free presentation to all elementary schools who converted over to audio textbooks, and the Cambridge Five-Inch Shelf of Tape Classics was thrown in for those who acted promptly. The response was overwhelming.

Even before they had consolidated their educational campaign, the audio interests launched their assault on the business world. The office dictating machine was fine, they conceded, but the business of transcribing and mailing a typewritten letter was highly inefficient. The new audio dictator did away with all that. The tape was dropped into a mailing package without any intermediate transcription. Even the address on the package was dictated, and was easily "read" by an audio mail sorter in the Post Office. An entire secretary was thus eliminated, not to mention the typewriter she used and the space she took up. The savings were tremendous. The commercial world promptly converted. Only company presidents kept their secretaries. There are *some* things, they explained to the chairman of the board, that a machine just can't do.

There followed soon the replacement of bill boards and election posters by roadside audio advertisers. At first, these were equipped by signalers that automatically and brazenly turned on the earplug of the innocent passerby, but later all this was regulated by audio legislation. The National Audio Association withdrew their objection to the legislation when customers refused to wear their earplugs on the street and the billboards started coming back. But while it lasted, the Burma Shave audio ad was really something.

Following the new trend, street signs were replaced by audios. Even the names of buildings changed over to audio. The TV programs did not have to change very much. NBC dropped its initials, but the peacock stayed.

Within a couple of years, libraries had converted over to audio, although most still had space in the basement for books and technical journals.

Audio quickly received the sanction of the courts. The written signature for checks, deeds, and contracts was quickly replaced by taped voice-print, which, as was proven in a landmark legal decision, was as unique as a fingerprint. Taped records promptly became admissible as evidence in litigation, and as a proper corollary, the printed record became suspect, and required certification and taped translation by court-licensed readers.

And then a mild reaction set in. And it came from audio's first patrons, the schools.

English teachers were beginning to complain about the impact of audio on the language. The Culture Section of the National Audio Association admitted that there was an impact, but they insisted that it was a good impact. Audio, they claimed, had freed language from the fetters of the printed form. The English language, for the first time since the days of Caxton, was flowering freely and was finally liberated from the silly chains of spelling and syntax. They pointed out, with considerable logic and force, that the language had been growing and developing all along, anyhow. With audio, it was just doing it faster. Good usage would continue to be whatever language forms were used by the educated classes. "It don't hurt," said the Association's chief lobbyist, "if we want to quietly dangle a few participles, like we always have."

The National Curriculum Conference of the year 2,000 was stormy. The big issue, of course, was whether reading and writing should be dropped from the elementary grades.

The deadlock following the 14th ballot was broken by a compromise: these two subjects would be retained as electives. The pupils could take them if their parents made a special request, approved by the principal. It was the beginning of the end. Within five years, reading and writing were dropped altogether in nearly all the public schools. And soon there was very little writing of any kind to read. And then people who once knew how to read and write now began to forget. There was no need to know, any more.

Reading and writing were in the process of disappearing from the civilized countries of Terra, and indeed from the whole planet. Emerging nations took pride in the fact that, by the new standard, they were suddenly one hundred percent literate.

The phase-out of the old skills was marked by a number of curious incidents.

Item—a schoolboy was hauled into the principal's office for painting a dirty word on the school building. But he had to be released. The only person on the premises able to read the word was the librarian, a maiden lady on the verge of retirement, and she refused even to *whisper* the word into the principal's ear.

Item—there was the case that went up to the Supreme Court, where a teacher had been caught explaining the letters of the alphabet to her first grade class. Her conviction was finally reversed when the high court could find no legislation expressly forbidding this activity.

Item—a curious and rather general mental phenomenon occurred: the loss of ability to read and write was as complete as if the cranial lobes had suffered organic damage. Doctors even coined a new medical term, "alexiagraphia," meaning loss of ability to read and write. But the syndrome became hardly worth mentioning, because it eventually hit nearly everyone, and also because it was no handicap at all. Audio more than made up for everything.

Chief, let me now give you a typical day in the life of a typical schoolboy.

After breakfast he plugs an earphone into his right ear, tosses his audio-texts in his school bag, and trudges off to the bus stop. (Note: The Terramerican Army Medical Corps reported the rejection of over two million draftees in 2007 for otoitis. Half of these were stereo addicts and had inflammation in both ears.)

When the bus lets him off at the school, he doesn't need a sign to know he's at the right place. The transmitter at the front door is broadcasting many messages simultaneously.

"Students, this is P.S. No. 107. Proceed quietly to your audio-rooms."

On another wavelength: "Motorists, you are in a school zone. Slow to fifty miles per hour. Courtesy Squeezo Orange Concentrate."

Inside, the student receives instruction by closed-circuit TV, and later recites by audio teaching machine. Only one real live teacher is needed for every thousand students, a great savings for the taxpayers. (This teacher spends all his time filling out reports.)

And then home. He looks over his mail. There are a couple of tape letters from his chums. He snaps these immediately into his shirt pocket unit and plays them by earplug. The content of these letters is invariant. TV shows. New recordings.

Homework is generally easy, although a few dullards may have to struggle for the better part of half an hour on it. No English Composition. No term papers. No spelling. American Literature is managed in a few minutes during supper; Edgar Allan Poe is plugged into one ear, Robert Frost into the other.

After homework, the color stereo TV programs. There is a wide variety of cultural selections for the discriminating viewer:

Galactic Ghouls
Space Doggie
Pirates of Pluto
Carnivorous Plants of California
Microbe-Men
Snooping Camera

And so to bed.

During this day, he has not been exposed to a single printed word. He does not even know what one is.

This generation moved into college (where things were not greatly different) and finally out into the world of commerce and industry. These young people became Terra's bright young leaders in science, law, the arts, government, and education.

Twenty eleven was a year to remember. In that year was printed the last:

Supreme Court Decision
Chemical Abstracts
Congressional Record
Telephone Directory
Bible
United States Patent
Science Fiction Magazine

And so vanished from this great planet, within one generation, the greatest single achievement of six thousand years of human progress.

After the changeover to audio was complete, it was suddenly realized that a vast body of past printed records would have to be promptly micro-audioed, or lost forever. The Office of Hygiene, Audio, and Welfare successfully wangled an appropriation from Congress for the design and construction of a device to read the printed word electronically and convert it to audio on microtape. The machine was duly created (complete with printed Maintenance Manual) by the only electronics expert alive who was still able to read, a retired M.I.T. professor, and it was immediately applied to micro-auditing the ancient U.S. Supreme Court Reports. It had got to volume 40 and was in the middle of "Holmes and Brandeis dissent," when it broke down. The professor, never having been paid, refused to repair it. And no one else could read the Maintenance Manual, so the whole project was junked. But no one really cared. As the president of the Audio Association pointed out, "Actually, it's a blessing. Our judiciary is now freed from all inconvenient precedent. And anyhow, what nobody knows, hurts nobody."

I have just now reverently returned the professor's ill-fated Manual to that horrid pile of books, here in front of the great Library—which is no longer a library. It once had over fifteen million books. And now, not one. Everything had to go, to make room for tapes. That's what this big stack of books is about. They were dredged up from nooks and crannies, and they are the only books left in the world. Audio's victory is complete. They're celebrating with a book-burning.

There's a Gutenberg Bible there on the edge, bound in white pigskin. The old vellum gives a cheery blaze.

It's time now for me to add some volumes from our own shelves:

Procedure for Admission to the Confederation of Galaxies
Elements of Intergalactic Flight
Biota of Some Representative Extraterrestrial Systems

And some of our most popular items:

Triple your I.Q.
Live to be Five Hundred
Become a Millionaire in Your Spare Time

I wish we could understand voice. Sometimes it's frustrating to be native to an airless world, without the possibility of communicating by atmospheric compression waves generated by holes in the head.

See you in twenty years, chief.

5.
CRITICAL ISSUES IN CONTEMPORARY EDUCATION

Contemporary education faces a number of critical issues. But here, as in the other sections of this book, the major theme of the social foundations of education rings true: the social conditions external to the school system affect fundamentally the nature and the issues of education.

The definition of contemporary issues—how intense their impact upon people and what portion of society they affect—depends upon regional variations in social, economic, and political conditions. Urbanization as one major critical issue, for example, means something very significant in New York City and is not an issue at all in Pahokee, Florida.

Yet, on a national basis, there are several overall issues which affect most schools. Among these are: (1) the battle over community control of schools; (2) the impact of urbanization upon curriculum and organization; (3) the lingering effects of racism and discrimination with their concomitant of school integration and bussing; (4) the inadequacy and, in some cases, the inequity of school finance and taxation; (5) teacher unionization and militancy; (6) the role of special interest groups within the educational system; (7) the perennial issue over *what* is taught in the curriculum; (8) the role of the federal government; (9) the role of religion and prayer in school; and (10) the question of the "quality" of education.

Rather than focus on each specific issue and problem, the student of the social foundations of education should understand the *sociology of educational issues.* This perspective implies that he view an educational issue as a symptom of a set of social variables. The social framework from which the issue emerges should be the principal focus of analysis and not the issue itself.

NADA

Thomas M. Disch

The two central characters of this story are Nada, a Puerto Rican child in a large city, and Oveta Wohlmuth, her teacher.

Nada is an "exceptional child." This term has been applied equally to slow learners and to the gifted student. Both categories seem to be increasing in size as psychological testing discovers more and more children who require special attention. Reaching and assisting these students is one of the most difficult tasks facing our educational system.

Nada's home life is grim. Her environment is one of garbage, poverty, and danger. Unfortunately, her environment is not fictional for several million of our fellow citizens. The inner-city child often comes from a large family, with many children competing for the attention of their parents, one or both of whom may be away from the home for long periods. The parents are usually poorly educated, sometimes unemployed, and the social organization of the family may be heavily matriarchal, with the mother making most of the major decisions for the group.

This contrasts with the suburban child, whose environment is almost the opposite of a youngster like Nada. He or she comes from a smaller family, with a better educated father who is steadily employed. Furthermore, the suburban child lives in a nicer, cleaner area, partly because municipal services there are much better than in the large cities.

In addition, the minority child often has a negative self-concept —he doubts that he can adequately compete with the performance level of other children. In many ways the minority student is trapped —self-doubt leads him to act in ways which cause him to fail—thus reinforcing his doubt and establishing a pattern of failure.

The desegregation decision of the Supreme Court in 1954 was in part an attempt to create a better educational environment for the deprived child. A number of devices to promote integration have been developed, including the pairing of schools, educational "parks," metropolitan school districts, and open enrollments. The teachers who work in these schools face many difficulties, such as the hostility of many of the students. Teachers spend much of the day maintaining order, reducing conflict, and adapting the curriculum to the needs of inner-city children.

Miss Wohlmuth is obviously a devoted teacher. She takes a special interest in Nada, visits her home, and takes her on field trips—exposing her to a world she would never normally see. She is a model of what the inner-city teacher should and can be, in spite of the frustrations and difficulties involved. Her dedication is an example of the progress that can be made with students who appear to be "hopeless" cases, even though Nada constitutes a very special case.

FOR FURTHER THOUGHT OR DISCUSSION

1. What are the problems faced by the inner-city child? What can be done to help him?

2. Compare the family and social environment of the minority student with that of the suburban child.

3. Is integration raising the educational level of minority students?

4. How can the racial problems faced by many schools be solved?

5. What educational techniques did Miss Wohlmuth use to reach Nada?

NADA   *Thomas M. Disch*

"What word begins with *J?*" Oveta Wohlmuth surveyed the twenty apathetic faces confronting her, the forty dull eyes that watched her only because the seats in the classroom did not comfortably allow them to focus on anything else. "Jill—"

Jill Coldfax looked down at the maple slab of her desk, stolidly silent, invincibly ignorant, resigned and resentful.

"*J*—can't you think of a word that begins with a *J*-sound? Jill?"

Three children laughed; Oveta, for the moment, ignored them. The remaining sixteen faces had sunk, weighted by shame, to contemplate the varnished surfaces of their desks, where, as in mirrors, they were confronted with their own natures: blank tablets upon which years of abuse had left a few beautiless scars as the only evidence of their passage—sixteen faces thus, except for one, which stared at Oveta with disconcerting steadiness, avoiding her glance; which had stared at her so all that day and for many days past.

"Nada—what begins with *J?*"

Nada had been gazing at the monogram on Oveta's collar. Since she had been moved, in November, to the front row (where it was harder to go to sleep) Nada Perez had learned to achieve trance state without even closing her eyes.

"Nada!"

"Kangaroo. *K* is for Kangaroo."

"We were on *J*, Nada." For all that, it was a kind reproach.

"I thought you asked that already. *J* is for Jam." Nada's eyes slipped back from the ironic twist of Oveta's lip to the soothing nothingness of the silver O.

"And what is a kangaroo?"

Nobody knew. She sketched one on the blackboard and pointed out Australia on the Repogle globe, but the forty eyes rested on these artifacts of their education with the same glazed and weighty disinterest that they had evidenced for anything that came before them in the guise of learning.

These children were the special problems in a school for the exceptional: special in the sense that all the other teachers there had despaired of them. All, that is, except Oveta Wohlmuth, who, partly because they were her job and partly because it was natural to her, was more optimistic. "I *can* teach them to learn," she had said once to a friend, once her fiancee, now only a colleague, a specialist himself in exceptional children—but exceptional for their talent rather than their lack of it.

"Why bother?" he had scoffed. "So that they can, after great labors, achieve something else than mediocrity?"

"Why ever bother, John? I bother because others won't, because someone must."

Sometimes, fortunately, it was worth her bother. Sometimes she would break through the apathy, see light dawning in eyes suddenly alive, watch the first floods of knowledge wash across the shallows of a retarded face. At such moments she could have answered her doubters more eloquently. Many years ago there had been Alfredo, who had become an Air Force officer and was occasionally mentioned in news accounts of Pentagon intrigues; and, more recently, Marion, who had married a novelist and was raising three dismayingly bright children. They, and their like, were the reasons she could not stop bothering, although she was now past fifty and, with her doctorate and years of experience with "special problems," could easily have retired to the relative ease of college teaching. That she did two evenings a week.

Now there was Nada.

A very special problem, Nada. The girl knew much that she would not admit to knowing: the alphabet, words like kangaroo. Oveta suspected that the real limits of her clandestine knowledge were far broader than her few accidental betrayals of it could lead one justly to believe. In fact, she suspected that Nada was a genius-in-hiding, and, like a hunter close on the scent, she was excited at the prospect of scaring that genius out of cover.

But Nada was a difficult quarry. She could be relentlessly, stupifyingly dull. Only once that Oveta had seen had Nada forgotten to be dull. It had been during art period, the day the class had tried watercolors. While the other nineteen special problems wrestled unhappily with the special problems of watercolor, Nada painted. She *painted.*

A picture of the gray Brooklyn tenements outside the schoolroom, not distorted into forbidding expressionistic shapes, but quietly real: full volumes in true spaces—beautiful. It reminded Oveta somehow of a seascape: the elemental rhythms of the calligraphy, the subdued colors, its peace.

So it was that that afternoon—the Day of the Kangaroo—Oveta asked Nada to stay after class. Nada stood before the teacher's desk, a dowdy twelve-year-old, fat, sallow, her clothes in need of laundering, her black hair hanging down to her shoulders in untended, greasy curls, dark eyes staring with steady, dull fixity on Oveta's silver pin.

"How do you feel you're coming along in school, Nada?" The girl shifted her weight with lethargic uneasiness. "I mean . . . you don't seem to take an interest in classwork. Perhaps it bores you?"

"No."

"Do you like school?"

"Yes, I like school."

"What do you like about it?" Oveta asked slyly.

"I—" Nada's mouth hung open as though she were waiting for Oveta to fill it with words she could not invent herself. Then, when the words did not come, it slowly closed.

"Do you like art class? You do very nice things, you know. With a little practice you could become a good painter. Would you like that?"

"I—" Then, slowly, it closed.

"Of course, practice is important. Do you practice at home?"

"No."

"Would you like to?"

"Yes. . . . " An uncertain *yes*, but for all that, Oveta had made her say it.

"Here, then, is a set of watercolor paints, and here is some special paper. The paints belong to the school, so take good care of them."

They lay in Nada's hands, like alien artifacts demanding explication.

"You can take them home—to practice with. Now run along, darling, and show me what you've done, tomorrow."

Oveta never called a child darling.

"A spaceship?" Mrs. Butler asked.

"Well, it didn't look quite like a spaceship," Oveta went on. "It was shaped a little more like a cornucopia."

"Do you still have the picture?"

"No, Nada took it back home with her."

"How would she know the exact dimensions of a spaceship?" Butler asked in a rhetorical tone. "Or anyone else, for that matter? Especially a twelve-year-old retarded Puerto Rican girl. Or, even if she had some idea from TV or the movies, her draughtsmanship might not have been up to the job."

"Her draughtsmanship is excellent. Judge for yourself; there's an example hanging in your living room."

In the living room at that moment there was a shiver of minor-keyed music, a voice that cried: *"But don't you understand? Earth is being invaded!"*

"Turn down the volume, Billy," Butler shouted into the living room. Then, turning back to Oveta: *"She* did *that!—*and I thought at first glance it was a Marin! Mmm. Is your plan working out with her?" A tone of professional interest had crept into his voice. "Is she doing better in school?"

"Not that I can see."

"Martians!" said the voice in the next room. *"Now I've heard everything!"*

"Don't be discouraged," Mrs. Butler said with perfunctory good cheer. "Would you like another piece of pie?"

"Thank you, no."

"There they are now—coming out of the sewers!"

"Would you tell Billy to turn down the TV," Butler shouted. "You can't hear yourself think. Oveta, that girl is *talented.* She'll waste away in that slum, marry some dock worker, and never be seen again if we don't do something for her—and soon."

"Billy, turn off the TV and come and have another piece of pie."

"Oh, how horr—"

Oveta smiled. "That's why I came to see you."

"Why does she have this block against learning anything. I've heard of geniuses camouflaging as average kids—but as a sub-normal?"

"Where is it?" Billy asked, taking his place at the table. His mother handed him the pie.

"She's a very strange girl," Oveta said. "I don't understand her at all."

"A pretty girl?" Mrs. Butler asked.

"On the contrary, quite unattractive. She lives with her mother; no father is mentioned on her enrollment card. . . ."

Mrs. Butler tssked. "And the mother's on relief, I suppose."

"I suppose," Oveta grudged. "A slum background. No books in the home. She probably didn't learn English till she came to school. It's not unusual."

"She's unusual, though," Butler insisted.

"Dad, do Martians have tentacles?"

"Don't interrupt the grown-ups, Billy," Mrs. Butler scolded. "And don't be silly—there's no such thing as Martians."

"He's only asking a question, Bridget. And we don't know there aren't any Martians. When we land a spaceship on Mars, Billy," he explained, "we'll find out whether there are Martians—and if they have tentacles."

"On TV," Billy explained patiently, "they showed one. It wasn't on Mars. It was in the sewer, and it had tentacles and big eyes. . . ."

"That was just a story. They weren't the *real* Martians," Mrs. Butler added sarcastically, for her husband's benefit.

". . . and they were going to conquer Earth," Billy concluded.

"Martians are a much-maligned people," Oveta said with mock seriousness. "Always the invaders. If I were a Martian, I think I'd settle down and take it easy."

Butler's eyes twinkled. "Like Mrs. Perez?" he suggested.

"Yes," Oveta returned, "like Mrs. Perez." Mrs. Butler's cooking was beginning to have its usual effects. She felt the first spasm of indigestion.

"If you folks will excuse me, it's time I started on my way home."

"Watch out for the Martians!" Billy shouted to her when she reached the door. Billy doubled with laughter. His father chuckled.

Outside, the air was misty—verging on rain. Oveta raised the hood of her coat.

—Is it too late to go there? she wondered. As though there were ever really a proper time for it!

Once already that week, when Nada had shown her the watercolor of the odd, cornucopean spaceship (starship, she had called it) circling above a distant, moonlit Earth and then had returned the watercolors and left the classroom with a mumbled "Thanks," Oveta had given way to an unconsidered impulse and followed the girl home. Just to see, she had told herself, what Nada's neighborhood was like. She had kept a block's distance between her and her quarry, careful of the film of ice that slicked the streets, preventing herself from thinking of anything but the mechanics of pursuit and concealment; on her right hand, an unending, undifferentiated facade of brick and brownstone, on her left, a monotonous procession of parked cars or, sometimes, banks of soot-crusted snow; and Nada always a block ahead.

She had been too ashamed of her senseless pursuit of Nada to mention it to Butler that evening. She was still ashamed—and upset—remembering Nada's face at the moment before she had gone up the brownstone steps and into the tenement building, glancing back, not even *looking*, but knowing that Oveta was there and viewing her as casually as if she had been only a part of the landscape. With neither special recognition nor surprise, simply knowing Oveta was there and then turning away, while Oveta's face had crimsoned and blanched with shame.

Now, as the shame of remembering ebbed away again, Oveta climbed into her gray Renault (thinking again that her legs were really too long for a compact car), and set off in the direction of the waterfront.

It was nine forty-five. The drive, from Butler's apartment toward the waterfront, took her half an hour. She stopped the car by a candy store one block from Nada's building. It had begun to rain.

—In general, the evidence for telepathy is very slight, she thought, while, on the other side of rationality, her mind conjured up the image of a large-eyed, tentacled Martian. (If I were a Martian, she remembered saying, and then Billy's laughter, his father's chuckle: *Watch out for them!*) She pulled her cloth coat more tightly about her and set off against the wind that siphoned up the street from the East River.

By the time she reached 1324, Náda's address, she was chilled through. It was a narrow, six-floor walk-up, with a facade identical to five other buildings in the row. The half-flight of brownstone steps that projected from the doorway onto the sidewalk had been painted bilge-green, a color much-favored by Brooklyn landlords. The green shone with incandescent fervor in the light of the streetlamp overhead. Oveta hesitated at the foot of the stairs.

An old woman trundling a baby carriage passed on the sidewalk and stopped before the row of garbage cans stuffed full for the morning's collection beside the entrance way to 1324. She rummaged through the refuse, oblivious of Oveta, and fished out three nylon stockings knitted into a ball and a broken umbrella. These she put in the carriage and trundled on to the next hoard.

"Starlight, starbright, hope to see a ghost tonight!"

Across from 1324 was an asphalt lot, pretending with a few metal poles to be a playground, from which three small figures ran now, pell-mell, giggling.

"Ready or not, here I come."

It was *almost* Nada's voice. Oveta couldn't be sure. Hesitantly, she crossed the narrow ill-lit street. The girl who was *it* couldn't be seen now. Oveta thought she heard, from *somewhere*, a child's giggle.

"Nada?" she called out uncertainly.

The rain was now a steady drizzle that seemed to hang stationary in the air, haloing the streetlamps with coronnas of cold, blue light.

Across the street in 1324 Oveta saw the silhouette of a fat woman in a third floor window. As she watched it, it moved out of sight.

"Nada, are you here?"

"Lousy weather," a voice behind her piped. Turning to see who had addressed her, she became aware that her coat was soaked through.

"But not so bad for January." He cnuckled, as though it were the punch line of a joke, the rest of which he had forgotten or did not need to recount. A man's voice, though high-pitched, and wearing a man's clothes, but not the figure of a man. Sitting in the swing (a child's swing that adult hips could not have squeezed into), his feet dangled inches from the asphalt. A midget—or a dwarf. Oveta could not decide, for the swing lay in the shadow of the adjacent building.

"I don't recognize your face. New in the neighborhood?"

"Yes. I mean—a visitor."

"Thought so. I know most the faces on this street. I used to live over there . . ." he waved his hand in a vague arc. ". . . over there," he echoed himself. ". . . and I couldn't help overhearing you mention Nada. You know her?"

"Yes, I do."

"Nice girl. Make a good wife for some lucky fellow." He chuckled.

"Do *you* know Nada?" Oveta asked over-eagerly, for the little man made her feel uncomfortable, afraid that he might think she patronized him.

"Nice girl," he repeated.

"You've spoken with her?"

"Well, she doesn't have much to say—you know how it is. Women aren't great talkers."

"No," Oveta agreed reluctantly, for her experience had led her to the opposite conclusion.

"Men are the talkers. Men will make plans, have the big ideas, reach for the stars. Talking, all the time, like me."

She smiled, as a practical measure to keep her teeth from chattering. "Spaceships are certainly a man's idea," she volunteered.

"But it's the woman," he went on, beginning to rock back and forth in the enclosing seat of the swing, "that get things done. From day to day. Practical. A woman."

In the awkward interval of silence that ensued, broken only by the squeaking of the swing and the susurrus of the rain (which had become heavier, falling in distinct droplets on her cheeks), Oveta stood to leave.

341

"Nada," the little man began, and ended.

"Nada?" Oveta questioned. The momentum of the swing had died out. His head hung slumped onto his chest. "Are you all right?"

"I'm fine. It's nice weather for January. The rain. I pretend it's warm."

"Could I take you home?"

"I don't have a home."

"I'm sorry. To a hotel somewhere, then? I could loan you a little money. The rain isn't really very warm."

"My wife, you know," he continued, ignoring her offer, perhaps not even hearing it, "my wife died."

"I'm sorry."

"Well, that's the way the tide rises." He chuckled.

Slowly, Oveta retreated toward the street, stepping backward, her eyes on the man, whose hands now fell limply out of the sidebars of the swing. When she reached the sidewalk, she turned.

There was only one light on in 1324, in a third-floor window. Even in silhouette, she could recognize Nada, and she imagined her eyes, dull, impassive, and knowing, offering no recognition, as though Oveta were no more than a figure in a landscape of her own invention.

"She *knows*," Oveta whispered. She began to run.

In the car, she discovered that she had lost one of her shoes on the street, and she had to wait several minutes before her hand was steady enough to insert the ignition key.

"You mean you've *never* been in Manhattan before?"

"No," Nada repeated, "never."

"Amazing! Why, you're a pure specimen of the Brooklynite. I sometimes think that I've been parochial. . . . Do you know what parochial means?"

"It's a kind of school, but you mean narrow-minded, don't you?"

Oveta laughed. "The opposite of cosmopolitan—or international. And speaking of that—those are the United Nations buildings on your right. Are you interested in architecture?"

"No. I mean—it doesn't seem necessary. Nobody needs a building like that to live in."

"Nobody needs paintings for that matter."

"True."

Oveta was inebriated with her success. The hunt was over; her quarry had broken cover, and she would never be able to return to her pose of numbed stupidity—Oveta would see to that.

That morning, Saturday, Oveta had awaken with the beginnings of a cold and the conviction that she would never be able to speak to Nada again. For exactly that reason she had resolved to return to 1324 on the pretext of taking Nada to the Metropolitan Museum, a visit that Nada had once luke-warmly agreed to make. An unannounced visit to a student's home and then her virtual abduction were not professional tactics, but Oveta had convinced herself that, unless she openly declared herself to Nada, the girl would forever distrust her. Since Nada knew already she was being hunted, Oveta had to tell her *why.*

The plan worked smoothly. Nada had been delivered over to her abductress without the least fuss. Of Mrs. Perez, Oveta had seen only one suspicious eye when she had opened the door and a fat-wreathed forearm thrusting Nada outside. As soon as they had gotten into the Renault, Oveta had declared: "You know, Nada, I think you are probably a very intelligent girl and I think you're trying to hide it."

And Nada had replied without hesitation: "I know. I know you thought that." And then shrugged. But, ever so slightly, she had been smiling. Her eyes had not yet been glazed with their customary dullness but had examined the car with curiosity. "I've never been in one of these before," she had said, the first time, to Oveta's knowledge, she had ever spoken without being addressed a question.

"In a Renault, you mean?"

"In a car. Does it go?" Nada was smiling.

"Yes, it goes."

"The Metropolitan Museum," Nada had said dreamily. "Well, well...."

"Well, here it is, Nada: the Metropolitan Museum. How do you like it?"

"It's too big; it's ugly!"

"Don't judge a book by its cover."

"Why, Miss Wohlmuth, I don't judge books at all."

Oveta laughed, until she began to choke. Her cold was growing worse. "That must change," she brought out weakly, as they mounted the museum steps.

Nada pouted. Each new expression on the girl's face astonished Oveta, as though she were witnessing a prodigy of nature. She didn't feel entirely in control of the situation (as she had with Alfredo or Marion), but it was more exciting that way.

They hesitated in the Grank Hall, dwarfed by colossal Corinthian columns. Oveta felt awed by the sheer size of the space enclosed by the columns; unconsciously she began to breathe more deeply. Nada, on the other hand, seemed altogether unaffected.

"The paintings are on the second floor, and over to your right are the Egyptian rooms. Hieroglyphics, big basalt statues, and part of a pyramid, a small one. Even so, you'd probably find it all too oversized for your tastes."

"Oh, but I like the Egyptians. They never changed—their art, the way they lived. If it hadn't been for other people coming in, interfering, they would always have stayed the same."

"I suppose we're all like that."

"Let's see the paintings."

Nada gave one glance at the Renaissance paintings and snorted with contempt. Only once in these rooms did Neda show enthusiasm to any degree—for Crivelli's *Madonna and Child*. It was also a favorite of Oveta's.

"Look at the fly on the ledge—the shadow it casts," Oveta pointed out.

"Mmm . . . No, what *I* like is the thing hanging up at the top, by the apples. Its shape. What is it, some kind of vegetable?"

"Squash, I think," Oveta answered crestfallen. "Or maybe a cucumber. The draughtsmanship is beautiful, isn't it? Look at the Virgin's fingers, the curve of her wrist."

"Oh, but that's so *easy!*"

"You try it. You'll see how easy it is."

"What I mean is, it's already been done. Everything here has already been done. Why should I try to do something that's already been done?"

Like a witness going down the line-up at the police station, Nada was hurried past the accumulated centuries of painting. There was little that roused her interest. Bruegel's *Harvesters* inspired her to say respectfully, "It makes you feel sort of sleepy," but her response to Rosa Bonheur's *The Horse Fair* reawakened Oveta's worst fears. *The Horse Fair* was a large, furious painting of horses rearing and plunging and galloping on an arc that seemed to sweep out of the picture-plane toward the spectator. One could almost hear the shouting, the stomping, the neighing of the horses, the wind of their running.

"How awful!" Nada gasped.

"Why awful?"

"Oh, it's just too—I mean everything is going somewhere. It makes me dizzy. And a *woman* painted it!"

"Rosa Bonheur, about a century ago. How did you know? They were standing several feet back from the huge canvas, and at that distance the nameplate was illegible.

"I—" Her mouth hung open, waiting for the words to fill it. Oveta grew frightened, recognizing the characteristic expression of insensibility that was stealing over Nada's features: jaws slackened, e⸱ ⸱s fixed on a void, the flesh of her face utterly relaxed, inert.

"Shall we get something to eat? Nada! Listen to me! Would you like to eat now? Shall we go to the restaurant I told you about?"

"Yes."

In the museum restaurant, Nada regained some degree of alertness by being forced to select a pastry from the rack. By the time she had finished eating it, she seemed fully recovered, and Oveta relaxed again. She had let her coffee go cold before her, tasted once and set aside. Her throat was sore and dry, but the coffee's steaming bitterness repelled her. It's coming along nicely, she thought: I'll be in bed with a cold tomorrow.

"Well, I'm surprised at you, Nada," she said with forced cheer. "I thought you'd find a few Old Masters, at least, who could measure up to your standards. Your tastes seem to be pretty solidly formed."

"Not at all. I've never thought about painting before. But I *do* like the Flemish painters better than the Italian ones. Their women have better shapes."

(—Like squash, Oveta thought.) She said, "That's a pretty definite taste, it seems to me. Where do you learn all the things you know? You must do a lot of reading."

"I *can't* read. You know that. Isn't it time to go home."

"It's still early, Nada. Would you like to take a walk through the park? We could see Cleopatra's Needle and get some fresh air. And it's only a short way to the Planetarium."

"To see the stars, you mean?"

"Yes. The stars."

"No, that would be . . . boring." She yawned for emphasis.

"Are you tired?"

"Yes. Let's go home."

Last night's rain had frozen to the streets, and Oveta had to divide her attention between Nada and the mechanics of driving. Twice Nada fell asleep, only to be awaken when the car skidded uncertainly to a stop at icy street corners. Oveta manufactured commonplace conversation, pointing out the buildings along Fifth Avenue: St. Patrick's ("No," Nada said, "I don't go to church."); the Library ("No, I don't have a card."); and the Empire State Building ("How awful!").

Finally Oveta blurted out the question she had meant to introduce off-handedly, at an appropriate moment, but that moment had never come. "What are you going to do when you grow up, Nada?"

"Oh—get married, I guess."

"Do you have any boyfriends yet?" Oveta asked doubtfully.

"Mmmm." Nada snuggled into the chill plastic upholstery.

"But don't you want anything *else*? Painting, or some kind of job?"

"No."

"Nothing else at all?"

"No. Nothing. It's cold in here, don't you think?"

"We're almost home now. Do you suppose I could stop in for a moment to have a cup of coffee? It is, as you say, cold in here. Something must be wrong with the heater."

"I guess so," Nada said, with grave doubt.

"If it's too much trouble . . ."

"No. You can come in."

"And in good time! Here we are . . . 1324."

Standing in the garlic-weighted hallway, while Nada negotiated with her mother to let her into the apartment, Oveta listened to the chirruping and trills of what seemed to be a whole aviary of canaries in the apartment opposite the Perez'.

Nada came to the door. "Just a minute. Mommy wants to clean up."

"Don't hurry." But Nada had already disappeared into the apartment. Down the hallway, Oveta watched a fat woman with a shopping bag full of groceries labor up the narrow stairway to the next floor, stopping at every third step for breath. Over the trilling of the canaries Oveto could hear the strained tones of Nada's mother, tugging at something and uttering Spanish imprecations. "*Vayas con diablo*," and "*Muerto*."

"Come in." (—And in good time, Oveta thought.)

"Thank you." She offered her hand to Mrs. Perez, who regarded it as though she saw through the flesh to a particularly unwholesome tumor. "I'm so glad to meet you at last, Mrs. Perez."

"*No hablo Ingles*."

"She can't speak English," Nada interpreted.

Oveta repeated her lukewarm amenity in Spanish: "*Mucho gusto do concerla, Senora Perez*." Mrs. Perez turned her back on Oveta to throw a pile of unlaundered clothes from an armchair to the unswept floor. Cockroaches scuttered from the heap.

"Yeah," Mrs. Perez said, "the same to you. Have a chair."

"Why—thank you." Oveta repressed her scruples and sat in the threadbare armchair. There might be bugs, but she could take a bath later, at home.

"You wanna drink?"

"Just a cup of—a drink? Whatever you're having. Thank you."

"Nada, get some glasses."

While Nada went into the next room, her mother sat down on a mattress on the floor and stared at Oveta, who was herself staring at the room in which she found herself, like a Dowager Queen touring her dungeons, suddenly trapped. Oveta could not imagine what measures of tidying Mrs. Perez had taken with the room, for it seemed in a nearly perfect state of disorder: clothes, blankets, and what seemed no more than rags, in various conditions of dirtiness, were heaped over and stuffed under the few scant pieces of furniture. The walls were a pastiche of wallpapers (Oveta counted four distinct patterns) and green paint in various stages of discoloration. The patchwork of linoleum and bare boards on the floor presented a similar spectacle, like an uncared-for billboard in the warehouse district from which the rains had peeled the years' detritus of posters irregularly to create a ragged montage of meaninglessness. Yet, the final impression was not one of wild disarray, or even of untidiness, but rather, sedative, asleep, like a garden gone to seed.

Perhaps it was the figure of Mrs. Perez that produced that impression, for her figure certainly dominated the room. She was a gargantuan woman, of vast breasts and a stomach that hung, gothic and pendulous, over the edge of the mattress and rested on a patch of bare, unpainted boards. It was her face that most fascinated Oveta, for it was the nightmare image of the face that Nada's could become: devoid of expression, stuporous, and vaguely, almost obscenely sensuous, like a complete allegory of the vices, the more lethargic vices.

Nada handed her mother three grease-clouded tumblers, which the woman filled brim-full with gin. (Oveta presumed it was gin; the bottle, which she replaced at the side of the mattress, was unlabelled.) One tumbler she handed to Oveta, one she kept for herself, the last was Nada's. Oveta sipped warily at her drink; it was gin. Nada drank from her glass as though it contained, at the worst, a sweetened medicine.

Outrageous! Oveta thought. But she kept the thought to herself.

"Mud in your eye!" Mrs. Perez mumbled into her glass, which she proceeded to drain in two swallows and a switch of her tongue.

"Cheers," Oveta returned.

A smile faded from Nada's lips. Her eyes began to take on the glazed, benign indifference of her mother's .

"Nada has told me so much about you," Oveta lied.

"Yeah, kids talk too much."

"Really? I've always thought her a very *quiet* girl. Until today," she added, smiling at Nada, who lowered her eyes to stare at her tumbler of gin and seemed to blush.

"Whadya say?" Mrs. Perez poured herself another tumbler-full.

"Nothing. Nothing at all."

"Mud in your eye."

"Cheers," Oveta replied gloomily, taking a sip of gin. Actually, the liquor felt good trickling down her sore throat, but she felt that she would lose any advantage she possessed in Nada's eyes by seeming to enjoy it.

"Nice apartment."

"Like hell," Mrs. Perez said.

"I beg your pardon?"

"Like hell," Nada repeated. "But I think it's a nice apartment too. Mommy's joking."

Mrs. Perez no longer made a pretense of sitting up. She lay back on the mattress, her eyes closed, and began to snore.

"Your mother seems to be quite . . . worn out."

"She's always that way."

Only a few rays of the afternoon's dying light penetrated the grime-coated windows to spend their power dimly and to no purpose upon the montage of floor and walls and heaped clothing; darkness spread over the room like a rising tide.

"Nada," Oveta whispered, "you don't want *this*." Her hands gestured awkwardly, but her tone conveyed her disgust eloquently. "You can't. Nada, let me help you get away from this."

"But, I do."

"Nada, please."

"This *is* what I want. I *like* it."

Mrs. Perez rolled over on the mattress. "Get out of here," she grunted. "Go on, get out."

When Oveta reached the door, she imagined she heard a chuckle, high-pitched and mocking, but she realized it was only the canaries trilling in the next apartment.

Oveta Wohlmuth's living room was untidy. It could never have been called untidy before, but now there was no other word for it.

Oveta had been in bed (or on the sofa) for four days with her cold. Saturday evening, after returning home in a high fever, she had had to call in a doctor. Sunday she could not remember at all, and the rest of the week until today she had spent impatiently convalescing from what threatened constantly to become pneumonia. Breathing was still slightly painful. Coughing was an agony, but holding it back was worse agony. The doctor had been strict: she could not leave her apartment.

She had contented herself with phoning the substitute teacher twice a day. Nada had not come to school on Monday, or on Tuesday, or yesterday, or today. Perhaps, Oveta thought, Nada had caught cold too, but it was a very faint *perhaps*. The school nurse had visited 1324 and claimed that she couldn't find the Perez apartment.

Oveta had made another series of phone calls while she was confined to her apartment, breathing in the medicated fumes that steamed out of the vaporizer. She had called Butler and social workers she knew and, by force of will and patient and repeated explanations, had extorted from them the papers she would need to remove Nada temporarily from her mother. Temporarily—while that woman was tried for incompetence and a number of other charges that Oveta had not too closely inquired of. She had also persuaded the welfare agency to allow her to call for Nada, when the legal process had been completed. Now she was waiting for Butler to arrive with those papers.

To pass the time, she made a few ineffectual gestures of housecleaning, but she quickly exhausted herself and ended up on the sofa, fighting to regain her breath. Butler found her not quite recovered.

"Are you sure you're well enough to leave the house?"

"Positive. Now, help me on with my coat, will you? God, I still feel so *guilty!* It's my first legal kidnapping. Usually, I'm against meddling."

"From what you told me about Mrs. Perez. . . ."

"I know. But I still feel guilty. It's irrational."

In Butler's car, with a travelling blanket over her legs, she pulled the hood of her coat close about her fever-reddened face. Butler could see the trembling of her hands even beneath the bulky fur mittens.

"Oveta, if you're too sick—"

"Damn the sickness! We've got a job to do. Now let's get on with it."

The car pulled away from the curb. Oveta kept glancing to Butler's face and away; several times her lips parted to speak. Then, hesitatingly, she began: "When I was sick, John, I couldn't help thinking about Nada. I couldn't read. My eyes would begin to smart, and my mind would wander. I kept thinking of Nada.

"I was sick. I'm still sick, for that matter. What I mean to say is, I don't really *believe* what I'm going to tell you. . . . No that's not true either. The commonplace common-sense Miss Wohlmuth doesn't believe it, but I think I do. At least, it's *possible*—and that's bad enough."

Butler made a *moue* of impatience. "Get to the point."

"Well, then. Imagine a race, John—an alien race, telepathic, living on another planet, in another part of the galaxy. Imagine that they have spaceships—no, starships. They've travelled everywhere, seen everything—or enough to satisfy them that they've seen all they need to. Telepaths can share their knowledge. What one has known and seen, they all know and remember. Their minds are filled with it: knowledge, memories, piling up through the generations."

"A dismal picture," Butler commented.

"So dismal that they might decide just to blot it out."

"You're shivering, Oveta."

"And you're trying to humor me. Just listen for a minute. Nada is such an alien. She's telepathic. I've seen that for myself. And I've already told you about that starship she painted, drawn, probably, from a memory in her mother's mind. And her attitude, her uncanny quiescence—her background—can't be explained in any other way."

"You explained it well enough another way—gin."

"No, let me finish. Mrs. Perez is not human: she doesn't look human or act human. She's a vegetable on two feet. She has only one purpose in life: homeostasis, physiological equilibrium, Nirvhana. She eats, she drinks, she sleeps, she breeds more vegetables, and that's all she wants out of life. A Homeostat. There are thousands more like her, and God only knows how many of them are. . . ."

Butler laughed indulgently. "It's a nice theory. It fits the facts. But a simpler theory will fit the facts just as well."

"It doesn't fit the way I feel about Nada—and Nada's mother."

"Look, Oveta—you've been sick and that scene with Mrs. Perez upset you. We all feel uneasy about the Mrs. Perezes of this world. She's a Homeostat, as you put it, and she's turning Nada into another. That doesn't mean she's an alien telepath, for God's sake."

"Women," Oveta went on dreamily, "*women* are more likely to be vegetables, you know. Squash and cucumbers. I'll tell you something else. It was explained to me by a widower of my acquaintance, but I didn't understand him at the time. They are married to little men—midgets. It was the men who built the space ships in the first place, but the women got their way in the end, when the men were ready to give up, when they'd seen all there was to see, when their minds were filled up until they couldn't hold any more."

"So they came to Earth to go on relief?" Butler asked mockingly.

"Because it was the easiest thing to do. They could leave the shell of their own civilization behind. It was too much trouble to keep it intact, and they only wanted homeostasis after all. Well, they've got it."

"Oveta, if I didn't know you better, I'd think you'd cracked under the strain."

"That's why I told you and not someone else. I know it's a theory for the casebooks, but when I lay in bed thinking of Nada, all the pieces began to lock together, by themselves. I feel like the victim of my own idea. It's not just for Nada's sake that I want to get her out of the nightmare she's living in. At the hospital, they're bound to discover any—anomalies. I hope I'm wrong, but if there are aliens. . . ." Oveta began to cough, a lung-ripping cough that brought the conversation to an abrupt end.

"1324," Butler announced, as they stood before the door of the tenement, "where two civilizations meet. Do you think you can get up the steps?"

"I'll make it." On the second floor landing, where she was attacked by another fit of coughing, she was almost proven wrong.

In the third floor hallway, the lights were dim, the air heavy with garlic, and the canaries were still to be heard. "You knock," she asked Butler. "I feel slightly *deja vu.*"

The door was answered by a woman Oveta had never seen before. She was very fat; her eyes were dull. "Perez? Perez don't live here any more."

"Where have they moved? It's very important that we know."

"I dunno. They just *moved.* Away."

"But *where?*" The door was closed in Oveta's face.

Her eyes burned with an intensity: of fear; of sickness; of understanding too well. "We *won't* find her new address either. Did you see her? She was one of them. I could tell. They knew I'd come back for Nada. I must have been thinking about it when I left them, and they read my mind."

Behind them, down the hall, there was the patter of a child's steps ascending the stairway.

"Now I'll never find out. They've won!"

"Oveta, be reasonable. Mrs. Perez didn't need telepathy to figure you'd be back. Oveta? Oveta, for God's sake, what's the matter!"

A boy edged by them in the hallway and entered what had been the Perez' apartment. He was not quite three feet tall, and he wore a moustache.

351

Oveta had fainted.

Then she was outside again, and the weather seemed milder than it had a minute ago. Children were playing in the asphalt lot, and down the street Oveta recognized the old woman with the baby carriage.

"Are you all right, darling?"

Oveta smiled at the unfamiliar tenderness, then, remembering what she had just seen, the smile stiffened into a rictus of terror. "That midget in the hall. Did you see him? He had a moustache."

"That was a boy—just a little boy. His moustache was probably painted on. Little boys will do that." He rested his hand on her brow.

"You've helped me so much, John. I don't know how to thank you."

"Oveta, look—in the ashcan. Isn't that an art pad?"

"Do you think—?"

Butler removed the tablet of watercolor paper from the garbage pail and shook off the coffee grounds that covered it. A drawing fell out.

"The spaceship," they said in chorus. And, indeed, it was the spaceship, poised, above the hazy globe of Earth, at the instant before its descent, like an enormous apple just caught in the grip of Newton's Laws.

"Is there anything else?" Oveta asked, hoping there was, and hoping, as well, against it.

Butler opened the pad and grew numb, as before a basilisk.

"Let me see!"

"It doesn't mean anything. A child's imagination. Nothing . . . at all. *Oh, how horr—"*

Oveta grabbed the watercolor pad. She began to scream, and then to cough.

Underneath the picture, in an almost illegible scrawl, Nada had pencilled the words: MOMMY AND DADDY.

"They aren't from Puerto Rico, are they," Butler said expressionlessly. "Farther, much farther, much farther away."

The woman was recognizably "Mrs. Perez." Nada had captured perfectly the stuporous expression, the ponderous weight of the breasts and abdomen. Of the man, only his face was visible: eyes twinkling with an ageless wisdom and unwanted knowledge, an ironic smile on his thin lips. The rest of him—his dwarf body—was nestled securely in Mrs. Perez's marsupial pouch.

UP AGAINST THE WALL

Robert Thurston

We live in an era of protest. Dozens of groups in American society are protesting against what they believe to be injustice. These groups range from the Black Panthers to the National Organization for Women to the Students for a Democratic Society.

The protest movement reached the educational system first at the college level. During the 1960s our campuses were swept by wave after wave of unrest. The major issue behind this protest was not directly related to education. The Vietnam War and American involvement in it produced sometimes violent demonstrations. Soon, other issues, like the free speech movement (whose genesis preceded the war), student participation in decision-making, and the generalized demand for "student-power" became commonplace. These issues and demands have now spread to the high schools.

At the high school level, student protest has most often taken the form of racial demonstrations and criticisms of school officials voiced through "underground" newspapers. Students for a Democratic Society (SDS) has high school chapters throughout the country. Some student organizations, such as the New York City High School Coalition, exist to promote the interests of specific ethnic or racial groups. We can expect to see continued efforts at organizing high school students in the years ahead.

The phenomenon known as the underground newspaper is another relatively recent development. Those papers contain much more than just demands for reform; they carry news of the counter-culture into the schools and print material which the school-sponsored papers cannot. Estimates of the number of these papers run from six hundred to over a thousand. Attempts by school officials to stop the distribution of these papers often produces another issue leading to student demonstrations.

Student demands are varied, but they include the following:

1. Demands for ethnic studies—black, Puerto Rican, Jewish, and others.

2. Demands for more teachers of various ethnic and racial backgrounds, and the removal of teachers and administrators who do not belong to specific racial or ethnic groups.

3. Improvements or additions to school facilities. The quality of food available and its content is an issue in some schools.

4. Demands for student participation in curriculum and other matters.

5. Demands for changes in the grading and testing system.

Many of these issues have had to be settled in court. Such controversies as the right of the school to determine the dress of students, to censor school newspapers, and to search students and their property have often produced conflicting decisions from our judicial system.

In "Up Against the Wall" we encounter a school administrator (in this case at the college level) as he attempts to cope with the protests and demonstrations of his students. The story has some interesting things to say about the psychological motivations of the leaders of the student movement.

FOR FURTHER THOUGHT OR DISCUSSION

1. What are the major issues which have produced the student movement in this country?

2. How can a school most effectively deal with protest?

3. What are the motivations of student leaders?

4. How do you reconcile student rights with student responsibility?

5. What rights do students have? What rights should they have?

6. Do minority students have the right to demand minority teachers and school administrators?

UP AGAINST THE WALL   *Robert Thurston*

Whatever happened to Culligan? You remember, the student leader of a few years back? He was the man of the hour, always had a microphone pointed at him. It seemed as if he'd be around for years, as spokesman for his cause on TV and all that. You know, chatting with Carson and Cavett and Walter Cronkite. It's hard to believe he could just disappear from public view so easily, he must be up to something somewhere.

"Up against the wall!" Culligan shouted from the doorway of the dean's office.

"Which wall?" the dean asked.

Attempting a firm step forward, Culligan stumbled and fell sideways against a bookcase. As he tried to regain his balance, his foot slipped on the freshly-polished floor, and he fell forward. His face sank into a high-pile rug. With the quickness of a trained revolutionary, he rose to a kneeling position, ready to fend off attackers. But the dean, staring down at his captor, remained impassive.

Behind Culligan, Lester Martin made no effort to hide his laughter. For months Lester, the official recorder of Culligan's campus movement, had been angling for top position. Lately he'd been even more open about it, whispering sarcastic comments to some of the other followers. This stumbling incident would be used to advantage in Lester's retelling of the day's adventures. "Fearless leader initiated attack by kissing the floor in front of the dean."

There was plenty of time to show that fink a thing or two. Wait until the cameras arrived. In front of a camera Culligan was Lester's superior, which was why Culligan held his leadership so easily. In the country of the zoom lens, charisma was king.

Culligan stood up and walked toward the dean's desk carefully, as if he expected to find bear traps in the rug. The dean smiled as if he watched the approach of an old friend.

"You can stay seated, dean," Culligan said. "You stay with me, Lester. Everybody else form a line of defense in the hallway."

Culligan put a cigarette in his mouth. His strong fingers wrinkled the paper, bending the cigarette in his mouth. An expression of grim defiance fitted the situation, so Culligan narrowed his eyes and tightened the line of his lip. His cigarette bobbed upwards like an uncoiled spring.

Arrogantly he picked up the dean's Hong Kong desk lighter, a grinning cat made of China (the flame came dragon-like out of the smiling mouth). Sliding out of his hand before it reached the cigarette, it hit the desktop at an angle and bounced twice before shattering into several pieces. Lighter fluid spilled over the desk blotter and onto the monthly budget sheets. A glimmer of sadness broke through the dean's passive mask as he stared at a fragment of Cheshire smile.

"Okay, dean," Culligan said, searching his pockets futilely for matches, "how soon before the fuzz arrive?"

"I couldn't say."

"We've got a long list of demands and I want to know how much time we can allot to discussion. So let's not play put-on games, dean."

"I am not trying to trick you. I don't know when the police will arrive because I have asked them to stay away until their presence is absolutely necessary, and they have complied with my request. As have also the local press, and the radio and TV stations."

The still-unlit cigarette fell out of Culligan's mouth.

"No cameras?" he asked. Wistfully.

"There will be no recording, film or tape, of these proceedings. In a moment you will be glad of that."

"Is that some kind of threat?"

"No. A compassionate truth."

Culligan waved his arms in frustration. His left hand tipped over a fluorescent desk lamp, which in turn sent a gold-embossed pen and pencil set careening against a telephone.

Lester, who roamed about the office as if planning the arrangement of its destruction, seemed amused by Culligan's helplessness. They exchanged distrustful looks.

"Dean," Culligan said, "we can not establish a meaningful dialogue if you try to cloud the basic issues with semantic expertise."

"Mr. Culligan, we both know that your incessant pleas for communication are fraudulent. You employ the camouflage of dialectic for self-aggrandizement. For you meaningful dialogue would be a disaster."

Culligan frowned. The dean's insights were always a surprise to him. Originally he had not figured the old man to be so sharp. In fact, until recently the dean had always seemed rather vague. The age-old rumor, as told by generations of alumni, was that the old man spent only the minimum time required on college matters, just enough to dispatch them efficiently, because he preferred to tinker with trivial inventions. The decor of his office was often marred by pieces of rusty tubing or metal constructions. Right now Lester was busily examining the latest monstrosity, a thin boxlike structure which looked like a wardrobe with buttons and dials on the side and a shower nozzle coming out of the top. In the shade of the college's nuclear reactor the dean struggled to create the safety pin. No wonder, Culligan thought, that there were rumors that the Board of Trustees planned another attempt at removing the eccentric old man from office. If Culligan's plots were successful, the Board would have no trouble this time.

Gazing at the dean now, seeing the age in his wrinkled face, Culligan realized that the gap between them was not simply a generation gap. It was an abyss of centuries. The dean was a nineteenth-century man who could not cope with the future.

"So I think," the dean continued, "you could have the courtesy not to bore me with your rhetorical overkill. As they say, time is precious, too precious to listen to that endless litany of demands. Without dialogue of any sort, I accede to *all* your demands."

"And, Lester," he added as a footnote, "please don't lean against the time machine."

Culligan wheeled around, his arm flooring a picture of the dean's wife and children from the corner of the desk. He saw Lester backing away from the dean's latest conglomeration of metal.

"Dean, I do believe you're spaced. You hear that, Lester? Keep away from the time machine, baby."

"How does it work, dean?" Lester, who was Phi Beta, said.

"Ah, come on, Lester, don't groove with him." Culligan feared some new ploy on Lester's part.

"The yellow button activates the mechanism," the dean said. "Press it and whatever is under the transporter, that nozzle above, will be sent into the future. The machine is presently set for an unpolluted Spring day eleven years from now."

Lester pushed the yellow button and disappeared.

"He pushed the button and disappeared!" Culligan, expert at stating the obvious, screamed.

"Yes, I knew he would," said the dean.

"Knew?"

"Yes. For me it's already happened."

"What? What's already happened that I don't know about?"

"When Mr. Martin pressed that button, he was transported eleven years forward in time. Turning away from the time machine, he found himself still in my office with me at my desk, but you no longer in evidence. At first he didn't believe he had traveled through time, but I gave him several proofs. Then we had a pleasant discussion and he returned to the past, or will return here in about fifteen minutes."

"I can't dig it, dean. How, if the meeting between you and Lester takes place in the future, or is taking place *now* for him, how come you remember it in the *past*?"

"It did occur already in *my* past. On my way back from a trek to a farther future, I absentmindedly set the year gauge incorrectly and, instead of returning to this year, materialized at a point eleven years from now, that bright Spring Day I mentioned. I suppose it was a sort of Freudian time-slip, since I had already learned it was the year of my death."

"Your death? You know when you're going to die?"

"Yes."

"And it doesn't bother you?"

"It did at first. But it's eleven years away. I doubt that anyone, knowing the date of his death, would feel very much anxiety about it until the last year or so, when he's added up all the things he didn't do."

"God, I'd hate to know when *I* was going to die."

"I'll keep that in mind."

"You know?"

"I didn't say that."

Culligan began to pace. Pacing was useful to him in a crisis. The rhythm of his footfalls, to which he listened intently, provided a beat that helped to organize his thoughts or to avoid the obstacles of logic.

"I became quite nostalgic when I realized I stood in my office on one of the last days before it would be changed by my successor. It occurred to me that all of these relics left behind would, in one way or another, be disposed of. Stupidly I moved to the desk as if it were a longlost relative. It was at that moment that Lester Martin appeared."

Culligan could hear the crowd in the anteroom and hallway. They were restless, eager for something to happen. They had wanted to tear up the dean's office, but Culligan eschewed such tactics, however desirable they might seem, as out-of-date.

Why was the outcome of his dreams always so tedious? he thought. He'd imagine himself scoring a big victory—all signs pointing to a smashing coup—but each time he was thwarted, or only half-successful. Several months ago it had seemed simple to garner a mob and sweep through the Establishment maze armed with a multiplicity of causes. Instead, the route turned out to be laborious. Surely, he'd slowly (too slowly) built up a reputation with his shrewd publicity sense and timing. Students all around the country were beginning to look to him as a leader they could gather around, a sort of Super Mark Rudd or Abbie Hoffman.

But what had he done? With his timing, popularity, and quotability, what actually had he accomplished? Each time he had challenged authority, as represented by this screwy inventor-dean, the old man had deftly countered in a mood of easy accedence and a show of gentleness. What Culligan wanted most in the world was a dramatic conflict, a real fistslamming screaming confrontation through which he could slide to power with worldwide coverage. Instead, all he received were conciliatory blows from the dean's powderpuff artillery. Nothing he could use to any effect.

And now—how could he tell his impatient followers that not only was the dean refusing to oppose them, but that he'd stalled the entire maneuver with a time machine! Other leaders went up against formidable administrative talents, Culligan had to deal with the mild irrelevancies of a glaze-eyed eccentric.

"If you are willing to listen, Mr. Culligan, I have a few things to say to you. Sit down, it will only take a few minutes and it will be our last talk, I hope."

Culligan, unusually submissive, nodded and walked to the nearest chair. As he sat down, his foot brushed against an authentic Old West spittoon. It spun around a few times. Dazed, he listened to the dean.

"I spotted you as a potential troublemaker from the first day you set foot on this campus. When you began your little exercise in radicalism, I was pleased rather than filled with tyrannical anger, as you stated to the press. The spirited grail-quester for knowledge must often protest. It's a healthy reaction to outmoded practices. So I was not too unhappy when you began stirring up a little action around here. Gave some spirit to the place."

"Until you first confronted me, then refused to *listen* to my views, I did not fear you in the least. I saw then that your words did not match the expression in your eyes, that your gestures were egocentric rather than idealistic. In short, I glimpsed your future in your actions and I recoiled in terror."

The uncharacteristic harshness in the dean's voice surprised Culligan, who only understood emotional voice shadings as tools for communication. The dean continued in a softer voice:

"They say that important inventions come at a time when they are most needed even though the capability for their creation has been in existence for a long time. While the idea of the invention germinates, there is limited possibility for fruition until the inventor is spurred on by a dire need, personal, social, or otherwise. That view would no

359

doubt seem poppycock to your generation; in these days of financed group research and discovery by committee, the accidental insight of the individual working alone seems remote. Yes, the romantic old notion of the Edison-like genius toying with spare parts in his spare time seems like a fading illustration from an ancient magazine—if you handle it too roughly, it'll crumble.

"You see, I'd been tinkering with a time machine idea for some months. Like all my other projects, this one also seemed doomed to failure. But looking into your future that day gave me the incentive I needed. Somehow the principle blended with the material and I devised the workable model. The day of its completion was the day of our second confrontation. You'll remember that well, I expect."

Culligan nodded, a vacant look in his eyes. He remembered disappointment, frustration, a sense that his every move was anticipated. At the time he'd suspected an Establishment spy within his ranks, so he had stopped divulging his future plans to others. Nevertheless, the dean had continued to counter his moves effectively.

"As an initial test of the machine, I went a couple of years into the future. Immediately I noticed a few perceptible changes in the decor of this office. A couple of new pictures, the trophy cabinet was moved to the opposite wall, that sort of thing. Hesitantly I took a little trip around campus, causing no little confusion, since I—the future me—was away on a trip. People who saw me that day were frightfully upset."

"But these are inessential details. I'm sure *you're* not interested in the little comedies of time travel. I assume you'd rather get down to the nitty-gritty. What's important to the two of us is the newspaper I bought, the newspaper that revealed that William Culligan, nationally-known student leader, etc., had successfully gained control of a coalition of national student groups and vowed revenge against the repressive elements of Establishment society. At that time, evidently, the radical stars were in eclipse. The old pendulum swinging, I expect."

"I read further and found out that you had been launched on your road to national leadership by a takeover of this college begun when I'd fought you tooth and nail on the day of our second confrontation."

Culligan looked up. His eyes spoke all the words stuck in his throat.

"Yes, of course I did not fight you that day. I acted toothless and nailless. But that's jumping ahead of my story and, when you range all through time, it's difficult enough to keep the chronology of a story straight. You see, although I recoiled at the thought of you as a national figure, I was not especially disturbed by it. Then I made more jumps into the future, watched time pass like a TV special, at the same time tracing your rise in your own ranks, your entrance into state politics . . ."

"That's a lie," Culligan exploded. "I'm against all forms of organized politics, all structuralized institutions. I'd never become a politician, an Establishment fink!"

"You neglect the force of your ambition for power. Such ambition propels one into the most fantastic compromises."

"Compromise is an obscenity. My movement rejects such obscenities."

"Maybe so. Now. But later, when the golden apple dangles on the limb, ready to fall, you'd risk anything, even compromise. But let's skip present polemics which are, as you will see, irrelevant now. As I said, I watched your rise. It was something like extracting the substance from one of those multiscened, lightning fast movies that are all the rage now (they'll be oldhat within the decade, by the way). At each time-stop I found you somewhere else on the ladder of success. In many ways you were a most mercurial politician, in action and statement. As many people sense the times and structure their actions according to what they deduce as the prevailing trends, you similarly had good insight into what the trends would be, *but* you acted in *opposition* to them. Continually stirring up trouble and initiating violent action for which you took no blame, you in a sense became the Great Radical, a William Jennings Bryan of revolution, always in opposition to whatever measures were taken politically and socially."

"Your actions made a perverted kind of sense. You knew that, with the population exploding in all directions, there'd always be a majority of youth, ready to rebel, ready to follow a leader who offered whatever was necessary to nurture their natural desire for rebellion against previous generations. However the Establishment changed, you remained permanently anti-Establishment. The biggest irony in your rise to power was that your fiercest opponents were largely from the generation which are now your followers. They'd grown older—more conservative, if you will—and suddenly had found themselves to be the Establishment."

Culligan listened to the crowd growling outside and tried to imagine them turning against him. They seemed so idealistic, so dedicated. How in hell did idealism turn to pot bellies and wagging fingers in the space of a generation? Ridiculous. How could he take this oddball so seriously?

"Finally I reached what I suppose was the inevitable point: your election as U.S. President with a big electoral push from the youth of that day. Taking the bull by the horns, I chanced a trip to the White House to see what you'd become. When you saw me, your face went white and you dropped a boxful of official signature pens. You were to age well, a violent shock of white hair crowning a face unravaged by the years. I hadn't known that radicalism contained preservative ingredients. After you got over your shock, we had a long talk. You were mad, I could see that. Already your programs were terrorizing new minorities. You were considering a brand new brushfire war. You had no feeling for your people who were merely lines on the patterned circuit of your success. All the time we talked, you were planning my assassination, which would have succeeded if I hadn't slipped through your police lines."

"Police lines? You gotta be out of your tree. I hate pigs!"

"When they're tuned in to your squeal, you'll like them well enough."

Irritated by the dean's inference, Culligan sprang out of the chair which, in recoil, skidded two feet and into the trophy cabinet, starting a small crack in its glass front.

"The White House, eh?" he said, after pacing awhile. "Wow! And I thought maybe I could just be kingpin of my own political group. But *President*—Man, I don't know why you're telling me all this, but it's a good trip."

"But you're not going to *be* president now."

"What? How can you stop me, little fish?"

"I already have. Let me remind you again of our second confrontation. You stormed in here expecting rigid opposition, a continuation of our first encounter. However, I cooperated, thus blocking your takeover of the college, thus cancelling the action which gave you the impetus that led years later to the presidency."

"How the hell do you know I still won't make it? I'm gaining a national rep. I can use it as a springboard."

"No, the timing's not quite right anymore. After the second confrontation I returned to the future and someone else was president. Since I had skipped the intervening years, it took a while to find out what did happen to you."

Culligan, frustrated, kicked at a corner of the dean's desk, the metal toe of his boot leaving a permanent scar on the mahogany.

"What happened? I become a conformist school administrator like you, due no doubt to your example and inspiration?"

362

"No, I'm afraid not. If that had been the case, there'd be no necessity for this conversation. I could have forgotten you and returned to running this school quietly. What I found instead was that, shortly after another incident, our board of trustees had forced me to expel you from school, using for an excuse the fact that you'd stolen thousands of dollars of sound equipment from our communications center."

"You know about that? Well, I'm no thief. I just borrowed the equipment to help accelerate certain phases of the movement. I'm no thief."

"Maybe, but the board is especially sensitive to violation of public property. Public announcement of the theft brought enough discredit on you that many of your followers turned against you, and you quickly lost power."

"I'd think that's what you'd've wanted, a hatchet job that'd put me in the background."

"Normally, yes. But you didn't stay in the background very long. Embittered, you drifted around the country, making random connections with other aging radicals. Evidently their formulaic slogan-spouting tired you, for you rejected your revolutionary background and drifted into the Patriots, a newly-formed right-wing group."

"Now come on!"

"Sorry if it pains you. You might be comforted to know that your revived abilities brought you instant power, and the love and respect of your followers. However, one political failure after another made you completely callous. Gradually the Patriots, which were to the right of the Birchers, became under your leadership a corporation of assassins. A sort of political Murder, Inc. My source, which may have been biased, blamed you for the murder of two U.S. Presidents, among other world figures, and calculated that many significant social movements had been set back years by the Patriots. So I came back, got to the board of trustees in time to block their actions, and demanded that you be kept in school."

"I'm touched. I suppose this effectively stifled my future?"

"Not exactly. Some people slip into grooves and affect few people by their lives; others have such volatile energy inside them that, however their circumstances are restructured, they find their way to the top. You're obviously one of the latter type, Mr. Culligan. My trips to the future have repeatedly shown you to emerge from my little alterations of the present with new plans, new objectives, and new routes to a tainted success."

"Trips? How many times have you mucked up my future?"

"This is the fifth. In the third, in a fit of dejection caused by my action, you met Linda Tymon by the quadrangle water fountain, and the two of you struck up a friendship."

"Linda Tymon? The beauty queen? But she's insulted every pass I've made at her. And she's against the movement."

Precisely. That's how she diverts your interest away from it. Together you join forces and, under her influence, settle the problems here through peaceful and orderly means."

"Saved by the love of a good woman, eh? I'd think you'd like that."

"I did, or would have, and I said some very laudatory things about you to the press. But, you see, you weren't sincere. Linda Tymon was another pawn in a different sort of power game. Using connections made during your college years, you took Linda to Hollywood where, through clever manipulation of the media, you made a star out of her and a famous personality of yourself. Again your effect on society was evil. The two of you became the vanguard of an anti-morality movement which made today's sexual revolution seem puritanical. And basically it was a political move. You didn't care about morality, you just needed to wield power. The subsequent decadence set this country up for a nearly-fascistic reaction which rocked foundations and, more importantly, ruined uncountable lives. There were tragic suicides and a rash of terrible mass murders."

"All because of li'l old me? No way, dean. No single man can be held responsible for the aberrational actions of members of society. Nor can the, as you say, decadence of a society be caused by one man's actions."

"Perhaps. All I know is that you were so forceful you came to symbolize the decadence. In the midst of the reaction you went completely insane and poor Linda Tymon, a spiritual and physical wreck by that time, committed a particularly horrible suicide. Note also that the wave of decadence does not occur in any of your other futures."

"Well, hell, I didn't like that future anyway. What next in your ever-changing crystal ball?"

"The ministry, oddly enough. You became a religious fanatic, using doctrines that appeal to the dispossessed. Mainly you convince your followers that, whatever insight they find within themselves is right not only for themselves but for others as well. Your church is what people have always wanted churches to be, a chaotic madhouse where the congregation not only flail themselves but each other. Your religious revival sweeps the continent and, again through an adroit use of television, you get more power than you had in your first future as president. Each of your congregations insidiously gains control in their respective communities, forming a network of power across the country. Heretics are burned at the stake."

"It seems that, while I can change the events of your life, I cannot alter the pattern. Your lust for power is so keen, it emerges no matter what obstacles are placed before you. But no matter, it is a fascinating study, and I think I may have found the solution."

"Study? Solution? You hypocrite, this is just an experiment for you, isn't it? But this time, instead of a pile of metal, you've got a human life to tinker with, to *destroy*. Click click, set up a cycle of events; results negative; cancel. You're killing me before I've got a chance to live, altering the chain of events until you find the circumstances that make me kneel down to authority. It isn't fair!"

"In principle I agree with you. It is not fair. However, in each of your lives your fascination destroys too many others. I'm afraid most people would sacrifice one life to save others. At least, that's what they always say."

"You . . . you fascist!"

Culligan made a threatening gesture but succeeded only in knocking over a lamp.

"We haven't much time," the dean said. "The last trip I came back discouraged, upset at the way things seemed to be getting worse each time. Perhaps because I was preoccupied, I made the mistake I mentioned earlier and encountered Lester Martin on a byway of time. The solution came to me at once. I had always left you free to pursue your power quests, and your resiliency helped you to find new outlets for it. But, I realized, a competitor would, at the least, make the going rougher."

"Competitor? Lester? He couldn't compete in a paper airplane race."

"I'll admit that Mr. Martin seems more qualified for shadow than substance. But he *is* ambitious. Until now he's been waiting for an opportunity to develop. That's his weakness, patience. He hasn't the flair for capitalizing on circumstances which you've shown in all your futures. You may have noticed, however, that lately he's become bolder. Also, it seems, a direct result of my tampering, since it comes from the fact that he's been getting more and more impatient with your leadership."

"He can't do anything. He hasn't enough guts."

"He may surprise you. You see, when he returns he comes with the knowledge of your various futures. I told him everything. As the voice for moderation within your group, the information is tactfully useful to him. Further, he knows that if you, as he put it, 'blow this one,' those friends of yours out in the hall can be swayed away from you. In their eyes this is a showdown play. And you are about to lose. Lester will take control."

"We'll see about that." Culligan paced along a border of the rug. "And what if he does? What about my famous resiliency? I'll find a way to destroy you and Lester Martin and the whole system. You've found no 'solution,' dean, you've just forced one puny minor setback. Not only that—knowing what I know, *what you've told me,* I'm more unbeatable than ever."

"Perhaps, but I doubt it. You see, Lester will have an advantage you've never had. He'll know his enemy. He's vowed to keep tabs on you, and do everything in his power to keep you from establishing a power base in any organizations, fanatic groups, even PTA's. You may still find some route to power, but we'll cross that bridge when we come to it—or, rather, we'll stand on the bridge and forbid you passage."

Culligan stopped pacing. The dean stood up.

"That's about it, Mr. Culligan. Mr. Martin will be back in a few seconds. Then we'll see . . ."

Culligan started several sentences, but words would not logically fall together for him. The crowd rumble outside had increase in volume, as if to taunt him. The dean toyed with fragments of his smashed lighter. The time machine made a couple of small noises and Lester was back, a foolish grin on his face.

"Hi-ho, fearless leader," he said.

"No, man, no, I won't—You think you've beat—But no, no, I'll—I can—You know what this is—what this is—You think, both of you, that you can each have a piece of me until—until there's nothing left until—But you can't, you—It's against all the laws of—it's against—Lester, man —man—you can't—"

"Yes," Lester said quietly, "I sure can. And I sure will."

Unable to regain coherence, Culligan backed away from the dean and Lester. Turning, he ran out of the room, tripped on a tangle of feet, and fell like a child into the arms of his followers.

Both the dean and Lester quickly walked to the doorway in order to watch.

"You were right," Lester said, as they watched Culligan look up from the floor, apparently studying several of the faces around him.

"Right? Right about what?"

"When you told me there was a streak of madness in what we were doing, and I might feel some regret."

"When did I say that? Oh, *then*. I forgot—it was just now for you, but so long ago for me. Days, anyway."

Members of the crowd tried to help Culligan to his feet. He rolled away from their reaching hands, to a cleared area in the middle. His followers looked down at him, and muttered among themselves. Their mutterings seemed distinctly hostile to their leader.

"You think you've really beaten him this time?" Lester said.

"I suspect so. The pattern's there."

"Pattern?"

"Yes, well, in our first confrontations his sureness extended to perfect control of his body. He moved almost gracefully, and his gestures showed a leader's confidence. But, as you saw today, he was as clumsy as an ox, a mark of the deterioration caused by my successive alterings of his future. I think that's a sign. He can't seem to cope any more, just as he is now flailing on the floor in the midst of his own people. If that's not a definite sign, it is at least an interesting development."

Lester felt an involuntary shudder, together with a desire to move physically away from the dean. He glanced at the old man, who smiled in return, then turned away from the doorway and went back to his desk. Lester continued to observe the hallway events.

"Culligan's getting up now. He's talking to the people around him. He looks okay." Lester turned around and faced the dean. "Is *that* a sign?"

No emotion registered on the old man's face.

"Might be. No reason to worry anyway. I'll check things out on my next time-trip."

A cheer, half-hearted but definitely on the positive side of things, came from the hallway.

"You may be surprised, sir. Listen to that." Lester took a couple of steps towards the dean. "And, when you get there, when you get to your future checkpoint, I suppose it is quite possible that you'll be checking me out. That is, making sure my future satisfies your Olympian judgments on our behavior."

For the first time, as he stared into Lester's eyes, the dean looked troubled. Worried, maybe.

"Could be that I'll do that," the old man said. "Could be."

Another cheer, louder than the first, went up in the hallway. The dean moved away from the desk, toward the time machine.

"But I don't think we have to worry about you, Mr. Martin. Patience, as they say, is a virtue, a virtue you seem to have in abundance."

Lester watched the old man walk slowly to the machine which

now looked more than ever like a mere conglomeration of junk. He felt frightened for the first time since the dean had bestowed confidence on him, in this same room, several years from today. What would Culigan do now, he thought. Zonk the old bastard a good one on the skull probably. Lester looked around for a wieldable weapon. Everything looked either too light or too heavy. Anyway, the risk was too great, everybody knew he was alone with the dean. Definitely too risky, a real invitation to a jail cell. Maybe he should demolish the time machine instead, he thought. But immediately he knew that he was just as afraid to do that. He had too much respect for science which, after all, had earned him his Phi Beta Kappa key, his honors degree, and an assured job with the top company in his field if he chose to take it. No, this was not the time for smashing the old man or his invention. This was the time to wait and see what the old bastard came back with, to stay here until he materialized and then examine his eyes closely.

The dean turned and waved goodbye before pressing the button. Lester walked around the desk and sat on the administrator's comfortable padded leather chair. The dean faded out. Lester, responding to the soft comfort of the chair, put his feet on the desk. He felt perfectly relaxed and knew he could put up with the long period of staring at the time machine.

He could hear the crowd outside moving away, down the hall. They cheered once more, with some energy, and then seemed to laugh their way out of the building.

PUBLISH AND PERISH

John Thomas

There is a rumbling in the educational land. Teachers are taking stands on a wide range of issues which affect them, and doing so with a militancy unprecedented in American history.

The issues which have aroused this new teacher militancy are many and diverse. Among them are:

1. *Economics.* As inflation eats away at income, as the price of consumer goods rises, teachers are demanding what they consider to be a fair return for their efforts and status. Teachers remain among the lowest paid professional groups in the United States.

2. *General working conditions.* This factor has many dimensions to it, including status. In an earlier era, the school teacher was among the most educated members of society; in some small communities he or she was *the* most educated individual. This is no longer the case. Millions of Americans have college degrees and more are being added to this list each year. Furthermore, the social status attached to being a teacher has fallen with the rise in the educational level of the country. In addition, many schools, especially those in large cities, are unpleasant, impersonal, and even dangerous places to work.

3. *Specific working conditions.* Teachers are voicing concern over the size of their classes, protection against hostile students, the institutionalization of grievance procedures, and the right to academic freedom.

4. *Job security.* Teachers are seeking guarantees against arbitrary removal, the maintenance of tenure, and, for the younger teacher, access to a decent teaching position in a time of diminishing opportunities.

The rising militancy and demands on the part of minority groups, women, anti-war protesters and college students have influenced the tenor and tone of the educational "movement." The teachers have responded in typically American fashion: they have *organized* and *unionized*.

The two major teachers' organizations are the National Education Association and the American Federation of Teachers. The NEA is the larger group, with a membership of over one million. However, the AFT has been more aggressive in its pursuits of teacher demands, and has sanctioned the use of strikes to obtain its goals. Both organizations are becoming more militant as the problems faced by their memberships mount.

"Publish and Perish" depicts a university in which the issue of job security is the dominant issue facing the professional staff. It is a self-contained social system which has developed its own methods for dealing with the traditional problems of which teachers to retain and which to promote: just let them fight it out!

FOR FURTHER THOUGHT OR DISCUSSION

1. What are the major social issues facing the teaching profession today?

2. What role do the NEA and the AFT play in public education?

3. Should teachers have the right to strike?

4. What are the most effective ways of determining a teacher's performance?

5. What is tenure and why should it be or not be retained?

PUBLISH AND PERISH   *John Thomas*

The last cars had pulled into Clark W. Kerr Memorial Parking Lot for the opening session of his new Physics I course, and Gleason was still searching frantically for the rest of his notes. Today of all days he could not afford to be late for class. It had taken all the pull he could muster to get prime time on the closed-circuit TV, and he'd surely be relegated to the early morning hours or even cancelled if he were late the first day. With only one hundred and twenty-seven research papers to his name he was lucky to have made assistant professor anyway.

Quarters were dropping into parking meter slots, and the air filled with the buzz of hungry machinery clicking off the time. The big screen at the front of the lot lit up hopefully, then went dark again as Gleason, seated in his office a half-mile way, shook his head at the engineer on his monitor. He was digging hurriedly through the stacks of Physical Abstracts that had been delivered that morning, the six-foot bundle representing summaries of all the papers in his field published during the preceding week. Under one of the piles he found the missing pages of his notes and, with a relieved sigh, fitted them into the sheaf of papers in his hand. Using the camera lens as a mirror he smoothed down his rumpled hair, then nodded to the waiting engineer. The red light went on, and he saw his own owlishly bespectacled face staring out from the monitor.

"The pursuit of knowledge," he began, "has always been the province of a handful of lonely, dedicated men..."

He felt better once class was over. It hadn't gone badly at all. There'd been some disturbance on the screen from a passing jet, and one of the filmstrips had run out before he'd finished explaining it, but otherwise the show had been technically competent. He sighed, put down his notes on the desk, and began to burrow through the piles of abstracts that filled most of the small office. Buried in a corner he found a two-cup coffee maker, now empty. Again Gleason seethed with the consciousness of his inferior status. Associate professors rated five-cup coffee makers and didn't have to go hunting water all the time! He thought of borrowing the larger size from the office of Professor Morgan, who had died only yesterday, but decided against it since the theft would soon be discovered by Morgan's successor, and it could mean Gleason's job. If he wanted a cup of coffee there was nothing to do but trek to the graduate students' lounge.

He unearthed a chipped and blackened coffee cup, shoved a pile of abstracts away from the door and ventured into the hallway of the physics building. A sharp hiss from the office to the right of his brought him up short. Turning he found the department's other assistant professor, Gridley Farrington, peering out at him through a partially opened door. The other man, shorter than Gleason with a sharpened nose and slick, black hair, slipped from his office and confronted his colleague with a broad and strikingly insincere smile. "Off to the kiddies' lounge again?" he inquired, staring pointedly at Gleason's cup.

Gleason could understand Farrington's hostility, as the poor man had published a scant one hundred and twenty-three research papers and was thus even lower on the multiversity social scale than he. Of course seventeen of Gleason's publications had been purchased from graduate students who had dropped out before getting their degrees, but Farrington wasn't likely to have done all his own work either.

"Just thought I'd get some coffee," Gleason replied, waving his cup vaguely. "It's a chance to keep in touch with the students, see what they're thinking. It's hard to get to know anybody teaching your courses over television."

"Oh, sure," Farrington grinned unpleasantly. "Well, Gleason," he went on, turning apparently to what was really on his mind, "what do you think about old Morgan dying?"

"Terrible thing," Gleason mumbled.

"Oh, I don't mean that! I mean who do you think will get his job?"

Gleason had thought of little else since Morgan's death, but he wasn't going to let Farrington know that. "Well, I suppose there are lots of choices. Hunnicutt could bring in a man from outside."

"Ridiculous!" Farrington snapped. "Silly idea! Surely they'd choose a faculty man, someone with an—er—adequate publication record."

"Well, probably," Gleason admitted, shifting nervously from one foot to the other. He himself had been at the multiversity only a few months, a replacement in fact for Morgan, who had been promoted to an associate professorship after nineteen years on the staff. He wasn't familiar with all the nuances of departmental rivalries yet.

"You'll go for the job, I suppose," Farrington ventured.

"Well, if they offer it to me . . ."

"Oh, don't play modest with me, Gleason!" The little man smoothed down the back of his slick hair. "If you want the job you've got to fight for it! Nobody can afford to wait for offers any more. Are you going to fight or not?"

Gleason didn't quite understand the implications of the question. Farrington must want the job for himself, but surely the four-publication margin would be decisive if the chairman chose to recruit from his own staff. "Well," Gleason said finally, "I'll probably do whatever I can to get the job, if that's what you mean."

Farrington smiled nastily, but at the same time turned rather pale. "That's what I thought," he said and disappeared into his office, snapping the door shut behind him.

Gleason shrugged and continued on down the corridor to the graduate lounge, where he found four anonymous students and a lukewarm urn of coffee. He sipped some of the coffee and attempted to make conversation with the students, none of whom appeared to see any advantage in talking to an assistant professor. The belated entrance of a fifth student, however, left Gleason somewhat less than pleased. For the boy was Alec Throckmorton, a shambling, beetle-browed graduate student of minimal intelligence and doubtful competence, whose attempts to make up for his lack of brilliance through an anxious, almost fawning desire to please rendered him doubly odious. But, since his father happened to supervise the awarding of grants through the National Science Foundation, Throckmorton was assured not only of his degree, but of a soft berth as lab assistant to the least prestigious member of the staff—Gleason.

"How ya doin', professor?" the boy demanded, slapping Gleason's shoulder and dislodging most of the contents of his coffee cup. "All ready for the big spearmint tomorrow?"

Gleason recalled with a chill that the boy was scheduled to assist him the following day in a critical and perhaps dangerous investigation into the properties of one of the newer synthetic elements. "All ready, Throckmorton," he sighed. "I hope you can set up the equipment properly, this time."

Throckmorton nodded his head vigorously. "Don't worry, professor. Sometimes I get confused about where the wires go, but I've got it all straightened out now."

"Green wire to the red coil, remember?"

"Oh—uh—yeah, I remember." Before the boy could generate further unwelcome conversation, Gleason hurried away.

After awhile he wandered back to his own office carrying a tin of water for his coffee maker. Though he had closed his office door on leaving it was now ajar, and Gleason wondered idly if he had missed a visitor. Pouring the water into the coffee maker he added some grounds from a jar in his desk. He plugged in the percolator and stepped around a stack of abstracts to get his cup.

The explosion wasn't very loud, but it was powerful enough to lift the abstracts and deposit them solidly against the small of his back. Gleason went down across another pile of papers as a fusillade of deadly fragments rattled angrily against the walls. In the sudden silence he sat up and stared at the smoking hole where the coffee maker had been sitting.

His door flew open, and for a moment Farrington's ratlike face was momentarily framed, an expectant grin fading to dismay as he saw Gleason staring back at him. Then the face was gone, and Gleason heard rapid footsteps in the hallway. A few moments later the door again swung open to reveal the department chairman, Professor Hunnicut.

"Starting sooner than I'd expected," was Hunnicutt's only comment as he helped Gleason to his feet. "Bomb in the coffee maker, eh? Not really ingenious."

Gleason examined the remains of the percolator mutely. Only the heavy stack of abstracts had prevented him from being slashed by flying metal and glass from the explosion. Hunnicutt came up behind him and peered over his shoulder. "Looks like the bomb was connected to the heating element, went off when the coil started to warm up." Hunnicutt shook his head disapprovingly. "Not really a good job. Always takes a few seconds for heat to get to the element—long enough for the intended victim to walk away from the bomb. A really top-notch man would have connected the bomb directly to the electrical circuit."

It occurred to Gleason that the chairman's remarks were not entirely appropriate to an instance of attempted murder. He turned to stare at his boss, a tall, white-haired man impeccably clothed in gray pinstripe. "What," he demanded, "is going on here?"

Hunnicutt slipped a fatherly arm about Gleason's shoulders. "I keep forgetting you're new here, my boy. Not really conversant with the multiversity traditions." He kicked aside a stack of abstracts with a well-polished oxford. "Come up to my office for a few minutes. I think we can easily straighten this out."

The chairman motioned casually to a bored custodian who had

suddenly materialized and led Gleason into the hallway and down the long corridor to the left. Gleason noted that Farrington's door was tightly closed and that no sound issued from the sealed interior.

Hunnicutt seated himself at his desk and leaned back comfortably, moving a ten-cup percolator to one side. "Bit of a shock for you, I suppose, coming without warning and all. Warning from me, I mean. I assume Farrington did check with you to make sure you wanted to compete before he planted the bomb."

Gleason was thoroughly disoriented now. Something rather unusual seemed to be going on within the walls of what he had come to think of as a rather staid multiversity. "I—I don't think he really..." Gleason began and then recalled the peculiar conversation with Farrington of an hour before. "He said something about *fighting* for the appointment...."

"Yes," said Hunnicutt brusquely, "the appointment." He leaned back, making a tent of his fingers. "It's a real problem for me. Need a really top-notch man for the job, if you know what I mean. So many Ph.D's these days, so many publications, one can't really keep up with the qualifications any more. Don't want to go outside the present staff if I can help it. But, you know, I need some real evidence that I've got a top-notch man to fill the vacancy."

Gleason had a feeling that he didn't completely understand the conversation. "You know my qualifications..." he began.

Hunnicutt waved him aside impatiently. "Know it all; no better or worse than Farrington's except for a small difference in the publications index. Really couldn't choose on the basis of what I know now. Farrington's got seniority in service, of course, but I never let that influence an appointment." Hunnicutt's manner softened a bit. "It's ingenuity I like to see, my boy. Farrington's trying hard, but that coffee-maker stunt isn't really the sort of thing to convince me. The heating element, you know. Now, I wonder if you could think of some better way...."

"Better way, sir? To do what?"

Hunnicutt laughed nervously, tamping tobacco into a professorish pipe. "Why, to kill him, of course! He's had his chance, now it's your turn! If you can think of a more ingenious—and successful—method than his, you'll not only have convinced me of your own abilities, but you'll have eliminated your only departmental rival!"

Gleason stared at his boss. "Kill him, sir?"

"Well, that's the tradition!" Hunnicutt snapped with a sudden return to his mood of irritation. "Can't fight a good college tradition, I always say. Besides, it's really the only way. How can I tell who's really top-notch without some kind of test?" He paused, reflecting. "The whole thing began really as a kind of accident a few years ago. Milton and Borofsky had decided to duel for the post being vacated by Anderson, but Borofsky cheated by devising a way to assassinate Milton with the chimes in the college bell tower even before the duel took place. Read it in some mystery story, I believe. Of course we couldn't turn Borofsky over to the police, top-notch men being hard to get as they are. So I promoted him to the job—rather admired his ingenuity, as a matter of fact.

"Well, couldn't do much a few months later when Leonard electrocuted Borofsky to get Blassingame's job. A sort of precedent had been set, you see. Anyway, that's the way it grew, from small beginnings, as these traditions often do. Nowadays I wouldn't consider making appointments any other way." He was friendlier now, smiling an encouraging smile at Gleason. "I think you've got the stuff it takes to carry on the old tradition, my boy. Farrington's good, but not really my type of research man. Heating coils! Think up something a little better, and you won't have to worry about that associate professorship."

Gleason was still trying to make some audible comment as Hunnicutt ushered him briskly to the door. "To tell the truth," the chairman was saying, "I've been a little disappointed in the quality of assassinations around the department the last year—too messy, too routine. Now, if you could come up with something really top-notch on your first time out. . . ." His voice dropped to a friendly confidentiality. "Well, you'd have a head start on a really outstanding career in science." Gleason found himself standing in the corridor as the chairman's door sighed shut behind him.

He drifted back down the hallway and into his office, peering apprehensively at Farrington's closed door before he entered. The custodian had just finished cleaning up his office, and a shiny new two-cup percolator had already been installed in one corner. Gleason noted with relief that several bales of shredded abstracts had been removed.

What was he to do now? He couldn't go along with Hunnicutt's plan—simply couldn't! He'd never killed anybody in his life and wasn't going to start now. Yet apparently his own life was in danger, and if he didn't try some kind of counterattack the assistant professorship would surely go to Farrington. He'd heard vague rumors of the kind of cutthroat competition that had developed in the multiversities over the past decade, but he'd never anticipated anything like this. A little sabotage to divert government research funds—that was common enough. But murder! If this was the kind of game they were playing, he wanted no part of it.

Gleason glanced at his watch and saw that it was almost time for his next class. He went over to the wall case and racked out the TV camera. Removing a sheaf of notes from his desk, he sat down in his chair and turned toward the camera; only a half minute to go, he noted. Suddenly he realized that he was still a mess from the explosion, his hair on end, his clothing rumpled. He looked about for a mirror, then remembered the trick of using the camera lens as a last-minute mirror. He peered at the camera, trying to catch his reflection in the darkened lens.

There was no lens; only a slim, blackened tube.

Gleason sat for a moment digesting this fact as the clock hand crept toward the hour. The absence of a lens might mean several things, but only one occurred to him at the moment. He dived for the floor.

The red light winked on, and a high-energy laser beam spat from the tube, passing just over Gleason's desk and burning a hole in the wall behind it. Overloaded circuits began to whine, and the camera burned itself out within seconds, the beam vanishing as its power supply was cut off. After a few moments the top of Gleason's head rose warily above the level of the desk, round eyes fixed on the smoking hulk of the television camera.

The phone rang. It was Professor Hunnicutt.

"What's going on in there," Hunnicutt demanded between audible sucks on his pipe. "You're twenty seconds late getting on the air! Students are waiting—knowledge calls, my boy!"

"It's Farrington, I think, sir." Gleason sat down on the floor cross-legged, not quite ready to leave the shelter of his desk. "He seems to have installed a laser beam in my TV camera. He—he nearly burned a hole in me!"

"No!" came Hunnicutt's shocked voice over the wire. "Used a TV camera, did he? That sort of thing won't do at all!"

"No, sir," said Gleason, brightening.

"No man has the right to interrupt class programming for personal business," said Hunnicutt, righteous anger thundering in his voice. "Not a really top-notch kind of thing to do. Shows the sort of degeneration of standards in the academic community the last few years."

"Yes, sir."

377

"All violence must take place outside class hours, committee meetings and conference periods," Hunnicutt said firmly. "I'll have to talk to Farrington about this."

"Er—sir. . . ."

Hunnicutt's voice rasped with impatience. "Well, what is it? I've got to get back to work."

Still crouching, Gleason cradled the phone to both hands. "I—I was thinking, sir. I'm not sure I really want that associate professorship after all. I've only been here a few months, and. . . ."

"Nonsense!" Hunnicutt roared. "You're a top-notch man. Want to see you move ahead!"

"Yes, sir. But you see, murder's not really. . . . I mean, I'm not the type for this sort of thing."

"What's that?" Menace edged Hunnicutt's voice.

"What I'm trying to say is, I'm not really the type to kill someone just to get a job."

A long silence stretched across the wire. "Not the type, eh?" Hunnicutt sighed wearily. "I'd thought better of you, my boy. Really top-notch, I thought. Felt sure you'd come through." Another silence. "You understand, of course, that we can't keep a man on the faculty who scorns our department's hallowed traditions."

"Sir?"

"I mean, Gleason, that you do not yet have tenure."

"No, sir."

"Plenty who'd like your present job, Gleason. And no other multiversity is likely to hire you without a recommendation from me. Think it over." The wire went dead.

Gleason put down the phone and rose cautiously to his feet. He circled the desk to peer at the fused camera, then turned to stare at the neat hole burned in the far wall of his office. A peaceful grouping of trees and ivy could be glimpsed through the aperture.

Gleason stood thinking about Hunnicutt's words, the long struggle to get his present job, his unfitness for any real work in the outside world. Hunnicutt was right—no other multiversity would hire him without a recommendation, and surely no one would believe his story if he tried to use it as an excuse. It was either get out of this situation somehow or face a diminishing career at some backwater city college, stripped of research funds and despairing of the future.

Still sunk in misery, he called the TV studio and cancelled all classes for the rest of the day, since it would take that long for his camera to be replaced. Then he returned to a serious consideration of his problem. What was he going to do? He couldn't kill anybody! And how could Farrington...? There was a thought! Was it possible that Farrington was no more enthusiastic about murder than he? Perhaps the poor man had made the two attempts on Gleason's life out of nothing more than a pathetic loyalty to his department. If the two of them could get together and make a deal....

A few moments later Gleason was knocking timidly at his neighbor's door, a cautious optimism in his heart and a heavy paperweight in his hand should the optimism prove unjustified. Gleason heard footsteps inside the office, then Farrington's hoarse whisper at the door. "Who's there?"

"Gleason! I've got to talk to you!"

He heard a hasty scuffling, then silence. "Don't bother to try shooting through the door," Farrington's muffled voice called finally. "I've got an energy field around my desk!"

"For God's sake, man, I don't want to hurt you. I just want to talk this thing over!"

"There's nothing to talk about," Farrington snarled. "You won't get me to open this door!"

Gleason stepped to one side of the door in case Farrington decided to do some shooting himself. "Let's be sensible," he called in a stage whisper. "Why should we go along with this crazy scheme when the stakes aren't worth it? Maybe we could work something out!"

"There's nothing to work out!" Farrington snapped back. "I need the job! If I knew how to do anything else I wouldn't be a college professor!"

Nervously Gleason shifted the paperweight from hand to hand. "But, look, Farrington. We must be able to make some kind of deal. If we could just talk rationally about this I'm sure—"

"There's nothing to talk about, and even if there were...." A sudden, protracted silence fell. Gleason eased up to the door and put his ear against the panelling. He thought he could hear the faint sounds of hurried movement inside. "On second thought," Farrington went on, "you may be right. At least we can talk it over. Come on inside, and let's discuss it."

Gleason straightened, shifted the paperweight to his left hand and reached for the doorknob. He froze in that attitude, reflecting. After a few moments he ventured, "Maybe you'd better come out here instead, Farrington. The—er—light's better."

"No," Farrington's distant voice replied, "you come in here. We want to keep this private."

"We can have some coffee in the lounge."

"I've got a coffee maker in here."

"I think you'd better come out here."

A half-hour later Gleason gave up and returned to his office to sit brooding at his desk. Farrington seemed determined to kill him, and he still couldn't work up much enthusiasm for a counterattack. At any rate he couldn't think clearly about the problem with Farrington plotting actively next door. Kicking aside a pile of abstracts, he exited quietly through the hole in the wall.

After a sleepless night in a rented hotel room (in case Farrington had his home address) he rose bleary eyed and despairingly to face what would surely be another miserable day. He still had no plan, no hope. Perhaps there was some way of merely *disabling* his rival. . . . But no, he couldn't consider violence at all. Still, wasn't one of Farrington's arms or legs worth his own life? It was only a small concession to principle.

He arrived at his office early and found that the new TV camera had been installed and the laser hole sealed up. Of Farrington there was no sign. Gleason boiled some water in his percolator (after a thorough inspection), but soon discovered that his container of coffee had been shattered in one or more of the recent office catastrophes. There was nothing to do but go to the graduate lounge again. He slipped out quietly, pausing only to make sure Farrington's door was closed, and ran tiptoe down the hallway, dodging around a bit in case of pursuit by missiles. In the lounge he found no one but Throckmorton, snoring on one of the couches.

"The spearmint," said Throckmorton, opening one eye to peer dully at his boss. "Today's the day!"

In his anxiety over the murder attempts, Gleason had forgotten the experimental work scheduled with Throckmorton for that day. He felt a twinge of apprehension; the equipment that were using was dangerous, and in his present mood he could make any one of a number of errors. Still, if he tried to put off the experiment today his standing with Hunnicutt might be damaged irreparably.

"Go ahead and set it up," he said. "I'll be down later to work with you."

The shaggy boy unfolded himself from the couch, grinning vacuously. "I'll get started on it right away, professor. Count on me." He stumbled into Gleason, spilling the cup of coffee the man had just poured for himself, and shambled off toward the stairway. The research lab was downstairs in the basement, almost directly beneath Gleason's office.

"And Throckmorton," Gleason called after him, "don't forget—it's the red wire on the green coil."

"Green wire on red coil," Throckmorton assured him and increased his pace, trying to appear enthusiastic.

Gleason's head buzzed with the effects of little sleep and much worry, so that he barely heard the boy. All his remaining emotional energy went into the task of drawing himself another cup of coffee. It wasn't until he was back at his desk that the boy's last words finally registered.

He recalled at the same moment the possible result of attaching the green wire to the red coil.

Suppressing a howl, he headed for the door, twisting frantically at the knob.

The door refused to open.

Gleason stood momentarily transfixed, the doorknob still in his hand. The door had never stuck like this before. He rattled the knob experimentally, bent over to peer through the keyhole. Something was blocking it from the other side, something that was not a key. At the same moment he felt the doorknob grow warm beneath his hand.

Gleason snatched his fingers away and stood up, backing away from the door. The knob was turning cherry red, and smoke had begun to issue from the door itself. Could Throckmorton already. . . . Then he heard a bubble of wild laughter from next door, and he knew.

"Got you this time!" Farrington screamed at him through their common wall. "My heat converter will fry you alive within the next couple of minutes! The job is mine!"

Gleason wiped his damp brow with the back of his hand, searching about for some means of escape. Since the physics building was determinedly modern, it had no windows whatsoever; the door was the only way in or out. He glanced upward at the footsquare grill of the air-conditioning unit. Was he slim enough to worm his body through that passage? Desperately Gleason shoved his desk under the opening and clambered up to test the grill. Six strong screws held it firmly across the outlet, and Gleason had no screwdriver.

He peered down, spied the telephone on his desk. He might still be able to summon help. He had crouched down and was just reaching for the receiver when the phone rang. Lifting the receiver he heard Throckmorton's dull tones. "Everything's all connected up, professor. When ya comin' down?"

"Throckmorton, get help! I'm locked in my office, and Farrington is trying to kill me!"

"What's that, professor?" the boy shouted. "I can hardly hear ya with all the noise from the equipment!"

"I said Farrington—" Gleason's voice froze. "Did you say 'noise from the equipment?' "

"Yeah, professor, I got it goin', all right."

"It's operating—with the green wire on the red coil?"

"Sure, right now it's—"

But the sentence remained uncompleted as the phone went dead and the right wall of Gleason's office vanished. He dropped the receiver and stood staring at the vacant spot where Farrington's office— and Farrington—had stood. About fifty square feet of floor space had been vaporized instantly. The laboratory, Gleason now recalled, was almost directly beneath his office. But just *almost* directly. Actually it was beneath Farrington's.

The door had stopped smoking, and Gleason threw it open easily, the now harmless attachment to Farrington's heat converter clattering to the floor. He saw Hunnicutt scuttle down the hall toward him, pipe bouncing nervously between his teeth. The chairman halted and stood awestruck before the hole in his building. At last he turned to Gleason, tears brimming in his eyes. "My boy, this is the most absolutely top-notch piece of work I've ever seen in this department."

"But—"

"Oh, it'll be rather expensive to replace this much of the building; but we've got government money, and I must say the loss is really worth it, under the circumstances. Never seen a cleaner, more humane liquidation since the tradition began."

A ragged figure appeared at the head of the basement stairs and lurched toward them. Apparently the force of the beam of destruction, or whatever the thing was, had been directed almost entirely upward. "It was really Throckmorton, here—"

Hunnicutt majestically placed an arm about the shoulders of the frightened boy. "This young man gave you a hand, did he? Pulled the trigger, so to speak, while you were the bait. Brave lads, both of you!"

Throckmorton, who had never in his entire life been addressed by anyone above the level of associate professor stood open-mouthed, basking in the glow of sudden recognition. "You will no doubt benefit from this, too, Throckmorton," the chairman went on. "Naturally there'll be two assistant professorships vacant now, and I'm sure we can arrange a spot for you while you're completing your doctoral requirements."

Perhaps, Gleason decided, there was no point in rocking the boat after all. With the coveted associate professorship his, and the beginnings of a new and infinitely murderous weapon created by attaching the green wire to the red coil, he was well on his way to a brilliant career in science.

"Come into my office, both of you," Hunnicutt was saying. "Got to get started on the paperwork for your appointments."

Watching his boss chew vigorously on his pipe, a foolproof idea for a booby trap slipped unbidden into Gleason's mind. The whole thing was ridiculous, he told himself. He wouldn't be in line for the departmental chairmanship for years! Still, it didn't hurt. . . . "Do you have a pencil and paper, professor?" he asked. "I'd like to jot down a little idea I just had."

"Certainly, my boy," Hunnicutt smiled, handing him the pencil and paper. "It's the mark of a top-notch scientist that he's always thinking, always searching for new ideas, always looking toward the future."

"I'm afraid you're right, sir," Gleason said; he was still scribbling furiously as he passed into the chairman's darkened office.

GORMAN

Jerry Farber

As an integral part of our social and political system, public education in the United States is subject to a vast array of political pressures. First of all, the division of powers in education between local, state, and federal levels of government makes political conflict inevitable as each component bureaucracy struggles for supremacy. Added to this conflict are locally-elected school boards who often attempt to influence educational policies. It is a political rule of thumb that units which do not generate their own internal funds, but rather must compete for them, have to engage in political activity.

At the same time, the traditions and myths of education demand that the schools be somewhat *separated* from government so that academic freedom and independence can be assured. This means that the schools must be very cautious in their political activity, and this factor may reduce their political effectiveness.

There are many actors in the political arena of American public education. Among the more important "players" are:

1. *Local school boards and boards of regents,* some appointed and others elected, who represent the mass of citizenry in educational issues. They, in turn, are subject to varying degrees of pressure from their constituencies.

2. *State governments,* who must raise and apportion the funds necessary to the functioning of education and who are themselves subject to lobbyists and pressure groups.

3. The *federal government,* who assists the states and localities and who, through the decisions of the Supreme Court, must occasionally intervene directly in the schools.

4. *Pressure groups* of all kinds and descriptions, ranging from teacher groups like the American Federation of Teachers, to civic

groups like the Parent-Teacher Associations, to special-interest groups, such as those demanding local control of education. All of these groups interact and conflict with each other and with the other groups on this list.

5. *Students,* who are organizing as a group, especially but not exclusively on the college level, to make their wishes known.

But there is more to educational politics than this. Each individual school is also a political system, in which individuals and points of view compete for power and status.

Among the issues which produce political activity is the *curriculum* (curriculum can also be an issue which involves groups outside of individual schools). What is taught and who should teach it has long been of crucial importance in the schools. In some systems, the curriculum is system-wide. In others, department heads determine its rationale. In still others, whole departments debate and decide this issue in semi-democratic fashion. Whatever the system, the issue is usually a controversial one.

In higher education there is a trend toward student participation in curriculum matters: students sit as either voting or non-voting members of curriculum committees, or are consulted through the use of questionnaires.

"Gorman" presents a department meeting in a university of the future. Most teachers have spent or will spend time in department meetings at which the issues will be controversial and divisive, but none will (hopefully) spend as political an afternoon as Professor Gorman.

FOR FURTHER THOUGHT OR DISCUSSION

1. To what political pressures are the schools in your city subject?

2. What are the major political issues affecting education?

3. What are the major political issues *within* schools?

4. How should the curriculum be determined in a free society?

5. Can education be separated from politics?

GORMAN   *Jerry Farber*

There were several taps at the door. Gorman finished printing "2ND QUIZ" at the top of a blue-lined column. He closed the record book and called out:

"Who is it?"

"Chuck Fernandez."

"From my eight o'clock?"

"Yes, sir."

"Just a sec. I'm on the phone."

Gorman moved quietly to a filing cabinet by the door. He eased open the top drawer a few inches and took out a revolver. Then, holding the revolver in his right hand, he stepped up on Ferguson's desk, which was next to the filing cabinet. From the desk he lifted himself on top of the cabinet and kneeled on its narrow summit, his head almost touching the ceiling. Turning his face away from the door, he called out:

"Come in."

The door flew open, slamming against the steel cabinet. Gorman peered down over the top of the door. It was Grunewald, of course. Grunewald's right hand was stuffed in his coat pocket; his head pivoted wildly from side to side as he scanned the empty room. He froze when he heard Gorman's voice coming from almost directly over his head.

"Don't move or I'll shoot you, Grunewald. Not the slightest move. Good. Now do exactly what I say. Take your empty right hand out of that coat pocket. Now reach your left hand in there and take that gun by the barrel. OK. Shut the door behind you with your right hand. All right, now hand the gun up to me. Thank you."

Gorman dropped Grunewald's pistol into his own left coat pocket; then he stepped down and sat on Ferguson's desk, watching the other man all the while.

"Take my chair and sit in it facing me."

Grunewald sat. "So I'm sitting. Congratulations. What are you going to do, shoot me, Gorman?"

Gorman was silent.

"Look, figure you picked yourself up a pistol on the deal. Goodbye. Good luck."

"Gorman" by Jerry Farber, published in *The Student as Nigger*. Copyright © 1969 by Jerry Farber. Reprinted with permission of author.

"Don't get out of that chair."

"Gorman, think! Plan ahead. Hold me here and you miss the meeting, too. What have you gained?"

"Don't worry about it, Grunewald. Now pick up my Trilling from the desk and read it—quietly."

"Shoot me, Gorman. I won't read Trilling."

Gorman reached into the open file drawer again, took out a silencer and began to fit it on his pistol. Grunewald, meanwhile, had located the Trilling. He began to read. It was quarter to three. The next fifteen minutes passed in silence punctuated by Grunewald's ostentatious sighs, snorts and tongue clickings. A minute or two after three there was another knock on the door. Gorman waited.

"Professor Gorman?"

He waited.

"Marshall, are you all right?"

"It's OK, Pam. Are any of Grunewald's people out there?"

"Yes, that clod, McGriff. Oh, and I passed Dr. Peaster in the hall but he's gone now."

Gorman whispered to Grunewald, motioning with the gun. "Tell McGriff to go away."

"McGriff, go away."

They heard McGriff call softly just outside the door: "Dr. Grunewald? Listen, if there's anything wrong . . ."

"McGriff, just go."

After a few moments Pam spoke from the corridor. "Marshall? He's gone."

"OK, come in."

She opened the door and shut it behind her as she looked at the two men. Without stepping between them, she walked over to Gorman and kissed him on the cheek.

"Ciao, Marshall. Hello, Dr. Grunewald. Marshall, aren't you going to your meeting? It's after three."

"That's all right. Look, I want you to stay here and watch Dr. Grunewald while I'm gone. When I leave, lock the door and don't open it till I get back. OK?"

"OK. Don't worry about it."

He gave her his revolver. "If he gets out of that chair, shoot him. Can you do it?"

"Shoot him! Oh, my God, Marshall. Ask me something difficult why don't you!"

"Pam!" He looked at her for a moment. "We're voting on curriculum today."

She nodded soberly. "I'm sorry, hon. I'll be all right. Just take care of yourself."

"Sorority girls, Gorman?" Grunewald asked. "Are we going to see you at the prom?"

Pam leveled the gun icily. "I'm *not* in a sorority, Dr. Grunewald."

Gorman reached for his briefcase and opened the door. "Listen, Pam. McGriff or Professor Peaster or one of the others will be back. Make Grunewald send them away. Off campus somewhere. In the meantime, Grunewald, be quiet—and read."

He crossed the corridor into the men's room, patted his hair in front of the mirror and entered an empty stall, shutting and latching the door. He checked Grunewald's pistol to make sure that it was loaded. Then he put it in his right coat pocket. A swinging door had opened and shut. Gorman lowered his head below the top of the stall door.

"Marsh, it's Joel Peaster. I saw you come in. I'd like to talk to you for a minute."

"Just a minute, Peaster. I'm coming out." Gorman sank to his hands and knees and crawled silently under the partition into the next stall and then into the one beyond. One more partition brought him into the end stall. Its door was open a few inches, enough to reveal Peaster standing in front of the stall Gorman had been in. Peaster gripped a heavy glass ashtray in his right hand, which was poised at shoulder height. Gorman reach into his right coat pocket and spoke softly:

"Freeze, Peaster."

Several minutes later, his briefcase bulging with Peaster's clothes, Gorman raced up the escalator to the second-floor men's room. He dropped Peaster's underwear, shirt and tie in one toilet, his trousers in another and his coat in a third. He stepped on the flush pedal in each stall, then left the men's room and hurried down the corridor toward Lecture Hall 5. A few other latecomers were approaching the door. He entered with them and chose a seat on the aisle in the back row. About forty department members were already seated in front of him, scattered throughout the descending rows of padded, permanent seats.

They were winding up Old Business: allocation of out-of-state travel funds. When it was done, Gorman rose and introduced a motion to eliminate the second semester of the two-semester literary criticism requirement, and to substitute for it a required senior course in Chaucer. As Gorman stated his motion, the chairman, Wainwright, was scanning the rows of seats intently. When Gorman concluded, the chairman left his rostrum and walked over to the side wall where Roger, the departmental clerk, was standing. He spoke with the clerk briefly and then returned to the rostrum and addressed Gorman.

"Marshall, I wonder if you'd mind holding off on that motion for a few minutes. I notice that we're still missing several department members who have expressed particular interest in curriculum matters. Joel Peaster, for example, and Sid Grunewald . . ."

Wainwright was interrupted by shouts from the floor. Someone called out. "That's their problem!" A number of others, however, agreed with the chairman. Gorman spoke out over the hubbub.

"As a matter of fact, neither Professor Peaster nor Professor Grunewald will be able to attend at all. They both asked me to relay their apologies."

The shouted remarks from the floor, as well as a number of whispered conversations, continued. When they had subsided slightly, Gorman, still standing, reintroduced his motion to substitute Chaucer for second-semester Criticism. The chairman, Wainwright, however, ruled Goman's motion out of order on the grounds that proper written notice had not been given ten days in advance. Gorman appealed this ruling of the chair; from his briefcase he produced and distributed xeroxed copies of an affidavit from Donna, the departmental secretary, affirming that a notice of intent had been placed in each professor's box two weeks previously. Nevertheless, Gorman's appeal, though it won a majority vote, narrowly missed obtaining the necessary two-thirds' approval.

Gorman waited. A few minutes later he found an opportunity to reintroduce his motion as an amendment. Van Pelt had moved to add a new lower-division requirement: Great Issues in Criticism. Gorman's amendment stipulated that no more than one semester of criticism be required for the major, and it added as requirements a senior course in Chaucer and a lower-division survey of Middle English poetry. Before Gorman had completed his amendment, there were a number of shouts of "Point of order!" Wainwright quieted the meeting and ruled Gorman's amendment out of order on the grounds that its thrust ran counter to the thrust of the Van Pelt motion.

At this point, however, Ronceval, the parliamentarian, slipped his right hand into a coat pocket which was already heavily weighted and sagging, and slouched from his seat in front to converse with Wainwright behind the rostrum. He stood partially behind Wainwright and whispered in his left ear. Wainwright listened to Ronceval for a minute or so. Then he addressed the meeting:

"I have decided, on advice of the parliamentarian, to reverse my own ruling. Professor Gorman's amendment, which would limit our criticism requirements to one semester and would add required courses in Chaucer and Middle English poetry, is a proper amendment and may stand. Is there any debate on the amendment?"

"What do you mean debate? Van Pelt was on his feet shouting. "That's not an amendment. It's sabotage! What is this?"

Wainwright spoke, almost whispering. "Stanley, I have ruled it a proper amendment." Wainwright's glance slid to the far left corners of his eyes, then rolled back to focus intently on Van Pelt. "I hope you can understand my position."

"You're damn right I understand your position. Tell Ronceval to get his hand out of his pocket."

There was an outbreak of murmuring and whispered discussion. Ronceval remained where he was standing. The chair called again for debate on Gorman's amendment.

Three speakers on each side had been heard and Wainwright had already asked for ayes when Schlemmer rose and requested a secret ballot. Gorman stood up in opposition, pointing out that the vote was already in progress; he called for a ruling from the chair. Ronceval, who was still standing behind Wainwright, whispered a few words in the chairman's ear. Wainwright ruled in Gorman's favor. There were a number of calls for the parliamentarian to sit down and to take his hand out of his coat pocket. Then Roger, the departmental clerk, who had moved over against the back wall of the lecture hall, plunged his own right hand into his own sagging coat pocket and moved swiftly up behind Ronceval, where he whispered something in the parliamentarian's ear. Ronceval listened for a moment, then slowly raised his hands in a theatrical yawn and let them come to rest casually behind his head, where they remained. Elbows up, back arched, apparently frozen in mid-yawn, Ronceval in turn whispered to Wainwright, who promptly announced that he was reversing his ruling and would allow a secret ballot after all. He called for Van Pelt and Schlemmer to count ballots.

Schlemmer, however, announced, after a brief whispered exchange with Gorman, who was seated behind him, that one of his contact lenses had popped out, rendering him incapable of counting ballots. He insisted that Gorman take his place.

Someone called out, "Schlemmer, what is this? Since when..."
He was interrupted by Van Pelt, who was racing up the aisle toward Schlemmer. Van Pelt ran awkwardly. His right hand was stuffed in his coat pocket and his left was waving above his head, with the thumb

and forefinger pressed together at the fingertips making a circle. He shouted:

"I've found your lens, Schlemmer. Get moving. Never mind Gorman."

However, Gorman had already sprinted down to the rostrum and had taken a position behind Roger, the deparmental clerk. He whispered to the clerk, who jerked promptly and convulsively into Ronceval's frozen-yawn position and walked, elbows still in the air, back to the side wall. Ronceval, in turn, dropped his arms and whispered to Wainwright.

Wainwright announced that Gorman and Ferguson would count ballots. Donna, the departmental secretary, prepared the ballots and was distributing them when one of the doors of the corridor burst open and Grunewald entered. He apologized for his tardiness, conferred briefly and softly with Van Pelt and took a seat in the back row. A minute or two later, after the ballots had been handed out, Grunewald lurched to his feet and clawed at the air, shrieking unintelligibly. After a moment, he fell back against the wall, stared blankly at his colleagues, mumbled, "It's my heart" in a cracked whisper and pitched forward over the row of seats in front of him. The department members remained immobilized, all but Gorman, who was at Grunewald's side in an instant. He bent over Grunewald briefly, then looked up and spoke:

"He's all right, actually. Call for the question."

At this point, a number of things happened.

Grunewald, still collapsed over the seats, screamed, "What the hell do you mean all right. I'm dying here. Stop the meeting!" Then an explosion reverberated in the lecture hall, followed after a momentary hush by perhaps a dozen more, as faculty members scrambled in various directions over the seats and through the aisles. Van Pelt, his right hand bloody, scooped up a pistol from the floor with his left and dived behind the rostrum, shouting "Second-semester criticism, *over here!*" Ferguson and Fowler were standing toe to toe in the fourth row, battering each other in the face and head with briefcases. Peaster, who had been absent from the meeting, appeared striding down the right aisle, barefoot, in cap and gown, and bellowing, "Where IS that son of a bitch?" Gorman meanwhile was crouched in the last row of seats, Grunewald's pistol in his hand. Schlemmer was sprawled face down near the rostrum, as were Ronceval and Roger, the departmental clerk. Grunewald, holding Gorman's gun with the silencer attached, stood in the doorway, screaming "McGriff! McGriff!"

SELECTED BIBLIOGRAPHY

CHAPTER 1: THE PURPOSE OF EDUCATION

Bailyn, Bernard. *Education in the Forming of American Society.* New York: Random House, 1960.

Brubacher, John S. *Modern Philosophies of Education.* New York: McGraw-Hill, 1962.

Spindler, George D., editor. *Education and Culture.* New York: Holt, Rinehart and Winston, 1963.

Welter, Rush. *Popular Education and Democratic Thought in America.* New York: Columbia University Press, 1962.

CHAPTER 2: TEACHING AND LEARNING IN SOCIETY

Adams, Sam, and John L. Garrett, Jr. *To Be a Teacher: An Introduction to Education.* Englewood Cliffs, N.J.: Prentice-Hall, 1969.

Alberty, Harold B., and Elsie J. Alberty. *Reorganizing the High School Curriculum,* 3d ed. New York: Macmillan, 1962.

Barzun, Jacques. *Teacher in America.* New York: Anchor Books and Anchor Science Series, Doubleday, 1946.

Biber, Barbara, and Patricia Minuchin. "The Role of the School in the Socialization of Competence." In *Achievement in American Society,* Bernard C. Rosen, Harry J. Crockett, Jr., and Clyde A. Nunn, editors. Cambridge, Mass.: Schenkman Publishing Co., 1969.

Bigge, Morris L., and Maurice P. Hunt. *Psychological Foundations of Education.* New York: Harper & Row, 1962.

Brinkman, Erwin H., and Ruth A. Brinkman. "Group Influence on the Individual in the Classroom: A Case Study." *The Merrill-Palmer Quarterly of Behavior and Development* 9 (July 1963): 195–204.

Bruner, Jerome S. *Process of Education.* New York: Random House, 1960.

Clark, Burton R. *Educating the Expert Society.* San Francisco: Chandler Publishing Co., 1962.

Elder, Glen H., Jr. "Family Structure and Educational Attainment: A Cross-National Analysis." *American Sociological Review* 30 (February 1965): 81–96.

Eyerly, J. *Dropout.* Philadelphia: Lippincott Publishing Co., 1969.

Gardner, John W. *Excellence: Can We Be Equal and Excellent Too?* New York: Harper & Row, 1961.

Getzels, Jacob W., and Philip W. Jackson. *Creativity and Intelligence*. New York: Wiley, 1962.

Hentoff, Nat. *Our Children Are Dying*. New York: Viking Press, 1966.

Hullfish, H. Gordon, and Philip G. Smith. *Reflective Thinking: The Method of Education*. New York: Dodd, Mead, 1961.

Koerner, James D. *The Miseducation of American Teachers*. Boston: Houghton Mifflin, 1963.

Moore, G. Alexander, Jr. *Realities of the Urban Classroom: Observations in Elementary Schools*. New York: Anchor Books, Doubleday, 1967.

Morse, Arthur D. *Schools of Tomorrow—Today!* New York: Anchor Books, Doubleday, 1966.

Passow, A. Harry, ed. *Education in Depressed Areas*. New York: Teachers College Press, 1963.

Phenix, Philip H. *Realms of Meaning: A Philosophy of the Curriculum for General Education*. New York: McGraw-Hill, 1964.

Ripple, Richard. "Affective Factors Influence Classroom Learning." *Education Leadership* 22 (April 1965): 476–480.

Rogers, Carl R. *On Becoming a Person*. Boston: Houghton Mifflin, 1961.

Rosen, B. C., H. H. Crockett, and C. Z. Nunn, editors. *Achievement in American Society*. Cambridge, Mass.: Schenkman Publishing Co., 1969.

Rudy, Willis. *Schools in an Age of Mass Culture*. Englewood Cliffs, N.J.: Prentice-Hall, 1965.

Shostak, Arthur B. "Education and the Family." *Journal of Marriage and the Family* 29 (February 1967): 124–139.

Spindler, George, and Louise Spindler, editors. *Case Studies in Education and Culture*. New York: Holt, Rinehart and Winston, 1967.

Stiles, Lindley J., editor. *The Teacher's Role in American Society*. New York: Harper and Brothers, 1957.

Torrance, E. Paul, and Robert D. Strom, editors. *Mental Health and Achievement*. New York: Wiley, 1965.

Tuckman, Bruce, and John L. O'Brian, editors. *Preparing to Teach the Disadvantaged*. New York: The Free Press, 1969.

Turner, R. H. *The Social Context of Ambition*. San Francisco: Chandler Publishing Company, 1964.

Yamamoto, Kaoru, editor. *Teaching: Essays and Readings*. Boston, Mass.: Houghton Mifflin, 1969.

CHAPTER 3: SCHOOL AND SOCIETY

Brookover, Wilbur B., and David Gottlieb. *A Sociology of Education*, 2d ed. New York: American Book Co., 1964.

Carver, Fred D., and Thomas J. Sergiovanni. *Organization and Human Behavior: Focus on Schools*. New York: McGraw-Hill, 1969.

Gordon, C. Wayne. *The Social System of the High School: A Study in the Sociology of the Adolescent*. New York: The Free Press, 1957.

Perry, Charles R. *Group Conflict and School Organization*. Chicago: Reprint Series

No. 124, Industrial Relations Center, University of Chicago. Phi Delta Kappa, January 1966.

Westby-Gibson, Dorothy. *Social Perspectives in Education.* New York: Wiley, 1965.

CHAPTER 4: TECHNOLOGY AND EDUCATION

Alexander, W. M., editor. *(The) High School of the Future.* Columbus, Ohio: Merrill, 1969.

Allen, D. W., and K. A. Ryan. *Microteaching.* Reading, Mass.: Addison-Wesley, 1969.

DeCecco, John P. *Educational Technology: Readings in Programmed Instruction.* New York: Holt, Rinehart and Winston, 1964.

Deep, Donald. "The Teacher's Changing Role." *The Elementary School Journal* 69 (November 1968): 84–88.

Footlick, J. K. "How Computers Will Change the Teacher's Role." *The National Observer.* Editorial (May 9, 1966): 11.

Skinner, B. F. "Why We Need Teaching Machines." *Harvard Educational Review* 31 (Fall 1967): 377–398.

Torkelson, Gerald M., and Emily A. Torkelson. "How Mechanized Should the Classroom Be?" *NEA Journal* 56 (March 1967): 28–30.

Trow, William Clark. *Teacher and Technology: Design for Learning.* New York: Appleton-Century-Crofts, 1967.

CHAPTER 5: CRITICAL ISSUES IN CONTEMPORARY EDUCATION

Anderson, James G. *Bureaucracy in Education.* Baltimore, Md.: Johns Hopkins Press, 1969.

Bernstein, Saul. *Alternative to Violence: Alienated Youth and Riots, Race and Poverty.* New York: Association Press, 1969.

Bolner, James, editor. *Racial Imbalance in Public Schools: A Basic Annotated Bibliography.* Baton Rouge: Institute of Government Research, Louisiana State University, 1968.

Crain, Robert L. *The Politics of School Desegregation.* New York: Anchor Books, Doubleday, 1968.

Dentler, R. A., and M. Warshauer, editors. *The Urban R's.* New York: The Center for Urban Education, 1969.

Doherty, R. E. *(The) Law and Collective Bargaining for Teachers,* Reprint Series No. 197. New York: New York State School of Industrial and Labor Relations, Cornell University, 1968.

Douglass, Bruce. *Reflections on Protest: Student Presence in Political Conflict.* Richmond, Va.: John Knox Press, 1967.

Frost, Joe L., and Glen R. Hawkes, editors. *The Disadvantaged Child, Issues and Innovation.* Boston: Houghton Mifflin, 1966.

Fuchs, Estelle. *Teachers Talk: A View from Within Inner City Schools.* New York: Anchor Books, Doubleday, 1969.

Hall, Donald R. *Cooperative Lobbying—The Power of Pressure.* Tucson, Ariz.: University of Arizona Press, 1968.

Hill, Roscoe, and Malcolm Seeley, editors. *Affirmative School Integration*. Beverly Hills, California: Saga Publications, 1968.

Janowitz, Morris. *Institution Building in Urban Education*. New York: Russel Sage Foundation, 1969.

Kozol, Jonathan. *Death at an Early Age*. New York: Bantam Books, 1967.

Lee, Gordon C. *Education and Democratic Ideals*. New York: Harcourt, Brace, and World, 1965.

Lieberman, Myron. *The Future of Public Education*. Chicago: The University of Chicago Press, 1962.

Lutz, F. W., and J. J. Azzarelli, editors. *Struggle for Power in Education*. New York: Center for Applied Research in Education, 1968.

Martin, Roscoe C. *Economics and Politics of Education, No. 2: Government and the Suburban School*. Syracuse, N.Y.: Syracuse University Press, 1962.

Mayer, Martin. *The Teachers Strike: New York, 1968*. New York: Harper & Row, 1969.

Moore, G. Alexander, Jr. *Realities of the Urban Classroom: Observations in Elementary Schools*. New York: Anchor Books, Doubleday, 1967.

Nordstrom, Carl, et al. *Society's Children: A Study of Resentment in Secondary Education*. New York: Random House, 1967.

Racial Isolation in the Public Schools, A Report of the United States Commission on Civil Rights, Vol. 1. Washington, D.C.: U.S. Government Printing Office, 1967.

Rosenthal, Alan, editor. *Governing Education: A Reader on Politics, Power and Public School Policy*. New York: Anchor Books, Doubleday, 1969.

Rudman, Herbert C., and Richard L. Featherstone. *Urban Schooling*. New York: Harcourt, Brace and World, 1968.

Stinchcombe, A. L. *Rebellion in a High School*. Chicago: Quadrangle Books, 1964.

Stinnett, T. M. *Turmoil in Teaching—A History of the Organizational Struggle for America's Teachers*. New York: Macmillan, 1968.

Warden, Sandra A. *The Leftouts: Disadvantaged Children in Heterogeneous Schools*. New York: Holt, Rinehart and Winston, 1968.

Wildman, Wesley A. *Collective Action by Pubic School Teachers*. Reprint Series No. 119. Chicago: Industrial Relations Center, University of Chicago, 1968.